201

Gilda, Promise Me

To Tim,

Your enthusiastic support is much appreciated. Let us continue having adventures in the library.

Gilda

ISBN: 978-0-9984873-8-0
Library of Congress Control Number: 2018936538

Published by: Idea Press (an imprint of Idea Graphics, LLC) — Florida (USA)
www.ideapress-usa.com   email: ideapress33@gmail.com   editoreusa@gmail.com
Printed in the USA - First Edition, April 2018

A Memoir by

CAV. GILDA BATTAGLIA RORRO BALDASSARI, Ed.D.

Gilda, Promise Me

To Pope Pius XII,
"My promise to you has inspired me
throughout my life. I dedicate this book to
you with gratitude in your memory."

Acknowledgements

I am grateful to my loving parents Drs. Angelo and Mary Battaglia, for giving me the wonderful opportunities that crafted this memoir. They share in whatever good I have achieved.

Kudos to my daughter, Dr. Mary Celeste Rorro, for her skillful review, editing, and interest throughout the book's development.

I gratefully acknowledge the insightful guidance of my friend Ellen Stark who had her husband, author Albert Stark, Esq., review the memoir. He shared his valuable time and expertise generously and meticulously. His cogent comments were greatly appreciated.

This book would not have been written without the unstinting persistence and encouragement of my friend and consummate educator, Dr. Cheryl Simone. Since 1976, when I was a student in her English as a Second Language class at Trenton State College (College of New Jersey), she has continuously urged me to record my life experiences.

Technical support was graciously and skillfully provided by her talented physician sister, Dr. Jill Simone, by editing and formatting the document. Her insight and infinite patience were most valuable.

I wish to give my deep gratitude to the following individuals for their encouragement and editing: the Hamilton Public Library Memoir Writing Group members, our group's moderator, Rodney Richards, for his editing and ongoing mentorship, and former college president, Dr. Michael Riccards. My friends Linda Prospero and Tara DeLotto Paster were also encouraging.

My appreciation is also extended to my sister Victoria, Timothy Crawford, Ronnie Sternberg, and Magda Gelaszus, for reviewing several chapters.

Special appreciation is extended to Associate Justice of the Supreme Court of the United States, Hon. Samuel A. Alito, Jr., for composing the singular Introduction.

Introduction

History is the composite of the lives of individual human beings, and Gilda Battaglia Rorro Baldassari's fascinating autobiography, "Promise Me," not only recounts an adventurous life well lived but provides a valuable contribution to the history of the Italian American community.

The book's title consists of words uttered to Gilda in her youth by Pope Pius XII, Eugenio Pacelli. On a family visit to Castel Gandolfo, the pope asked her if she spoke Italian. When Gilda said that she did not, this was the pope's response: "Gilda, will you promise me something? Promise me when you return to your marvelous country across the ocean, you will learn Italian and never forget your Italian ancestors."

As her autobiography recounts, Gilda kept that promise. She not only mastered Italian, but she worked tirelessly to preserve the heritage of the Italian American community in New Jersey. Among other things, she served as Honorary Vice Consul for Italy in Trenton; she was appointed by the Governor of New Jersey to the state Italian American Commission and chaired the Commission's curriculum project, "The Universality of Italian Heritage"; and she worked doggedly and effectively to infuse Italian cultural heritage into the schools. In recognition of her dedicated service, the president of Italy named her a "cavaliere," the Italian equivalent of a knighthood. It is the highest honor bestowed by the Italian Republic—and one that Gilda richly deserved.

Listing these accomplishments and honors, however, does not do justice to Gilda's rollicking book. She provides memorable and poignant sketches of relatives and their struggles in their new homeland. And she tells the story of her generation, "the last to have direct contact with the Italian immigrant experience in the United States after World War II." Gilda and the members of her generation felt the pull of the past and tug of the present, and Gilda labored to make a life that combined the best of both. Always spirited and adventurous, she blazed her own path, which she recounts in lively prose: her teen-age infatuation with a suave Venezuelan, her decision to give up the study of nursing and study languages at Beaver College; modeling and movie roles in Mexico City; teaching Spanish in person and on public television; a trip around the world with her sister Vicki; the whirlwind courtship of a Spanish diplomat; turning down the opportunity for movie roles in Egypt; her marriage to Dr. Louis Rorro; moving to the Trenton area, which would be her permanent home; motherhood; Dr. Rorro's unexpected death; marriage to Giovanni (John) Baldassari; and much more. I don't want to spoil the story.

I first met Gilda when she befriended my mother shortly after my nomination to the Supreme Court. I had mentioned that my father had been born in Italy and had been brought to the United States as an infant, and a rumor then began to circulate that this was a fabrication and that my father had actually been born in the United States. The Boston Globe even hired a professional genealogist to investigate. Gilda knew my mother from her work for the Board of Education in Hamilton Township, where my mother taught for many years. So, the Italian consul in Newark asked Gilda to contact my mother, then in her 90s, and get the name of the town in Calabria where my father had been born.* Gilda and my mother then struck up a friendship. Gilda frequently visited her and took her to many interesting cultural events. They even rode together in a Columbus Day parade, something my mother relished. During this time, I was in Washington, and my sister was in northern New Jersey, so Mom was often alone. Gilda's friendship greatly enriched Mom's old age. When I called her to check up, one of the first things she told me was almost always about a recent adventure with Gilda. I am sure that Gilda's kindness to Mom is just one example of her many good works over the years.

As the title of her autobiography makes clear, Gilda took her promise to the Pope very seriously. And her book completes her obligation.

---

*An aside: after my confirmation, the Italian Embassy gave me a framed copy of my father's Italian birth certificate, which I proudly display in my office.

She has not forgotten her Italian ancestors. Her book tells the story of one remarkable, talented, elegant, determined Italian American woman. And in doing so it makes a lasting contribution to the story of the Italian American people.

Samuel A. Alito, Jr.
Washington, D.C.
September 2017

I

Early Childhood and Adolescence

*The Papal Promise; I am in the white beret,
front row second from right.*

CHAPTER ONE
PAPAL PROMISE

Just two words. I did not know they would change my life. I remember that special day they were uttered to me in Italy by Pope Pius XII, Eugenio Marìa Giuseppe Giovanni Pacelli.

Dad kept his word about taking me to his homeland. Six years after World War II, I was 13 years old and in Rome. What could be more glorious? The telephone rang in our room in the *Massimo D'Azeglio* hotel.

Unlike the lobby decor with ornate marble floors and chandeliers, our rooms were unadorned. A chestnut-colored hardwood floor supported a bed and chair covered with chartreuse fabric. On the side of the window there was a desk with a lamp. What impressed me were the bath, face and hand towels made of delicate white pressed linen with lace trim.

These aren't absorbent like the terrycloth ones at home. They are almost too pretty to use.

"Yes. Yes, Mr. La Bella. You are most welcome to come here now," Dad said in Italian. "Mary, get the girls ready. We're going to have a visitor from the Vatican in a half-hour."

"Hurry. We have to get this place tidied up right away," my mother said nervously.

Our mini-suite was messy with opened suitcases and handbags strewn across the sofa and chairs. My two sisters and I worked feverishly to make the place presentable, throwing our bags on the beds in our rooms.

Mom set about tidying the parlor in anticipation of our special guest. While we worked, my mind was racing.

The highlight of our trip to the Eternal City will be to have a private audience with his Holiness Pope Pius XII in his summer residence. I've seen him via the newsreels at the Walton Cinema two blocks away from our house in Germantown. Everything I see of the outside world is at the movies.

To meet the "Head of the Church" was the experience of a lifetime for a Catholic family. At the Walton, we would watch in awe as the pontiff appeared in all his regalia carried on men's shoulders in Saint Peter's Square on the ceremonial throne, the *sedia gestatoria*, a Latin term I learned on the trip. Thousands of the adoring faithful struggled to get a glimpse of him. The truly fortunate succeeded in touching the *sedia* platform, his shoe, or even the hem of his garment, as he blessed the throngs.

Seeing the Pope on the big screen will be the closest thing to witnessing God to me. And to think, tomorrow I may even speak to him. How incredible!

The doorbell rang and Signor Vincenzo La Bella entered. He was a handsome, slender, youthful official at the Vatican whose father was Chamberlain to Pope Pius XII (manager of the Papal household). His dark hair and eyes were alluring to me but it was my older sister Gloria who attracted his attention. Signor La Bella came to our hotel to give instructions on papal protocol.

Dad greeted the young emissary with a warm handshake. My father, like Mr. La Bella, wore a dark blue suit and matching tie. His eyes shone with excitement at the visitor.

"Welcome, Signor la Bella," Dad said.

"Please, call me Vincenzo."

Mr. La Bella approached my mother and kissed her hand while fixing his eyes on Gloria, who returned his gaze. Next, he addressed my 14-month-younger sister Vicki and me, explaining protocols we were to follow.

Vincenzo is the one arranging our private audience with the Pope. It seems important we be well prepared. I better listen and follow all the rules. This is exciting and scary.

"When the Holy Father approaches you personally, you must kneel and kiss his ring. Refer to the Pope as 'Your Holiness.' You ladies are to wear modest navy blue or black clothing, long skirts, slightly above the ankle and have your arms and heads covered."

When the emissary exited, Vicki and I chatted into the night in anticipation of the next day.

"We must remember all of the protocol, Vicki. We cannot make a mistake. It would be humiliating."

At 8 a.m. the following morning, the big day had arrived. Dad proudly drove us in our black Buick he had shipped from New York on the Queen Elizabeth, to Castel Gandolfo, the Holy Father's summer residence, located 15 miles southeast of Rome. I had imagined the type of castle with crenelated towers I had seen in Robin Hood movies at the Walton. Instead, Castel Gandolfo was a tasteful, unadorned building covered in cream-colored stucco with white shutters. A grey stone arch surrounded the entrance.

The term, "Sunny Italy," was well deserved. The lapis sky was cloudless. Avenues flanked by slender cypresses, pointed and dark, swayed gently in the serene setting.

We passed the ceremonial Swiss Guards with their grey caps and brightly-colored uniforms of blue, gold and red striped fabric, extending from their neck to mid-calf, resembling knickers boys wore in my class. They looked disciplined as they held six-foot, wooden spears. We were greeted by a formal host dressed in a black suit, tie and white shirt. He recited our names from a list he held in his hand and led us silently through a long bright corridor where cream-colored arches highlighted splendid murals of Italian landscapes with graceful tree branches and rolling hills. At the end, he beckoned me to enter the reception area which was so elegant it was intimidating. I felt overwhelmed and speechless. I trembled and looked at Vicki. We dared not speak.

The stately room's vaulted ceiling was gilded. The walls were covered in molded panels and the inlaid floor showcased intricate swirling designs of hand-cut marble and travertine. A red velvet throne with a golden canopy dominated the area where the Pope would surely be seated.

Are Mom and Dad so important to have a private audience?

That question was answered when men with yarmulkes (a brimless cap) entered. Others followed. Not a sound was heard in the chamber as we anticipated the grand entrance.

Will the Pontiff be wearing the jewels and robes we saw at the Walton? I feel nervous. I cannot imagine what he could possibly want to say to me, a 13-year-old girl. If I have a chance to speak with him, will I be too emotional to answer?

The doorway opened. All conversation stopped as the Pope appeared donning only a simple white cassock, skull cap and crucifix resting on his chest. He blessed us in fluent Latin—the language I often heard at Mass from Father Nipote at the Holy Rosary Church in Germantown, Pennsylvania.

Everyone seemed mesmerized. I fixed my eyes on the slim figure as he addressed each delegation in their own language. His demeanor was formal, yet gracious. He conversed with ease in German, English, French and Spanish. He never sat upon the imposing throne. My heart pounded as he approached my family.

What will he ask? What should I say? Maybe nothing would be best.

While these thoughts whirled in my head, the Pontiff approached my father. He looked at a list he held in his hand. Learning our surname was Battaglia, the Pope addressed my parents in Italian.

"Dottor Battaglia, Lei parla italiano." (Dr. Battaglia, you speak Italian.)

But hearing Dad respond in the *Margheritano* dialect of his *paese* (town), and then my mother, in her working knowledge of the Neapolitan variety, a bewildered look spread across the Holy Father's face. He raised his hand, signaling a pause.

"Forse è meglio continuare in inglese. (Perhaps it would be better to continue in English)," he suggested politely.

I heard Eugenio Pacelli was a scholar and had a superior command of many languages. I was in awe of his vast linguistic ability.

The Pope does not want to hear my parents' dialects. I wish they knew proper Italian. It's embarrassing.

As the Pontiff spoke briefly to my older sister, then to Vicki, I was next in line. I stood perfectly still. I lowered my head.

When he stood in front of me, all I saw was the flowing white of his cassock. I knelt as the Pope extended his hand and I kissed his deep-blue sapphire ring, encircled by diamonds.

It seems strange a man would wear such a piece of jewelry, but for once, follow the protocol of silence.

"What is your name?"

With the warmth of his voice and the benevolent look on his face, his smile melted me.

"Gilda, Your Holiness."

"Gilda, that is a beautiful name. Tell me, are you a good girl? Do you obey your parents?"

The last man who asked me that was Santa Claus.

But I had grown up. Was I experiencing another fantasy?

"Yes, Your Holiness," I said, looking fleetingly toward my parents in the hope they would not betray me by proclaiming I was a holy terror.

"Gilda, do you speak Italian?"

"No, Your Holiness, I am an American."

His piercing blue eyes narrowed. Standing erect, he joined his fingertips with both hands, moving them up and down in an Italian gesture of frustration which I had seen my father make many times: "*Che peccato!*" (What a pity!) I felt embarrassed.

"Gilda. Will you promise me something?"

"Anything, your Holiness," I mumbled.

"Promise me when you return to your marvelous country across the ocean, you will learn to speak Italian and never forget your Italian ancestors. Promise me!" His tone was kind but firm.

"I promise, Your Holiness."

MY ITALIAN AMERICAN WORLD

I had a head start on the second half of my promise to the Pope because I always loved asking my older family members about their lives in Italy and how and why they came to America. They welcomed my questions and their answers captivated me. My generation is privileged to be the last to have direct contact with the Italian immigrant experience in the United States after World War II. We witnessed several of our relatives and friends transition to this country. We did not experience the initial struggles and hardships of the earlier immigrants like those during the Great Depression. Ours was a time of postwar prosperity, deep patriotism and respect for America at home and abroad. The Americans of Italian descent embraced their new homeland with pride and loyalty.

I was born in the Germantown section of Philadelphia in 1938. There were many Italian Americans living there, especially on Haines Street, since it was a Little Italy enclave. One did not need to venture out of such a neighborhood where all needs were met. The banker, dentist, doctor, grocer, and most importantly, the parish priest, all spoke Italian. Some of the inhabitants, especially the older women, never learned English.

I looked forward to going to nearby Haines Street where, on Saturday afternoons, Daddy would take Vicki and me to Pasquale (called Patsy by friends), the butcher. He was a middle-aged, portly, jovial man who took his artisanal style of meat carving to a high art form.

"I'll have ten pounds of club steaks," Daddy ordered. "You got it-a, Doc," Patsy retorted eagerly, as he easily removed an entire side of beef which hung from a jutting iron hook on the wall.

I looked on, mesmerized as Patsy deftly cut out thick portions from the carcass and tenderloin Daddy always wanted. His fingers moved with precision. He discarded chunks of fat and cut each thick, red portion to perfection. As Patsy plied his trade, Vicki and I liked swooshing our shoes in the thick layer of sawdust on the floor of his shop where several other halves of cows hung unceremoniously across the wall. He made his job look easy although two missing fingers, one on each hand, were a reminder of the hazards of his occupation.

Like most Italian neighborhoods, the church was the heart of the community. Most activities emanated from its traditions and celebrations. The Holy Rosary Church was on Haines Street. We would go there on Sunday where Father Nipote celebrated Mass in Italian, often lapsing into his Piemontese dialect.

"*L'umanità è il fango!*" he would declare in a stentorious voice, his entire body shaking in emphasis. He stressed that, because of Adam and Eve, our sins could only be cleansed through the Eucharist.

"What does *fango* mean, Mommy?"

"It means human beings are mud," she uttered matter-of-factly.

"Does Father Nipote think we are dirty?" I queried.

"Only our souls."

"Are our souls muddy?"

Mommy was getting weary of my questions, so I just kept quiet, thinking of what she used to say to Daddy in Italian, "*Eh, Beh!*" (Oh, well!).

I was always fascinated by the life-size statues of saints which lined the walls. Saint Sebastian, his body pierced with arrows, and Saint Jude, a flame rising from his head, fascinated me most. Although I understood little of the significance of the religious figures, I always loved going into that church.

After Mass, Father Nipote often greeted my parents in Italian. Despite the disparate dialects, they communicated in hand gestures and words.

I understand what most of the hand movements mean, but not the words. I wish I could speak the proper Italian with Patsy and Father Nipote. I feel like I am left out.

We were educated by newspapers, the radio, or cinema. For example, at the outbreak of World War II, we'd go to the Walton Theater in our neighborhood where I would view Frank Capra's depiction of Mussolini looking pompous on a Roman balcony, surrounded by throngs of cheering Italians.

Some of the kids in the neighborhood taunted me relentlessly about my heritage.

"You Italian?" they would ask, derogatorily. "Mussolini lover, Meatball, Wop, Dago!"

Why are they calling me those mean names? I hate those names. How could I love Mussolini? I don't even know him. If they knew how nice my family is, they wouldn't say those things. Now I understand how my colored classmates must feel when kids call them names for no reason.

I loved my family and culture with its complex, tangled relationships, yet I soon realized that in the Germantown of those days, being Italian was not popular and that was painful to me.

I am a first-generation Italian American. My father was born in *Margherita di Savoia*, in Puglia, in 1905. My mother was also born that year, in Mays Landing, New Jersey. Both sets of their parents hailed from the *Mezzogiorno*, or southern region of the peninsula. My mother's father was from *Casola di Napoli* and Grandmom hailed from *Basilicata*. I loved being with all those who emigrated from the Old Country. I'd listen for hours as they spoke among themselves in their diverse dialects laced in English with stories of how hard life was and how hard they worked during their childhoods in Italy.

"We went to the fields from sunrise to sunset, six-days a week, with a scythe to thresh wheat. There was no school, doctor or dentist in our village. We buried the dead ourselves," a new arrival from Basilicata used to say."

Many expressions in different dialects were widespread among the Italian immigrants in our community and the country. Most Americans of Italian descent understood several common expressions from coast to coast: *Acida; Arrivederci; Managgia; Mangia; Madonna (Maronn)* and *Ciao*, were among them. One often heard *Musciad*. Loosely translated, it means mushy. If someone is feeling *musciad...* you get the message. Trentonians also called tomato sauce "gravy," *penne pasta* "pencil points" and enjoyed "tomato pie." Without a calendar, one could guess the day of the week by what our Italian neighbors had for dinner. Tuesday, Thursday and Sunday were usually reserved for various pasta dishes. The word *pasta* was not commonly used. Italians referred to the farinaceous delight as *macaroni*. On Friday, by church rules, fish or another meatless meal was prepared, as meat consumption was considered a mortal sin. *Pasta vasul* (in proper Italian *pasta e fagioli*)(pasta with beans), ceci (chick peas) or lenticchie (lentils) often appeared on the table any day of the week. The pungent smell of frying peppers and baking bread wafted through the narrow streets.

Sunday was devoted to attending Mass, followed by an *abbondante* family meal in the afternoon. In my family, the men did the bulk of the cooking, making a cauldron of tomato sauce, and 150 ravioli stuffed with ricotta and a hint of nutmeg. In the summer heat, they would perspire and wipe their faces on their white aprons which extended to their knees. They were uncomfortable in a 10x12-foot kitchen with water boiling and a hot oven full of roasted meats and potatoes, but they were jovial and always laughing.

I would anticipate that meal all morning. At Mass at the Church of Saints Peter and Paul in Mays Landing, while the priest held up the Eucharist, my thoughts would wander sinfully to the ravioli topped with the steaming tomato sauce, sprinkled with Parmigiano-Reggiano cheese.

Everyone had to arrive at the designated home, usually that of the grandparents or parents, to say Grace together before eating. We always went to Grandpop Sorrentino's house.

"You kids go into the bar and bring in the chairs," Grandmom would say.

We dutifully carried 14 chairs from the bar area of 'Sorrentino's Bar and Grill,' into the dining room where two tables were joined to accommodate us 14 grandchildren and at least 20 other hungry relatives. Their six-room wooden country house was filled with commotion and laughter as the men commanded in the kitchen and the women scurried to prepare the table.

I was always hungry, but no one could begin to eat until a certain ritual took place. When everyone was seated at table, Grandpop would say Grace.

"In nome del Padre, del figlio e dello Spirito Santo (In the name of the Father, the Son and the Holy Ghost)." After his opening prayer, he would put food on each plate. Grandmom was the first to be served, then the next oldest person to the youngest. When each dish was full, Grandpop would say, "Buon appetito!"

The *pranzo* (meal) in my family began with assorted antipasti, minestrone, macaroni, a roast with potatoes sprinkled with rosemary, and the ever-present homemade wine. We nibbled on fruit, *dolci* (sweets) and nuts. Piping hot espresso with anisette liquor for the adults ended the meal.

"God bless Gilly," the relatives would say, encouraging my hearty appetite. So, I ate to win their admiration, but also because the food was delicious. In those days, plumper was prized.

"In Italy, we ate meat only once a year, at Christmas or the New Year. Our diet consisted mainly of beans and macaroni," Grandmom's brother, Daniele, told us.

"When I received a steady paycheck in America, my wife was proud to prepare and serve dishes with generous portions of assorted meats. Life was good for us in our new country," he added.

Italians preferred their children marry other Italians—especially those hailing from the same *paese* (town). In Italy, before the Vespa and automobile became ubiquitous, the custom of *Campanilismo* (provincialism) was the norm. If a man wanted to court a woman, he usually walked as far as the church bell sounded, in other words, within walking distance or by riding a donkey. Living in remote, isolated villages, geographical restrictions remained a reason for the myriad variety of dialects in the country and adherence to the customs of one's own *paese.*

Those attitudes often prevailed in the New World when the Italian immigrants arrived in the late 19th century. In Mays Landing, where my grandparents lived, when an engagement was announced, one question was always asked.

"Is he or she one of us or an *Amerigan?*"

If the latter were true, disappointment was evident. They were concerned that, if a spouse did not share the same culture, conflicts could erupt, or a son or daughter might lose interest or respect for the customs of the parents. Regardless, they always welcomed the newcomer, some more enthusiastically than others.

"Can she cook? I don't want my son to starve," the mothers exclaimed.

"Is the person Catholic?"

One cousin was going to marry a Polish woman. "At least she's Catholic and the Polish people are clean," his parents said.

Many of the young men and women later wanted to marry non-Italians to integrate more rapidly into American mainstream society. Being Catholic was an important consideration, but even that could be overlooked.

When I grow up, I want to marry an Italian. I want someone who loves and will carry on our ways—especially ravioli.

Keeping my promise of learning to speak Italian was another matter because my parents spoke disparate dialects. I remember when Uncle Phillip came to visit us for the first time. *Zio* (uncle) Felippo DiCorato, my father's uncle, emigrated from Margherita di Savoia, to Philadelphia in 1944. As a six-year-old, he mesmerized me. He sat erect in the living room with Dad; they spoke their common *Margheritano* dialect. Zio was a spiffy dresser, decked out with a starched white shirt and stiff collar, a dark silk tie, beige vest, tailored jacket, striped trousers and shoes, blanketed with beige spats. A generous black handle bar moustache complimented the ensemble and, as everyone remarked, "He looked real sharp."

"*Come stai?*" (How are you?), Gilda," he asked, fondly, patting me on the head.

"I'm good but I don't speak Italian, Uncle Philip," I answered, embarrassed.

I would sit on the floor beside *lo zio*, and listen for hours to the duo converse, trying to decipher a word or two, but the dialect of Margherita di Savoia eluded me.

Often, I'd ask my parents to teach me the language, but to no avail. Mom spoke the Neapolitan dialect rather well, being the oldest daughter living with her immigrant grandparents. Dad's *Margheritano* version was laced with Spanish lexical influences from the time when the region of Puglia was under the reign of the Spanish Bourbons during *Il Regno delle Due Sicilie*, (The Kingdom of the Two Sicilies.)

"Mom, how do you say, 'frying pan' in Italian?" I once asked, before frying an egg.

"*Sartana.*"

"That's not how we say it, Dad retorted. It's *azarteszena.*"

"That's wrong, Angelo," Mom said, correcting him.

"No. You're wrong, Mary."

My question resulted in an argument that would go on for half an hour, so I left the room, ignorant as ever.

Often Italian Americans lament not having learned Italian as children.

"Speak English!" their parents frequently said.

I believe it was not because they did not want their offspring to learn Italian, but because they spoke their local dialect for which there was no formal grammar or schooling. Many children in agrarian regions of Italy either did not receive academic instruction or had very little because they had to work in the fields or other laborious occupations, as did their parents, six days a week. Speaking only a dialect relegated one to a lower station in life.

I am determined to learn proper Italian and keep my papal promise.

CHAPTER TWO

MY FAMILY

Mommy was proud of her Italian roots. Mary Rose Sorrentino was born in 1905 in the village of Mays Landing, New Jersey, to Raffaele and Nicola (May) Minnone Sorrentino. She was their second daughter. The first, also named Mary, died shortly after entering the world.

Mommy possessed a keen intellect, a contagious sense of humor, a loving and forgiving nature, a slight penchant for gossip, and a sturdy, healthy body. Regarding the latter, my sisters and I always marveled at how she was never sick in bed a day. Our mother loved life and she adored her family. To her, her parents, five siblings, assorted aunts, uncles, and cousins were paragons of virtue. Of course, that was not true, and I used to accuse her of being unrealistic.

"You see the world through rose-colored glasses," I'd say. "Your brother Ralph was a holy terror when he was a kid, and you know it."

But no matter what the facts were, to her, he could do no wrong. He would always be her "Faluccio" (Little Ralph). To attest to Mommy's tendency to idealize, she'd often recount her happy memories in the Mays Landing Cotton Mill during the summer where my grandfather was a weaver. When school let out, Grandpop's children would sometimes join him to work in the factory for extra wages. It was a noisy, unhealthy environment where the heavy machines clanged their metallic percussion mercilessly and cotton particles permeated the air, seemingly suspended in the humidity. Mom's siblings complained vociferously about the harsh working conditions, but not Mommy. She was happy being near her "Pop."

"The white flakes skittering in that stifling atmosphere, resembled snowflakes. I'd think it was winter in July and it made me feel cool," she'd say.

Mommy felt she was not beautiful. She really was a beautiful person. Mommy's brown, olive shaped eyes always seemed to sparkle as she found delight in just talking or undertaking some task. Her nose was slightly uneven, as was her full mouth. Her skin was white marble, free of blemish. Mommy resembled her father, Raffaele, a sturdy, squarely built, stocky Neapolitan, full of health and vigor. Her needs were simple as she did not care for clothes, jewelry or heavy make-up. Her parents didn't permit the girls to "paint their faces" anyway, but the sisters would pass a communal lipstick among themselves. My mother would put lipstick, not rouge, on her cheeks throughout her life, probably a habit she learned from her early days of prohibition. She always wore costume beads. If anyone wanted to reward her with an expensive piece of jewelry, she'd protest. "I like my plastic beads. I'm content with my lot."

Mommy told us often about the time her mother was speaking with a lady friend, commenting on the daughters.

"Mary is a pretty girl, May."

"Oh, Mary? She's all right, but you should see my Millie. She's really beautiful!" Grandmom said boastfully.

Mommy always seemed to favor good-looking people, regardless of their character. I think I always understood why. Although Mommy told that story with supposed humor, it saddened me to think how one thoughtless statement from a parent can affect a child's whole life. I vowed if I had a baby who was not so physically attractive, I would love it even more.

Many of our relatives gravitated to Mays Landing in the 1920s. They all seemed happy there, although, at first, they were forced to live in a segregated area of town called "The Grade." Italians were not highly regarded in those days.

Mommy loved to study. In the one-room Uptown School House, she absorbed her studies like a sponge. Soon she was assisting the teacher by tutoring her classmates. Although she was smart, I used to tease her that she spoke "Piney," the register used by some of the inhabitants of the New Jersey Pine Barrens near Mays Landing. She'd lapse into using some of those words like "yes diy (Yesterday), "Wens diy" (Wednesday), "res trint," (Restaurant) and "fair a midlin," when she was conversing with family or close friends.

The girls in the family were dutiful daughters. When they turned sixteen, Grandpop had them leave public education in tenth-grade to attend Hardcastle Business School, in Atlantic City. Grades 11 and 12 were available in Atlantic City High School, not in Mays Landing. When they completed two years at Hardcastle, they were all employed as secretaries in the Atlantic County Clerk's Office in Mays Landing. My mother excelled and won prizes as the best and fastest typist. She hated, however, having to type a Restrictive Covenant on deeds which stated that the property could not be sold to a Negro, a Jew, a Catholic or an Italian.

"Did you always do what your parents wanted?" I'd ask.

"Yes, most of the time. But there was one time I didn't," she said emphatically. Pop wanted me to marry the son of the Mayor of Atlantic City. He was a fine young man from a very good family, but he was so short, and he'd wheeze when he talked. One Sunday afternoon my parents invited him to dinner with some friends. I was to serve a tureen of minestrone to the guests. As I bent over to ladle some soup in my intended's dish, he began to wheeze. I was so startled my bosom fell right in the hot broth." She began to laugh. "Whenever I meet one of the guests who was there that day, he starts by saying, "Hi, Mary. Ain't seen you since you burned your tit in the soup!" She'd then howl, and I'd laugh with her.

Mommy's self-assertion was tested one rare day when she was home alone. There was a knock on the back door where a stranger would ask for directions. She went to open the screened portico and there, before her, stood the tallest, handsomest man imaginable. His dark eyes, enchanting smile, made more prominent by a thin, ebony moustache, instantly enchanted her.

Mary, behold the man of your dreams; she sighed silently.

Her Pop thought otherwise. He resisted my father's attempts to seek permission to court my mother. Grandpop held out for as long as he could because his Neapolitan code of honor required a person to live up to a promise, even if it were just a verbal one he made to the mayor of Atlantic City. But Mommy held her ground. She would have my father or no one.

Mommy and Daddy's Wedding.

Reluctantly, Grandpop capitulated. Daddy "came calling" on Sunday afternoons for two hours. He and my mother had to sit on the sofa in the parlor with Grandmom in the middle. There would be no touching or holding hands.

"Skin on skin makes sin," was Grandmom's admonition.

If Grandmom had a necessity, requiring her to relinquish her spot temporarily, a sibling or other designee was called to sentry duty in the middle.

Daddy was always calculating how he could find time alone with Mommy and one night he had his chance. It was raining and dark. He, with several members of the Sorrentino clan, was marching two blocks to the Victoria Cinema to see Rudolph Valentino in "The Sheik." Daddy somehow led Mommy to the rear of the line. When they were passing a small church cemetery, Daddy whisked Mommy behind a tombstone and planted a kiss firmly on her eager mouth.

Ah, what bliss! she thought. *Valentino could be no better.*

It was September 18th, 1929, when the happy couple was married in the Saint Vincent De Paul Church, in Mays Landing. Grandpop did not escort my mother down the aisle. His sense of honor would not permit it. But that did not spoil the day. My parents looked ecstatic in their wedding picture.

After the Mass, a luncheon was held for family and friends in my grandparents' home. Several lady friends had roasted chickens while others made pasta. The joyful couple set off on a honeymoon to Niagara Falls. They were so happy. It was good they didn't know what was in store for them and the nation.

THE NOT SO GOOD "GOOD OLE' DAYS"

Since our audience with the pontiff, my interest in "Italianità" became more intense. I continued to ask any relatives to tell me all they could about where they came from in Italy and what life was like in their *paese*. Some preferred to forget the hard times they knew while others, like my maternal grandfather, were eager to recount details of their experiences. My main source of information emanated from my parents. They welcomed my insatiable interest. I was always intent on hearing their stories, even when they repeated the same accounts over the years.

Daddy's life was the most heart rendering to me. He had overcome overwhelming odds and was the role model I wanted to emulate throughout my life.

"The best thing about "the good ole' days," Gilly, is that they're gone!" Daddy would often say.

I didn't understand the full impact of what he meant at the time. Angelo Fortunato Battaglia, the first son in a family of 18 children, was named after his paternal grandfather. Being born on 13 January 1905, his middle name became Fortunato because 13 is a lucky number in Italy.

Daddy was six-feet-tall, lean, with dark hair and hazel eyes. His upper lip was blanketed by a black mustache. Several of my girlfriends confessed to having a crush on him.

"You have a crush on my father!" I retorted in disbelief.

"Yes, Gilda. I can't help it," the teenage neighbor in the corner house confessed.

My earliest memories were of Daddy returning from a long day at his Naturopathic office, after riding the Broad Street Subway and then a trolley car to Chew Street, in the Germantown section of Philadelphia. His arms were loaded with stuffed animals. Vicki and I laughed with glee as he'd bark like a dog, meow like Felix the cat, or pretend to smell like the skunk before he would toss the soft critters to us. My father liked to fire our imaginations with made-up stories like "Chocolate Boy and Peppermint Girl," an adventurous duo who did daring deeds and solved many mysteries. We'd listen in rapt attention, imagining the bravery of such a diverse pair, but we were most captivated by accounts of his childhood in Italy and Philadelphia.

"I was born in a small town in Puglia on the Adriatic Sea, Margherita di Savoia, named after the first Queen of Italy. A pizza was also named after her."

"Will you take me there, Daddy?"

"Yes, someday, sweetie."

Daddy was always educating us. In 1948, when I was ten-years-old, most Americans did not know what pizza was. Italian food to the *Amerigans* consisted of spaghetti and meatballs.

"We want to go to Italy, Daddy. Why did you leave and come here?" I used to ask, anticipating the story he repeated so many times.

"Italy was beautiful but day-to-day life was hard. Many workers in my town were not even paid with money. Some toiled 12 hours a day, six days a week in the blazing sun in the local salt industry earning a salary of coffee and cheese, which they bartered among themselves. Your grandfather was one of them for a while until he decided to leave and come to America."

"Why didn't they want money instead?" I'd interrupt. He didn't answer.

Dad and young siblings arrive in the United States.

"What was your life like when you came here?" I would ask, knowing the question would prompt him to tell us about one of the bleak jobs he held from the time he was eight years old.

"In Margherita, it never got very cold and never snowed."

"Never?" I'd ask in disbelief.

"No. Never! We came to Philadelphia by ship in August 1913—not to Ellis Island like many other Italian immigrants. I had a pair of short pants to wear every day. My mother made me a nice suit with long trousers reserved for church on Sunday. I had to get up at 4 a.m. and sell newspapers at the North Philadelphia Train Station, with my legs bare up to my knees. It was not bad until winter came. The snow covered my bare legs; my skin turned red and chapped. When all the papers were

My father, Angelo Fortunato Battaglia, cleaning trolley cars.

sold, I went home for breakfast. All we had was coffee and milk. Sometimes there was a hard piece of bread which my brothers Santo and Giuseppe would throw at each other like a ball. The only way we could eat it was to dunk it in the coffee."

"I hate coffee," I said. "I'll never drink it."

Daddy loved to take long walks with us. Every excursion had an educational purpose. He'd talk about botany as we passed ferns.

"Take a look at this; the little coiled green plant shows alternation of generation. When this small one dies, a new, big fern will grow."

"What is he talking about?" I whispered to Vicki. "How does he know all that stuff?"

"Stay in school. Get an education!" he'd exclaim to his impressionable walking companions. "If you don't, you might have to work in places like I did."

"Like what, Daddy?"

"Like in the Ball Bearing Factory. After school, I had a job in a place where they put a heavy, long black rubber apron around my waist. I had to dip metal equipment in a vat of acid. After the first day at work, my apron was full of big holes. I was so scared." I was too, imagining wearing something riddled with gaping holes from acid.

"As a teenager, I cleaned trolley cars. One of the worst things I had to do was in the winter at the train station. We worked on the steel rails. Our hands got so cold they'd bleed. I used to be so tired I'd fall asleep in class, yet I never quit school."

"Why didn't you quit those awful jobs?"

"My mother died when I was 14 years old, and we always needed money. A friend and I dreamed of running away out West and becoming cowboys to live free under the open skies. He succeeded in doing it, but I could not because I had to take care of my five siblings. I wondered what happened to him. I am glad I didn't follow him because I wouldn't have had you."

I never quite believed his sacrifice story, but loved listening to it. The occupation I liked most was the one I could relate to, Italian water ice.

My paternal grandmother, Marìa Mezzetti Battaglia

"When I was 15, my father had me stationed behind a 100-pound pushcart in the summer. My job was to shave a huge block of ice for making Italian water ice. I enjoyed watching the purple, red, orange or blue syrup whirl through the frozen crystals. If customers wanted it to be extra sweet, I'd charge them double and they were happy to pay. I made good money, though it was tough work. Get an education."

"Yes, Daddy."

THE KLAN CAME CALLING

Mommy's childhood stood out in sharp contrast to that of my father. She was jovial and grateful for being born into a family that was loving and supportive. She seemed to know everyone in her village of Mays Landing, and remembered details of their lives with precision. Telling us about those experiences made her less homesick when she moved to Germantown. Although living and working conditions in Mays Landing had not been easy for her parents and grandparents, Mommy sported an optimistic attitude.

"Life in Mays Landing was beautiful. They were the happiest days," she would exclaim.

Mommy loved her brothers and sisters, but I think my Uncle Ralph was her favorite. He was "ornery", but fun to be with. Like Mommy, he often told me that he was forced to live in the segregated Grade in a modest wooden house without running water, gas, heat, or electricity, with a wood stove that only warmed a few of the rooms downstairs, and an "out house" where papers from the Sears and Roebuck catalog were used in lieu of Charmin. He told me several stories of the Italian immigrants, who, upon arriving in Mays Landing, were constantly called *Dagos, Guineas and Wops*. But it was Uncle Ralph's harrowing tale about when my grandfather opened his bar and grill that impacted me most.

"The family was enjoying dinner when a brick crashed and sailed through the dining room window. Rushing to the gaping space, everyone was horrified. We did not want to scream for fear the perpetrators would attack us. Members of the Ku Klux Klan, bedecked in their intimidating white robes and hoods, shouted from the grass, 'You dirty Dagos; go back to 'ITLY' where you belong!"

"Pop, why do they tell us to go back to Italy when I was born here?"

"Don't say or do anything, Raffaele. Never mention this to anyone; show them that you are better than they think," Grandpop advised in his heavy accent. "Somehow the Klan never 'visited' our family again. I often wondered if other Italians were targeted in town, but it was not a subject of conversation at our house."

Uncle Ralph's First Holy Communion.   *Mary Sorrentino, my mother.*

Despite being unwelcome, Italian immigrants continued to gravitate to the Cotton Mill of the Mays Landing Water Power Company. So why did Mommy say they were "the happiest days?" To her, the answer was simple.

"On Sunday, after Mass at Saint Vincent De Paul's Church, my extended family and friends convened at my parents' home where my grandparents lived with us. The house came alive with music, dancing and laughter. All the generations joined in entertaining themselves. No one was left alone or isolated on Sunday or any day, and were shown love as members of a true clan. They knew the secret for the happiest days."

MY GRANDPOP SORRENTINO

Like most Italian Americans, my parents' families had little money but lots of pride. My maternal grandfather, Raffaele, was no exception.

Sunday at Grandpop Sorrentino's house.

Like most of my relatives, he was strict, but totally devoted to his family. I prodded him to tell me about his life as I did my parents. Grandpop enjoyed sitting alone with me in a quiet corner to tell his stories.

"My family had a textile franchise in Naples. When the Italian economy collapsed in the late 1880s, I immigrated to the United States."

"How did you get here, Grandpop?"

He recounted what it was like crossing the Atlantic by ship for three weeks in steerage class.

"I was seasick most of the time. A large cauldron of *pasta e fagioli* (pasta and bean soup) was wheeled into the steerage dining area daily, but I could not swallow one spoon of it. The ocean was rough and being in the cramped quarters below with all those other sick people was unbearable, so I would try to sleep on the top deck. When we arrived in New York City, I found work in an Italian bakery where I made and delivered bread. For a while I slept on the floor near the ovens in a six-foot wooden bread box.

"I soon left Manhattan and went to Yardville, New Jersey, to work in a textile factory, then I subsequently left for Mays Landing where I heard there was a larger facility: The Mays Landing Water Power Company; it was strictly a cotton mill. When I arrived, I was employed instantly as a weaver. I could afford to buy a house, so I married, working six days a week, 12 hours a day from 6 a.m. to 6 p.m., and 7 a.m. to 12 p.m. on Saturday, earning six dollars a week. On Saturdays, my six children would accompany me to trim the long strings hanging from the ends of large rolls of cloth, which had to be cleaned before I would be paid. The mill rented to its workers houses that had a plot of land for each employee to plant vegetables and fruit trees. During the fall harvest, area farmers brought bushels of tomatoes and grapes to nearby Hammonton for the Italian locals to jar tomatoes for sauce and make wine."

Somehow, Grandpop managed to save money and sent for his parents and siblings, Gabrielle and Rosa, to join him in the village. Grandpop was the undisputed *Pater Familias*, a fact Mommy admired. It made her feel secure.

"As long as my Pop was around, nothing bad could ever happen to the family," Mommy often said.

Grandpop was interested in politics and was president of the Giuseppe Verdi Sons of Italy Lodge number 1085 in town.

"Local politicians asked me to be appointed under-sheriff in Atlantic County, but I was too embarrassed because of my Italian accent."

"You should have tried, Grandpop."

"No. I did the right thing."

I never agreed with him about that decision. He would have been an honest politician.

THE GREAT DEPRESSION

Stock market crashes! Those headlines struck panic in my heart," my mother said. "Your father and I had had enjoyed our Niagara Falls honeymoon up to that point. Daddy had worked hard to invest a few thousand dollars for his education and marriage. I had given all my earnings to Grandpop, as was the custom. There we were, standing before the spectacular Horseshoe Falls on the Canadian side with only enough funds to go to Philadelphia where Daddy was to begin his studies at the school of Naturopathic Medicine. That expectation was crushed. On arriving to the city after our shortened trip, we found a cold-water flat on top of the Unity Frankford market. Daddy immediately began to look for scarce day labor. I was soon pregnant and did not venture out. Paying bills became difficult as the country was thrust into the 'Great Depression.' Our financial situation did not improve on the birth of your sister Gloria in 1930. Her delivery had been hard. I was in labor over three days and the doctor asked Daddy to decide whether the baby or I should live."

"I can't make that decision. Do your best to save them both," Daddy directed.

"We were rewarded with what the family said was the most beautiful newborn they had ever seen. Gloria's enormous ebony eyes and raven ringlets were beautiful. We doted on her, especially after my obstetrician's warning."

"You should never risk another pregnancy. This must be your first and last child."

"We named her Gloria, because she was a glorious miracle. Caring for little Gloria was another matter. In winter, our meager quarters were frigid because we could not afford heat. Food was also scarce. I used to go into the store below and look at the jars of plump olives. My mouth was watering. We could barely afford bread and coffee."

Daddy told how much Mommy craved a cup of hot coffee. It cost only five-cents at Horn and Hardart's Automat, but he didn't have even that.

"I reached into my jacket pocket. There was a hole in it. Fumbling with my finger in the opening I felt something hard in the lining and pulled out a nickel. "Mary, we're going to Horn and Hardart's after all. You'll have your coffee," I told her. When I inserted the five-cent coin

Grandpop's mother and sister Rosa.   *My parents and Gloria.*

into the slot, several nickels poured out. I never took anything that didn't belong to me in my life, but I scooped up those nickels and we rushed out of the restaurant."

"Times got bleaker," my mother said. "One day, while looking for work, Daddy fainted in the street from hunger. That same day, a rabbi went to our shabby apartment door seeking a donation to the Jewish Milk Fund. When I appeared, my gauntness startled the rabbi. I was disheveled because I had spent most of the day in bed, trying to keep Gloria warm with my body heat.

"I'm sorry, sir, but we have nothing to give you."

"That's all right. I see you are in need. God will provide."

"The rabbi kept his word. After that visit, a bottle of milk was delivered to our door every morning. It was a godsend for Gloria."

"Why didn't you tell your parents how bad things were, Mommy?"

"We were too proud. They might have criticized me for marrying your father and not the mayor's son. I couldn't bear that."

"I was always grateful to Jewish people for providing milk for Gloria," Dad added.

But Grandmom and Grandpop found out about my parents' plight after Mommy's brother Louie had made a surprise visit to see her and Daddy in Philadelphia. Grandpop and Grandmom had not seen Gloria since her baptismal day in Mays Landing and decided to go unannounced.

"Traveling the 52 miles from Mays Landing to our Philadelphia apartment was hard for my parents, as well as leaving their business for a day. They managed to travel because my brother Ralph just got a car and offered to drive. When I heard Mom and Pop's voices outside my apartment, I thought my heart would stop. There was no food or even heat to offer. I hesitated to open the door out of shame."

"Mary, what is this?" Pop said in shock. "You have nothing. Where is Angelo?"

"He is out looking for any work he can find."

"Don't worry. Everything will get better," Grandpop reassured.

My grandfather kept his word. They had come with the car filled with fresh food from the farm. Grandpop went to the store downstairs and loaded the rickety table in my parents' apartment with the jars of olives and other foods Mommy longed for.

"My parents never criticized Daddy. Instead, when he came home looking so thin and weak, they praised him for his effort to support his small family. From that day on, our lives changed. Daddy saw an advertisement for an artist who knew the silk-screening process for the National Flag and Banner Company on Vine Street."

"Where did he learn to do that?"

"He didn't, but necessity makes you learn new things. He told the owners, Harry and Pinkus, that he was experienced."

"Show us samples of your work," they said.

"I can't now. Let me into your studio this evening and by tomorrow morning you will have a finished product," Daddy assured.

"We took Gloria with us and Daddy worked all night until he figured out the process of designing on a stencil and using a squeegee to paint artwork onto cloth. Your father always excelled in drawing and the next morning he made a sample banner for a movie at the Earl Theater. Harry and Pinkus were pleased and he was hired. My kid brother Ralph moved in with us to work on the squeegee, while my brother Louie came to sell pencils on the street for a dollar a day. Times were looking up for all of us."

"Through those hard days, I was always grateful to Jewish people for helping us. We will never forget what they did," Daddy always said. I was happy to hear that.

"When did Daddy become a doctor?"

"As soon as we could pay our expenses, he saved once again to enroll in the Naturopathic School. God kept giving, in abundance, and in 1938, you were born. Disregarding the doctor's warning, I wanted another child. Daddy and I had not planned that 14 months later, your sister Victoria would be born. Surprisingly, both deliveries were normal and quick, and we were very happy."

Their story makes me feel proud. They struggled, but most of all, they stayed together. Never did I hear one of them complain, criticize or threaten to leave the other. They showed us what true love is.

CLOSE FAMILY RELATIONSHIPS

An aspect of Italian American life that appealed to me was that Italian families preferred to live together in one building or close by. It was a custom I admired. Grandpop's brother, Gabrielle (Gable, to us), for example, lived in the village of Mays Landing, as did his sister, Rose. Their extended families formed a strong network of support and nurturing for all their offspring.

Grandpop's middle brother, Luigi (Louie), wanted to provide more social opportunities for his family than were available in that South Jersey village. On one of our visits to the Bronx, I cornered Uncle Louie and asked him to tell me some things about his life.

"In Italy, I had entered the seminary. I love my religion and wanted to become a priest. After a few years there, I had second thoughts and felt the need to marry and have a family. When my brother Raffaele left for America, I wanted to join him. Mays Landing was such a small community. I wanted to give my family more choices to expand in life.

"When I moved to New York, I met Aunt Adelaide and we married. I bought this three-story house in the Bronx. We occupy the middle floor while our two daughters, Ida and Carmella (Millie), live on the upper and lower levels with their families. We always want our families to be as close as possible."

Uncle Louie's daughter, Cousin Millie, did not marry until she was 52 years old because she wanted to be at home to care for her parents.

"I would never marry because Mom was a diabetic and needed regular insulin injections," she said in her New York accent. "She needed a lot of care and I could never neglect her."

When Aunt Adelaide died, Cousin Millie married a man her age, who had taken care of his mother also. They decided not to wed until their filial obligations had been met. Uncle Louie had two other daughters who lived nearby.

"Every spring and fall we sisters go to clean each other's homes. Every day we eat together and always after Mass on Sunday," cousin Ida would say.

It was a treat for us to visit them because everyone congregated in the capacious kitchen in the basement. I never knew why so many Italians maintained a pristine kitchen upstairs and a working kitchen in the basement. The lower-level kitchen was packed with people and the irresistible aroma of homemade bread baking, sausage, meatballs and *braciole* (stuffed flank steak) frying, sauce bubbling, and a roast with potatoes, sizzling. The culinary delight lasted the entire day and sometimes into the night.

Italian Americans were indeed very loyal to their family and friends. At times, however, misunderstandings could erupt whereby individuals and/or families would cease to speak to one another for days, months or even years. If one member of the group was angry at someone, the whole clan could be expected to get involved, but that was more the exception than the rule with my relatives because they all loved to talk and could not bear to be silent for more than a few minutes, regardless of the circumstances.

Whatever the situation, I loved growing up as an Italian American. To me, what made the experience so special was the *calore umano* (human warmth). I knew of no other people who were more loving and caring for one another and for others than they were, once you became a part of their biological or social circle. The Italian way of life, impregnated with art and an implacable passion for life and food, created beauty and joy. A cup of espresso, expertly prepared, became the perfect vehicle to express romance, do business or solve the problems of the world. Most Italians took their greatest pleasure in breaking bread and enjoying a glass of wine while being surrounded by loved ones.

"Alla salute," they'd say, clinking their glasses.

It didn't get better than that. Within that complex culture, I will tell my story.

BETTER LUCK NEXT TIME

Mommy was her family's oral historian, tracing the genealogy of all its members back several generations. She was a great narrator with a wealth of personal anecdotes and important data associated with almost everyone in the village of Mays Landing in the 1920s. She had a knack for telling and retelling the same scenario with original enthusiasm, excitement and humor. We'd hear her stories at home, in the car, when we took trips cross country or to Florida, on cruise ships, or taking the three-mile trek walking home from the Penn Fruit market in Germantown, our arms laden with heavy, bulging grocery bags that seemed lighter with our laughter. The telling was so familiar I would request her accounts based on an identifying introduction.

"Mommy, tell me about the time Uncle Joe was naughty and Grandpop punished him by making him put on his sister's dress and tying him to a tree for all to see."

"Mommy, I want to hear when I was two years old and jumped in the deep end of a public pool in Philadelphia with all my clothes on, and you went in after me wearing a chiffon dress. Tell me how your dress shrunk high up and you kept trying to pull it down on the trolley car on our way home."

With those clues, her eyes would widen and sparkle as she'd begin to spin the ever-familiar yarn. The text was so known to me I'd remind her if she skipped a passage. If she tired of telling such familiar material, I was unforgiving in my insistence she would continue and include all the details.

Mommy always wanted to entertain us with the antics of her family and childhood friends. She missed them so much when she moved to Germantown with Daddy. Her stories made them seem close. But one of her tales did not leave me laughing.

"My mother had given birth to 13 children—only six of whom survived. All the children were delivered at home and their entrance to this the world was met with mixed reactions. It all happened in my parents' bedroom."

I used to love to go into that room smelling of pine where all the babies were made. Like the rest of my Italian relatives in Mays Landing, New York, Philadelphia or Italy, the bedrooms all had common features. A large crucifix hung over the bed. Rosary beads and scapulars (two pieces of cloth on a string representing a religious devotion) were on the bedposts. A bible was placed beside statues of Jesus, the Blessed Mother and other related saints. Some relatives had doilies where they placed the child Jesus of Prague, with its embroidered gold gown, red-lined cape and crown. The holy image was surrounded by stiff, crocheted triangles of white which often reminded me of shark fins circling in the ocean.

My grandparents' room was always darkened, even during the day. There were venetian blinds and sheer, simple beige curtains on the narrow windows, which were invariably closed. The furnishings were of sturdy, brown oak. The pieces seemed too large for the 10 x 12 area. There was a dresser in which Grandmom hid a box of candy in the second drawer. I knew the place of her cache and strategically removed butter creams and caramels one at a time to avoid being caught, or at least I thought."

"Who took candy from this box?" she'd ask, scowling, knowing full well it was I.

Her low-lying bed's headboard was massive and unadorned. A dresser in the corner boasted a hand-hammered silver brush and comb set, the only fancy, feminine item in the area. Even the carpet was a drab, thin, brownish-blue square.

One feature fascinated me most, laying on the night table next to where Grandmom slept. It was a framed picture of Saint Gerard. His portrait was intriguing. His delicate features had a greenish-grey pallor. He clutched a crucifix in his graceful, slender fingers and looked heavenward. A human skull lay on a table in the background.

"Who is that man, Grandmom?" I would ask.

"That is Saint Gerard, the Patron Saint of Pregnant Women. He is my favorite."

"Why do you like him more than the others?"

"He was born in the small hill town of Muro Lucano, in the poor region of Basilicata, Italy. I also come from Basilicata," she would add. "He ran away from home to become a priest. He taught and ministered to the poor and sick."

No one in the family ever mentioned the exact place from where Grandmom hailed. Uncle Ralph said he used to hear the name Muro Lucano mentioned frequently, but he wasn't sure if his mother was born there or in another local hill town. The exact location would remain a mystery.

Could she have been from the same place as her beloved saint? It would make sense. When I look at the picture, I often wonder if she prayed to him to have 13 children or did she pray not to get pregnant? I'll never know because no one in the family ever discussed those matters. Daddy's mother had 18 pregnancies and only five of her babies lived. I wish I could have known her.

Mommy often informed my sisters and me of how her mother had her infants delivered at home by a midwife.

"At the time of labor, most relatives and friends gathered in the parlor, awaiting the cries of a newborn. What would it be? Some people bet on the gender. Toasts were made for "un figlio maschio!" (a boy). The whole room was abuzz with anticipation. When a cry was heard from Grandmom's bedroom upstairs, there was a silent pause downstairs, as though time had stopped.

"It's a boy!" a jubilant voice would proclaim from above, and repeat as its bearer descended the stairs to herald the good news over and over to the assembled guests.

Cheers would erupt in the crowded room. There was much back-slapping, congratulations for the father, cigar-passing, toasts and liquor slugging. Coffee sport flowed; it was made by spiking espresso with hefty doses of anisette or brandy.

If the infant's cry signaled "It's a girl." an opposite response took place. There was no jubilation, back-slapping or cigars. There were no liquors. Instead, heads were lowered. Women passed out ginger ale and the guests discretely began leaving the room, often offering condolences."

"Better luck next time," they'd say, with sympathetic smiles.

But that was then. It's 1950 and I'm 12. Do they still think like that?

"Mommy, weren't they ever happy to have a girl?"

"Oh, yes," she'd say. "Your father and I wanted girls. Daddy always says he's not a sportsman. He doesn't fish and he can't play baseball; he wouldn't know how to relate as well to sons as daughters."

Mommy's explanation did not convince me. I never smiled on hearing that story. I wondered how Grandmom felt lying in her bed and hearing "It's a girl?" She must have felt like Ann Boleyn.

That story makes me feel second class. It's not fair. It isn't my fault I was born a girl. All I know is that I will show all of them that I am as good as any boy. Well—almost.

MY GRANDPOP BATTAGLIA

In contrast to mommy, my father was often embarrassed by his father, Andrea Battaglia. Born in the town of Barletta, a *contadino* (farmer), his life had been one of hard work and scant education. He always spoke in a loud voice, like many of the *contadini* in Margherita di Savoia, where he later resided.

Like Grandpop Sorrentino, he was a husky man of medium build. He had a quick smile and a temper to match. He was a tough guy whose life had been one of relentless hard work in the fields of Puglia, and later, in American factories and small businesses.

Many Italians in those days bated their children and grandchildren to urge them to fight back. They knew the world was a tough place and they wanted to prepare their young to survive in it. Feisty offspring were respected more than passive ones. I won Grandpop Battaglia's esteem by being defiant.

Grandpop Battaglia visited our home in Germantown on rare occasions, always accompanied by other family members because he did not drive. One afternoon, after a typically hearty family meal, Daddy told me to clear the table. He hadn't asked Vicki to help, only me.

"That's not fair. Vicki should help too or I won't do it."

Daddy could not let such public rudeness go unpunished or he'd lose face in front of his parent. As expected, Daddy removed his belt. It stung the back of my right leg and the pain made tears come to my eyes.

"You should cry for speaking to me like that," Daddy said.

"I won't cry. You can try, but you can't make me," I retorted.

I walked over to the staircase and sat on one of the steps. Everyone watched me fight back the water welling in my eyes, especially my grandfather who was grinning from ear to ear.

"Good-a-gal, Gilda. Try-an-a-get-a," he said.

He meant to repeat my dare of "Try and make me."

While Grandpop did not want me to be disrespectful, he admired my spunk. From that day on, every time he saw me, he'd smile with pride, calling me "Try-an-a-get-a."

CHAPTER THREE
THE DREAM CASTLE

When I was six years old, in 1944, Mommy entered our bedroom smiling.

"I have wonderful news, Gilly and Vicki. Today, your father paid off the mortgage to our "Dream Castle" house. Now we own our home. Aren't you excited?"

Her enthusiasm was contagious, so we answered, "Yes!" Of course, we did not know what a mortgage was, but we figured home ownership was a very good thing.

Mom worked hard with Dad in Center City. They put Vicki and me under the "care" of our older sister. They did not know that Gloria was more often absent than present from the house after school, leaving us younger siblings alone for long periods to fend for ourselves. Our senior sibling was strikingly beautiful, with enormous dark eyes and long, flowing hair, which she rolled onto a "rat" to create a glamorous hairdo. She'd spend time admiring herself in the mirror as she'd apply makeup and don clothing that would accentuate her curvaceous body. Once satisfied with an ensemble, she would strut out of the house, confident that she would soon be admired by passersby.

Vickie was a quiet, obedient child. Unlike Gloria, she had lovely, soulful hazel eyes which reminded me of a fawn's, delicate and a little skittish. I was the assertive one, always inventing new ways to get into mischief and bearing Vicki along to shoulder the blame, even though no one ever scolded her for anything because I was the obvious culprit. Being unsupervised for long stretches granted endless opportunities for me to explore our house, the community and the lives of our neighbors, and create mischief.

McMahon Street was a diverse neighborhood in the 1940s. There were Scots, Irish, English, Germans, Jews and Italians, all living in

Vicki and I in front of the Dream Castle.

proximity. The "colored" were relegated to a separate section, close to downtown Germantown. Their community, as ours, was modest, with clapboard houses and tidy streets, through which we passed frequently to go to "The Avenue," a term to designate downtown Germantown.

McMahon consisted of two rows of houses on opposite sides of the street. Both sides were kept in pristine condition. All residents took pride in maintaining their six-room, one bath "Dream Castle" homes, as they were advertised in local realty offices. The fairy-tale name for these row houses with small, sloping lawns was inspired by their massive, grey granite columns in front, which supported a small roof. Jagged granite trim joined one house to the next. They didn't look at all like the castles I saw in the Robin Hood movies, although I heard, "A *man's home is his castle.*"

Compared to our neighbors, the interior of our house was luxurious.

"Girls, your father and I bought this crystal chandelier for the dining room. We want you to wash each piece and keep it clean," Mom said with pride. "We bought this mahogany dining room set from Van

Sciver's so be careful not to scratch it."

I do not know where or what Van Sciver's is, but it sounds important.

Our living room had a mirror trimmed in gold leaf. I loved looking at my reflection in that gilded frame. Dad loved art work and adorned our walls with paintings of a ship at sea and flowers in a vase. One wall was covered in bright paper with red roses nestled in decorative cream-colored molding.

This is pretty. The roses reflect in the mirror on the other side.

Outside, flowers were planted near the top ledge of the lawns, which I often uprooted to sell back to the owner of the house. Although there were no buyers, I persisted, and the inhabitants complained often to Mom and Dad. The small porches were furnished with comfortable, green or white metal chairs and brightly colored striped awnings.

McMahon was a vibrant street. The Abbott Milk Wagon was a daily sight, pulled by a brown-spotted horse. I loved patting him and felt the gentle animal knew me.

"He really likes me," I'd say to the milkman.

"You're right about that, honey," he'd answer, good-naturedly.

I'd watch it patiently eat oats from the feed bag attached near his mouth as he pawed the pavement, and observed with curiosity the "road apples" he subsequently left behind. Vicki and I would take the bottles of milk into the house. The cream had risen to the top and froze. I liked scooping the white delight into a bowl and drizzling syrup on it, claiming I was enjoying a sundae for breakfast. Hucksters came weekly, bringing a variety of fresh produce in their open trucks. In the blistering summer heat, they would unplug a juicy watermelon for a potential customer.

"It's not sweet," Dad would sometimes say.

"That's okay. Let's try a different one," and another wedge was instantly produced.

Bushels of ripe tomatoes would sell quickly to the Italian neighbors who would jar the red fruit for making sauce and tomato paste for consumption throughout the long winter. The porches seemed permanently occupied by the elderly ladies who inhabited these intergenerational households. Mrs. Di Pompei, Mrs. Sarnese and others would sit for hours with arms folded across their bosoms, scrutinizing our every move. Most of the Italian women in our area wore their hair in a neat, severe bun. Some kept the Italian tradition of wearing black for an extended period after the death of a close relative. Their straight drab house dresses were unflattering, hiding any hint of a waistline or alluring curves. Their shoes were "sensible," that is, thick and laced up the middle and ugly. To me, the ladies looked like book ends— square and sturdy.

Mrs. Di Pompei was such a woman. She arrived from Naples, Italy, and lived with her grown children; she never learned to speak English. Every time we met, she said, "God-a Bless, and Nice-a-Gal." Her vocabulary never deviated from these two expressions.

Other "chair detectives" were not as kindly. They often scolded us and told our parents of any slight transgression. Of course, I gave them more fodder for disciplinary action than the Abbott milkman's horse ever consumed.

One of the "vigilantes" saw me hiding, waiting for Mrs. Litwack to return home from work. The Litwacks had a hat factory in Center City, Philadelphia, and Mrs. Litwack proudly modeled her beautiful millinery laden with vibrant colored flowers. As she was passing our house, I decided the floral spray atop her head looked wilted, so I took our hose, turned it on high, and sent the flowers and our unsuspecting neighbor flying in all directions.

"Oh! What is that?" she yelled, in shock from the sudden deluge.

When the informant notified my parents of my latest escapade, I too ran in all directions, trying in vain to avoid Dad's belt.

McMahon Street was my entertainment center. Every day after school, I'd play in the street, stepping aside for passing cars with Rosalie, Patsy, Mary and Domenic Sarnese, Eddie and Merle Rice and a raft of others. Hop Scotch, jacks, Double Dutch jump rope, roller skating and stick ball were commonplace sports on the pavement.

"We don't want you on our ball team," the boys used to shout, so I discovered other forms of amusement.

One of my favorite made-up games was "Sheena of the Jungle," where I'd pretend to wear a stunning, sleek leopard skin. Vicki wanted the same imaginary outfit, so we would quarrel before the game began. I'd then play at "Sheena," climbing trees and dangling upside down from sturdy branches until it grew dark.

No one locked their doors. Neighbors and friends would just walk in, clanging the front screened portal in the summer. They would join us for heaping plates of ice cream from the Breyers store nearby, often speaking Yiddish, German or Italian.

"Why do the Jewish kids call their Grandpops *Zadeh*? And why do the Italians say *Nonno*?" How I longed to understand and speak the exotic languages!

At home, Gloria would entertain the neighbors and us by playing her accordion. *Lady of Spain* reverberated annoyingly in my sleep. I liked her storytelling more. On summer nights, we'd sit on the front steps and she would tell us and other kids tall tales which were continued the next evening. I always remembered the details and reminded her if she skipped a part. In cold weather, we'd sit in the living room and listen to the radio. With lights turned off, we'd shudder and squeal at the popular, scary sound of the squeaking door and deep voice of the narrator of *The Inner Sanctum*.

Playing tricks on Vicki was another of my favorite pass times. One day, I was in an inventive mood, planning to shock my little sister. I thought of the perfect scenario.

"I can fly, Vicki."

"No, you can't!" she answered, emphatically.

"Yes, I can," I retorted, matching her determination. "I'll show you."

I climbed up one of the jutting columns, onto the roof with a large umbrella under my arm. Peering down at my incredulous sister, I opened the parasol with a dramatic flair. Balancing on the edge of the roof, I examined the verdant hedges below. My legs began to wobble as I was on tip toe. Vicki gazed up, speechless.

This is scary. What if I break a leg or something? I started the dare and now I must finish it. I don't want Vicki to think I'm not tough.

I took a deep breath, held my parachute high and leapt. The umbrella turned inside- out as I fell into the protective branches of the arborvitae. Scratched and a bit shaken, I took stock of my physical condition.

Good. No bones are broken. Stand and act like you demonstrated a flying lesson.

I got up unscathed and struggled out of the greenery. Vicki was wide-eyed, her mouth agape.

"You really can fly," she exclaimed, awestruck.

"I told you so!" I answered haughtily.

THE TIN MAN KNEW

War raged in Europe. As children, we were acutely aware of suffering in the world. Everyone had a ration book: coffee, sugar and butter were in short supply. We had a Philco radio and we listened intently each day to the broadcasts, which transmitted grim news. Our cousins Pat (Pasquale), Muzzy (Antonio), David and Daddy's brother Sandy (Santo), served in the United States army. My parents, two sisters and I prayed at home nightly for their safe return.

It was at the Walton Theater two blocks away where gruesome, visual details of concentration camps came alive to me. I cringed at the images of frightened families being herded behind barbed wire as terrified children were yanked from the protective arms of their mothers. Those sights haunted me in my sleep. There were times I woke up screaming after vivid nightmares.

Mommy was home less frequently. She went with Daddy to help him as a receptionist in his naturopathic practice on Walnut Street in Center City. She had started taking courses in science during the day and sometimes at night at a place called Beaver College.

"Mary, you will be the bread winner when I am gone," Dad used to say. "Go to college and become a Naturopathic physician." I hated her being away.

"Gilly, I'm going to be out for a while. Be a good girl and don't fight with Gloria while I'm gone."

"No, Mommy. Don't go!"

"I'll be back soon."

She smiled sweetly and donned her one grey suit, high heels and small-brimmed hat with pink rosebuds and short veil obtained from our neighbor, Mrs. Litwack's millinery establishment. I ran after her crying, begging her not to leave me like the children in Europe. Gloria and her sympathetic school companions from the neighborhood restrained me and tried to console me but this was a familiar sight on McMahon Street.

It was September when Mommy made a statement I did not want to hear.

"Gilly, I have wonderful news for you. In a week, you will be going to school."

Gloria, then a student at Roosevelt Junior High School, had attended Francis Daniel Pastorius Elementary School on Chelten Avenue, where Vicki and I were to go. It was named after the German born founder of Germantown. The building resembled a picture of the French Bastille Daddy had shown me in a book, a horseshoe-shaped structure with solid grey-granite walls.

Mommy spent countless hours preparing me for the big day. She'd tell me how she had loved her one-room schoolhouse, the *Uptown* in Mays Landing, and what a good student she had been.

"In those days, Mr. Bailey was my teacher. He taught three grades, first through third simultaneously in the one-room building."

My quick-minded Mommy would listen to what the older students were learning and soon Mr. Bailey had her assisting his advanced pupils. It was there that she memorized the entire poem *Evangeline* by Henry Wordsworth Longfellow. I remembered one line she often recited to us.

"This is the forest primeval. The murmuring pines and the hemlocks. . ."

The day arrived that would change my life forever. Mommy parted my hair and wove two neat plaits. She had also made a new dress on her treadle sewing machine. It was pretty with miniature rose-colored flowers and bric-a-brac trim on the collar. It was time to go.

"You'll love school as much as I did," she kept repeating. We crossed the trolley tracks on Chew Street as she gripped my hand tightly.

Two blocks from our neighborhood, Chew Street was a bustling thoroughfare. Maimon's Drug Store with its soda fountain was on the corner.

The Cooper and Fitton Hardware Company across the street had a display of metallic objects outside. In front was a full-sized tin man standing guard, his lips frozen in a perpetual silver smile.

As we passed Mr. Tin Man that day, the gaze from his dark, hollow eyes seemed to follow me as though he knew where I was going. He saw I was not happy and that I had no choice. My mother's cheerfulness irked me. I felt like telling her to stop trying so hard to convince me I would like elementary school. But I walked on, hand-in-hand, in submissive silence.

As we trudged up a hill, the austere destination loomed on the horizon. My heart sank with each step. As we approached the entrance, groups of children appeared with their mothers. They looked like prisoners behind a high metal fence. The closer we got, the more I wanted to bolt and go home to our living room where Vicki would be playing with her Chinese checkers. Mommy had to be home all day to take care of my younger sibling. I longed to be with them, but no, I too had to join the ranks of the captives.

Entering the school yard, I took in my surroundings. Flanking a massive grey stone wall was a row of outdoor water fountains. They consisted of ivory-colored porcelain cups where the liquid streamed down in a pathetic trickle, leaving ribbons of rusty, orange stain behind. What upset me most was the metal fence circling the property which resembled the barbed wire in the newsreels at the Walton.

Mommy released her hand and smiled benevolently.

"I have to go now. You'll love kindergarten, Gilly."

She's wrong. I won't like it. Whatever you do, don't cry in front of all these kids.

Outside, a teacher separated us into rows of boys and girls and told us to stand straight. Mrs. Price, the Principal, greeted us with a smile, which did not reassure me.

We entered the building and marched through a dark brown corridor to arrive at our class. The room was bright in contrast to the dim hall and was full of toys, a play kitchen, stacks of coloring books and crepe paper. The middle-aged teacher told us to sit in tiny wooden chairs with decals of cheery animals while she would call our names. I chose one with a happy-faced brown bear cub.

When the instructor came to my name, she could not pronounce the first or last.

"Guilda, or Golda, is it?" she asked.

"No. It's Gilda," I said, emphasizing "Jill-da," with the soft "G" in Italian.

"Oh, yes. Gilda," she repeated, with the hard, Germanic sound. Battaglia became a jumble of consonants I did not even attempt to correct.

I hate my name. Everyone I meet mispronounces it. Why wasn't I called Mary or Jane? Where did my parents get Gilda?

After roll call, I raised my hand meekly and asked the teacher if I could be excused.

"Yes, the girls' room is next door."

This is my chance. I'm getting out of here.

Walking quietly and swiftly down the gloomy wooden corridor, I rushed out the metal door and bolted beyond the cyclone fence to freedom. I kept running the mile to get home without looking back or sideways lest it slow my stride. Rows of houses and little stores whizzed past my peripheral vision. At Chew Street, I purposely avoided the Tin Man's disapproving, steely stare as I skirted Maimon's.

Arriving home, I breathlessly, but cautiously entered through the back entrance near the kitchen. My mother was there and saw me come in. She looked at me in silence, with a mixture of wonder and understanding.

"Why are you home so soon, Gilly?"

"The school burned down, Mommy."

"Oh, I'll have to call the principal to hear what happened."

"No. Don't, it's not there anymore."

It's no use. She knows full well I am lying. She will call and then send me back to the Bastille.

Once again, we trekked the mile to Francis Daniel Pastorius Elementary School in silence. This time I looked directly at the Tin Man. He glared at me, his metallic face shining knowingly in the sunlight.

Before long I was back in the bright classroom where the other pupils were enjoying cutting crepe paper objects. The teacher motioned for me to sit in one of the little chairs. She smiled, and like Mommy, didn't scold me.

Everything seemed small there, even the light brown mole on my right knee which I kept staring at with head bowed to avoid looking up and facing my shame for telling a big lie on my first day of kindergarten.

MY SISTERS

For as long as i could remember, Mom put Gloria in charge of Vicki and me. She even gave my older sister an allowance for doing so. That eluded me because Gloria was absent from the house most of the time. Where she went, Vicki and I never knew.

On the rare occasions Gloria was home after school, she was a taskmaster, relegating us younger ones to the position of house maids. We had to clean the kitchen, bathroom and make the beds daily. Regarding the latter, after we did our best, the "inspector general" entered and, without commenting, removed the spread and blankets in one fell swoop.

"Make it over."

"Why?" I protested.

"Because I said so."

"No!" I retorted, defiantly, knowing I was in for a pummeling.

While Vicki avoided confronting Gloria, I became more resistant.

My sister Gloria (center) and Vicki (right) with me at home.

This resulted in the inevitable blows, with Gloria pinning me down on the floor, helpless under her eight-year-older frame. She had the advantage, but I always fought as hard as I could. The stress resulted in my getting a migraine headache, yet I never backed off.

Maybe we have arguments because each of us has a strong personality. She wants to be boss of Vicki and me while I want to be boss of myself.

When I'd complain to Mom about Gloria's abusive behavior, she always answered the same way.

"Oh, that's not what she says."

That ended the conversation.

Mom is too tired after working 12 and 14-hour days to want to be bothered with our disputes. Instead of being angry with my mother, I feel sorry for her because I know how hard she toils each day to provide for our necessities. I feel sorry for Gloria too. She must be unhappy if she wants to fight with me all the time, but I love her and I always will, no matter what she does to me.

Gloria, paradoxically, could also be capable of acts of kindness and affection. She took us to the dentist and to violin lessons. On Wednesday evenings, Mom and Dad worked until 5 p.m. Gloria would prepare a

Gloria in her fur trimmed coat.

copious meal for the family. On Friday nights, she would ask a familiar question: "Would you like me to take you to Linton's cafeteria to have warm sticky buns topped with vanilla ice cream?"

Despite her authoritarian attitude, I always looked up to my older sibling. She was charismatic, always the center of attraction, she looked mature for her age. She also had a flair for the dramatic and joined the Germantown Theater Guild, where she appeared in several productions.

Gloria would apply red lipstick to accentuate her voluptuous mouth. Vicki and I knew that Dad idolized her. She was his first born and the first grandchild in the family. Everyone admired her, even me. Vicki and I never resented the fact that Gloria was Dad's pet. It somehow seemed natural. Dad tried in vain to persuade Gloria to go to college.

"Become a Chiropodist; you could make a good living," Dad advised.

Gloria did not want to study; she liked drama. Since an acting career was out of the question, our parents told her she could stay at home to watch Vicki and me until she decided on a profession. I was ten years old when she graduated from Germantown High School.

Vicki, on the other hand, was the opposite of Gloria and me. She seemed to live in her own world, one that was gentler and more tranquil, where there was no wrangling among siblings.

"Vicki was our 'surprise,'" Mom often said. "After two girls, we expected a boy. His name was to be Victor."

Well, the surprise was another girl. No matter what my parents said about preferring female offspring because they are not as rambunctious, I always felt they were disappointed not producing a male heir in an Italian family. I don't know if Vicki shared my feelings on the subject. She never mentioned it.

Vicki had a delicate, slender frame, which brought comparative criticism from Mom and other family members.

"Mary, make Vicki eat more. She is too skinny. Make her plump, or just right, like Gilly."

Because Italians thought being robust was beautiful and a sign of health, I used to overeat just to gain approval while Vicki's slim figure enabled her to be a great walker and to enjoy a lovely figure. She loved going on errands to the Penn Fruit Market on Germantown Avenue, which was two miles from our home. Her energy was boundless. I, on the other hand, preferred a more sedentary existence at home, reading a book. Then again, Vicki also liked to read; she was smart and liked to study. Unlike Gloria, she intended to go to college.

Vicki resembled my father's mother. We had only one photograph of our paternal grandmother next to an artificial lemon tree. She had died when Dad was 14 years old. Dad was proud of her and said she had been an artist in Italy, painting the statues of saints in churches in the town of Barletta, near Margherita di Savoia. The lemon tree was said to be one of her creations. Like her grandmother, Vicki inherited hazel eyes, which sometimes appeared green in the sun, and her angular, attractive features.

While Dad showed a penchant for Gloria, Mom could not repress her pride in my resembling her side of the family, the Sorrentinos.

"You look exactly like me," she'd say. "You are 100 percent Sorrentino."

Of course, that was not true, but in her eyes, it was a compliment.

Sometimes I feel sad for Vicki. Gloria is Dad's favorite; I'm Mom's favorite. If I have children, I will never have a favorite. I will love each one for being special no matter who they look like.

Vicki and I were often dressed the same so that many thought we were twins. I didn't mind wearing Mom's hand sewn clothes and I don't think Vicki did either. We were inseparable companions, going and coming from school together. We kept each other company in the house while our parents worked long hours and Gloria disappeared. I was never lonely because Vicki was always at my side.

GOING INTO PHILADELPHIA

Contrary to the Italian American stereotype of protecting daughters, my parents encouraged Vicki and me to be resourceful and independent. "Gilly, you are seven years old. When I was your age, I helped my mother cook," Mom said. "Let me show you how to fry eggs."

Before long, I was cooking my meals when Mom and Dad were at work. Traveling unescorted into Center City was another example of what Vicki and I had to do.

My parents' Naturopathic/Chiropractic office was in Center City at 16th and Walnut Street on the second floor of a bank building. When I was seven and Vicki six years old, Mom took Vicki and me aside.

"I am going to teach you how to use public transportation to get to our office. You will travel one hour and a-half. Take a trolley car to the Olney Subway. Once you are on the subway, count 14 stops before you get off at Walnut Street," Mom told us.

We rode the noisy train to the Walnut Street exit and walked three blocks to their office. I never liked the trip, especially when there was a line of clients streaming out from the staircase of the bank building and circling around the corner as far as Chestnut Street. I never saw a doctor's office as busy.

"Oh, Vicki," I'd exclaim. "The line is like that at Radio City Music Hall in New York, when we would go to see the Christmas show. They won't finish work until midnight."

I resented the fact that their schedule was so packed because our home life was not like that of the other kids in the neighborhood. Most of my friends had fathers who worked from nine to five. Their mothers were home to cook dinner when they returned from school. Vicki and I went to an empty house most days and remained alone until our parents arrived later in the evening or at night. But our lives were also enriched because of my parents' work.

Observant neighbors often hurt my feelings with critical remarks. "Your mother doesn't love you. She'd rather go to work than to stay at home where she belongs," some liked to say.

I know Mommy loves me, but she may love Daddy more because she's always with him.

Unlike most children in the late 1940s, my parents could afford luxuries. We were the first on the block to have a new, shiny green Buick. Ours was the first dishwasher and TV. Their prosperity also resulted in our taking extended vacations and eating in the finest restaurants and attending concerts, the opera and ballet, but I would have traded it all to have Mommy home after school, cooking something special.

MAJESTIC MAURITANIA

My parents arrived home late as usual one October evening in 1948. We kids were waiting for them to eat dinner together. This night they were not their jovial selves. We knew something was amiss when they told us to sit before dinner because they had something important

Our family posing in front of the Mauritania.

to say. I was ten years old and had resented having to cook most of my own meals for the past three years. In 1948, most of my friends' mothers were home, preparing dinner when their children arrived from school. But not Vicki and me; we were latchkey kids, pulling out boxes of Mrs. Grass' dehydrated soup or a can of baked beans. The tiny piece of salt pork on top of the latter always fascinated me and I'd scoff it down before my sisters noticed. Tonight was different, as the serious look on my parents' faces bore witness.

"We've got some bad news and some good news to tell you," Mom said, drearily.

"The bad news is your father has a heart condition and the doctors told him today he has six months to live."

The announcement was like an electrical shock surging through my body. Dad saw my reaction and that of my sisters. He smiled bravely and hurriedly wanted to break the mood by announcing the good news.

"Cheer up! I've booked us all on a cruise in December to Cuba, Curaçao and Venezuela on the *Mauritania*."

Realizing we did not know what a *Mauritania* was, he explained it was a large ocean liner that was built in England and was one of the best and fastest in the world. If he were going to pass on, Dad was determined to leave us with a wonderful memory. "Wait until you see that ship; you'll be so thrilled."

I'll pretend to be excited and grateful for this vacation of a lifetime, as he described it, but to be honest, I don't care at all about going to South America. Where is it, anyway? I just feel so sad thinking of Dad's heart.

When our teachers were notified about our pending cruise, we became the talk of Francis Daniel Pastorius Elementary School.

"Do you realize how lucky you are?" asked my third-grade teacher, Miss Boyer.

"Yes." I replied, but really didn't.

The day before our December sailing, we stayed in a suite at the Royalton Hotel in New York City. It was an old place with plush accommodations, spacious rooms and overstuffed velvet chairs. Vicki and I would punch the arms and backs of the furniture sending billows of dust flying and hovering in the air. Beams of light from the windows illuminated the shimmering, suspended particles.

The next morning, a Yellow Cab drove us to the pier.

"Here she is, the *Mauritania*. What a bute!" said the cabby.

Indeed, she was and even more. Our home for the next two weeks was majestic. Its enormous black hull and jutting smoke stacks left us speechless. We had never seen anything like it. Stepping off the gangway, we entered a new world. The main lobby featured a circular, mahogany staircase with brightly polished brass fixtures. Huge vases with fresh flowers decorated the inlaid wooden end tables as lilting music welcomed us from what I later learned was a string quartet. Such elegance only existed in the movies at the Walton Theater. I felt like I was starring in a real movie, dazzled by all the elegance surrounding me.

Our family in Caracas.

A steward escorted us to our adjoining cabins. Gloria, Vicki and I shared one stateroom. I took my shoes off and climbed on the bed to look out the portholes where flocks of people gathered to wish a *Bon Voyage* to their friends and relatives. Gongs from the crew signaled it was time to sail.

"All visitors must leave the ship," was broadcast via a loudspeaker as revelers filed out reluctantly.

"I bet they wish they were in my shoes," I thought, selfishly.

Dad knocked on our cabin door.

"Girls, let's go on deck and see what's happening. You don't want to miss this. How do you like it so far?" he asked, beaming.

Dad seemed transformed embarking on this wonderful adventure. I felt so proud of my father who never complained about his six-month sentence. He only wanted to share an unforgettable memory with us.

The smokestacks belched billowing clouds of black smoke as the *Mauritania* slowly separated from the pier, guided by diminutive tug boats. What a contrast! A giant of the sea being led by such tiny vessels.

Confetti rained on our faces as the swelling group of onlookers wished us a happy trip. The ship navigated slowly along the Hudson River and passed the Statue of Liberty. Everyone on board seemed to quiet down, paying respect to the magisterial lady holding her torch high.

"Girls, get ready to eat now," Mom said. "We'll meet you outside the dining hall at 12 o'clock."

I wondered if they serve Mrs. Grass' soup in pretty bowls?

Pleasant chimes heralded lunch and boy, was I hungry! But en route to the dining area, we sisters eagerly explored many of the attractions we were going to enjoy aboard. There was a cinema, a pool and even a children's theater.

Like clockwork, our parents were waiting for us at the designated spot. Dad took my hand and kept looking at my face as we entered, wanting to see my reaction. He slowly led me in to what seemed a food fantasy land. At the entrance, a stuffed pheasant stood guard on a gleaming silver platter, its plumage splayed in a kaleidoscope of color. On another tray, there were monstrous-looking creatures with orange shells and formidable claws. Dad did not wait for me to ask.

"Those are lobsters," he instructed. "They may not look pretty but they have a wonderful taste."

"They're ugly! I'll never eat lobster," I retorted, emphatically.

"Someday you'll change your mind," he said, knowingly, with a gentle smile.

"Never!" I answered defiantly.

My attention was suddenly diverted from the crustaceans to long flaming skewers a waiter held, rapidly crossing the room.

"Daddy. That food is on fire," I exclaimed dumbfounded.

"Those are flaming kebobs."

This was a place with food I never knew existed. Even though I didn't want to eat pheasant, lobster or anything on fire, it was magical to watch. It was like a theater where waiters weaved between tables balancing wide trays and lifting silver domes on plates with a dramatic flourish, revealing mystifying morsels. My palate needed to be educated and Dad said this was the ideal place to learn. There was no Mrs. Grass' soup in sight.

At breakfast the next morning, Gloria, Vicki, and I ate alone as our parents wanted some time together. Ken, one of our servers, addressed me in his beautiful British accent.

"What would you like to order?"

I was confused and shy. Ken was so good looking, and his voice made my heart flutter.

I wanted to impress him with my knowledge of breakfast fare.

"I'll have scrambled eggs, bacon, ham, sausage, pancakes, waffles . . ."

"Stop!" Gloria ordered. "You can't eat all that!"

Ken winked my way and said he'd bring everything I mentioned just for me to sample. Platter after platter was put before me and I gobbled up as much as possible not to be wasteful, but I was uncomfortable doing so. Gloria was right. I couldn't eat it all.

Gloria asked Ken about his duties aboard this sailing paradise.

"I have several jobs. I rise at 5 a.m., scrub the main staircase, polish all brass knobs, plaques and ornaments, and then put on my waiter's uniform. After serving in the dining room, I work on deck in a variety of functions, completing a 10 to 12-hour work day."

Life is hardly paradise for the crew aboard, but they always have a ready smile for the passengers. I wonder if they get to eat what we are served.

I felt even more ashamed of what I had done at breakfast. I could imagine my teachers scolding and telling me there were so many starving children who would never waste food like I did.

After our hearty morning repast, the *Mauritania* encountered rough water off North Carolina. The high swells caused the vessel to lurch and pitch. My stomach followed the same rhythmic pattern and I no longer had thoughts of eating, quite the contrary. Mom, Gloria, and Vicki felt the same way, but Dad had his "sea legs." He strutted along the promenade deck in all his glory, looking heartier and healthier than ever.

Perhaps my prayer for him was really working as we sailed on the *Mauritania.*

CHAPTER FOUR

GROWING UP ITALIAN AND CATHOLIC

MRS. MAC CREA'S BIBLE CLASS

Religion played a major role in the lives of most Italian Americans. My relatives in Mays Landing and New York were avid church-goers. My parents were not, but they wanted us to receive the sacraments. First Holy Communion is a milestone in one's journey as a Catholic. At nine, I prepared for it at the Immaculate Conception School in Germantown, an imposing granite structure located across from the public school. Religion was not taught in Francis Daniel Pastorius Elementary School.

At first, I was curious about receiving religious teaching. In my public school, we started each day with a passage from the Old Testament of the Bible. I was proud to read aloud when the teacher called on me. Proverbs and Psalms taught me valuable life lessons. The message from First Corinthians made an impression on me.

"When I was a child, I thought as a child . . . , but when I became a man, I put away childish things."

I knew that one day I would have to assume a lot of responsibility, but for now, I was glad I was still a child. The 23rd Psalm was comforting. I used to recite "The Lord Is My Shepherd" mentally, before entering math class, hoping for divine assistance.

On entering the parochial school, the Mother Superior greeted us pleasantly and led us to a classroom where a priest was present. The nun smiled and complemented us for being ready for our significant sacrament.

"Congratulations for coming to prepare for your First Holy Communion. God loves all people, but He loves Catholics a little more."

On hearing those words, my hand waved in the air.

"Yes," she asked.

"Doesn't God love everyone the same?"

"As I said," she continued, visibly annoyed. "The Lord loves everyone, but He has a special place in his heart and in heaven for Catholics."

Unable to control myself, I blurted, "Do you think that's fair to everybody else? If God created all people, why would He bother to make some more likeable?"

The eyes of the priest and nun met and narrowed, communicating in a silent language. They simultaneously turned to scrutinize me and glared without answering my question. I never raised my hand in that class again.

Walking home from school one day a classmate told me about an after-school program he attended every week. It was a Bible class held midway between our school and McMahon Street.

"You go and hear Bible stories every Wednesday afternoon from 3 to 4. When they're over, the lady of the house gives you the biggest and best oatmeal raisin and chocolate chip cookies you ever ate!"

That sounds good. I'll go home to an empty house anyway, so why not venture to Bible class and sample the cookies?

The following Wednesday we went to visit Mrs. MacCrea, a sweet-faced, pleasingly plump lady who reminded me of a kindly grandmother. She wore a rose-colored house dress and lilac cologne. On her kitchen table, I noticed a tray of freshly-baked cookies whose enticing aroma was irresistible. Mrs. MacCrea saw me eying them, hoping she would break the custom. Before class began, she offered us the large, yummy confections.

A young woman escorted us and other youngsters into the basement area of the attractive, single red brick two-story house with blue shutters. She would place figures of Bible characters and animals from the Old and New Testaments on a felt board to keep our attention. I loved listening to stories about Daniel in the lion's den and Joseph's cloak of many colors. They were far more interesting than hearing about our sinfulness in catechism class at the Immaculate. Neither the story teller nor the matron of the house objected to my being Catholic as the latter introduced me lovingly to the other children.

"Everyone, this is our new friend, Gilda (hard "g," of course). All are welcome in my home."

That's good news because I really like it here.

Three months passed, and I never missed a Wednesday at Mrs. MacCrea's. Simultaneously, I had to prepare for first Holy Communion and my fellow classmates and I had to go to confession in preparation. I loved being in church. The atmosphere made me transcend to an ethereal, beautiful world. Waiting in line to enter the confessional was another matter.

"What are you going to say?" I asked the boy ahead of me.

"Oh, I don't know. I punched a kid in the playground once, but he started it."

"That'll be good."

"What are you going to confess?" he asked.

"My parents say I'm mouthy. Guess I'll start with that."

When I entered the dark chamber, a soft voice emanated from an invisible man behind a screen. It made me feel uneasy having to mention my sins. I didn't really know what I had done wrong, so I made up something.

"Forgive me, Father for I have sinned. I stole a Chiclet from the Food Fair market. I spoke back to my father and dared Vicki to say a bad word and she did."

"Do you regret your sins?" asked the voice, almost in a whisper.

"Yes, Father."

My confession seemed to go well until I made a terrible error. After my Act of Contrition, I somehow mentioned to the confessor that Jesus had brothers and sisters. The priest was aghast at my declaration.

"Where did you hear that blasphemy?" he exclaimed, hyperventilating.

"In Mrs. MacCrea's Bible class," I answered timidly.

"Who is Mrs. MacCrea and why are you going to her Bible class?" he demanded.

Of course, I couldn't mention the cookies, so I told him the stories were interesting. His manner did not soften. He was outraged.

"You are never to go back to that house. You are Catholic and don't belong there. Never, never return!"

"Yes, Father," I said with a combination of fear and sorrow.

No matter what, I must go back to that cheerful home, but only to bid a sad farewell to the woman who was so welcoming to me. I've been happy there and I am very fond of Mrs. MacCrea.

When I returned to her friendly red brick house, the sweet woman noticed my troubled expression.

"Is anything wrong, Gilda?"

"I can't stay for the class and I can never come here again" I said, peering into the dear lady's eyes. "Why not?" she asked. "The priest told me that I can't come anymore because I am a Catholic and you taught that Jesus had brothers and sisters." Tears welled and streamed freely down her cheeks. She was truly sorry I would not be continuing with the group. "I will miss you, Gilda. Here, dear, have one last cookie before you go. I made oatmeal raisin, one of your favorites."

It looked and smelled so good, but I resisted. It didn't seem right to accept it. That would be my sacrifice to let Mrs. MacCrea know how much I would miss her. Whether Jesus had brothers and sisters didn't matter to me. What I cared about was the love that kind woman shared with me and everyone who came to her Bible class. Surely Jesus would not be mad at that. Would He?

MY FIRST KISS?

"You're growing nicely, Gilly," Mom said.

I was 12 years old and in the fifth grade. It was apparent that several boys in my class liked me because they went out of their way to tease.

"Hey, can I walk you home or does your younger sister have to be your bodyguard?" "Will you invite me over to eat spaghetti sometimes?" They'd laugh foolishly while I would act as if I never heard them.

One day our routine class was interrupted by the arrival of a new student named Carla. She had moved into our neighborhood from Abruzzo, Italy. She had black, olive-shaped eyes and a cascade of long, dark curls, which her mother made by wrapping Carla's twisted locks in strips of cloth. Her dark features contrasted with the white, curly wool coat she wore. Since I was of Italian descent, the teacher called me to the front of the room.

"Gilda, tell Carla in Italian that we welcome her to our group," Miss Allen said.

My face felt hot with embarrassment and I knew my cheeks turned scarlet.

"I don't speak Italian."

"Well, try anyway. Surely you must know some words."

Recalling my parents always said *Buongiorno* (Good Day) on greeting someone, I uttered that phrase. Carla's reaction amazed me. Her face lit up. Smiling, she repeated the salutation and rattled off a lengthy dialog.

"What did she say?" Miss Allen inquired curiously.

"She said she likes this class and especially you, Miss Allen."

"How nice! I'm putting you in charge of taking care of Carla and helping her with homework."

My new assignment made me feel proud. Carla and I became inseparable. Vicki liked her too and we invited her to our house and we visited hers on a regular basis. Every Tuesday, Thursday, and Sunday, her mother prepared a savory sauce made from fresh tomatoes she had jarred over the summer. Mrs. Fonte did not speak English, yet she managed to work full time in a garment factory in North Philadelphia.

Mom and Dad generously included Carla on our weekend day trips to Baltimore to eat seafood or to Pennsylvania Dutch country for waffles with creamed chicken and shoo fly pie. When the boys in class saw that my Italian friend absorbed all my attention, they stopped teasing. I did notice increased male attention elsewhere, however, on our Saturday food shopping sprees in South Philadelphia with Gloria. Her stunning beauty evoked loud whistles from the virile male vendors at the stalls. I was aware that several also began to look admiringly at Vicki and me.

"Tu sei bella (You are beautiful)," the fruit seller at Giordano's produce store said to me one day. I liked the attention and secretly enjoyed the young men smiling and blowing kisses. But I recoiled instinctively if one cast a lingering stare directly into my eyes.

Because I was unable to learn Italian from my parents, I concentrated on helping Carla acquire English. She was a quick learner and we always managed to communicate. We continued to be very close into the next school year. We were then both 13 and still enjoyed day trips, family dinners and sleepovers together. One night in late September, Carla asked me to spend the night at her house. I liked being with her parents and 20-year-old brother, Pietro, who was studying for a Ph.D. in Philosophy at the University of Pennsylvania. I seldom saw Pietro because he often was at school or in his room piled with books, but we did exchange pleasantries from time to time. That night, or should I say, 4:30 a.m., Pietro had another type of encounter in mind. I lay asleep next to Carla. Suddenly, I was awakened by a silent presence at my side of the bed. I felt a pang of panic, realizing that someone was sitting in the dark directly in front of me. I didn't want to open my eyes and face the uncomfortable reality, so I feigned sleep while peering out ever so slightly to see who the still figure was.

It's Pietro! What am I to do? Why is he here?

My heart began to race.

I'll act as though I'm not waking up. Maybe he'll go away.

Pietro did not intend to leave. After a few agonizing minutes, he tugged gently at the bed sheets, wanting me to stir. I was too frightened to move. Pietro grew more impatient. He came close, so near I could feel his hot breath on my cheek. He touched my shoulder and the light pressure startled me and with a faint gasp, I opened my eyes.

"Kiss me," he said, moving even more forward from his chair.

"No."

"Don't be afraid. I won't hurt you. I love you. I loved you the first day you came into this house. I want to marry you someday, so kiss me."

God help me. Maybe I should scream and wake everybody up and they'll find him here. But that would be so embarrassing for his family and for Mom and Dad. I don't know what to do.

"Kiss me," he whispered insistently.

"If I kiss you, will you go away?"

"Yes."

"You promise?"

"Yes."

"Okay. Do it, then go."

I closed my eyes and mouth tightly. My body stiffened, prepared for the dreaded happening. Pietro bent over, pressing his lips on mine. His breathing quickened, and I knew he was eager to prolong the contact.

I pushed him away. "Stop! You did it, now go away." My voice rose slightly above a whisper, but Carla did not hear.

Pietro was heaving heavily. He reluctantly sat up, rose and quietly left the bedroom. My heart was pounding. I looked at the slumbering Carla who was enviably oblivious to what had transpired.

It was 4:45 a.m. and all I could think of was to run away.

Get out of this house before anyone wakes up. Never come back—ever.

I put my street clothes over my pajamas and tiptoed out of the room and down the stairs. I was thankful the front door opened easily and quietly, unlike our squeaky one at home.

Once free, the cool, morning air propelled me as I ran the two blocks from Chew Street to McMahon. I pounded the metal knocker of our front door and grew anxious that it was taking Mom a long time to open.

"Gilly. What are you doing here so early? It's five o'clock. Did something happen?"

I recounted what occurred with every detail. When I finished, Mom looked displeased. Her bubbly personality was averse to confrontations. My story put her in an uncomfortable position.

"Are you sure that's what happened? You're not making things up, are you?"

Mom doesn't believe me or, she doesn't want to believe me. I know what I went through and I'll never forget.

Expectedly, the phone rang later that morning. It was Carla's mother questioning why I left her house.

"Gilda is here, Mrs. Fonte; I'll let her talk to you. Here, Gilly," Mom said, thrusting the receiver in my hand. "Tell Mrs. Fonte what you told me."

"No," I said, horrified. "You tell her," and I ran upstairs.

I listened as my mother repeated my words almost apologetically.

Mom's sounding like I did something bad and she's sorry for my behavior. I don't know what I should have done. Should I have screamed and have everyone come and catch Pietro by the bed or should I have kept this a secret?

"Come down, Gilly," Mom said, after her chat with Mrs. Fonte concluded. Mom looked at me sternly. "Mrs. Fonte asked Pietro whether your story was true, and he denied it. You're not imagining things, are you?"

"No, of course not and I'm never going to Carla's house again."

"All right, but know that it would be a terrible thing to accuse someone of something they didn't do."

I don't know what's worse—having Pietro terrify me or not being believed by my own mother? Why am I the one made to feel ashamed right now? What did I do wrong? The saddest thing is that I cannot be close friends with Carla anymore and I will not go to her nice house or see her parents. Pietro's actions changed everything and I must kiss my friendship with Carla goodbye.

THE LESSON FROM MY ITALIAN NEIGHBOR

When I was 14 years old, a young woman from Calabria and her two young daughters moved into the neighborhood. Their house was across the street from ours. After several days, I befriended her six and eight-year-old girls and got to know their 38-year-old mother, Lucia.

One day, I was returning from Roosevelt Junior High School, carrying my book bag. Lucia admired it and wanted to explore its contents.

She looked at the titles of each volume with admiration, although she could not read them.

"I get tired of lugging so many books and having to do a lot of homework," I confessed to Lucia. At that, my neighbor's eyes widened, then narrowed. Scowling, she pointed a finger at me. "Don't-a-you complain about-a school," she scolded. "I'm-a-so ashamed to tell you I never been to school-a one-a day. In my *paese* we girls had to work all-a time. Ever since I was-a little, I wash-a clothes and-a bed sheets in the river to earn a few cents for-a-my family. In the winter, the water, it was-a so-a cold-a, like-a ice. Look-a-my hands-anow. I can hardly move-a dem," she said, exposing gnarled, arthritic appendages. "You-a- 14-a years-a-old and you got-a nice-a finger nails. Go to school; you a lucky girl."

Lucia's misshapen hands bore witness to her hard life in Italy. An illiterate woman, speaking the local dialect, could not read or understand legal documents nor defend herself in a court of law among other disadvantages. How could she systematically teach her offspring a language in which she was never instructed? She knew firsthand the importance of an education. I never complained about having to carry books after that day.

ROSEMARY'S SECRET

In "the good ole' days" of Italian culture, women were strictly guarded by most traditional families. Virtue and virginity were demanded. A girl was either good or bad, based on those two "v's." There was no grey area.

When I was 14 years old and Vicki 13, Mom took us aside. We sat in the living room on a dreary, rainy afternoon. Mom did not put the lights on. Addressing us, she looked grave, so unlike her jovial self. We suspected this was going to be a serious conversation.

"Girls, you are becoming ladies now and there is something I must tell you. But first, promise me you will keep what I have to say a secret."

"We will."

Mom went on, slowly.

"In 1925, at age 15, in Mays Landing, an older married man from out of town, took advantage of my best friend, Rosemary. She told me that he had attacked her in the dark when she went outside to throw trash away. She confided to me that she did not get her period for almost three months and she did not know what was wrong.

"I don't know much either. You should tell your mother," I suggested.

"No! I'm afraid to tell her what happened."

"Rosemary was right. Such a deed in that small community could not go unnoticed or unpunished. The news would spread faster than the influenza, infecting everyone in her family. Who would marry a sibling of one who had fallen so far, and she had two sisters and three brothers? Soon, Rosemary's condition was starting to show. Her father took control of the situation before anyone could detect his daughter was with child."

"What did he do?"

"With the encouragement of the local parish priest and my father, who was a paesano (townsman) from the same town in Naples, he did what he thought was the only definitive solution, one that would change the life of Rosemary forever."

"Your daughter has to disappear for a while," my father urged.

"Yes. She could be sent to live with my mother's sister and brother-in-law who live in a village in upstate New York. It is a remote place in the mountains," her father suggested.

"Yes, good," said Grandpop, proud that his suggested solution could be finalized.

"As strict Catholics, Rosemary's father and my father knew abortion was out of the question. The only solution was that the pregnancy would have to be brought to term and the baby given up for adoption. A girl was born in the New York village and was taken from her mother and handed over to Catholic Charities. The infant was named Rose Saunders." Mom's eyes welled with tears.

"Rosemary's father believed that once his daughter had known sex, she would be unable to resist having it, marriage or no marriage. To ensure my dear friend would never again get pregnant outside of wedlock, whatever the circumstances, her father had her fallopian tubes tied immediately following the birth."

"What are those and how do you tie them?" Vicki asked.

"I don't want to give an anatomical explanation now. Tying her tubes meant she would never have a child again."

"That wasn't right. It wasn't her fault she was impregnated. Why didn't they have the man's tubes tied?" I interrupted. "I would not want a baby at my age, but if I had one, I would never give it away. Did she see her little face? Did she hold her close and feed her? When they took her, did she cry knowing she would never cuddle her again? If that happened to me I would fight and scream or go insane."

Mom didn't respond to my ranting. She sat silently for a moment, reflecting on what to tell us next. Resuming the conversation, she spoke haltingly.

"When my friend was permitted to return home, her parents continued her punishment by making her work hard at home, scrubbing floors on her hands and knees and performing other arduous chores. For several months, they barely spoke to her. Communication was via angry stares, even from her mother.

"Rosemary married five years later, but never had a child. She claimed she had had a miscarriage and there were complications which prevented a pregnancy."

How horrible! Hadn't she suffered enough by having to give up her daughter?

Her husband did not always treat his wife kindly. I wonder if he knew the secret. His parents were from Abruzzo, so he must have felt a sense of Italian honor too. Through Mommy, Vicki and I knew Rosemary. We visited her house on holidays. Her wedding picture was prominently displayed in the parlor, with her white gown and veil. Seeing that photograph made me feel the weight of carrying her terrible secret.

Mom's attitude toward her chum's plight was another aspect of dismay to me.

"While I am sincerely sorry for Rosemary, I admired her father for protecting his other daughters and the family name. His Abruzzese code of honor cleared the path for all of them to marry."

"Was Rosemary ever resentful about what her father and Grandpop did? I would be."

"No. she was always a loving, dutiful daughter. She loved her home and was always trying to please her parents and everyone in the family."

Rosemary is a saint. I would not be forgiving if they had my child taken away. I wonder what little Rose was told later in life? Did someone say her mother gave her up because she didn't love her? How untrue and cruel that would be! Did she ever have that agonizing thought as well?

My only consolation is to hope Rosemary will be reunited with her daughter in the after-life. I shudder to think of how many women suffer because of some inflexible, moral code. I also wonder if the baby had been born a lusty boy, would the two men have been so eager to have him adopted?

"Why are you telling us this sad story, Mom? Do you think we will go and get pregnant before we marry?"

Mom ended the upsetting conversation with a caveat: "Whatever you girls do, never lose your honor and bring disgrace on your family name."

"Rest assured Mom, we won't."

GRANDMOM'S WARNING

"Gilly, I want to talk to you. Come with me to the parlor."

What could my grandmother want? Why the sound of serious urgency in her voice? This was something new.

I loved being in my grandparents' country home where the comforting scent of pine reminded me of evergreens and sandy soil outside. It was nothing like our home in Germantown, where the "Dream Castle" homes had cold, craggy granite exteriors.

My parents and I looked forward to our weekly visits with my maternal grandparents. Sundays were always special; after our afternoon feast, selected members of the household were invited into the parlor to hear my grandfather's prize collection of operatic 78-inch records playing on the Victrola. Grandpop and my father would listen to Beniamino Gigli, Enrico Caruso, Renata Tebaldi and others, with eyes closed, absorbing each aria with rapture.

But today there was no musical interlude. Grandmom wanted to talk to me alone. Entering the parlor, she motioned to me to sit on the sofa, worn from the use of 14 grandchildren who often used it as a trampoline.

I sat next to this 72-year-old woman, who also looked worn. Grandmom had birthed 13 children, of whom only six survived. She always appeared aged with her salt and pepper hair, densely wrinkled face and translucent skin revealing blue ribbons of veins pulsating through her delicate fingers. I loved stroking her soft hands.

She was strong, however. Among the two overstuffed fuchsia armchairs in the parlor, was her prize possession, a black, wooden player piano. Grandmom had worked in the cotton mill for the money to buy that ebony instrument. She wanted the sound of music to permeate her home as it would surely bring many happy times to her family.

At this moment Grandmom was not smiling. She looked serious and intent on what she was going to say to me. We sat in silence for several minutes. Her hands lay still in her lap.

Gilly, you are 15-years-old and growing nicely. There is something I must tell you now."

"What is it, Grandmom?"

Her hands then began to fidget, and it was difficult for her to speak.

"When I was young, we didn't know about anything. No one ever spoke about personal matters, if you know what I mean?"

"No, I don't know what you mean."

Could this conversation be about "The Birds and the Bees?" I heard grownups use that expression, but no one ever expounded on it to me.

"Then let me put it this way. When I became a lady, I thought I was dying. I was so scared, but I was too ashamed to talk about it with my mother. You are growing up fast; it's my duty to warn you about something."

She clutched her hands rigidly on each knee as though they were giving her the necessary support to get through this uncomfortable conversation.

"Gilly, when you go out with a boy, never let him... never let him touch your..."

Silence reigned again as Grandmom paused for a much-needed breath and reflection on how to proceed. She began to wring her hands as though that motion would make the words burst forth. She tried again.

"Never let a man touch your... " Again, her words ended abruptly. Now I was really curious.

"Touch what, Grandmom?" I asked, my voice rising with impatient curiosity. "Never let a man touch your... knee. That's where it all begins!" I looked down at one of my kneecaps in wonder.

If a man were to touch it, would it fall off, or something?

"That's where what begins, Grandmom?" But there was no answer. I looked up and Grandmom had disappeared.

II

Early Adulthood

Jamie in Caracas.

CHAPTER FIVE

VENEZUELA

CARACAS: FIRST LOVE?

To go or not to go? Donna asked me to her birthday party but the thought of venturing out in the blustery December evening and shivering on the corner of Chelten Avenue to take the trolley to Chestnut Hill was not inviting.

"The weather's bad but you should go, Gilda. Donna is a good friend and she may be disappointed if you don't," Mom said.

My mother was usually right, so I bundled up and traipsed two blocks in the snowfall and waited impatiently for the clanging trolley to arrive. It grew dark early that December 3rd, 1955. I was 17 years old and looking forward to graduation from Germantown High School in January. Thoughts of receiving my diploma and perhaps the annual nursing scholarship, raced through my head during the bumpy ride.

On arriving at the party, Donna was genuinely happy to see me. The festivities had begun. Several of my school chums were in attendance; all were in a cheery, holiday mood.

"Gilda, there is someone special I would like you to meet. You took Spanish for six years; you can practice with him. He comes from Venezuela and is studying at the Philadelphia Textile Institute to be an engineer."

Donna went up to a broad-shouldered young man and tapped him on the back. He turned, tilted his head as she whispered in his ear, then looked up and approached me.

"Gilda, this is Jamie F.; he's from Caracas."

"*Encantado* (enchanted)," he said, taking my right hand and implanting a soft kiss. "*Encantada*," I responded, making sure I used the correct gender form. Donna left us as we eyed one another. He was muscular, of medium build, with olive skin, dark eyes and hair, but sans the Latin lover looks Mom admired.

Mom won't like him. He has a deep crease between his eyebrows which makes him appear both stern and sad. She is into appearance, but I don't care. He has lovely manners and seems nice.

He proved to be more than nice. He was solicitous to my every want. He made sure I had something to drink, then to eat. He complimented my limited command of Spanish, laughed at my attempts at humor, overly praised my pithy comments and danced divinely. His innate Latin sense of rhythm made the intricate movements of the rumba and samba easy to follow. I was having a grand time.

Thanks Mom for telling me to come. I would have hated to miss this party.

At 10 p.m., I excused myself to Donna. The trip home would take at least an hour and perhaps longer because of the weather.

"Where do you live?" Jamie asked. "You should not be out alone, unescorted in this weather. With your permission, I will accompany you home."

"I'll be fine. I don't want to bother you."

"It is not a problem. I will be pleased to spend more time with you."

His sincerity convinced me, and we set out in the cold. Although flakes of snow landed on my cheeks, I felt a warm sensation being next to him. We chatted easily, and I was captivated on hearing his life story. His parents had divorced when he was six-years-old, and his father sent him, an older brother and his sister to boarding school in the States. The two sons attended the Hill School in Pottstown and the daughter went to Shipley, both prestigious Pennsylvania prep schools. They were Jewish. Jamie had celebrated his Bar Mitzvah alone, as his father, a prominent businessman, was too busy to attend.

There was an air of melancholy about him that was endearing to me. He was telling me intimate things about his family and his feelings that I held precious. He was the stereotypic "poor, little rich kid," sent to boarding school in a foreign country, not to be in the way. He made me feel grateful for my gregarious, and at times, boisterous, Italian family.

He told me of the beauty of his country. His descriptions of the vast Andes Mountains, pristine beaches and stately palms of his Venezuelan paradise made me temporarily forget that I was stepping on snow and slush. They also made the trip home seem all too short as I could have listened to him for hours.

When we arrived at my front door, he asked if he could see me again.

"Yes," I answered, without hesitation.

"Please have dinner with me next Saturday."

"I'd like that."

Entering the house, Mom was waiting for me.

"Well, did you have a good time?"

"Oh, yes, a very good time. I met a nice young man from Venezuela."

"Venezuela? Tell me about him."

"He's studying to be a textile engineer and wants to take me out next week."

"What's he look like?"

"I like his looks. You might not, but he is polite and intelligent."

"Oh, Gilly. You always say things like that. I bet he is handsome."

Don't contradict her. She won't believe me until she sees him.

The following week, I was excited at the prospect of being with my new friend from Caracas, regardless of what my parents might think. My heart raced, and I felt giddy upon hearing the doorbell ring.

Will he like me as much this week as last?

Jamie entered carrying a rectangular, honey-brown carved wooden box.

"Hello, Gilda. This is for you."

He handed it to me with a lingering look, which reassured me his feelings had not changed.

"It's lovely. What is it?"

"Open it."

I lifted the lid, which had a romantic scene on top with a man on his knee, kissing the hand of a fair maiden, both dressed like characters I recently saw in a "Three Musketeers" movie. Inside there were two layers of assorted dark, milk and white chocolates. I wanted to sample one but dared not disturb the artful display until I could show it off to Mom and Dad.

"It's beautiful. Thank you."

"I bought it at Carol Candies on Chelten Avenue."

I pass Carol Candies every day and love to look in the window at all the confections. This has been their premier box all week, mounted on a pedestal in the center of the picture window, surrounded by butter creams and toffee in gold wrapping with red trim.

I heard my parents' footsteps on the porch. Jamie sat in a chair as I went to open the door. Dad entered first. I introduced him to Jamie. Dad shook his hand and left the room to get settled in the kitchen as he was more interested in having dinner. Mom, on the other hand, approached my new friend with a quick stride and anticipatory grin. When she got closer, her smile faded. Mom had expected to see Cesar Romero. Disillusioned, she was only civil toward my date.

"It's nice to meet you, Jamie," she said, unconvincingly.

Trying to impress Mom, I showed her the box of chocolates.

"Look what Jamie brought me."

Mom could not help but like the gift, but her disappointment was still evident to me.

"Dr. Battaglia, may I use your telephone? I would like to call a cab to take your daughter out to dinner."

"Where are you going?"

"To Fallotico's in downtown Germantown."

"Why take a cab and spend all that money? You can go by trolley and be there in 15 minutes."

"Yes, but it is cold, and I want Gilda to be comfortable."

The cumulative effect of the present and cab on Mom compensated temporarily for Jamie's appearance. My mother could not help but approve of his generosity and old-world manners.

I want her to like him. Mom's fixation on looks is annoying. His face is pleasing enough. I only care about the way he treats me, like the man on the lid of my Carol Candies box.

We were given a table for two in a secluded corner of the popular Italian restaurant. The red and white checkered tablecloths and brilliantly colored murals of the Amalfi Coast on the walls added charm to this spot.

"Is there anything special you would like to order?" the server queried.

"No. Just a simple dish of spaghetti."

I don't want to request anything too expensive.

"Will you allow me to make the selections this evening? I want our first dinner together to be a memorable one."

"Certainly."

When the waiter arrived, without referring to the menu, Jamie ordered assorted antipasti, lemon fettucine with *pecorino Romano* (cheese) and *osso buco* (veal shank). This was an auspicious start.

"Next Saturday I would love to see you again, but we can't go out.

"Why?"

"I'll be in Germantown Hospital to have a cyst removed from my back. It's not serious, but I will be there overnight. Will you come to visit me?"

"Of course."

The food tasted unusually wonderful and was indeed memorable, but most of all, I felt comfortable with him. Often, when speaking with young men my age, I was self-conscious and nervous, not wanting to say anything foolish. He made me feel important, deserving of special treatment.

I was again excited at the thought of seeing Jamie the next week. Not known for self-control, I told my history teacher, Mr. Finkel, about my Latin friend. I asked for advice about buying a small gift to take to the hospital.

"A Parker Pen set may be a good choice. He could write to his family in Caracas with it."

"Hmmm. Let me think" I responded, happy to share my enthusiasm with an interested teacher.

No choices seemed right until the Thursday before my visit. Next

to the Band Box Cinema on Armat Street, there was an intimate boutique. In the window, I spied several items for men. One was a tube of
rum toothpaste.

*That's it! He must brush his teeth in the hospital and this flavor should be
appealing to someone from the tropics.*

I couldn't wait to show my purchase to Mr. Finkel the next day.

"Yes, Gilda. You made a good choice. He's sure to like it. In fact, I
might buy a tube for myself."

Mr. Finkel's approval made me happy. I placed the present in a
white, rectangular gift box and wrapped it in green paper we had at
home. I had read green was the color of hope and I hoped my friend
would like the gift.

On Saturday, at 5:30 p.m., I went to Germantown Hospital and was
told what room Jamie occupied. When I entered, I was shocked. Jamie
stood with his back to me, wearing a maroon silk robe. Two young
women were standing in front of him, facing me. They had been laughing until I came in. The blonde and brunette stared at me inquisitively,
prompting Jamie to turn around.

"Oh, Gilda, come in. Let me introduce you to my friends."

"That's alright. I see you are busy. I'm leaving."

"No. Don't leave; stay a while."

"I have to go home now. I see you seem fine after your procedure;
that's all I wanted to know. Goodbye."

I rushed out of the room, clutching the green package, fighting
back tears.

*How could he do such a thing? Why did he ask me to visit him when he was
expecting other women? He embarrassed me. What will Mr. Finkel think? I'm
never going to see Jamie again. Mom will probably be glad.*

When I opened the front door of my house, the jingling telephone
interrupted my ruminations. It was Jamie.

"Gilda, why did you run out like that?"

"You were with those other women. I didn't want to be in the way."

"You weren't. They are engaged to friends of mine at the textile institute. I was happy you came."

"You were?"

"Yes. Please don't be upset. I love you, Gilda."

I was speechless. Many boys told me they liked me, but this was the first time a young man said he loved me. My hurt feelings quickly vanished, substituted by utter elation. I didn't stop to evaluate my feelings toward him. It was too exciting hearing those three words, though I wondered how he could fall so fast.

"You do?"

"Yes, from the moment I saw you."

"Are you sure; it's only been two weeks?"

"I just told you. I knew the moment I looked into your brown eyes."

I can't say I love him too because I'm not sure what it feels like. I do care for him, but is that love?

"I bought you rum-flavored toothpaste."

We both laughed.

"Next weekend I will be in Caracas with my family for the winter break. I would like to give you my hi-fi record player while I'm gone. You can listen to romantic songs from my country."

"I would love to have it."

When I returned home from school that Friday afternoon, there was a knock at the door. When I opened it, my eyes widened. A delivery man handed me a long, white box from the Germantown floral shop, secured with the largest red bow I'd ever seen. It looked just like the elegant gifts opera divas received in the movies.

I savored every second on opening it, revealing a dozen long stem red roses. I hesitated to put them in water lest I disturb the exquisite effect they had nestling in pink tissue paper.

He loves me and makes me feel more special than anyone has. I will wait till Mom and Dad get home before putting these into a vase.

Another knock at the door. This time, my heart skipped a beat: it was Jamie.

"I've brought you the record player with popular recordings from Venezuela and the opera Carmen. The toreador song sounds great on my hi-fi. I see my flowers arrived. Do you like them? If you do, I will send you bouquets all the time."

"How could I not love them? They are so beautiful."

Jamie was poised to make another remark when Mom opened the door with her key. It was rare for her to arrive home so early on a Friday, but I remembered casually mentioning to her that he might come by.

She left the office to see what Jamie was up to. I know her too well.

"Mom, look at the stunning roses Jamie sent me."

On eyeing the long, white box and its vermillion contents, Mom tried in vain to suppress her admiration.

"They're very nice," is all she managed to say.

She then noticed the record-player. "That hi-fi set is not another gift, is it?" she snapped, disapprovingly.

"No, Mom. Jamie wants me to look after it while he is in Caracas."

If it had been a present, she would have surely objected even more. I detected her frustration at having nothing to criticize.

During Jamie's two-week absence, I listened to the exotic recordings although I did not understand all the words. *La Historia de un Amor* (The Story of a Love) was my favorite. I played it often, picturing my Latin friend basking under tropical palms.

Gloria had invited the family to her house in Ambler, PA, for New Year's Day dinner.

"Gilda, when Jamie returns, bring him along," she said. My sisters liked him and that put me more at ease.

Jamie called as soon as he arrived at the Philadelphia airport. He was happy to accept Gloria's invitation.

"Come to my house tomorrow and we will go to Ambler together."

I'd thought of him often during the past two weeks and anticipated seeing him again.

He said he loves me. Those words still make me feel on top of the world. Being loved is wonderful.

When Jamie appeared at our front door, his skin had a bronzed glow. How I envied his being away in the sun during our frigid winter days. He gave me a lingering gaze.

"Let's get going," Dad said, impatiently. "We don't want to be late to dinner."

Jamie entered Gloria and JB's home carrying a bag from which he extracted presents for all. The men received electric shavers from Switzerland. Mom, Gloria and Vicki unwrapped bottles of Chanel #5.

My gift was in white tissue paper. Unfolding the delicate sheets, I discovered a white, hand-made lace mantilla. Until then, I had only seen those head coverings in the movies. Now I had one of my own.

"I'll wear this to church. It's so unique; everyone will wonder where I got it."

Jamie was outwardly pleased that I was impressed.

"I brought you one other present to wear with the mantilla."

Jamie handed me a semi-circular blue velvet box. The contents were more than I could have dreamed. I gasped on seeing an 18-karat gold pin, in the shape of a graceful orchid, resting on a bed of blue satin. In the center of the three delicate petals, lay an authentic cream-colored sea pearl. Two miniature gold earrings in the same design completed the ensemble. I was speechless.

No one ever gave me such a gift. This is stunning—perhaps too much so for my parents to allow me to accept. Jamie wants to show the family how he values me. It makes me proud and a little scared. He is serious about our relationship, yet I don't know how I feel. Of course, I care for him. What girl wouldn't want a boyfriend who is so attentive? Is this love? Maybe it is. Whatever, I want to keep this set and show it off.

"Look what else Jamie brought me," I said, passing the orchid grouping around the room.

"It's gorgeous," my sisters exclaimed.

Mom looked at my father, as though she were expecting him to verbally disapprove of my receiving such a costly present. Dad just seemed bewildered. On the one hand, I knew he thought it was too valuable for a teenager in "puppy love." On the other, he felt a sense of pride that his daughter was placed in high esteem.

I only want my family to appreciate Jamie for the kind and generous person he is. It seems that no matter what he does, my parents don't want to accept him. Their attitude makes me want to defend him even more.

My high school graduation portrait.

OBSESSED?

My parents had interesting clients in their practice, such as artists, dancers and sculptors. It was January 1956, and they were planning a special gift for my graduation from Germantown High School. Dad had asked a patient and well-known artist in Philadelphia, Cesare Ricciardi, to paint my portrait. Mr. Ricciardi had frequent exhibits at the Philadelphia Art Alliance in Center City and recently put the likeness of John B. Kelly, Sr. (Grace Kelly's father) on canvas.

What a great gift. I am so lucky.

"Gilda, come to my studio for the portrait. I'll require at least three sittings for a period of three hours each to complete it," Mr. Ricciardi said.

I did as he instructed and did not fidget during the long hours in one position. I didn't want anything to go wrong by moving. The artist was totally absorbed in his work and never spoke while applying his brush.

I don't mind being still because graduation and my future in nursing school are on my mind. All I want is to win the annual nursing scholarship. It would make Mom and Dad proud. I really want to please them as well as myself.

A week before the graduation ceremony was to take place, Mr. Ricciardi brought the portrait to my house. My parents praised it, but I was not as impressed.

The colors are vibrant. The red velvet blouse and black lace shawl are lovely, but I would have preferred my forehead were higher, my lips thinner and my chin smaller. I never like the way I look in pictures. Mom and Dad do and that matters. I will act as though I love it.

When Jamie saw the painting, he shook his head.

"It's lovely but no artist is capable of capturing your likeness, which completely overwhelms me."

While my parents seldom complemented Vicki or me, Jamie could not stop. I never believed all the flattering things he said because I had always been more self-conscious than confident.

A few days later, I received a phone call from the artist.

"Gilda, this is Cesare Ricciardi. I am pleased with your portrait and hope you are too. I was impressed by the way you sat for it. I would like to hire you to be my model. Just your face, and I will pay you by the hour. Will you accept?"

"I would love to, Mr. Ricciardi. First, I must ask my parents, but I'm sure they will want me to do it."

This is great! Nursing School starts next September. Modeling for him will fill time from January until then and I'll get paid. I was planning on getting some kind of job and never expected it to be this.

Jamie came to my house shortly after that telephone conversation. I couldn't wait to relate the good news. When I did, he glared at me. His reaction was startling. His face turned red; the crease between his eyebrows became a dark furrow.

"No. Absolutely not! I forbid you to model for anyone, even if it is just your face. Call the artist at once and tell him you cannot accept."

Why is Jamie so outraged? I don't understand. Does he think Mr. Ricciardi will start with my face and then want to paint more of me? It's absurd. I feel like telling him I don't want to go steady anymore, but is that what I want? He's so good to me in other ways I know I'd miss him. None of my girlfriends have a devoted beau like Jamie. Perhaps in his culture girls from nice families do not model. It would be embarrassing to his Latin relatives. That's it; it's cultural. I don't like it but I know I don't want him to be this angry, so I'll have to decline Mr. Ricciardi's offer.

Deeply disappointed, I sheepishly picked up the receiver and dialed.

"Mr. Ricciardi, I am sorry, but I cannot accept the modeling job. Please, don't mention it to my parents."

"Okay, Gilda. I'm sorry you can't do it; you would have been a perfect Saint Veronica with the head of hair you've got. She was going to be my next subject."

"I'm sorry too."

If I were to tell Mom and Dad what Jamie insisted I do, it would give them real ammunition to dislike him.

When the conversation ended, the line between Jamie's eyebrows softened. Although he was visibly satisfied, I felt deflated. I'm never going to forget this opportunity.

SENTINEL

"The women in white are doing a fine job for our country and lands overseas." I wrote that sentence when I was in the fourth-grade English class at Francis Daniel Pastorius Elementary School. The teacher praised it in front of the class as an example of a fine beginning for our writing about future career choices.

I wanted to care for the sick since childhood. My sister Gloria entered a registered nursing program in 1954, at the School of Osteopathic Medicine, where she met and married a young intern, Dr. J. B. Joye in 1952. I was 15 years old at the time and she influenced me greatly. Mom and Dad always encouraged us to become doctors there. I rejected the idea because I did not want to rear my children as "latchkey kids" like Vicki and me, alone in an empty house after school and most of Saturday.

Mom and Dad preferred the Osteopathic School of Medicine because it offered more modalities for healing the whole body by combining both medicine and Osteopathic Manipulative Therapy, or OMT. The latter alleviated much pain without drugs. Unfortunately, in the '50s and '60s, Osteopathic, Chiropractic and Naturopathic physicians were considered by some to be "cultists," but that did not dissuade my parents. I respected their philosophies and treatment methods and chose to enter the nursing program where I could fulfill my altruistic leanings and interest in science and have time to devote to a home and family.

Occupations for women were limited in the '50s and '60s. The standard careers were secretary, nurse or teacher. The rare ones like my mother, who became a Naturopathic/Chiropractic physician in 1948, were few and far between and were badgered by their male counterparts in professional school, from admission to graduation.

"Go home to your children where you belong," Mom heard from the male students.

"A woman shouldn't be a doctor," they taunted.

But feisty Mom persevered, graduated, and joyfully worked side by side with Dad in their practice.

Several young ladies in my senior class at Germantown High School aspired to be nurses as well, and relied on the one available annual high school scholarship to attain their dream. Tuition was 350 dollars for a three-year diploma program, a significant sum at the time.

On the night of my graduation ceremony in January 1956, Mom and Dad sat with Vicki near the stage in the auditorium. When the moment came to award the scholarship winners, I was nervous. My heart was beating wildly as names were being called for various prizes in alphabetical order. It was time for the nursing category and as the announcer spoke, I could barely move.

"It gives me great pleasure to announce this year's winner of the nursing scholarship is Miss Gilda Battaglia."

Oh, thank God! The pressure is over; I can breathe now.

*My high school graduation photo
from Germantown High School.*

It was a joy to see my parents' faces glowing when my name was announced as the award recipient. They would soon contact everyone in the family with the news.

How wonderful Dad has lived to see me graduate and receive the award! His frequent vacations are what have kept him alive these past years. May he have many, many more travels. He certainly baffled the doctors.

My elation was momentarily dampened by the pained look on the other aspirants' faces. I felt unworthy and often wondered if any of them would be able to achieve their dream of becoming a nurse.

Jamie came to my graduation ceremony. He also seemed proud that I won the scholarship. My parents planned a small family party at an Italian restaurant in South Philadelphia where Jamie gave me a Parker pen set.

Because I would not be modeling for Mr. Ricciardi, I wanted to get work that would meet Jamie's approval. Perhaps I could be a receptionist? I mentioned the possibility to him, sotto voce, after we ordered our entrees.

"No! In my family, a woman doesn't work outside the home unless there is a necessity."

"We're in America and here women work."

"No! When we're married, you'll never work."

I thought my parents would criticize Jamie and be glad I wanted to make a financial contribution to the family before nursing school began. Their reaction disappointed me.

"Gilda, you won the scholarship, so you don't have to get a job for only a few months. Enjoy your freedom while you still have it. You'll be more than busy in nursing school."

I was disappointed there was no one in favor of my seeking employment so I resigned myself to pleasing others.

Jamie insisted I be at home to answer his telephone call each afternoon. He wanted to speak with me during his lunch hour. One day I dared to go out on an errand and he became extremely angry.

"Where were you when I called today? Were you seeing someone else? I want you home when I call."

Prepare yourself. When he comes here after his school day, he will be wearing that expression of silent rage. How I hate it and having to defend myself.

As anticipated, Jamie arrived looking greatly disturbed. The crease between his eyebrows seemed even harder. He wouldn't speak. He just glared at me in disapproval.

"Why do you have this unreasonable jealousy, Jamie? Why do you insist I not go out of the house?"

"I can't help the way I feel. I only want to know you are safe. I need to hear your voice. Do not leave until I come and we go out together."

It was easier for me to comply than to argue, so I never ventured out during the day again. To keep me occupied during the day, Jamie brought me books to read like "Doña Perfecta," a novel by the famous Spanish author, Benito Pérez Galdós.

Jamie spoke French, as his grandmother was from Tunisia.

"Teach me French," I pleaded.

"I'd love to."

Jamie brought me a French grammar book and made daily assignments. He would sit and tutor me in the evening. I loved those sessions. He was patient and encouraging. He almost made me forget his controlling nature.

While I enjoy that he spends time with me discussing Spanish novels and basic French, I wonder how he gets his studying done. Isn't the coursework for a textile engineer demanding and difficult?

Jamie became obsessed with protecting me; from what, I don't know. My parents wanted him to leave our house by 6 p.m. He would stand guard outside, across the street until Mom and Dad returned. Sometimes they didn't come home until 10 o'clock or even later. He was steadfast and didn't leave his post under the street lamp. "Boy, he's got it bad," Dad would say.

They, as I, both admired and were leery of Jamie's attention. None of us knew what to make of it or how to react. It was extreme, but it was evident the young man was deeply in love. My parents continued to disapprove of him. Yet, rather than tell me just to stop going steady, Mom would criticize Jamie in any way she could.

"He is so quiet. He never has much to say, does he?"

Jamie treats me better than anyone in the family. I love him for that and I want others to care for him too. Is caring being in love? I don't know. Mom might answer that question, but she is so against my being with Jamie that I won't ask. What more does he have to do to make my parents see the good in him?

One evening, when Mom was home, I was cleaning the kitchen floor with a spaghetti mop. Jamie walked in unexpectedly. When he saw what I was doing, he came up to me and grabbed the utensil from my hand.

"Give me that. When you marry me, you will never touch a mop again," he said, angrily.

His words were welcome to me, but Mom was incensed. When Jamie left the house, instead of congratulating me on finding such a considerate man, she scolded me.

"I think it's awful that he doesn't want you to scrub a floor. Everyone should do it."

Mom always found something negative to say. It was not easy for her to carp because Jamie took me out to eat at the best restaurants. The Barclay and Bookbinders were typical destinations. We went to the Academy of Music for concerts and operas. For my 18th birthday, we went there to see Andrés Segovia playing his exquisite guitar.

Jamie often escorted me to New York City to Carnegie Hall, the Metropolitan Opera and elegant restaurants. We'd ride the horse-drawn carriage in Central Park. At Central Park South, near the Plaza Hotel, he pointed to a luxurious duplex apartment he said his father owned.

Jamie continued to lavish me with presents from fresh flowers almost daily to a TV set for my bedroom.

"I don't like this," Dad would say aloud to Mom. "He gives her too many expensive gifts."

Although my father said such things, he didn't forbid my seeing Jamie. Inwardly, he must have known Jamie hailed from a fine family. Why else would he have had such refined taste? Who else would treat me the way he did? All I wanted was for my parents to like him. What could he possibly do to make them change their minds?

VILLA REGINA

The burst of flowering trees made springtime glorious. Dad had just purchased a new, sleek, Buick Roadmaster. He took Mom, Jamie and me for a pleasure ride near Fairmount Park. We went up a steep incline. At the summit, Dad stopped the car.

"There was something I saw on the road and I want to check it out. Jamie come with me; this will only take a minute," he said.

The men exited the auto, leaving Mom and me in the back seat. It would have been fine if not for the fact that Dad had failed to engage the brake. The front of the car was teetering toward the edge of a cliff, slowly rolling forward, rendering Mom and me helpless and horrified. We were too afraid to scream.

Thankfully, Jamie turned and saw what was happening. He had the presence of mind to run to the vehicle. He managed to open the driver's door; hurling himself across the front seat, he put his hand forcibly on the emergency brake. The car came to a halt with one-half of the front tires exposed in the air. Dad stood behind, witnessing the near-disaster, unable to move.

"Oh, Jamie," Mom exclaimed with relief. "You saved our lives today."

I am so proud of my boyfriend. At last, Mom has something good to say about him. What greater feat could he accomplish than rescuing us from certain death? Maybe what happened today will make my parents finally accept him.

On the ride home, Jamie was quietly basking in the approval of his heroic act. He kept smiling at me and I at him.

Jamie is courageous and brave.

In the following days, however, Jamie's jealousy became extreme. I never tried to give him cause. He would become angry if he thought a man even looked at me. His reactions to any perceived flirting resulted in an icy silence, which caused the crease between his eyebrows to deepen. I'd always try to appease him, but it did not seem to matter. A case in point was Vicki's 17th birthday in May 1956. Jamie invited both of us to dinner at Falotico's. While the three of us were strolling toward the restaurant, Vicki and I were chatting gaily when Jamie's body suddenly stiffened. He stopped walking and glared at me.

"What's the matter?" I asked.

"You know."

"No, I don't. What is it?"

As usual, Jamie refused to speak. He sulked from the time we entered the eatery until we left. On the trip home, he finally revealed the source of his quiet rage.

"You saw that man ogle you on the street."

"What man? I wasn't aware of anyone."

"Yes, you were; you had to be."

It didn't matter to me whether I convinced him or not; Vicki's birthday was ruined. He had made us both feel uncomfortable all evening.

At first, I thought his jealousy was flattering and part of Latin culture.

Now I can't stand it. Because of it I gave up modeling for Cesare Ricciardi. What's next? It's time to tell Jamie I don't want to be going steady any longer.

The following morning, Mom and Dad gave me news that hit me like a lightning bolt.

"Gilda, your relationship with Jamie is going too far. We've decided to take you and Vicki to Venezuela next month to show you what you would be getting into if you continue. There are frequent revolutions in Venezuela and many people are extremely poor. If you go to live there you may become 'morta di fame (dying from hunger).' The only way you'll understand is if you see it for yourself."

I never expected this. Today I was going to tell my parents that I am ready to break up with Jamie, although the thought saddens me. I'd love to see Caracas again. I'm not going to say anything to them or Jamie about not going steady. Going to Venezuela may be just what I need.

When I told Jamie of my parents' plan, he was excited. Several days later, he made a welcome announcement.

"I am so happy you will come to my country. I spoke with my father. He said, "When they arrive at the Port of La Guaira, my car will be waiting to take them to lunch at my house.""

"Jamie, that sounds lovely."

I've always wanted to meet his family and see where they lived in Caracas. For months, I've been imagining it. I can't wait.

From the time of Jamie's invitation to our arrival in Venezuela, I could think of nothing else.

Jamie was at the pier in La Guaira, when our vintage ship, "The Southern Cross," docked. I was excited to see him, and he greeted the four of us warmly.

"Welcome to my country. My father's car is waiting. The driver will come to take your bags."

The driver was not an ordinary workman, but a chauffeur in a formal outfit. The "car" was a luxurious limousine with a moveable glass panel separating the chauffeur from the passengers. Communication took place through a microphone attached to a wooden panel on the door. We had never been in anything like it.

The vehicle climbed through cloud-capped mountains, a scene I remembered vividly from our first trip there on the *Mauritania* cruise where the clouds looked so full I felt as though I could float on one. The chauffeur headed toward the city of Caracas.

The buildings flanking the spacious boulevards in the metropolis were a modern wonder. They appeared sleek and colorful in the tropical setting. The driver continued until he approached an outlying area of secluded homes with sprawling lawns, flanked by elegant palms. He pulled into a driveway where a sign read "Villa Regina."

"We've arrived," Jamie announced.

As we approached the massive front door of the villa, it was opened by a butler. He, like the chauffeur, wore a formal outfit with "tails," like the ones I saw in the movies at the Walton.

Oh, my gosh! Look at this home. Mom and Dad must be awe-struck too. Be composed. Act as though you are used to this kind of life.

The next surprise came when the butler led us to a sunken, marble living room. Seeing similar mansions in the movies, I always wondered if people really lived in such places. This was proof that some do.

We were subsequently escorted to an atrium where there was a long, winding staircase with an ornate wrought-iron banister. A beautiful woman in her early 40s, emerged and slowly descended, fully aware of our admiring gaze.

This must be "la Regina" (the queen).

Jamie's stepmother looked totally royal. Her dark brown hair and eyes were alluring. Her slim figure glided toward us in ebony tulle couture. Her gold cuff bracelet was studded in diamonds, complimenting an eight-carat brilliant diamond ring.

Regina proved to be a sophisticated and gracious woman.

"Before my husband arrives from his office, would you like to see some of our canvases? I am most interested in art and I love to paint."

The regal lady led us to a sitting room where the walls were lined in art.

"These are my favorite pieces. The Anthony van Dyke, Jan van Eyck and Vincent van Gogh are originals. They are my treasures."

They are indeed treasures. This is a museum, not a home. It's incredible.
"Come, we will dine now."

The dining room was predictably handsome. We were seated at table on which the lace cloth appeared too beautiful to eat on. There was no plastic sheet to protect it.

Most of my relatives put oilcloth on the table, not priceless hand-made lace. The black marble column in the room reminds me of the Philadelphia Art Museum. I have never seen so much marble outside a church before.

A tall, dark and extremely handsome man appeared. The look on Mom's face when she saw Jamie's father bore witness to his singular good looks. Her eyes widened, and she struggled to conceal a gasp.

Mr. F. sat next to me. He spoke to Dad initially, asking questions about his work and what hotel we were staying at in the city. Dad was proud to say we were at the Tamanaco Hotel, one of the best. When it came to questions about any matters related to business, Dad's answers were more modest because he was a solo practitioner with Mom, not a business man.

Our host's attention then switched to me. Sitting next to me, he wanted to know what food I liked, what artists I admired and what my plans were for the future. His cogent questioning intrigued me, and I enjoyed our conversation. He seemed truly interested in my life.

The butler served our food on a long silver tray, stopping for each person to take what they wanted from the *lomo* (beef tenderloin) and roasted potatoes. Our stunning hostess had prepared a *merengue* (meringue) dessert for which everyone lavished praise. With a bevy of cooks in the kitchen, any effort on her part to prepare a dish was appreciated.

Mom, Dad and Vicki are as overwhelmed by all this as I am. What a beautiful couple amid these lavish surroundings. I would love to be part of this world.

"Let us go to the patio," Mr. F. suggested.

The outdoors was also a feast for the eye. We sat at a Lalique crystal table as the butler brought a tray of assorted liquors, nuts and petit fours. The petit fours were luscious. Our hosts thanked Mom and Dad for showing hospitality to Jamie. They wished Vicki and me success in our future endeavors.

"You intend to be a nurse," Regina said to me. "In our country, after high school, young women are generally expected to marry and have a home. We do not consider it necessary for a woman to have additional education."

I smiled at her, not wanting to contradict a word she uttered.

The luncheon ended, and Jamie accompanied us to the Tamanaco Hotel, a luxury oasis in the heart of the city. The chauffeur tended to our luggage while Jamie said goodbye.

"I hope you enjoyed your visit with my family. You must rest in the afternoon here as it gets very hot. Dr. Battaglia, with your permission, I would like to return at 6:30 p.m. to show Gilda our sunset over Mount Avila."

I couldn't wait to get to our rooms, so I could quiz my parents on what they thought of our visit to the villa. Surely, they would be thrilled to see me live like a queen and not *morta di fame*. But once again, my hopes were dashed.

"Jamie belongs to a fine family, but you don't belong here," Dad said.

"Why do you say that? Is it because they are Jewish?"

"You know it's not that with us, although I don't know whether they would object to your being a gentile."

"What is it, then?"

Dad did not want to discuss the matter and neither did Mom. I went for a nap, anticipating Jamie's visit with an uneasy heart.

When 6:30 arrived, Jamie was his punctual self.

"Let's go to the terrace bar."

He took my hand and led me there. We sat outdoors in the tropical evening air; Jamie looked handsome to me.

If he resembled his father, I bet Mom would have no objections to my marrying him.

I was comfortable sharing a bistro table with Jamie in his exotic country. The sunset was a glorious display of crimson and gold. Jamie took my hand, came close and kissed me. I liked his kisses. They were warm and comfortable, although there were no bells ringing as I'd heard some people experience.

It is nice to be with someone who loves me. I've grown close to him. That's a form of love. He doesn't care that I live in a six-room row house in German-town. He would be willing to share everything with me. How I'd love to visit his family in the villa often. I would be fortunate if they'd accept me into their circle. Jamie's shown me the high standard he is used to, but it hasn't swayed Mom and Dad and that really bothers me. Maybe what they object to is that they would not feel comfortable here. How would they entertain someone like Jamie's father and Regina in our small house sans masterpieces? It is they who would not fit in.

After visiting the villa, the rest of our two-week trip seemed anti-climactic. Jamie came to swim in the hotel pool each day. We five did some touring together. A sight that touched me greatly was the respect shown to the statue of Venezuela's liberator, Simón Bolívar. In the Plaza Bolívar, male pedestrians would approach the equestrian figure and tip their hats in reverence. I had never seen anyone in the States do that for our national heroes.

One day, Jamie took me to have lunch with his mother while my family went on an excursion in the city. We entered a modest building and ascended a flight of stairs to her apartment. This time there was no butler opening the door.

"*Buenos días! Pasen Vds.* (Good day; come in)," his mother said.

The matriarch wore a pleasant smile. Her dark hair and eyes were kind, but not like those of the raving beauty, Regina. She was middle-aged, of medium build and had a strong resemblance to her son. There was a sadness in her eyes, that of a woman abandoned, living with a parent for dignity and consolation.

In lieu of a sprawling mansion, his mother lived with her father in a middle-class apartment. The furnishings were comfortable and immaculate, but not luxurious. Her cotton dress was plain, and she wore no outstanding jewelry.

Jamie's grandfather was a charming octogenarian and I enjoyed speaking Spanish with him. His mother had prepared lunch, with the assistance of a servant, consisting of fried plantains and rice with ground beef.

His mother is a lovely lady. I feel sorry for her being cast aside in favor of a younger, more vibrant model. She is to be admired because she exudes dignity and devotion to her family. It is evident that she, her father and Jamie are close.

When I returned to the hotel, Jamie left. I went to talk to my parents about their sightseeing experience. Mom did all the talking.

"Oh, Gilly. What a day we had! We got lost in the city and took a public bus we thought would bring us to the hotel. Instead, we traveled through incredibly poor neighborhoods with ragged children and adults. Tell her about what it was like, Vicki."

"Gilda, at one of the bus stops there were men in uniform with rifles. Everyone around them seemed nervous. No one smiled. I felt scared."

"Not everyone here lives in a villa or ultra-modern buildings in the city," Mom added. "We witnessed other sights that would greatly disturb you. You better think of what you are doing and what you really want in life. Don't be dazzled; be smart."

She may be right, but I don't have to think too much now. I'm going to nursing school in September, where I'll spend three years. Who knows what will happen after that? Jamie will be more mature; he'll become an engineer and hopefully not be as jealous. Why can't my parents just let me be for a while? I can't bear this constant pressure and negative reinforcement.

After two seemingly long weeks with my disgruntled parents, we left Caracas. Jamie accompanied us to the dock, this time in a small red car his cousin owned.

"Gilda, I will miss you so much. Look at the moon each night at 8 o'clock and know that I will be gazing at it too. It will bring us close." During the first three nights at sea, I did gaze at the moon, but friendly passengers would pass and ask if I wanted to join them in the salon. "She can't," Vicki retorted. "She has to look at the moon for an hour." I was teased and on the fourth night, I accepted their invitation.

DECISION

From the time we returned home from Caracas to the last week in August, my parents voiced relentless objections to Jamie. Among those repeated were that he was a product of a divorced family and lived in a country where there was significant instability and rebellion.

"Venezuela is beautiful, but you live in the greatest country in the world; why would you want to be so far away?" Mom would proffer.

Their harping makes me feel miserable. I know they genuinely care about my well-being. Even though he is excessively jealous and controlling, I don't know if I could ever find another man who would care for me as much.

Jamie returned to school in Philadelphia at the end of the month. He came to my house the day of his arrival, dressed in a casual white sport shirt and khaki pants. His face was relaxed and radiant with anticipation.

"Gilda, I missed you more than you could ever imagine. I gazed at the moon every night since you left Caracas and felt you close. Did you feel that way too?"

"Yes, Jamie. Moon watching was a great idea."

I feel ashamed that I only looked at it three nights.

"Here, I brought you a small gift."

A solid gold "Lady Omega" wristwatch was embedded in a rectangular black velvet box.

"Jamie, it is beautiful, but I cannot accept this expensive gift. My parents will surely object."

"I do not think they will," he said, with a twinkle in his eye. "When we are married, I will give you a present every day, I promise. This is nothing compared to what you will have. Gilda. I love you more than I love my mother."

"Jamie, please don't say that."

His feelings are too intense and make me feel uncomfortable. I do not want him or anyone to love me more than their mother. It isn't right.

His voice took on a more insistent tone.

"I can't help it. I want to marry you. I talked to my father before leaving Caracas and he agrees with a decision I have made about us."

"What did he say?

"Eat all the spaghetti you want!"

"Gilda, now that I have my father's permission, let us get engaged at once. My studies will end next June and then we will be man and wife." His voice carried a certain urgency.

The look on his face was pleading, leaving me befuddled and feeling anxious.

"I do not know what to say. I love you, Jamie, but like a brother. I always told you so, and it may not be sufficient for you or me."

"Don't worry. I love you enough for both of us. In time, you'll feel the same toward me. Think about my proposal. I will not wait long. To-morrow night I will call you for your answer. It's now or never, Gilda."

"All this is happening too fast, Jamie."

He was not smiling when he opened the door to leave. Turning to me, his demeanor was serious.

"Hasta mañana, Gilda."

I could not sleep that night. Jamie's words of now or never, kept repeating in my head. Instead of being ecstatic with his proposal, I was wracked with anxiety.

This is all too sudden. Mom was right. I did not want to see what I was getting into. I was selfish, happy to accept Jamie's affection and generosity, flat-tered to have such a doting boyfriend to show off to family and friends. Yet I also have deep feelings for him, but they are not romantic. When he is not jeal-ous, he is so kind and I feel more at ease with him than I do with anyone else.

Some of my chums from high school have already married, but am I ready to make a lifetime commitment at 18? I want to enjoy my youth and find out what I can accomplish before "settling down." How I hate that term; it almost reminds me of dying. I want to go up, not down. I must sort this out to give him the right answer.

The next day, Jamie called, awaiting my decision. I told him I needed one more day. I was too conflicted. I did not want to confer with my par-ents; I knew what they would say. The answer would have to be mine.

I spent another sleepless night tossing and thinking of the pros and cons of Jamie's ultimatum. Scenes of the trip to Caracas filled my mind as I compared my possible life there to the one in Philadelphia.

When I saw Regina descend that elegant staircase, I imagined myself in my regal palace with an adoring husband who would shower me with gold and diamonds. But what would I give in return? Would I play the part of an enamored wife? Mom had always loved Dad unconditionally. She went through the Great Depression and never wanted to leave his side in their miserable apartment with no heat. Would I feel like that toward Jamie if there were no gold or diamonds? What if we had to face difficult times together in Venezuela?

And what about my nursing career? I am 18 years old and I would still like to study and have new experiences before becoming a housewife. An ultra-jealous husband could make me feel like a caged bird, unable to fly, let alone soar.

Gilda, would you be so confused if you were madly in love—like Mom was with Dad? Be honest for your sake and for Jamie.

Jamie called the following evening. I dreaded what I was about to say when I picked up the telephone.

"What have you decided?"

I answered in a shaky voice.

"Jamie, I truly love you, but not the way you deserve. The lucky lady who accepts you will have won the lottery. I know that if we were to marry, I would not be able to cherish you the way you would expect. Please, please forgive me."

My words were followed by a long, painful pause.

"Oh, Gilda, I can't talk now. Goodbye."

With a heavy heart, I put the receiver in its cradle.

Oh God, what have I done?

A miserable feeling of remorse ensued and continued until the telephone rang the next afternoon. I answered the call with trepidation. Jamie spoke deliberately, without even saying hello.

"Gilda, I've made a decision too. I cannot be in the same city with you and not have you belong to me. I am leaving the Textile Institute at once and returning to Caracas to work in my father's business."

"You mean you will not become a textile engineer? No! Do not leave school because of me. I am not worth it. Don't forfeit your career and abandon your dream. Please reconsider. I do not want to carry such guilt the rest of my life."

"I cannot talk anymore. *Adiós.*"

"Jamie, wait!"

"Goodbye, Gilda."

With that click of the telephone it was over. Have I tossed away the greatest love I may ever know? I do not want our relationship to end his way—all or nothing. Can't we at least be lifelong friends?

The last thing I want him to do is to leave school because of me. That is a burden I do not want to carry. He is suffering from loving me. I only wish he would give me the chance to express how deeply he has touched my life. He has given me so much—not just material things, but his heartfelt affection. I will never toss that away, no matter how long I live.

CHAPTER SIX

EMBARKING ON MY CAREER PATH

WOMAN IN WHITE

Breaking up with Jamie left a pall over my emotions. He had returned to Caracas leaving me with a feeling of emptiness. Gone were the lovely outings, presents, and most of all, loving words and compliments which made me feel special. My parents were satisfied that I had returned to a normal life, but 'normal' was not as satisfying as my days with Jamie.

Why does making others happy not make me happy? I don't miss Jamie's fits of jealousy and pressure to marry, but I do miss him. I hope this awful, pernicious remorse will end soon.

But it didn't end. On my 19th birthday, five long, white, rectangular boxes were delivered from the Germantown Florist. The sweet scent of sixty vermillion roses permeated the house. I was touched, but my parents were not.

"Send him a "Thank You" note and nothing else," Mom warned.

I did as she instructed, but longed to tell him how much he was missed.

The months passed. I concentrated as much as possible on starting nursing school the day after Labor Day. When I entered the Osteopathic School of Nursing, at 48th and Spruce Streets in Philadelphia, I had never lived away from home before. Mom and Dad were proud I was going there. They enjoyed a close relationship with the staff and often referred their patients to that hospital.

A brief orientation session was held. The students introduced themselves. They were friendly and eager to begin. Concentrating on my career would help me forget my ex-Latin boyfriend.

I was assigned a single room in which there was a bed, a desk and a chair. It was not capacious, but it was functional. My first night sleeping away from home was uneventful. I was not as excited about the prospect as I had anticipated.

The next morning, we dressed in our new grey uniforms, white aprons and stockings and marched off to class. The head of our program entered the room first and instructed us to stand and greet our professor from Germany.

"When he enters the room, you are to stand and say, "Good morning, Professor.""

The tall figure strode in toward his desk and we recited on cue.

"Good morning Professor!"

He did not return our greeting and motioned for us to be seated.

"Ladies, you are to be congratulated on choosing a noble profession. There are women who want to become doctors. They take the food out of a family's mouth. By natural law, the man should be the breadwinner. For every seat occupied by a female in medical school, a man is deprived of supporting his family. Women are not equipped to be physicians because of their menstrual cycle. Every month, as you know, a woman may become dysfunctional, even hysterical for one to five days, and therefore unfit to make the life and death decisions of a doctor. You have chosen the proper path for your gender."

Like my classmates, I wrote his words down.

So, I shouldn't become a doctor because I could become hysterical five days a month? That's one I haven't heard before. Remember your catechism class. Don't stand out as a rebel on the first day; it would bother Mom and Dad.

"When you educate a woman, you educate a family," Dad often said. "You girls must get a good education. I suggest you become doctors."

The professor made me appreciate my father even more.

I am grateful my parents want us to be educated, although they too are starting to pressure us not to wait too long to get married.

"Eventually, the bloom will be off the rose," Dad would say. I disliked that expression, but I was proud of all the other ideas he espoused. We had direct contact with patients on Tuesdays, Thursdays, and a half day on Saturdays. Mondays, Wednesdays and Fridays were reserved for class, from 9 a.m. until 5 p.m. My first assignment with patients was in the male ward.

"Good morning, Glory!" the men would cry out as we novices entered the area.

Our assignment was to record a patient's temperature, pulse and respiration, followed by a bed bath, massage and a change of clean hospital gowns and sheets. We shaved those who were unable, brushed their teeth, combed their hair and fed them, if needed. I was assigned to eight beds each morning. Patients had all types of infirmities which often made providing basic hygiene difficult. There was a man with brain cancer. Maggots swarmed in the infected area of his exposed skull. Badly burned victims required special skill. I tried my best not to faint at the sight of the horrific images. The nurses deserved admiration and respect. I felt shame at my weakness and tried always to conceal it.

Heading for anatomy instruction on the upper floor of the hospital, my young colleagues and I would exit the elevator and find ourselves among a group of medical interns who were changing classes. They scrutinized us and uttered their "catcall appraisals" within hearing range. It made me uncomfortable to be stared at from head to toe, although the majority were truly handsome, and I secretly admired them in their white clinic jackets. I kept my eyes down, focused on the floor when passing them until one singled me out, calling in a loud voice.

"Hey, Miss! Why is your head always down; are you looking for dimes?"

On hearing that, it seemed the entire male student body laughed, mockingly. My face felt so hot, I knew I must have turned scarlet. From that moment, I never raised my face to any of them again.

In the Anatomy class, we sat on stools in front of long, narrow tables occupied by cadavers covered with oil cloth sheeting. I'd rest my notebook on a cold, solid limb for writing. The professor lectured us as he did the medical students. His descriptions of the human body were so detailed, and he spoke so quickly, most of us were clueless as to what he was saying. Luckily, the head of the nursing school provided us with a basic anatomy text which was comprehensible and from which we would be tested.

Once ensconced in the program during the first semester, it became increasingly apparent I hadn't made the right career choice for my personality. The sciences were fine, but I also wanted to study art, history, literature, French, Latin and, of course, Italian. I missed the French grammar exercises I used to do with Jamie. Also, working with the male and female patients was enjoyable but problematic because I bonded with many of them. When one suffered, or died, I felt deeply saddened. The mood continued throughout my first semester until it affected my health. I had frequent colds and seldom smiled or laughed. Finally, I knew I could not remain.

I'm miserable. Jamie is out of my life. I can't confide in him. I feel like I am letting so many people down, especially Mom and Dad and the scholarship committee. What am I to do and where am I to go?

Unbeknown to my parents, in December 1956, at the end of my first semester of training, I had visited the director of nursing and told her I contemplated leaving the program. She tried to convince me to stay. "Miss Battaglia, you are too hard on yourself. You have a fine rapport with the patients and you are an excellent caregiver. You will make an outstanding nurse. Please reconsider."

I was steadfast. My greatest regret was having received the only nursing scholarship available at graduation, thus depriving a worthy student of the opportunity to realize her dream of becoming a woman in white. Abandoning this career was not easy and there was no alternate plan. This was the most difficult decision of my life.

When I went home that evening I told Vicki to break the news as I was too upset to face my parents. Their disappointment would compound my misery.

An hour later, the familiar sound of the front door closing signaled the arrival of Mom and Dad. I sat alone in the dark on my bed awaiting the explosion, and it came.

"What!" Dad exclaimed in a loud, agitated voice. "She quit? What will all our friends at the hospital think? This is a disgrace. Where is she?"

"She's in her room," Vicki confessed.

"Well get her down here right now."

I didn't wait. When I descended the stairs, my sorrowful demeanor softened my parents' hearts. My eyes welled with tears when Dad addressed me in a normal tone of voice.

"Gilda, why did you do such a thing?"

I looked into his disappointed eyes and spoke from my heart.

"I had to, Dad; it was not what I want to do for the rest of my life. Being there with those sick people made me sad all the time. I'm so sorry to have disappointed you both."

There was a pause as Dad pondered what I had said. His attitude changed from rebuke to consolation.

"Don't worry about letting us or others down. There are other choices in life and we will help you find your way. Go now. Get some sleep."

I went to bed relieved but with a heavy heart.

I'm scared because now I must strike out into the unknown. But Columbus sailed into the unknown and discovered something great. Perhaps I will too.

THAT SMILE!

"It's a girl!" Mom announced happily on the telephone.

Gloria had just given birth in November 1956 at the Osteopathic Hospital in Philadelphia. I was so glad she had a daughter. My nephew Mark had come along in 1955 and, in true Italian fashion, as a *figlio maschio (masculine child)*, was greeted with jubilation. I intended to make the same fuss over a *figlia (daughter)*.

The nursing school I used to attend was adjacent to the hospital on 48th and Spruce Streets; I knew the way. Mom and Dad had already been there to welcome the infant. I grabbed my coat and set out toward the hospital. En route, I couldn't help but think of all the taunting my father endured by having three daughters and no son.

"What kind of a man are you to have only girls?" or, "You gotta' try again. You might get lucky. You must have a boy to carry your name."

Even the women made similar remarks to my mother. "You have to give your husband a boy," they'd scold, as though she could produce one at will.

I heard of a family that had eleven daughters before a son was born. I would have named him Finale. Gloria is fortunate. She got lucky the first time having my nephew Mark.

When I arrived at the hospital I had a wonderful feeling of anticipation.

Will the baby look a little like me?

I walked into Gloria's room, where she was smiling contentedly. She acquired even a broader one when I handed her a bouquet of pink roses. Her eyes traveled to the bassinette beside the bed in the sparsely furnished hospital room. I approached the darling little bundle she and her spouse fittingly called Mary, after our mother. The traditional Italian custom is to give the first girl the name of the paternal grandmother. But in this case, my brother-in-law, Jennings Bryant Joye—J. B. for short, was not Italian. Regardless, he was willing to follow the custom. He was one of those *Amerigan* mixtures of English and several other things —even French Huguenot. His mother's name was Guyola. He did not want that name for his daughter. Guyola was the quintessential southern belle, feminine, frilly and fun. Family members used to say, "Guyola could charm a snake."

His family was Methodist from South Carolina, so you can imagine they did not rejoice when J. B. married a northerner, an "eye-talian," and a Catholic. But Gloria was strikingly beautiful, a great cook and soon managed to captivate her new in-laws.

"Do you want to hold the baby?"

"Sure."

She seems so fragile; I am a little scared to lift her.

But embrace her I did, marveling at the adorable, diminutive circular face of my niece, *Mariuccia,* the Neapolitan version of "Little Mary."

She didn't look much like me, but it didn't matter.

"Her face is so round, she looks like the winking man-in-the-moon on the *Conte Luna* spaghetti box," I laughed. "I'm going to call her *Conte Luna*" (it sounded better than the correct 'Contessa Luna').

"Oh, only you give such silly names to everybody," Gloria joked. Just then, the little *luna* smiled back at me.

"Look! *Mariuccia* likes to be called *Conte Luna*, I said, and was rewarded with another captivating baby grin.

That tiny, toothless beam beguiled me, and her delicate, almost diaphanous digits gripped my pinky finger. From that moment, the baby and I bonded.

Gloria is as lucky this time as she was with the first.

It was starting to get dark. I hated to leave that warm, joyous maternity room with *Mariuccia* secure in her bassinette. I went into the hall of the hospital to take the elevator to the ground floor. It was slow, so I kept pressing the "down" button impatiently, knowing full well it would not speed the process. While I was waiting, I overheard two men speaking Italian. Rather, one was talking fluently while the other was struggling to be understood.

"Hey, you!" a voice called to me.

Turning in its direction, irked at the abrupt tone, my annoyance dissipated once I saw to whom the voice belonged. Before me stood a handsome, dark-haired, young doctor in a white clinic jacket. Marcus Welby, M.D., Dr. Kildare or those blond TV heartthrob physicians couldn't hold a candle to this guy. He smiled at me with a perfect set of "pearly whites," which seemed to light up the drab, beige corridor.

Oh, God! Is this the man I'm going to marry?

I was 19 years old; he was decidedly more mature, maybe 10 or 11 years? There were neither bells nor bolts of lightning. There was just that smile.

THE TELEPHONE CALL

The riotous upsurge of spring can bring in joy or melancholy. The colorful season arrived in late March 1957 with the golden glory of forsythia in bloom. Sitting on our stiff, green metal porch chair on McMahon Street, I watched the unfolding of nature with a sense of inexplicable melancholy. My mind wandered back to when I left nursing school and the young doctor I met at the elevator.

Most likely, I will never see the intern again. Why do I remember his smile? Thinking about him makes me feel sad, as does remembering Jamie. This is my youth and I am not enjoying it.

Sitting there, my thoughts began to wander. I thought of when I left nurses' training. I had needed to look for a full-time job. It was January 1957. I took the bus to Olney Avenue for the Broad Street Subway, en route to Center City in my quest for employment. There was standing room only on the rambling vehicle. Securing an overhead hand strap, I saw a chum from my class at Germantown High School. She was of slight build. Her amber-colored hair was dull and hung straight around her square face, but her beguiling smile made her look pretty.

"Hi Linda! Where are you going?" I asked, glad to see a familiar face.

"To the Curtis Publishing Company. I'm a secretary there. It's near Independence Hall. Where are you headed?"

"To any place that will hire me. I need a job and think I'd like to be a receptionist because I can't type well."

"Aren't you studying to be a nurse?"

"Not any more. I tried but it wasn't right for me," I answered, with no small sense of embarrassment.

"There's an opening at Curtis for a receptionist. Why don't you apply, and we can see each other for lunch? Come with me and I'll show you where to go."

"Curtis. They publish the *Saturday Evening Post* and *The Ladies Home Journal.* I'd like to try out."

Linda and I exited the subway and walked to South 6th and Walnut Streets near Independence Hall toward the iconic publishing company. The Beaux Arts style structure occupied a city block. We passed massive, white marble columns and entered an expansive atrium with faux Egyptian palm trees. The interior inspired awe.

"This place is incredible, Linda."

"I felt the same when I first came. I'm used to it now. Follow me to the employment office."

Linda led me to the place where a stern-looking woman seated behind a square desk quickly scrutinized me from head to toe.

"This is my friend. She would like to apply for the receptionist position," Linda said, smiling.

The lady handed me a test packet and told me to go to the first cubicle on the right to take the qualifying exam.

"You have one hour to complete this," she said in a laconic voice.

The questions were easy for me and I finished in half the allotted time.

"You're done already?" the woman in charge commented suspiciously.

"Yes." I replied confidently.

She scrutinized each page and saw all answers were correct.

"You are seeking the receptionist position?"

"Yes."

"Take a seat and I will call you shortly." She rose and exited the area for a few minutes, then returned.

"Congratulations, you can begin tomorrow!"

Oh, happy day! That was easier than I thought. At least I can deliver some good news to Mom and Dad this evening. I have let them down and I feel awful. I hope they'll realize I am trying my best to be a responsible person—just not a nurse.

A staff member was summoned to lead me to the second floor, where my station was an attractive, welcoming open space. There was a comfortable sofa covered in a purple and mauve paisley print. A desk faced out with a captain's chair behind, where I was to sit and greet regular clients and newcomers.

"You should like it here," my guide said, graciously.

"Oh, I know I will," I responded.

Wow! Wait till Mom sees this. She'll be impressed and so will Dad.

That evening I shared the news of my full-time job with my parents. They were pleased I had found employment in a prestigious company and that I would have an independent income, but there was an observable lack of enthusiasm because I had abandoned nurses training.

"Being a receptionist is nice, but it is not a profession, young lady. You should seriously consider becoming a doctor," Dad expounded.

"Oh, Angelo, let her be. She is trying to find her way. She's got time. She's young," Mom retorted in my defense.

They always allude to time. I know they want me to have a profession prior to marriage. **Tempus fugit,** *and I feel pressured to get some sort of a degree and a husband as quickly as possible to please them.*

Settling into the new position at Curtis was easy. The duties were few and the surroundings lovely, but I was not fulfilled. I realized I did not want to be a doctor. Leaving the nursing program was traumatic because I had never thought of preparing for another profession and I would not want to be a receptionist the rest of my life, no matter how beautiful the setting. I felt alone and directionless.

While I continued to sit on the porch, my daydreaming was abruptly interrupted. At 5 o'clock, the telephone rang inside. For some inexplicable reason, I felt it might be the handsome doctor I encountered briefly at the hospital during my nursing school days. I rushed in to answer.

"Hello!" I said.

There was no response.

"Hello!" I repeated.

Another pause. I was going to hang up when a male voice asked, "Do you remember me?"

That sound sent a slight thrill through my being.

"Yes," I said, almost breathless.

"What have you been doing since you left nursing?"

I told him proudly of my new job in a posh office. He was unfazed.

"Do you have plans for college? May I suggest you become a teacher of languages like my sister, Celeste? You know some Italian and you mentioned you studied Spanish for six years in school."

"A teacher? I may consider it," I said, wanting to please him and myself.

"Good," he concurred."

Teaching? You liked language study. Teaching is a noble profession. You would be with young, healthy people all day and not be depressed surrounded by sickness and suffering. You must get an education and this would provide direction. Once in college, you could always change your major. Think it over carefully before you mention the possibility to Mom and Dad.

I thought about little else for the remainder of the week. We females had limited career choices: secretary, nurse or teacher. The latter seemed like my best and only other option. Classroom scenarios entered my mind.

I liked studying Spanish when I started in junior high school, but after six- years of grammar and translation exercises, it became dry and boring. I wanted to speak the language. If I become a teacher, I will stress conversation from the first day. Learning a language could be fun and exciting—but not the way I was taught.

At the end of the week, the doctor called again. This time he spoke readily.

"Well, have you decided?"

"I've been considering it."

"You should make up your mind soon to be accepted at a college for the fall semester."

"You are right. I will tell my parents."

He's really interested in my education. Most Italian men are not. It must be because his sister is a teacher. I want to make him proud of what I do as well as Mom and Dad.

That night I approached my parents with the alternate career proposal.

"Mom, Dad, I'd like to apply to college, maybe the University of Pennsylvania, because it has an excellent language program. I'd like to pursue becoming a teacher of French or Spanish, or both. I could even learn Italian and keep my promise to the Pope. If I have a family, an instructor's schedule would coincide with my children's school day and I'd have summers off to be at home."

The more I argued the case, the more convinced I became that it would be a good decision.

"No!" Dad exclaimed. You'd go to a university to learn a language? You already speak Spanish fairly well. I don't want to pay for it. As a teacher, you'll be *Morta di fame* (dead from hunger). Study to become a doctor like we always wanted. That's what you should do."

I disliked the atmosphere in the hospital, especially the smell of formalde-hyde in the anatomy lab. It was bad enough taking notes over a stiff cadaver, let alone dissecting one.

My recourse was to appeal to Mom. She always loved languages and had a flair for them since she was fluent in Neapolitan dialect. When Dad left the room, I went immediately to her, pleading.

"Please, Mom. If I take this step, I'll see it through; I promise."

Mom was on my side. With her as an advocate, Dad would eventually give in.

Grandpop was visiting us when I mentioned my intention of going to Penn, despite a recent exposé in the Philadelphia Inquirer newspaper of a panty raid at the Ivy League institution.

"What? You-a crazy! Dey have-a panty raid-a dere. What-a-do dey study dere? No good-a gal-a go to dat-a school," he ranted.

My parents concurred.

"If you go to college, you'll go to Beaver College where your mother went or you'll go nowhere," Dad reported authoritatively.

I was in no position to argue and I did not protest. If he was willing to send me to Beaver College I would accept because one thing was clear, I needed to prepare for a future profession.

Vicki and I had to take a college aptitude test, which we both subsequently passed. An appointment was made at an all-female institution. Mom accompanied me to my interview at Beaver with Admissions Officer, Miss Darling. She accepted me for the fall semester on the spot. Based on my performance, Vicki was also admitted, sight unseen.

My sister acquiesced but was not pleased with the news because she wanted to study Spanish at the University of Miami. She liked warm weather and preferred to study away from home. Initially Mom and Dad had told Vicki they might consider her going south but when I was admitted to an institution close by, they changed their minds.

"You too will go to Beaver or nowhere," Dad declared. They would offer no other option. Vicki did not protest.

A month had passed since the doctor's first phone call. I sensed he would contact me again. One evening the phone rang at home and I intuited who the caller might be.

"Have you finalized plans for college?" he quizzed.

I was so proud to relate my latest news and await his approval.

"By the way, what is your name, doctor?"

"Louis, but you can call me Lou or Louie. I am glad you will study languages and go to Beaver College. You are making the right choice. You'll be happy with your decision. Celeste teaches French and Latin at Trenton High School. She enjoys her career and I am sure you will also."

As he spoke, I experienced the same fluttering sensation surge through my body. I was happy he approved and wondered if he was wearing that same dazzling smile?

BEAVER COLLEGE

Dad finally supported my proposed career change. He and Mom were glad Vicki and I were admitted to Beaver College. Our parents never complained about paying for tuition because I had received a full scholarship to nursing school. Their generous attitude made me more determined to complete my studies and become an educator.

Once we matriculated, in lieu of congratulations, Mom and Dad heard many negative comments from our Italian family and friends.

"Angelo, are you crazy? Why are you wasting money on educating your daughters? They're only going to get married," or, "They'll never graduate. Save your money and use it for their weddings."

Gloria and J. B. honeymooning.

I was extremely proud of my parents when they resisted the naysayers and encouraged us even more.

"Don't listen to them. Do your best and take advantage of your education," Dad advised.

The Italian preference for educating males over females really irks me. It's no wonder. They keep girls ignorant and dependent. Their expectation for females is to marry. If they don't wed, they are to live with a relative and be dependent. I hope that attitude will change someday soon. I'm grateful to my parents and I'll try to make them proud.

I embarked on the first day on my new career with great anticipation. Vicki and I arrived at Beaver, in September 1957. Preparing for the big event, I learned a few facts about the college. It was a liberal arts institution founded in 1872 on the Beaver and Ohio Rivers, thus the origin of its name.

We enrolled as "Day Students," meaning we would not live on campus. That was fine with me because I preferred being more independent at home than in a dorm, although our six-room, one bath "Dream Castle" house seemed to get smaller by the day with no space for entertaining friends. What I preferred was privacy in the bathroom, the ability to receive many phone calls from gentlemen callers and go on week-night dates with Louie, who 'came calling,' without having to adhere to a 10 p.m. curfew at the dorm.

The main campus of this well-known institution was centered amidst an imposing, bona fide castle known as Grey Towers, which had been acquired in 1928. This singular treasure had been commissioned by William Welsh Harrison, an owner of the Franklin Sugar Refinery. The mansion design had been based on England's Alnwick Castle, the medieval seat of the Dukes of Northumberland, boasting crenulated turrets on the exterior and impressive coffered and strap work ceilings inside.

Beaver offered a significant perk to its alumnae. A student or family member could have a wedding reception at the castle. Because Mom was an alumna, Gloria had celebrated her fairy-tale nuptials and reception there in the elegant, gilded baroque ballroom. I was her 15-year-old bridesmaid, enchanted by the sumptuous surroundings. I admired the French Renaissance style ceiling paintings of women attended by cupids amid flowing garlands of pastel flowers.

"When you marry, someday, Gilly, I want you to have your reception at Gray Towers like your sister Gloria. There is no more elegant place."

I will not tell Mom now, but I do not want to be married soon.

Vicki did not share my enthusiasm because of Dad's prohibition of permitting a daughter to live away from her family.

"Young women should only leave their father's home for their husband's home," he'd exclaim. "No decent girl lives alone if she has a family."

So off we went together, majoring in Spanish: I, planning to become a teacher, while Vicki was undecided. We donned fall coats on our first day of orientation because of September's brisk wind.

"Look at these girls," I exclaimed to my sister. "They all seem to be stamped out by the same cookie cutter."

"You're right. There aren't any dark-haired Italian Catholics here. Almost all are blue-eyed blonde Protestants, dressed in beige camel hair coats with fox fur collars and white sneakers without socks."

"I'm glad I bought a blue mohair coat because I don't want to look like everyone else," I affirmed. "It's my Italian independent spirit." Vicki readily understood.

One item shared by all incoming students was a required, green beanie, a little cap which signified we were freshman. A staff member instructed us to wait outside on the grass before the orientation assembly. Once seated, we silently stared at each other, some with disapproving glares, evaluating our looks and non-conformist attire. They were making up their minds regarding these "exotic creatures" among them.

We followed our fair, fellow students to the auditorium for the president's address. In contrast to the interior beauty of the castle, the auditorium was a stark space. The unadorned room could comfortably accommodate 620 students sitting in individual chairs, the size of the entire college population.

The auditorium was abuzz with chatter in anticipation of the president. When he entered, and took his place behind the lectern, silence prevailed. He was tall, with an avuncular, albeit firm countenance. When he spoke, everyone listened intently.

"Congratulations, ladies! You are now part of the Beaver College family. I have two significant announcements: First, because it is accepted knowledge females are not as adept at mathematics as their male counterparts, there is no math requirement at Beaver."

At this, I readily applauded with the rest of those assembled.

While I am glad I do not have to take a course in Calculus, I know the president's statement was not academically appropriate. There are women who excel in mathematics.

"Secondly," the president continued, "per state law, the college must accept at least one Negro to its student body annually, therefore, we have admitted one."

No one applauded nor protested. Everyone seemed to accept the pronouncement because it was the norm in the 1950s.

How embarrassed she must feel being singled out like that, knowing they're forced to tolerate her. The colored kids in my classes at Germantown High were good students. She'll stand out more here than Vicki and I with our dark hair and eyes.

"Do you believe your ears, Vicki?"

"Some of the colored kids at Germantown said they had a very hard time getting into college. My friend Edith once told me, "Gilda, why do you think they want everyone to submit a photograph with the college application? When they see you are a Negro most often you don't get an interview."

"Edith, I find that hard to believe."

"My friend, where have you been all these years?" Edith asked.

I didn't want to accept her words because I didn't want to believe them. The President continued his speech.

"To graduate from Beaver College, you must pass a diving and swimming test. In addition, you are to take at least three courses in Bible study, another of life's essentials. No one is truly educated who does not know "The Good Book." Lastly, at Beaver we offer speech courses. You will be judged in life by the way you talk. An educated woman should not have a discernable regional accent such as the one in Philadelphia."

I don't mind the nautical part because I can dive and swim. The Bible stuff is okay too because I enjoyed the lessons at Mrs. Mac Crae's house. I think I speak without a Philadelphia accent because I like to imitate Catherine Hepburn.

But Vicki wasn't happy. She couldn't dive. In fact, she looked glum.

After our orientation, tea was served in the castle. Near the Grand Staircase and marble mantle, the freshmen could meet with faculty. Mom told us to seek out Dr. Cartwright, her favorite science professor. An instructor pointed to him. Dr. Cartwright was enjoying watercress sandwiches with his wife, who would become our Spanish professor. We approached the pair with anticipation.

"Dr. Cartwright, our mother, Dr. Mary Battaglia, told us to introduce ourselves. She always speaks so highly of you."

"Dr. Battaglia is your mother? She was the best student I ever had in chemistry. You girls have a lot to live up to."

At that, Vicki and I felt doomed. Mom was a whiz at science and it came so easily to her. She would sit and do chemical equations at home just for the fun of it. She had taken all her required science courses at Beaver, to be admitted to the Philadelphia College of Naturopathy.

Uh-oh. We are going to be compared to Mom in science class. Vicki and I are going to be compared to each other as students and we are also going to be compared to all the blonde, blue-eyed young women at Beaver. After my stint at nursing school and being a receptionist, I am motivated to do this no matter what, but Vicki isn't. She acts as though she is a prisoner in the Grey Towers. Dad should have let her go somewhere else. As for me, I'll prove wrong all those who said not to educate daughters. Whatever it takes, I will become a "Beaver-ette" and I will graduate.

WHAT WILL PEOPLE THINK?

The curriculum at Beaver College was demanding. I often groaned with having to study for: weekly quizzes, two, three-hour mid-term exams on two consecutive days, a mid-term research paper and a final examination and research paper. To graduate, students had to pass an eight-hour qualifying examination in the topic of their major. I chose the test required in Spanish. It lasted eight and one-half hours. I realized that the education I received at that institution had prepared me well for future study elsewhere.

One night, when I was in my room studying, I heard loud voices from downstairs. Dad rarely raised his, but this time he was yelling at the top of his lungs as he conversed on the telephone. I stepped out of my bedroom and crept into the hall, curious about the heated discourse.

"You did what? You are where? It doesn't matter. Your mother and I want you to return home immediately. Is that clear?" he demanded, slamming the receiver into its cradle.

"Angelo. What is it?" Mom asked in a quivering voice.

"Where's Gilda? I bet she knows what's going on. She may even be behind it all. Mary, get her down here!" I was already descending the stairs to inquire what the ruckus was about.

"Young lady, what's behind this?"

"Behind what, Dad?"

"Behind Vicki's decision; that's what!"

"What about Vicki? What's happened?"

"You mean you didn't know she left Beaver College after completing only one year? She just called to announce she decided to live in a Catholic residence in New York City. She found a job at Vanity Fair, not the magazine, but where they make lingerie. It sounds indecent!" he ranted.

No kidding! She never said anything to me. We all know she hasn't been happy at Beaver this year, but I thought she went to Manhattan today to meet some friends. Now it is clear to me; those friends are living with her in the Catholic residence.

"Angelo. What are we going to do? Everyone's going to talk."

Dad looked at Mom in raging silence for a nanosecond. I backed away, fearing the inevitable eruption.

This scene has all the components of the Old Testament tales at Mrs. Mac Crea's. There is wailing, gnashing of teeth and rending of garments.

Mom sobbed uncontrollably into her apron, while Dad sputtered words so fast they ejected like rapid fire from a machine gun.

"How could she leave a good home? What about her education? What will people think?"

Gee whizz! Vicki is 19-years-old, not a baby. She never wanted to attend an all-female school and being with me in class. She disliked living in this small house with no privacy. She just wants to be her own person. After all, doesn't the bird have to fly out of the nest?

Mom and Dad were so upset they did not even realize I left the scene to seek refuge in my room upstairs.

Why didn't Vicki tell me of her plans? She was always more private, unlike me; I always spew out more than people want to know. I would have blabbed it to Mom and Dad, ruining her plans. But where did she get the money? How did she find a respectable place to live and a job the same day? How clever of her to go to a Catholic residence! There no one could claim she left home to escape parental supervision; the nuns will be in control. Vanity Fair is a well-known company. It doesn't make kinky underwear. Mom and Dad are right about her education, though. Even so, she can always go back to school later on, when she's motivated.

Confess, Gilda. You often dream of having a place of your own without the TV blaring all the time. Even a little apartment would do, but after this debacle there is no way out. You could never put Mom and Dad through this again. From the sound of things downstairs, Dad's heart condition might not survive this episode let alone a second one caused by me.

They're so worried about what people will think they don't seem interested in what Vicki has to say. The reality is the only way out for you is through marriage — even if you don't wed until you're 50, like Cousin Millie in the Bronx who stayed home to care for "Mom-er and Pop-er" until they died in their 80s. Her husband did the same. He was 52 when cousin Millie and he were finally free to marry.

Good for you, Vicki! What you did takes courage—something I don't have now. Brava, little sister, no matter what people think.

SHE WANTS TO GET MARRIED

I had completed three years at Beaver College. Louie and I had been dating on and off during that time. We would go out on a regular basis every Wednesday and Sunday, Louie's days off. I was deeply in love with him, but our relationship was rocky. His manner was always disturbingly abrupt, unlike the gentility I was accustomed to from other gentlemen. This resulted in my breaking off with him several times, although I always went back to "my diamond in the rough."

Louie had rented a small apartment, while he was in medical school, from Jim Dunne in Center City, Philadelphia. The two subsequently became friends. Jim was always present during those rare occasions I visited with Louie for lunch. He was like a silent chaperone.

Jim would join us when Louie would prepare his signature spaghetti dish made from a can of Contadina tomato paste, a packet of *Spatini* (a variety of dried Italian herbs), and a copious amount of black pepper. He would end the carbohydrate-laden meal with cream and cake donuts from Eddie's Shop in Trenton.

Jim could sense when Louie wanted to be alone with me. Those few private moments were always special. Ours was an age of restrictions and innocence. Hugging and kissing were as far as we would go, but it was romantic. I was in love, so much so, I complimented Louie on his spicy sauce and managed to gulp the sugary donuts with a forced smile.

Liar! You know it was awful. We won't eat like this once we are married.

Louie never uttered a romantic word to me, nor I to him, but the look on his face when he saw me spoke volumes for his amorous feelings. I would never reveal my emotions until the man spoke of his first.

Tonight, we will meet Jim and Ruth's newborn son, Mark. I'm happy they married and have a child.

The metal knocker on my front door signaled Louie's arrival. I was ready to meet him with a sponge cake I baked, secure in a plastic carrying tray. We rode contentedly from Germantown to Center City where our friends lived in a two-story colonial row home near Cherry Street. Louie seemed pensive in contrast to my exuberance in anticipation of seeing little Mark.

When we arrived at Jim and Ruth's, Louie remained unusually quiet and reserved. I would have expected him to share my anticipation at seeing their baby, but he did not.

"Welcome! Come in," Jim said, on greeting us at the door. "What have you got there?"

"What a beautiful cake!" Ruth exclaimed. "Did you bake this or buy it?" Her words pleased me.

"I baked it."

"I am impressed, Gilda."

"First, you must come to meet our son," Jim said.

We admired the tiny infant who was in a sweet slumber.

"He's wonderful! God bless him," I said, making sure to say the latter to avoid the *Malocchio* (Evil Eye). I had learned that, in Italy's folk culture one must mention the Lord when seeing a newborn to avoid casting a spell. I didn't believe it, but mentioned God nevertheless.

We sipped wine and nibbled on hors-d'oeuvres, when Jim blurted unceremoniously, "When are the two of you going to get married and have kids?"

It was one of my cheek-reddening moments. Louie never spoke of love, let alone marriage. He was focused now on making a living and accruing some savings. His father, Michele (Michael), was a mechanic in Trenton. He had left the village of Monte Verde in the region of Basilicata for Trenton when he was 20 years old. He married Louie's mother, Filomena, and had five offspring. Filomena's brother, Angelo Guglielmelli, had become a doctor at Hahnemann Medical School. His sister had a dream of educating all her children, although she was a *donna di casa* (homemaker). The parents sacrificed much to send Louie and his older sister to college.

Upon graduation from Temple University with a major in Biology, Louie was drafted into the United States Army. His sister began teaching Latin and French. Her earnings went toward enabling one of her two sisters to become a physician, who, in turn, assisted the younger brother and subsequently, younger sister to also obtain a medical education. The G.I. Bill was instrumental in financing both brothers' medical studies.

Louie had completed his internship the previous year and opened a private practice on Hamilton Avenue in the Chambersburg section of Trenton. The 'Burg,' as it was called, was an ethnic enclave consisting predominantly of Italians and various sections of Polish and Hungarians. I was not concerned that he had no nest egg. His accomplishments were a source of pride. I would have lived on *pan e cipolla*, (bread and onions) to be with him.

"Come on. Set a date; what are you waiting for?" Jim insisted.

"I can't get married," Louie retorted, emphatically. "I know she wants to, but I have no money now, so marriage is out of the question."

Although seated, my knees felt week. My face was betraying me, because the blood surged to my cheeks in scalding scarlet. There was a boiling sensation in the pit of my stomach.

"Sorry we cannot stay longer. I have an exam tomorrow."

Jim and Ruth noticed I was visibly upset so they did not insist we extend our visit. We excused ourselves and entered Louie's car for the half-hour ride back to Germantown. Louie started the car without uttering a word while I lashed out.

"You humiliated me! How could you say such things? Did I ever say I wanted to marry you? Well, I don't, and I won't. In fact, I never want to see you again!"

As we rode along Broad Street, I began to ruminate about what Louie had said at our visit. I felt angry, hurt and disillusioned, but in my heart, I knew his words made sense.

Louie is right. He is the sensible one, being almost 11 years older. He is a very practical, responsible person, unlike impulsive me. I just wish he told me those things when we were alone. If he had asked me to wait for him a year or ten, I would have agreed readily. I would have understood, but not this way. How could he embarrass me publicly?

When we arrived at my house, I got out of the car and said, "Good bye!" as resolutely as I could. Louie sped off.

The very next day at Beaver, I noticed on the billboard an announcement for a summer scholarship to the National University of Mexico. I met with my Spanish professor and made an instant application. Ten school days later, she called me to her office and congratulated me for receiving the award. I was completing my Junior Year of college in 1960 as a French major with an Education minor. I had also taken courses in Latin, one in Italian and six in Spanish. If I were to take four courses in Spanish at the University of Mexico, I would have a dual language major and be more marketable as a teacher.

Mom and Dad supported this venture and within a week of Louie's public declaration, I was on a plane headed to Mexico City.

CHAPTER SEVEN

MARVELOUS MEXICAN ADVENTURE

INTERVIEWING PABLO CASALS

"Toma este perrito por tu viaje (Take this little dog for your trip)." My landlady handed me an adorable stuffed animal for my exciting new job in Acapulco.

"Muchas gracias," I answered with delight, cuddling the snow-white present.

Although I was 22-years-old, her gift would be my welcome traveling companion. I left the house in *Colonia Napoles* in Mexico City and went to the airport, heading to the international resort of Acapulco.

I was a little nervous embarking into the unknown as an interpreter at the 1960 *"Tercera Reseña Cinematográfica de Acapulco. (The 3rd Annual Acapulco Film Festival)."*

At the university, I was asked to apply for a position as an interpreter at the festival. On doing so, I was selected from among a bevy of candidates. My job was to interview famous people in English, French, Italian and/or Spanish. What an extraordinary opportunity for a summer semester abroad from Beaver College!

Until now I never even heard of the Acapulco Film Festival. I've learned it is the second largest after the Cannes Film Festival in Nice, France. Wait till the girls at Beaver hear about this; they won't believe it!

"Hola! Dónde va Vd? (Hello! Where are you going?) "

Startled, I looked up to several smiling faces of young men hauling commercial cameras and tripods. I told them I was going to Acapulco and their grins became even broader because they too were headed to that famous playground.

This is more fun than I imagined.

Interview with Pablo Casals.

Arriving at the Acapulco Airport, a car and driver whisked me to a luxury hotel. I was definitely going to like it there. Shortly after settling in, I received my first assignment, to interview the world's greatest cellist, Pablo Casals. At first, I thought someone was playing a prank on me. The Maestro performed at the White House a few months before at the invitation of First Lady Jacqueline Kennedy. Newsreels throughout the world gave the performance great attention and accolades. Could I, a visiting student in my senior year of college, be given an opportunity of that magnitude?

There was no time to ponder such questions because I was driven to the Papagallo (Parrot) Hotel where the artist was conducting the local orchestra. Stepping out of the auto, rousing music by Manuel de Falla greeted my ears. Following the sweeping sounds, I entered the garden area of the building. I walked hesitatingly along a path flanked by majestic palms and scarlet hibiscus swaying gracefully in the tropical breeze. My mind was a whirl, drinking in the sounds and colors of the glorious garden while simultaneously rehearsing appropriate questions.

I should be objective, but could I enquire about something personal? What should I ask to sound savvy and well informed?

A feeling of fright and flight overtook me but there was no time to dwell on it. The path ended, opening onto the group of musicians and their energetic leader. A male staff member awaited and silently escorted me to a chair next to Señora Marta Casals. The young spouse of the renowned octogenarian was featured in newsreels and on television shows in the States. On seeing her in the media, the apparent contrast in their ages led me to think she might be an opportunist. Why else would a woman marry a man more than 60-years her senior? People often laughed in the movie theaters when they witnessed the unlikely duo.

The serene brunette acknowledged me with a gracious smile as we sat next to each other. The music ceased, and the players took a break. The same escort whispered in the maestro's ear and they turned in my direction. The cellist approached with brisk strides and sat between his wife and me.

I introduced myself in Spanish and we continued in that idiom until I mentioned seeing pictures of him in the presidential residence in Washington, D.C. He then reverted to English. Trying to appear professional, I posed my first question.

"Who is your favorite composer?"

"Let's not talk about me. I am much more interested in learning about a lovely young lady like you," he insisted.

I can't believe my ears. Is he serious? How could anything in my life interest him?

"What are your dreams and ambitions?" he queried.

The rest of our conversation was a blur. We kept speaking. I was mesmerized by his gentleness, punctuated by affectionate glances toward his lovely señora who reciprocated with long looks of admiration.

Listening to this brilliant musician made me realize that love is not restricted by age. Like Martita, I too was drawn to his zest for living and value of all things, even the aspirations of a naive college senior.

"Martita," as he calls her in the diminutive, is no opportunist. It is obvious she idolizes her iconic husband. I can picture her as his talented student, clinging

to his every word in their cello master class. She must have been elated when he showed an interest in her as he did to me in our brief encounter. The age difference is bridged by his incredible charisma and their spiritual and artistic compatibility.

"I love life," he said, stroking his wife's hand.

Bending in his chair, he plucked a small flower.

"When I look at this blossom with its intricate detail I see a reflection of all the beauty in the universe and it brings a tear of joy to my eyes."

The concert master broke the mood by gesturing it was time to resume the rehearsal. Señora Marta and I embraced. Before the pair parted from the area, Maestro Casals took my hand, planted a kiss on it, and gently folded my fingers inward as a gesture of farewell. I clutched my hand to preserve the special moment.

As strains of the *Ritual Fire Dance* resumed I opened my palm slowly, revealing a fresh, golden buttercup gleaming in the Acapulco sun.

PHOTOGRAPHERS' QUEEN

It was my second day as an interpreter at the 1960 Acapulco Film Festival and I was spellbound. Movie stars from around the world were streaming into this renowned resort. Dolores Del Rio chatted with me in Spanish as did other Mexican celebrities like songstress Mona Bel and the legendary Emilio Fernandez. I was overwhelmed to be introduced to the Russian icon Sergei Bonderchuk and his beautiful wife, actress Helena Bonderchuk. I had seen the film idols in the classic *Voyna y Mir* (*War and Peace*), in a Philadelphia art cinema and was mesmerized by their performances in Tolstoy's masterpiece. Helena touched my cheek affectionately and said I was (*krasivaya*) pretty.

I will never forget this elegant, lovely lady and her bigger-than-life husband.

Chatting with the photographers of the film festival.

That evening, cinema greats were singled out at the Fort, where their international films were screened before thousands of adoring fans. The following afternoon, several of the photographers I had met at the airport in Mexico City approached me in the event office. They told me to prepare for a big surprise the next day. They were sworn to secrecy, so I would have to wait to find out what it was. I plied them with questions, begging the nature of their cryptic remarks. Worn down by my persistence, they revealed something which rendered me speechless.

"Every year we select the Queen of Press Photographers. Tomorrow you will be our new Queen of Photographers of the Acapulco Film Festival. The movie star Linda Cristal reigned last year."

I just saw her portraying Cleopatra in a movie in the capital city. Could this be real?

"Wear your best dress," they chuckled. "The program will be televised throughout Mexico."

Oh, no! I don't have a best dress—just a ten-dollar outfit a Mexican designer made for me from local, red cotton cloth. It is form fitting, but plain.

Viewing the Impacto magazine covers.   *Wearing my $10 red dress.*

On the third day of the festival, I was instructed to escort the famous German director Josef van Sternberg, Marlene Dietrich's former husband, on a short tour of downtown Acapulco. I rode in the back of a limousine with him, once again awed by the magnitude of opportunities this dream job afforded me. The vehicle turned onto the main square in the city. Suddenly, I saw a large kiosk strewn with *Impacto* magazines, the equivalent of *Life* in the U.S.

No! No! It can't be! My eyes are playing tricks on me.

But as we neared, there was no mistake. I was on the cover of the national publication wearing my ten-dollar red cotton dress. A photographer had snapped my picture at the University of Mexico after I went to receive a scholarship for summer school. How was it put on the cover of the leading national journal? Herr Von Sternberg noticed my image on the magazines. Registering genuine surprise and admiration, he took my hand, kissed it and congratulated me.

"Wunderbar, Gilda, how wonderful."

Oh, my gosh! If this was the photographers' surprise, what was in store for me tonight? Could what they laughed about be true after all? I'd better iron the red dress.

When evening came, I was escorted by a handsome gentleman into the San Diego Fort where throngs of fans assembled to see the popular movie, *The Apartment*, starring Jack Lemmon and Shirley MacLaine. My guide seated me on the end of a center row near the front of the stage. I was alone and surprisingly calm in this sea of people, strangers who did not know or care about me. Anonymity felt safe. Hopefully I would be left alone, unnoticed in my modest attire. I just wanted to see the movie and then retire to my hotel room.

Royal palms surrounded the Fort, swaying gently in the velvet tropical air. Dazzling light filled the stadium, illuminating countless spectators. There was a full orchestra and a stage as big as Carnegie Hall's on which a tuxedoed Master of Ceremonies appeared to thunderous applause. Ornate ebony cages were wheeled onto the proscenium. With a dramatic flourish, the host unlocked them, releasing flocks of white doves fluttering and shimmering in the light as they flew into the onyx sky.

A timpani roll signaled the start of the spectacle. Famous stars, directors and producers paraded onto the stage. The crowd went wild as cameras flashed, capturing the beautiful people bedecked in their fine couture.

Joining the movie stars on stage at the film festival (I am the third from left).

"And now," the moderator said, in a deliberate voice, "it gives me great pleasure to present the highlight of tonight's gala, the selection of *la Reina de los Fotógrafos de la Prensa* (the Queen of Photographers of the Press). This year it is not a woman from our country, but an Italian American from Philadelphia, Señorita Gilda Battaglia. Remember Rita Hayworth's film, Gilda? This is the real Gilda. La verdadera Gilda! Señores y señoras, I present to you the Queen of Photographers of the Press of the Acapulco Film Festival!"

I never saw the movie Gilda with Rita Hayworth. With all this fuss, she must have been quite a bombshell. I feel like an imposter up here. I'm totally unprepared for all the attention. It's like playing a part without a script. I'm simultaneously thrilled and scared to death.

Spotlights overhead blinded me. I felt paralyzed. The ceremony was being televised nationally. I was too terrified to move! Two guards came to my aid, literally lifting me under my arms and dragging me onstage where more glaring lights obliterated the thousands of onlookers who were clapping wildly. The Master of Ceremonies made more public remarks, but I did not pay attention because my knees were knocking uncontrollably.

Oh, my gosh! Now I know what it means to be so scared one's knees knock. I wonder if everyone can see them?

"Do you want to say something?" he asked softly, into my ear.

"No!"

Noticing my nervous state, he did not insist.

"Our Queen will appear later tonight at the Sportsmen's Club," the announcer exclaimed.

Oh no! There's more to come? I'm trying hard not to faint.

Admiring faces greeted me as I was led from the stage.

They like me. All I have to do is smile and people seem pleased. I must compose my nerves. If only I had a mentor to advise me what to do. Drama classes at Beaver never prepared me for anything like this.

"Before the movie is shown, we are to take you to your next assignment," said my two escorts. En route, they told me I did *muy bien*, and that I looked *muy bonita* in my basic local outfit. Their comments put me more at ease.

On arriving at the Sportsmen's Club, I was led to a large azure pool where circular pedestals floated. I was directed to stand in the center of one while swimsuit clad beauties surrounded me on the moving spheres. A water show extravaganza ensued as incandescent aqueous streams swirled around our pedestals. VIP guests filed in. The glare of camera lights was unrelenting, yet I became increasingly comfortable posing with each flash. My new title and the excessive attention emboldened me.

If only Mom and Dad could see me here. They would be spellbound. This is one of the grandest moments in my life. I feel sad there is no one I can share it with. No one in my family would care except for them. What would the blue-eyed blondes at Beaver say? It's hard to believe this is really happening.

The best part of being the Photographers' Queen during the remainder of the festival was that the public treated me like a real celebrity. Owners of upscale restaurants called my hotel, inviting me to be a guest at their elegant eateries. My sole obligation was to appear and be wined and dined. Cab drivers did not charge me a fare if I would only sign my autograph on the *Impacto* magazine cover bearing my image. I was in a motorcade with star Robert Cummings where cheering crowds lined the streets.

I understand now the lure this glamorous world holds for actors lucky to be part of it. It's intoxicating, and I am becoming addicted—dazzled as though in a dream. But I must always be cognizant of the fact that dreams can end abruptly.

RADIO ANNOUNCERS' QUEEN

The day after I received the title of *Queen of Photographers of the Acapulco Film Festival*, everything reversed. No longer was I sent on an assignment as an interpreter or interviewer, but I became an interviewee. Cameras flashed, capturing my every move. The press was anxious to know about my artistic background, but my experience was limited. In high school, like my sister Gloria, I belonged to the Germantown The-

As slave girl in Germantown Theater Guild play.

ater Guild, a local company with high quality and low budget productions. My parts were minor like playing a slave girl walking across the stage balancing a water jar on my head. I had joined the Drama Club in Beaver College.

"There are no small parts, only small actors," our drama teacher often told us and I took those words to heart.

At the end of my junior year, the theater instructor gave me the lead of Hera in Shakespeare's *Midsummer Night's Dream*. This was worth mentioning, but hardly the stuff to make headlines.

When the press at the festival wanted more substantive material they did not hesitate to invent it. An article was published claiming that I, like Anita Ekberg in *La Dolce Vita* style, climbed into the fountain in the Square in Cuernavaca (a charming colonial town outside of Mexico

City). I hadn't been to that locale nor had I ever stepped into a public fountain. When I protested the inaccuracy in the article which appeared in *Cine Mundial*, a national paper, I was told it was standard procedure to get the public's attention, and it worked!

The famous Mexican star, Emilio Fernandez, sent a four-foot bouquet of flowers and a telegram saying he was in love with me. Could he be serious?

I never answered him but secretly kept the yellow page in a small box under my bed. At every interview, I was queried about the fountain caper. Not wanting to fabricate yet another story, I just smiled and remained silent.

Let me try to look mysterious. They can write whatever they want.

One day an event organizer handed me an invitation to a breakfast at the *Presidente* Hotel with American celebrities. Actor Jack Lemmon was to be among them. His latest film, *The Apartment*, was going to be shown in the San Diego Fort that evening.

Would a star of his magnitude want to speak with me over a drink of papaya juice? Most likely not. I am an imposter and Mr. Lemmon will confirm it at a glance. This is all make-believe, but I intend to have fun while it lasts.

On arriving at the *Presidente*, an employee led me to a poolside table where the breakfast was being served. As always, the ambiance was lovely. The azure sky was free of clouds and the bougainvillea bloomed in vibrant colors. It felt again like paradise in December 1960. Mom had called my hotel telling me the winter in Germantown was very harsh and bleak. It was so delicious to be in Acapulco. What a lucky lady I was.

My breakfast companions greeted me politely. One was the son of Luis Buñuel, the renowned Spanish movie director of *La Joven and Nazarín*. Another was a young French filmmaker whose documentary on Rangoon, Burma, was to be aired that night at the festival.

Jack Lemmon soon arrived being propped up under an arm by a gentleman from the hotel who saved the star from falling into the pool. It was 10:30 a.m. and Mr. Lemmon was obviously inebriated and staggering. He was assisted to a seat at my table and the conversation turned to *The Apartment*. Despite his current condition, the actor spoke lucidly and long about several aspects of the film's production. It was impressive to see how the artist's passion for his craft overcame the influence of alcohol.

When the gathering ended, I was approached by a festival agent wearing a white suit. I thought he came to see Jack Lemmon. This time it was a representative of Mexican Radio Announcers and he stopped in front of me.

"Señorita Battaglia," he said formally. "It is a pleasure for me to inform you that the Radio Announcers of the Acapulco Film Festival select you as their Queen. Tomorrow evening, at the Sportsmen's Club, the event will be televised nationally. Award-winning actor Jack Lemmon will present the crown. You must prepare remarks for this important occasion, which will be shown on national television and in all cinemas of Mexico. Do you accept?"

Of course, I accepted and with pleasure as I no longer suffered from paralyzing nerves. The fantasy continued. This time I knew it was not a joke and I was swept along. A staff member of the hotel brought me a telegram at the breakfast. My sister Vicki heard of my exciting adventures from Mom and Dad and flew to Acapulco to join me at my hotel. I was happy to have an eyewitness at the festival because who at home would envision all this? My family always accused me of having a vivid imagination and describing my recent experiences would be met with disbelief.

No sooner had I read the message than a telephone was brought to the table.

"Gilda, Mom and Dad said you were having a great time here. I flew in from my trip to Japan and I'm in the lobby of your hotel."

"What a surprise! I'm so glad you are here. You won't believe what is happening. Nobody could. Come by the pool at the Presidente Hotel. It's within walking distance. We'll have lunch and toast your arrival."

Having Vicki with me will surely add to the excitement. I need to have someone I can share my insecurities with.

Soon my sister arrived. We were giddy as we sat at a table, hugging each other. Our chatter soon ceased when two tall men passed close by.

"Did you see those guys?" Vicki said. "They're gorgeous." I turned discreetly, but could not control blurting, "Oh, my God, it's Rock Hudson!"

Rock Hudson was seated at a table behind me, smiling at a male companion.

"He's the most handsome man I have ever seen. He looks like a statue of a Greek god! What an initiation to the festival for you, Vicki!"

During the rest of the day, we hobnobbed at poolside with Ernest Borgnine and his Mexican wife Katie Jurado, where I raved about his award-winning movie *Marty*. Karl Malden also joined the group, promoting *The Apartment*.

The glamorous people we saw on the big screen at the Walton Theater had come alive and we were in their midst. The dream continued.

That evening was spent writing my acceptance speech for the Radio Announcers gala. The following morning, I was asked to report to the office of Licenciado Miguel Alemán. He was the most eligible bachelor in Mexico and the scion of the former President of Mexico, Miguel Alemán, purportedly the 5th richest man in the world. A life-sized statue of his father stood at the center of the National University in Mexico City, where I was studying. The father purportedly owned the Waldorf Astoria Hotel in New York City and his son hosted the Acapulco Film Festival and served on the selection panel which had hired me as an interpreter. I entered the attorney's office and found him conversing with the international idol, Dolores Del Rio.

He rushed to greet me with an outstretched hand.

"So, you've been singled out to receive another significant title tomorrow. After the ceremony, if you are not tired, I would like to invite you to a party at my family home here in Acapulco. I will be waiting for you at the Sportsmen's Club."

Dolores Del Rio looked closely to see my reaction at such a tempting offer.

An invitation to go anywhere with 'Miguelito' Alemán would be prized. The handsome young bachelor was a national heart throb. His fair, European features, beguiling smile and impeccable manners were admired nationally and internationally.

Why would he want to go out with me? Daily newspapers are full of his romance with Cristiane Martel. Who could compete with Miss World? Besides, she's got to have a better wardrobe.

"Thank you. I'll be waiting," I said, glancing at Dolores Del Rio who was still scrutinizing me intently.

Vicki took no time in getting acclimated to the beautiful surroundings, wonderful food and the excitement that filled the air.

"This is going to be a big night for me, Vicki."

That evening, The Sportsmen's Club was decorated with dazzling lights and potted palms. More celebrities poured in from around the world to join the festivities. When my big moment arrived, an escort motioned for me to sit on a rococo throne strategically placed under a flower-strewn arch on a circular pedestal. A familiar drumroll heralded Jack Lemmon's appearance. My heart beat so loud I thought everyone could hear it and see it thumping in my chest. I tried looking composed and smiled demurely as the versatile star stood before me, holding up a glistening crown.

"The Radio Announcers of Acapulco have chosen their Queen of the Third Annual Film Festival this year. Ladies and gentlemen, it is my distinct pleasure to place this crown on the head of Señorita Gilda Battaglia."

My remarks were uttered perfectly in Spanish and on national TV.

"Gracias por este honor inmerecida." (Thank you for this honor for which I am unworthy...). Simultaneously, I felt both elation and an unexpected sadness that I was enjoying this incredible experience alone. Vicki had wandered off somewhere and I longed to share the moment with someone from home.

Real movie stars must get this feeling at times. It's both exhilarating and isolating. Despite all the attention, I feel lonely.

That emotion was fleeting because at the end of the ceremony a well-known film producer approached me.

"When you return to the capital, come to my office; I may have work for you in a movie." I'll always remember his last remark—*"Porque tu vales."* (Because you are worth it).

As planned, when the ceremony ended Miguel Alemán came for me. All eyes were on us as he extended his arm and assisted me into his convertible Mercedes Benz sports car. I felt proud to be at his side as we drove off.

He is the number one bachelor in the country and I am sitting beside him. What would the folks at Beaver College say if they saw me in this gorgeous setting with the most sought-after bachelor? What should I say to him? I'm tongue tied. This is my big chance to impress him. Don't ruin it.

My date did not initiate any conversation. Without either of us uttering a word, the young attorney veered the car onto an exclusive road off the highway. We rode for more than a mile before arriving at the entrance of his house built into a mountain overlooking Acapulco Bay.

"We have to take a funicular to the lower level. President Eisenhower and Gina Lollobridgida are house guests this weekend. I have to attend to them shortly."

Exiting the nearby cable car, we arrived at the main entrance where we entered a room filled with guests. Miguelito took my arm and led me to a bar area where Buñuel's son and the French Burmese documentary producer were enjoying tropical drinks. He had me sit with them. Excusing himself, he left me with the two outgoing filmmakers.

"*Viridiana* is a fascinating movie," I said, trying to appear worldly. "Your father is a brilliant director. He must be pleased you are following in his footsteps."

"Yes and no. What are you interested in doing, theater, film?"

"I'm going to be a teacher of Spanish."

"What! We thought you were enamored with the *farándula*" (show business).

They laughed good-naturedly and our conversation began to flow. My nerves and feelings of inadequacy dissipated for a while, but soon returned when Miguel re-appeared, gesturing for us to leave.

Why does he want to go so soon? I've been here less than an hour.

As he drove in the direction of my hotel, I was hoping he would comment about the crowning ceremony and my flawless performance in his mother tongue. Instead, he asked the unexpected.

"Would you like to go for an ice cream? Do you like chocolate or vanilla?"

"Vanilla is fine but it is too late for ice cream right now, if you don't mind."

Ice cream! I was wishing he would tell me he changed his mind about Miss World.

We rode on for 10 minutes when he pulled off the highway and stopped the engine of the car.

Is he going to get romantic? He is attractive. It might be nice, but I am beginning to feel nervous. Is his attention what I really want or am I only flattered to be in his company?

Looking directly into my eyes, he spoke deliberately.

"Gilda, you are a nice girl. You don't belong here. Being in the movies is not the place for someone like you."

His words stung, deflating my elation at the wondrous evening.

"I'll only be here for a little while. My parents expect me to become a teacher."

"Good. Listen to them. Go home."

El licenciado drove back and saw me to the door of my hotel room. He took my hand and gave me a serious smile.

"Good night, Gilda. Remember what I told you." He turned and left.

How can I forget? This is not what I wanted to hear, but he's probably right. I am flattered he showed me respect, but I'm going to stay and try a little longer. This kind of experience may come only once in my lifetime. I want to see what I am capable of doing. If I leave now, I'll never know.

Adiós ilusiones.

A RICH AND POWERFUL MAN

At the end of the Acapulco Film Festival, I experienced a slump. The incredible glamour and attention had ended abruptly. If I wanted to remain in Mexico and try out my fledgling new career while continuing my studies, I would need to make money. I had been happy in that mountainous land. The people treated me warmly and I enjoyed the faculty and studies at the university. Beaver College granted me an extended stay for the fall semester of my senior year. Vicki wanted to join me. We found a reasonable apartment in Mexico City. The lease was paid with a portion of the 240 dollars I earned at the festival.

Modeling jobs poured in. On Tuesday and Thursday nights on prime-time, I portrayed Cleopatra, advertising *Osart* beauty products on Mexican TV.

"From the time of the Queen of Egypt, exotic women have used *Osart.*"

An announcer repeated those words twice a week while I doused water on my wrists and arms seductively. My favorite commercials were feeding grapes to Marc Antony, played by an Italian American wrestler who held the *Mr. Universe* title. He was friendly and good-natured as I joked about wanting to squeeze his hypertrophied biceps. Once, only my hands were modeled. My fingernails always grew long, and the director of the commercial liked the way they looked holding a silver tray. No one saw my face when I would point to a bottle of Bayer Aspirin. *Sábanas de Reina* (Sheets of a Queen) was another popular ad shown in movie theaters. I was made to stand in front of a white backdrop with a pillow fastened to the wall. With eyes closed, I pretended to be asleep while a narrator said, "Use *Sábanas de Reina*; you'll feel like royalty and sleep like a queen."

For a high-end textile commercial, I was painted gold from my shoulders up. A makeup artist brushed the yellow liquid on my hands, arms and upper torso, above my green-satin, full-length gown. It was surreal meandering through rows of billowing sheer cloth, my skin glistening among the diaphanous fabrics. Unfortunately, the lovely gown was permanently stained with gold blotches and the paint was uncommonly difficult to get off my skin.

From 1960 to 1961, I appeared in 27 documentaries, playing among other roles an elementary school teacher in the colonial town of Puebla, a tourist in Guadalajara and among the spectacular Aztec ruins of

My prime time TV commercial as Cleopatra.

Tenochtitlán. I was embarking on a serendipitous career and financial independence. I wanted to prove Miguel Alemán wrong.

One morning, as I was walking toward a studio for another modeling position, an American gentleman approached me. He knew my name and said he was a filmmaker from California, working in Mexico, and that he had been following my career.

"This is none of my business, but I'd like to give you some advice. You've progressed rapidly so far, but to really succeed in this business you must align yourself with a rich and powerful man. It's impossible to do it alone."

I felt offended by his comment, but politely disagreed. Thanking him for his advice, I walked away, determined to prove him wrong as well.

My first role in a full-length movie took place in the Churubusco Studios in Mexico City. I was an "extra" in a musical featuring the popular singer/actress, Mona Bel. My scene consisted of being in a spa with several women, lip synching to her lyrics in steam cabinets with white towels wrapped around our heads. I went to take a place in one of the contraptions behind the other starlets but was immediately taken by the arm and led by a stage hand, who placed me in the appliance next to the leading lady. Our faces were moistened with wet sponges to simulate perspiration.

I apparently perspired so convincingly I was given the opportunity to appear in another film. It was a bit-part consisting of being outside a mansion where I had to walk down a long flight of circular, concrete stairs. If an actor missed a cue or flubbed a line as I was stepping down, I had to climb up and descend the narrow steps once again, panting in the rarified air of Mexico City. I had to perform that trek four times before the "take."

That film was to be called *Dos Madres (Two Mothers)*, although the title could have been changed as often happened. I was given a small speaking part as the grown daughter of Dolores Del Rio. The director explained that in the plot I had been separated from my mother in childhood and was reared in Brazil; ergo, I was given two lines to recite in Portuguese.

Eu gosto muito a música. (I like music very much). *A música e bonita.* (The music is beautiful).

The most memorable aspect of the experience was observing a consummate actress. Ms. Del Rio's timing and facial expressions were honed from years of practice. Her persona was stunning, and I felt privileged to be in her company.

Each subsequent film had brought me more speaking opportunities. The third movie I appeared in was a monster comedy titled *Frankenstein, el Vampiro y Compañía* (Frankenstein, the Vampire and Friends), produced by Jorge Calderón. By 8 a.m. I was on the set, made up and dressed as an odalisque (a harem woman). My part was an Italian woman attending a masquerade party. A valuable necklace had been stolen and I was accused of having snatched it. I was to deny the charge and look very dramatic with a heaving bosom. The director informed me my scene would be filmed in the afternoon, so I decided to wander among the varied sets in the studio and observe the action.

In a different locale, the cameras were being prepared to roll. I stood in the background and watched, fascinated by the preparations. My eyes settled on an elderly, portly man who rambled in wielding a cane. Everyone scrambled to make way for him. An armchair was provided post haste. He sat in a strategic spot behind the set and motioned a young actress to approach. She hesitated. He extended the cane and thrust the silver crook between her legs. Yanking on the wooden rod, he forced her to move forward. She hopped uncontrollably toward him with a forced, nervous smile to conceal her embarrassment and revulsion. He whispered in her ear and she nodded slowly in the affirmative, wearing that same artificial grin.

Is this the type of rich and powerful man my street counselor had in mind? Does she feel she must put up with this sleazy specimen to survive? Is there a child or an elderly parent to support? She would surely not endure such public degradation for an acting career? Or would she?

With that scene etched in my brain, the initial elation of the morning dissolved. I decided to concentrate on my script and recited it flawlessly, but the disgusting vision crept back.

No! That will never happen to me. If I make it, it will be without a rich and powerful man, Porque Yo valgo *(Because I'm worth it).*

ONE FINAL WORD

Christmas had come and gone a week ago, here in Mexico City. The "Posadas" portraying Mary and Joseph seeking room at an inn were enjoyable. Of course, the "inns" were private homes where lovely parties were hosted.

A *piñata* was always present. It was fun being blindfolded, taking turns with children and adults at swinging a bat at a distended cardboard bull or donkey covered with tufts of brilliant red, orange, yellow, green and blue crepe paper. When a thrust severed the toy creature, I'd giggle and join the rest in scrambling for the sugary contents skittering on the floor.

Yes. It was fun, but unlike last year when the festivities seemed somewhat magical, there was something missing now. The year 1961 was coming to an end. It had been a good one for me. I'd appeared in three full-length motion pictures, 27 film documentaries, numerous commercials and a daytime variety television show, *El Solar de Vagabundos* (The Vagabond Sun). It was all 'groundwork,' as far as I was concerned. My big break would come the following year because Señor H., arguably the best producer for cinema in Mexico, mentioned the possibility of a co-starring role. His latest movie, *Animas Trujano*, centered on an Indian from the region of Chiapas in the south. There were rumors it might win the "Best Foreign Film" category at the Oscars in Hollywood.

He assured me he could make me famous by giving me a part in his latest work starring the beautiful María Felix and Pedro Armendariz. The movie would be titled "La Bandida," and would appear in 1963.

What an opportunity! She is perhaps the biggest celebrity in the country. If I can co-star with her, my career will be made. He didn't promise me the part, so I shouldn't get too excited.

At 9 p.m., on December 29, 1961, I was alone in our room in Mexico City at the Hotel San Francisco, waiting for Vicki to return from visiting friends. We had traded our furnished apartment for a space in the hotel because it afforded us mobility without a long-term lease.

It grew dark. I sat alone in my black cocoon, and began to have ambivalent thoughts. I had loved being in this land of mountains and mariachis, but my mind kept zooming back to New Year's Day in Mays Landing, at Grandmom's and Grandpop's modest wooden house. As in a Dickens' tale, scenes opened, filled with gregarious, laughing people in a bright, warm dining room. It was my family, full of an assortment of distant relatives and friends, all awaiting a succulent feast. They had returned from Mass at Saint Vincent De Paul Church, where my extended family occupied the major portion of pews in the small structure.

On arriving home, I'd accompany Grandpop to the basement. He would remove two Langhorn hens from their coop outside.

"What are you going to do with them?" I'd ask, knowingly.

Without answering, my five-foot-five, robust grandfather held each bird above a drain in the concrete floor. His stocky fingers circled its brown neck, and deftly snapped it.

"EEE-WWW!" I'd squeal, with a combination of revulsion and fascination.

Scarlet specks splattered onto the brownish-red plumage. I wondered if killing them bothered Grandpop. He never said, probably because he believed everything in the Bible, even the part where God put animals on earth for man's consumption.

The poultry was then carried to the kitchen and given to the women for eviscerating and plucking. The warm insides exuded an unpleasant pungent odor, yet I remained, watching and sniffing as Mommy and Aunts Millie and Rose removed the inner and outer contents. From the two hens, Grandpop made a big pot of *minestra*, a thick soup of stock, savoy cabbage, spinach and tiny, hand-rolled meatballs. To make it richer, quartered hard-boiled eggs were added. Nothing was wasted. The feet went into a bubbling, red, tomato sauce, with chunks of beef, pork and veal. My favorite dish was homemade ravioli stuffed with ricotta cheese, flavored with a dash of fresh nutmeg and a copious quantity of *Parmigiano* cheese and a touch of fresh mint.

Grandpop always said Grace.

"In nome del Padre, del Figlio e dello Spirito Santo," he'd begin.

After the enormous repast, the men and boys would nap in chairs while the women and girls cleaned up. Later in the afternoon we would "go visiting." This would entail entering several homes of our relatives to see their *presepe* (manger scene) under the Christmas tree and to partake of their hospitality. I loved going to Uncle Gable's (Grandpop's baby brother Gabrielle) and Aunt Lina's house because it was full of their eight children and grandchildren. They usually served *struffoli* (small rounds of fried dough drizzled with honey) in the shape of a Christmas tree. There was always so much laughter and commotion there. Also, I enjoyed going to the farm house of Uncle Mike Cirigliano and Aunt Rose. The former was strong and burly-built. He seemed so big to me in my childhood, but kind and gentle as well. He worked for the Mays Landing Water Power Company where he delivered to local houses, four to five tons of anthracite daily. He shoveled the coal by hand on and off a truck. His wife, Aunt Rose, my grandfather's sister, always wore black, a sign of perpetual mourning. She used to sit in the parlor where there was an iron heater. We would approach her with the customary kiss and she would grin and say, "God-a-bless." She too was kindness personified.

How I missed them all now as I sat in darkness. In this capital city, we would probably eat *Mole Poblano*, with turkey, to welcome 1962. But that highly spiced, tasty sauce was no substitute for a dish of *ragú*, right now.

The metallic click of a key unlatching the door interrupted my reverie.

"What are you doing sitting alone in the dark?" Vicki asked.

"Oh, just thinking of New Year's Day dinner in Mays Landing," I retorted.

"Yeah," said Vicki. "That was always something. If we weren't visiting other relatives, we'd be so stuffed we'd fall asleep in a chair afterward and at about five o'clock, they'd bring out all the leftovers and we'd start to eat again."

"I used to like sitting around the table peeling roasted chestnuts and cracking walnuts, and giggling, almost drunk from so much food," I added.

We both lapsed into nostalgic silence. We were not near home. We were in a foreign country. There was no snow in Mexico City, a feature I preferred on arrival, but now strangely missed. A loud ring broke our nostalgia as the telephone sounded.

"It's 9:30 p.m. Who could it be at this hour?" Vicki asked, perturbed.

I lifted the receiver to the familiar "*Hola!*"

"Gilda, this is Manuel. I'm in Cuernavaca, heading for Mexico City. Forgive me for calling so late, but I've been very busy. The film is going to start soon, and I want to discuss something with you. Can I come to the hotel tonight?"

"Yes," I replied, hesitatingly.

"Good, he said. I'll be there in an hour."

"Are you kidding?" Vicki retorted. "He wants to talk business now?"

"I'll meet him in the lobby, of course. He's always been so formal and a gentleman," I said, to reassure myself.

"I still think it's odd," she snapped.

I went to touch up my makeup. Applying rouge took me back to Mays Landing once again, where Aunt Millie would watch me go through the ritual.

"What brand is this? I like the color; it's just right for your complexion. Do you mind if I try it?" she'd say.

Once again, a loud ring shocked me back to *la Ciudad de México* (Mexico City).

"I just want you to know I passed the *carnitas* (assorted fried meats) place you like. I won't be long now," stated the masculine voice, with anticipation.

Why is he so eager to keep me posted about his route?

While I tried to dismiss it, I had an uneasy feeling. The *Carnitas* was a roadside eatery where long strips of pork and beef were deep fried to a crispy, juicy goodness, hard on the arteries but good on the palate. Manuel invited me and a group of *artistas* there once and it was fun.

With "my face on," as they'd say, I was tackling my long, thick hair. Half-way through making a French twist, the telephone jangled.

What now? Is he going to announce he is almost at the hotel entrance? After five rings, I slowly lifted the receiver.

"Darling!" he responded in a breathy, seductive voice. "I am getting nearer and can't wait to be with you."

At hearing the word "darling," a shock permeated my body. I froze temporarily. This married, middle-aged man had seemed so serious and professional, not like the rest.

"Señor H., I am sorry, but it is not possible now. Something has come up and I can't leave my sister."

The disappointment in his voice was palpable, but he continued politely.

"Oh, well, then. I'll come to you tomorrow evening."

I hung up, feeling betrayal and profound disappointment.

Perhaps when he said "Darling," it was just Hollywood talk. Perhaps it was not. I will never know.

When I recovered, I gave my sister an order.

"Vicki. Pack your bags; we're leaving Mexico tomorrow on the first plane to the States."

"Why? What did he say to you?" she insisted. "Just one word. We'll be in time for New Year's dinner at Grandpop's."

CHAPTER EIGHT

DISCOVERING EXOTIC PLACES IN THE WORLD

SPANISH TEACHER INTERVIEW

On returning home from Mexico City, I felt a strong sense of letdown.

I'm glad to see my parents and relatives again, but I miss the attention I had in Mexico. It's like the time I broke up with Jamie. I always feel I am doing my duty, but it does not bring me happiness. I wonder how Louie is. Has he found another girlfriend, or will he be waiting for me? If he isn't, I would understand. I would never admit to Vicki that I missed him while I was in Mexico, but I did.

I was upstairs arranging for college, when Mom called from below. I detected a lilt in her voice. "Gilda, Dr. Rorro is here to see you."

He hasn't found another girlfriend. I wonder how he knew I was home. He must have calculated the starting date of classes at Beaver. I always told him he had the attention to detail of a detective. Despite all that transpired, I'm glad he is here.

When I descended the stairs, my heart began to quicken. I tried valiantly to suppress smiling too broadly and I felt Louie was doing the same, but we both looked happy to see each other. Mom was beaming in my peripheral vision.

"You haven't changed much. You haven't lost any weight," he said.

"You haven't changed either. You are still abrupt."

"Let's go to the Pub and have lunch," Louie said, revealing that dazzling smile.

"Okay."

Returning to Beaver College and anonymity after being the subject of so much attention in Mexico was an adjustment. I missed the life of the *farándula*. Going to the Walton to see foreign films was especially

Article in a Mexican newspaper stating I had left the country.

upsetting. There I saw many of the international stars I had mingled with in Mexico. They were on the big screen while I was carrying books to and from classes.

Although living at home with Mom and Dad was pleasant and I was grateful for their protective attitude, the transition from modeling, movies and TV was more difficult than I imagined. I missed that lifestyle and the friends I had cultivated south of the border.

I tackled my final semester of college full force. The increase in my verbal skills made the language studies easier. I performed the part of the youngest daughter in Federico García Lorca's play, *The House of Bernarda Alba*, in Beaver's drama class. It was well received and served as an anodyne to the pain of separation I felt far from a country and people I had grown to admire and love.

Louie was very pleased with my decision to finish college.

"Forget the movies. It's all nonsense. Believe me; you'll never regret becoming a teacher."

But I couldn't forget easily because of a letter I received from Mexico. The envelope had Películas H. on the front. It was from Señor H., admonishing me for leaving the country without notifying him. In it he wrote, "I was going to surprise you with the part in *La Bandida,* but you left without a word."

How I wish I could have had the co-starring role with María Felix. It could have made me famous. I might have real talent, but now I'll never know. I made my choice and I have to live with it. There is no going back. I must put such thoughts behind me and start a new life.

Graduation day came and went at Beaver College and with it the realization I needed to earn a living. With my diploma in hand, it was time to find a full-time job with benefits. Life was good in 1962 for a young woman with a college degree. A Liberal Arts education was well-regarded and opportunities for a teacher of French and Spanish abounded in the Philadelphia area and beyond. I did not have to seek a position: I received numerous calls from schools inviting me to visit their facilities.

"Come to our district. See for yourself all we offer. We think you will like it here and become a great addition to our faculty."

Those words were stated repeatedly from department chairs seeking language teachers. I could pick and choose.

One morning, the phone rang at home. It was the principal of Upper Moreland High School wanting me to apply for the Spanish teacher position. Upper Moreland was one hour by car from our home in Germantown. The commute would be long, but there were benefits. Gloria used to take us to Willow Grove Amusement Park, which was near Upper Moreland. My memories of the Alps Roller Coaster and the Whip were fond ones, so I decided to give Upper Moreland a try.

Who knows, maybe I would be close enough to revisit the rides at Willow Grove.

Dad insisted on driving me to the interview. I told him I preferred to go alone, although I knew he wanted to see the school where I might be working. He looked so disappointed, I acquiesced.

"All right, Dad, you can take me, but please wait in the car when I meet the principal. I want him to know I am an independent adult."

"Of course," Dad agreed.

On arriving at the modern, red brick school building, I entered the main door, leaving my father in the car. The principal, Mr. Wesley, was waiting for me in the hall to conduct the interview. He was of medium build and had light brown hair and discerning eyes. His beige suit complimented both.

As soon as he shook my hand, he was distracted and looked away from me. Before he could resume, Dad appeared.

"Excuse me, but I wanted to come in and see the place where my daughter may be working. I don't want to interrupt you."

What do you mean? You already bothered us and the principal might think I am immature.

I cast an annoyed glance at Dad for not remaining in the car, hoping it went unnoticed.

"Sir, you are not interrupting at all. I am delighted to meet you and admire your interest in your daughter's potential place of employment. It's an honor to have you here."

Mr. Wesley took us on a tour of the school and introduced Dad to everyone he met, bragging about the latter's paternal interest. "Look, here is a father who cares about his daughter so much he escorted her here. You don't see that every day."

The principal was sincerely impressed with Dad, so I got the job without any formal interrogation. Dad was beaming with pride as we rode back to Germantown. I smiled back at him, inwardly pleased.

That night, when my psychiatrist brother-in-law J. B., heard what happened, he disapproved stoutly. "Italian fathers are too protective of their daughters. They don't give them the freedom to become independent adults."

I often thought the same and frequently protested Dad's constant concern regarding my affairs. But in my heart, I was always grateful to have a father who cared deeply for me.

AROUND THE WORLD ON PAN AM

My first year of teaching high school Spanish was rewarding. I enjoyed the students and wanted to teach the language in an interesting and meaningful way—not the grammar/translation method I was exposed to. I spoke only Spanish in my classes and the pupils learned quickly. Their enthusiasm for language learning was rewarding to me. I was thankful for Louie's sage advice. Being with healthy, happy young people suited my personality. I had chosen the right profession.

One Sunday morning in October 1962, Vicki was reading the *Philadelphia Inquirer* newspaper and let out a yell.

"Hey, Gilda. Look at this! For 1,200 dollars, you can take a trip around the world on Pan Am Airlines. Let's go!"

"Let me read that announcement first."

It sounded unbelievable. We could make a complete circle around the globe and stop off at as many countries as we'd like along the prescribed route. We showed the ad to our parents who were avid travelers.

"Traveling is a wonderful way to get an education," Mom used to say.

"If you want to go, do it, but you must earn the money yourselves," Dad exclaimed.

"We have contacts for you in many different countries. In Spain, you can meet the relatives of the Consul of Uruguay, who live in Murcia. You could also see your high school pen pal in Sevilla, Eloy Alvarez Pastor. Stay with our family in Puglia. In Burma, Dr. Saw Nyun and his wife would love you to visit. Vicki's friend, Daisy, always invites you to be her and her husband's guests in Hong Kong."

Dad's excitement increased our own. Yes, there were wonderful people to see and the Philadelphia Society of University Women, of which I was a member, offered to arrange a welcoming tea for us in Delhi.

Dad was adamant about the financing for this trip. I was 24-years-old and teaching. Vicki had a job in New York. We should pay for what we wanted and not rely on the largess of our parents. I was giving Mom and Dad 15 dollars a week for board from my 98 dollar weekly income

Article on our world trip.

as a high school Spanish teacher. My starting salary at Upper Moreland High School was 4,200 dollars a year. A male colleague was married with two children when he started teaching there. With that sum, he could provide a modest, pleasant apartment and car for his stay-at-home wife and their two offspring.

Vicki and I will need to take a year off to complete such an adventure. I'll have to make more money to fund my portion of the trip and a tutoring agency may be a way to increase my income.

I found a company that obtained several after-school teaching jobs for me in various locales from City Line Avenue, Cheltenham, to South Philadelphia. I worked nights as a "coat check girl," for six weeks, at a restaurant on Walnut Street in Center City. My parents' office, three blocks away, provided a perfect place for me to sleep after my full-day teaching position, my 2-hour tutoring sessions, and the 2-hour coat checking gig. In all, I worked steadily from 6 a.m. to 10 p.m. daily, hoarding all the cash I could. The schedule was grueling. I was constantly tired, and my knees began to ache, but I persevered and managed to save 4,000 dollars at the end of the school year for the trip.

When Louie heard of my plans he expressed annoyance I would spend my hard-earned dollars on so frivolous a pursuit. I told him we would depart the first week of June 1963.

Louie called me early in May.

"Come to Trenton. There is something I want to show you," he said.

I complied to satisfy my curiosity because Louie was not one for surprises.

We drove to Yardville, a modest community outside of Trenton, where there was a newly-constructed housing development. Louie asked me to join him on a tour of a sample home. We entered a 2,000 square-foot split level model. It was pristine, with all the necessary amenities.

After examining all the rooms, we left and entered his car.

"What was that all about?" I asked.

"Can't you figure it out?" he retorted, somewhat dismayed at my naiveté. "Instead of traveling the world, give me the money you earned, and we'll buy this house."

"So, this is what you wanted to show me? And I suppose you are proposing marriage by asking me to give you my earnings?"

Once more Louie's abrupt way of expressing himself aggravated me. I knew it was difficult, if not impossible for him to show amorous feelings, but that did not lessen my irritation. I deserved a more romantic gesture of his intentions.

"My answer is no! If this is how you propose, I am going to spend my money going around the world."

If he had said this to me when I was 18, I probably would have jumped at the prospect of marrying him, no matter how he phrased the question. It is different now. I am not as starry-eyed, and I've been hurt by his bluntness. I understand the man: he is methodical. He wants to do everything in the proper sequence—finish school, start a practice, make a sufficient income to support a family. I respect him and, I must confess, I love him for those qualities. Nevertheless, his way of expressing affection is irritating to me, even though what he is requesting is practical. I do not disagree that we should pool our resources, purchase a house and "settle down," but say it tenderly. If I marry Louie, I will probably never go anywhere beyond Trenton. He is not used to traveling and has little interest in it. I don't want to feel like Madame Bovary, married to a country doctor, trapped in a life of boredom, her free spirit sublimated until she resorts to aberrant behavior. If I go around the world now, my wander lust should be satisfied, and I will be ready to settle in Yardville, or wherever, pending a proper proposal.

Once more, I left Louie and took the train to Philadelphia. My mind was racing in a whirl of confusion. On one hand, I felt if he had asked me differently I may have abandoned my travel plans. On the other, I was still displeased and held a grudge about his former comments to Jim and Ruth Dunne about my wanting to get married.

This time I am the one not ready to get married. There is a whole world out there waiting for me and I am up to the adventure.

MARRIAGE IN MURCIA

Our world tour in July 1963 had exceeded our expectations. Our first destinations were to London, Amsterdam, Paris, Zurich and Bern, Switzerland. We had met interesting people and enjoyed new sights and sounds, but no place provided the drama we experienced in Spain. "When you and Vicki arrive in Madrid, expect a big surprise." "Really? I can hardly wait." I answered with anticipation to Xavier's voice on the telephone.

Placing the receiver in its cradle, my mind momentarily wandered back to the time I had met Xavier in Philadelphia at a cocktail reception for the Organization of American States, the past October. At the soiree, I noticed Xavier, a heavy-set man, in his 40s, with kind eyes and chestnut-brown hair. He was staring at me. Our gaze met, but I turned my head out of shyness. Mom drummed into my head, "Never flirt; let the man come to you."

A few minutes later the event host, William Strawbridge, scion of the owners of the Strawbridge and Clothier Department Store in Center

City, approached Vicki and me, accompanied by my admirer.

"Ladies, allow me to present the Honorary Vice Consul of Uruguay, stationed in Philadelphia, the Honorable Xavier Nóvoa."

It's obvious the consul must be important.

"You are from Uruguay?" I asked, to open the conversation.

"Now, yes. But I was born in Spain and have family there. My brother is Consul General of Uruguay, in Rome, Italy."

"What does a consul do?"

"There are many duties, such as passport renewals, composing Power of Attorney documents, as well as inspecting imports on ships from Uruguay. Do you want to hear more?"

"We have an idea now. If I'd like to be a consul could a middle-class Italian American female without political connections ever become one?" I asked, disappointed my listener did not contradict me. I did not wait for him to answer. "I teach Spanish at Upper Moreland High School near Willow Grove."

"I know where it is," he said gently. "If you come to my office on Walnut Street, I will give you educational materials about Uruguay for your students."

"That would be convenient because my parents' office is on 1703 Walnut Street."

The evening passed pleasantly, and I never expected our paths to meet again soon, but two days later, a letter-sized envelope in thin brown paper was in my mailbox at school. I un-wrapped the delicate folds to find a beautiful black pen and ink sketch of me holding a scarlet rose on a chalk-white background of rice paper.

He's so talented! With a few strokes of a pen he captured my likeness.

A note was attached with his business card and phone number.

"Give him a call," Vicki said. "He seems really interesting."

Her words proved true. I eventually invited him to dine at our home where my parents enjoyed entertaining people from all over the world. Haitians, Burmese, Asians and others were frequent guests at our table.

Xavier enchanted our parents. He proved to be a bon vivant and connoisseur of fine food and wine. He practiced fencing, was an artist,

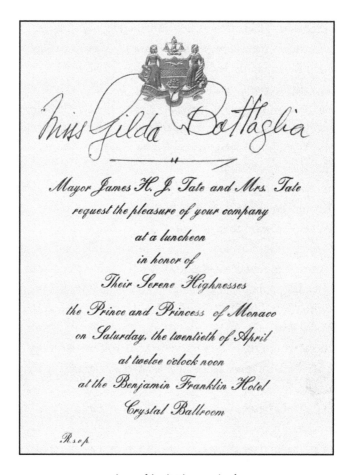

Miss Gilda Battaglia

Mayor James H. J. Tate and Mrs. Tate
request the pleasure of your company
at a luncheon
in honor of
Their Serene Highnesses
the Prince and Princess of Monaco
on Saturday, the twentieth of April
at twelve o'clock noon
at the Benjamin Franklin Hotel
Crystal Ballroom

R.s.v.p.

A royal invitation received.

a hunter, adept at playing cards and a designer of stunning jewelry he crafted from pure gold.

"Are you married? Do you have a family?" Mom asked at the first dinner he attended *chez nous*. She never hinted; she wanted an immediate answer. Mom's direct style of questioning was embarrassing to me.

"I have siblings in Uruguay, but I am a confirmed bachelor, Señora. I cared for my aged father for many years. My work takes me to many countries to live and I prefer to explore them alone."

That was fine with me because I still cared for Dr. Louis M. Rorro from Trenton, New Jersey, although our relationship took many turns. It was currently in a downward mode.

From his first encounter with my parents, Xavier became a regular guest at table. He subsequently invited Vicki and me to lovely dinners at Philadelphia landmark restaurants such as my favorites with Jamie, Bookbinders and the Barclay. We always admired the way the *Maître d's* would come to greet him and cater to his every whim. They knew Xavier was very fond of giant steamed lobsters and filet mignon. They also were aware he was a generous tipper.

One day he took Vicki and me to New York City.

"Where would you like to eat when we arrive?" he inquired with a twinkle in his eye.

"Oh, it doesn't matter. Any place you suggest will do," we answered. It wasn't exactly true, but we wanted to be considerate of our host.

"Would you like to dine at *Le Pavillion?*

"Le Pavillion?" I gasped. Its manager appeared on the Jack Parr show boasting how the French establishment denied entry to a famous movie star because he lacked a jacket and tie. Both items were offered to the actor, but when he refused, they in turn refused him access. *Le Pavillion* was arguably the most elegant, expensive eatery in Manhattan.

Xavier parked his car near the restaurant entrance. His diplomatic license plates allowed him to park wherever he wanted. Vicki and I exited his auto with a somewhat cockish air, but on entering the famous establishment, we felt a twinge of intimidation.

"Bonjour, Monsieur, Mademoiselles," said the francophone *Maître d'. "Suivez moi."*

We were led to a lovely table in the center of the room.

"This will not do," Xavier exclaimed. "Seat us at a place that is more private, more intimate."

The *Maître d'* obliged. That was only the beginning of Xavier's expectations. The Campari with soda was fine but the first bottle of *Veuve Clicquot* Champagne was sent back, to be replaced by one more pleasing to his discriminating palate. Before long, we were surrounded by a sommelier and a bevy of wait staff who aimed to please this demanding guest.

We dined on *escargots, soupe a l'oignon,* assorted *pâtés,* and my favorite dessert, *marrons glacé.* The assorted flavors made my palate dance.

When the luncheon ended, we exited the building and were treated to a horse-drawn carriage ride through Central Park. Shopping for gloves in Saks was followed by the Broadway comedy, *A Funny Thing Happened on the Way to the Forum* with Zero Mostel. Lastly, Xavier took us to an Iberian dinner at a Spanish restaurant in Greenwich Village with live Flamenco dancers.

My favorite outing with the Uruguayan was to a consular luncheon at the Benjamin Franklin Hotel in Philadelphia.

"Would you like to attend this affair with me?"

Xavier showed me an invitation written in ornate script where the guests of honor were the Prince and Princess of Monaco. Grace Kelly was incredibly popular in her native city and the media carried myriad stories of her fairytale wedding on the French Riviera.

Is he kidding? I would love to go. Vicki should come too. I would feel guilty leaving her behind. If I ask, Xavier will agree.

Exchanging pleasantries with royalty was an unforgettable experience for Vicki and me. We were seated near their table in a private dining room in the upscale Philadelphia landmark. Princess Grace wore a straight-line navy-blue coat dress and a matching turban covering most of her wheat-colored hair. While her couture exuded quiet elegance, it was an exquisite diamond and sapphire broach that caught my lingering attention, surely one of many sumptuous jewels of the Grimaldi family. They were the epitome of refinement and elegance and I was thrilled to take part in that magical afternoon.

Xavier had eclectic taste in gift giving. For Christmas 1962, he fashioned beautiful 24-carat gold pins for Vicki and me. Hers had an Asian design because she'd visited Hong Kong and Japan.

"I thought you would like this design, Gilda. It depicts Quetzalcoatl, the white bearded man god of the Aztecs."

It was perfect as I was in my Mesoamerican phase, after living in

Mexico. Xavier also loved classical music and treated us to a concert at the Academy of Music where we saw Flamenco dancers perform.

On 2 July 1963, when Vicki and I were departing for our long-anticipated trip around the world, Xavier gave me luggage from Bailey Banks and Biddle.

"You will need a sturdy bag for your lengthy trip. I've had your initials put on this."

What a friend! Everyone in the family loves him, even my relatives in Mays Landing. He possesses panache but most of all, he is down-to-earth, easy to talk to and sincere. His generosity brings back memories of my days with Jamie, memories I have tried to suppress.

It would be nice if he and Louie got along better. Neither seems to enjoy the other's company. When they come to the house at the same time, they tolerate each other, nothing more.

Before we left on our trip of a lifetime, Xavier said a big surprise would await us at the airport in Madrid where his cousin, José, would be waiting to escort us to his *finca* (ranch) in Murcia in southeastern Spain. What could the surprise be? Knowing him, it would be exceptional.

The day to embark on our journey arrived and we departed for London, then Paris, followed by Madrid. So many wonderful experiences occurred in the first two locales we forgot the mention of Xavier's "big surprise" until we were approaching the airport in Madrid.

"What do you think he'll do this time?" Vicki murmured.

"You never know with him."

The Pan Am jet landed and we were met by a tall, lean, tanned *caballero*, his cousin José.

"*Bienvenidas a Madrid (Welcome to Madrid)*," he said, gallantly kissing our hands. We identified ourselves, but he already knew us by photographs supplied by Xavier. José then announced in a formal tone, "*Señoritas*, a surprise awaits you here."

A small group of people then parted, revealing Xavier who sauntered toward us smiling. He gave me a long, furtive look I'd never seen before. That gaze was brimming with anticipation for reciprocation. He not only expected me to be surprised, but thrilled by his presence and hurl myself into his eager arms Hollywood style, where romantic music would reach its crescendo. Instead, I could hardly hide my consternation. His eyes confused me so.

Oh, no! This really is a surprise—no, a shock. I never would have guessed. Why is that sworn bachelor here looking at me as though I should fall into his arms? This is awful. I don't want to embarrass or hurt him. I don't know what to say or do. Maybe I should laugh as though it were a great joke.

Vicki caught on quickly: if he came to be our pal and adventurous companion that would be fine, but why those Latin eyes?

A driver took the four of us to the region of Murcia, a land of contradictions where stark, semi-arid plains were dotted with lush vineyards and crops of tomatoes flanked by lemon and orange trees. The landscape toward this southeastern region of the Iberian Peninsula unfolded. We passed the windmills, immortalized by Cervantes' *Don Quixote* and bull-rearing ranches where the brave beasts would one day endure the sting of *banderillas (barbed sticks in bullfighting),* the crimson and gold cape, and the sword of the *matador.*

After our sojourn in that sprawling, flat landscape, we arrived at the *Caballo Blanco* (White Horse) Ranch, where José was the proud *Padrón* (boss). His domain was a vast paprika farm where plump red peppers were strewn as far as the eye could see, basking in the relentless sun of Murcia. "*Bienvenidas,*" José's wife Angela called out as she exited the main house to greet us with several other female companions. She was a lovely brunette in her late 40s, eager to meet the *Americanas.* Speaking Spanish, she said we must be tired from our journey and should freshen up before lunch. Her 16-year-old niece "Yes Yes," was our designated chaperone.

The teenager escorted us to our new quarters. "*Este es su cuarto* (This is your room)," she said with pride.

We entered a capacious space with double beds, a dressing table, and happily, diminutive battery-driven hand fans, which offered a bit of cool air in the excessive, dry heat.

"You must be so excited to see Señor Xavier," said Yes Yes.

"Yes. It is delightful to be here. We've heard so much about Don José and Doña Angela, but first, tell us why you are called Yes Yes."

"My name is Cecilia, Si Si, for short. Translated into English, *sí sí* means 'Yes Yes,' and I want to speak English to you."

"So, that's it?" We laughed.

Our joviality was short lived when the young lady made her next remarks.

"You must be so excited about the wedding. Everyone at the ranch has been planning it for weeks. It will be catered here at the *finca*. A white tent will be erected. The *Dueña* and I will tell you more details later."

"How wonderful! Who's getting married?" I asked innocently.

At that, Yes Yes burst into fresh laughter.

"You are so funny," she declared, waving her index finger at me.

"Xavier is so in love. You are all he talks about. We couldn't wait to meet you."

Not wanting to appear rude during our first minutes at the ranch, we asked Yes Yes to allow us to rest a bit, to which she respectfully obliged.

Alone in the room, Vicki and I stared at each other, speechless. The heat was not the only intolerable thing there. When the initial shock waned, Vicki came to my defense.

"How could he?" she exclaimed angrily. "A confirmed bachelor, hah! He had us all fooled. Does he think he can trap you into marriage in Murcia?"

It was no laughing matter, only one of considerable confusion at our vulnerable position in a foreign place under these circumstances.

Could it be he was in love all the time he took the two of us out? He'd listen with patient interest at my talking about Louie Rorro. Surely, he knew where my affections lay. In my heart, I feel so sorry. I'd never want to cause him pain.

I was deeply fond of Xavier. He opened doors to the world of diplomacy and culture which are closed to most. He was always the quintessential gentleman, and everyone liked him, including me. But chemistry is chemistry and my heart was in Trenton, New Jersey, not in this compelling land of fighting bulls and windmills.

"*Es la hora de comer* (It's time to eat)," declared a voice knocking on the door.

Vicki and I were led to a spacious dining area where a splendid table was prepared in our honor. The family stood, waiting for us to be seated first. José, his wife, their two handsome adolescent sons and their lovely eight-year-old daughter, smiled at us, eager to display their legendary hospitality. Yes Yes, was among them with several other adult friends.

"*Esta es alta cocina* (High style cooking)," Xavier proudly proclaimed.

The table was a smorgasbord of delectable Spanish delicacies. Serrano ham, mortadella, manchego cheese, platters of lamb and barbecued pork, fresh grilled langostinos, mussels in a white wine sauce, succulent *chorizo*, seafood paella and *tortilla de papa* (potato omelet) were among the offerings.

As we were enjoying this Iberian feast, Angela interrupted. "We have much to talk about and to prepare for your big day."

I smiled politely, suddenly losing my appetite despite the culinary spectacle.

"*Después* (afterward)," I answered, as a smiling Xavier directed another adoring glance at me from across the table.

Vicki was visibly annoyed and kept darting disapproving looks my way. Her tolerance level was lower than mine, which concerned me. I didn't want her to make a scene. Thankfully she practiced self-control.

We were told it was siesta time after lunch. The blond sun was too strong for us to venture out. A maid came to our room to close the shutters, blocking out its cluster of golden arrows piercing the room. My sister and I readily surrendered to the "Arms of Morpheus" as Mom used to say. We'd always laugh at that expression she was so fond of quoting.

After I experienced two restless hours, a knock sounded on the portal. This time it was a worker who led us outside the house where José and Xavier were waiting.

"I want to take you on a tour of my *finca*. I am the paprika king of Spain. The McCormick Company in the United States buys my product for use in making lipstick," José boasted. Vicki and I never knew paprika went into lipstick for coloring.

The property covered so many acres we would not be able to visit it all by foot. As far as my sister and I could observe, there was an endless sea of red peppers drying like a sinuous, flaming blanket over the parched earth. The cloudless lapis sky loomed over the burnt sienna-colored soil, creating a backdrop of intense orange and blue, dotted by contrasting white stucco dwellings.

Following the tour, we joined the ladies on the patio, while the men went horseback riding. José and Xavier mounted sleek, ebony stallions and impressed us with their equestrian skill, "Macho" style, without saddles.

Angela had me dressed in a complete flamenco outfit, replete with ruffles of red and white polka dots, a short, colorful embroidered shawl called a *mantón,* and a delicate black lace mantilla supported on a high, bone hair comb.

"*Tu estás hermosa* (You look beautiful)," she said admiringly. Yes, Yes, and the other ladies readily agreed, but no one viewed my colorful attire as glowingly as Xavier, as he galloped toward us, bareback on the night-black steed.

They're preparing me in every way they can, and I am truly impressed, but I am not Spanish. I'm an Italian American and when I marry, my parents and family, as well as that of the groom will be present. How could I face Mom and Dad back home if I secretly entered matrimony in Murcia? Xavier probably suspects my parents would disapprove of our marrying because he knows Mom is very fond of Louie and neither parent would want me to live with a diplomat abroad. I must be able to speak to Xavier alone, without these chaperones. And how can I contain Vicki's frustration, so she doesn't make a justifiable scene?

The moment arrived that night after a light supper. At 11 p.m., everyone joined us on the patio and smiled approvingly as Xavier offered his arm for the two of us to walk along a path outdoors. I sensed they continued to stare behind us throughout our brief stroll.

A profusion of stars shone like diamonds in the dense, ebony sky. The air seemed to be warm velvet caressing our skin. Xavier and I strolled, arm in arm, neither daring to break the silence.

Posing in a flamenco outfit.

Could I learn to love this man romantically? My French friend in Mexico, Guy Le Brun, often said, "It's better to put a cold pot on a lukewarm flame, which will eventually boil than a boiling pot on no flame, which will quickly cool down." Xavier would place me on a pedestal and I'd have an exciting life. But I just don't feel my heart race like it does when I'm with Louie. Xavier deserves a woman who will love him unconditionally. I only wish I could, for both our sakes.

The silence was broken when I pulled my arm away and looked directly into my companion's impassioned eyes.

"Xavier, you always flaunted your bachelorhood. I never thought you had feelings for me or Vicki that went beyond a sincere friendship. You know I have been seeing Louie and care for him regardless of our ups and downs. What did I ever say or do to make you decide to propose such an important step?"

The dear man poured out his heart. His former declarations of being a contented bachelor were a protective device because of his age and my apparent interest in another man. But he could repress his feelings no longer and did not want me influenced by others. Obviously, he thought this magical setting, removed from my reality in Germantown, would be so intoxicating I would readily succumb to his wish of marriage in Murcia.

"Won't this make an irresistible tale for our children and grandchildren?" he chuckled.

He can't be so naïve as to think my strict Italian upbringing would condone such an action. But let's be honest, Gilda. Were you completely unaware of his feelings, or had you denied them because you were having such a good time, most likely better than you'd have with another man?

"You have given me a great honor Xavier, but I cannot marry you here or anywhere. Vicki and I are not prepared for this. Please explain to José and Angela. I only wish we could go on being great friends as before."

I knew that was not possible. Everything now had changed irrevocably. I turned him down as a husband; platonic friendship was no longer an option.

Xavier remained silent. His Latino pride prevented him from facing rejection. His reticence screamed out louder than words in the darkness. I looked up at the sparkling orbs in the heavens for support, but it was not forthcoming. Xavier just guided me back into the light of the house, passing the *murcianos* assembled on the patio, who now wore puzzled, curious expressions. Gone were their approving smiles.

"Did you tell him?" Vicki asked as I entered our room. "What did he say?"

"Yes" to the first question and "No" to the second. He never said a word. I feel so bad."

"Well, I feel relieved," she said with satisfaction.

"We shouldn't stay here any longer," I added.

Vicki nodded in agreement. Pangs of remorse and shame prevented me from sleeping. I lay awake with conflicting thoughts racing through my mind.

Here's a man like Jamie, who would love me unconditionally. Why couldn't my feelings change? Mom and Dad could fly here for the wedding. It could be the fairy tale Xavier envisioned. No, it could not. As Blaise Pascal wrote, "The heart has its reasons of which reason knows not." My feelings for Louie were my destiny. I had been selfish, happy to enjoy the best of both worlds and not wanting to part from the diversion and opportunities Xavier provided. A good man is hurt because of me and I must bear that guilt and its consequences forever.

Falling asleep was difficult. The next morning, I arose in a stupor, not wanting to face Xavier or his friends and family, but knowing I must. At breakfast, only José and Xavier were present. His cousin started the conversation, somewhat cheerfully.

"Xavier explained everything to me, but we agreed you should not leave this beautiful land yet. Stay. Visit it and you will come to love it. Paco, my young driver, will take the two of you all over the country. You are my guests for all expenses."

"No!" I exclaimed emphatically. "We couldn't do that. It is best we leave now."

Xavier looked at me pleadingly.

José must think by becoming enamored with Spain and this extraordinary family, I wouldn't want to leave it or Xavier.

The two men were insistent. They had arranged for box lunches to be prepared. The chauffeur was ready, and in a flash, we were whisked off to such enchanting destinations as the *Ramblas* in Barcelona, the *Prado Museum* in Madrid, the impressive *Roman Aqueduct* in Segovia, the graceful, Moorish *Alhambra* in Granada, the swirling mosaics on the pavement of the seaside town of Alicante and then to Santiago de Compostela in Galicia.

Spain is an aesthetic treasure trove of culture and singular beauty.

From Spain, Paco drove us to Oporto, Portugal, another colorful Latin country. In small towns, children ran after our car because an auto was a novelty in places where the mule still provided needed transportation. We loved the fishing village of Nazaré, where for 25 US cents, one could enjoy a large, freshly caught grilled sardine, a hard roll and a glass of red wine.

At a bull farm in Murcia.

Paco was a handsome young man in his 20s. He loved to drive and was tireless behind the wheel.

"I will take you anywhere you want to go. If you do not know where, I will decide for you."

"I would like to visit Morocco; it is so close."

"Of course. As I said, we will go wherever you want."

We crossed from Portugal to Algeciras, Spain, to take a ferry to Gibraltar, then to Marrakesh and Casablanca in Morocco. We were gone for two weeks. Each day José would call Paco, ordering him to extend our tour. I would have prolonged the venture even more rather than face our host with the inevitable decision, but it had to happen: I had to confront my destiny.

After two weeks, the tour came to an end. José had Paco returned us to Murcia and the ranch. When we alighted from the vehicle, and our body language said it all, José let Xavier speak to me alone. Before I could utter a word, Xavier motioned for me to be still.

I have made a decision," he said, resolutely. "When you return to Philadelphia, you can go back to Louie. He could never love or value you as much as I, but you can marry him because I let you."

"Yes. It is only because you let me," I said soberly, hiding my feeling of deep relief. Xavier was revealing another face of *Machismo*. He provided the solution for both of us to save face.

"Vicki and I will leave for Madrid tomorrow," I said to a silent, besotted Xavier.

There must be some way we could remain friends when we return to Philadelphia? I would hate to have our relationship end like this. I feel we meet people in life for a purpose. What good will come out of all this? Stop! Too many thoughts! Think of what Scarlet O'Hara would say:

"Tomorrow is another day."

FINAL FILM TEMPTATIONS

"Fasten your seat belts. We'll soon be landing at the Cairo Airport," the captain of our Pan Am jet announced on the loud speaker in September. Vicki and I exchanged excited glances.

Just think, we are in the land of the pyramids.

It was 10 a.m. as we exited the terminal and took a cab whisking us to the luxurious Nile Hilton Hotel.

"Do you want to convert US dollars to the local currency? If yes, I will give you a 30 percent higher rate than the bank," the driver confided. While his offer was tempting, we deferred.

These must be hard economic times for Egyptians, but I am wary of doing anything illegal.

As anticipated, the hotel lobby was gorgeous, replete with themes of former Egyptian splendor. Our quarters, however, were standard Hilton: Twin beds, a desk and two chairs.

"Let's take a walk and look around," Vicki said.

She was always one who could stroll for hours. We turned left from the entrance of our hotel and began to take in the sights of the bustling cosmopolitan city. A short distance from the hotel, we entered the *Musée d'antiquités*, or Cairo Museum.

"Let's go in; this must really be interesting, Vicki."

At the entrance, large lights were erected with camera equipment from the Magdo Film Company. They were focusing on one of the display cases containing ancient figurines, gold and turquoise jewelry and hair ornaments worn by the upper-class women of the era.

We proceeded to explore the breathtaking exhibits and passed display after display of 5,000-year-old amphora, shards and common household items used by the ancients. But nothing could prepare us for what we were privileged to see next: the extensive treasure, sarcophagus and gold burial mask of the boy king, Tutankhamun. The quantity, quality, and exquisite beauty of the objects were staggering. They were shown as they may have been when George Edward Stanhope Molyneux Herbert, 5th Earl of Carnarvon, first saw them, scattered unceremoniously throughout a diminutive space. There was no dramatic backdrop or special lighting—only magnificent artifacts to dazzle the eye. A golden throne shone in the darkness with depictions of the king's family life, his lovely wife and three young daughters. Mummies of his three infant daughters were also present. Golden sandals glowed next to his spear, chariot and accoutrements needed in the afterlife.

An imposing figure of Anubis, the "black dog or jackal god," stood watch. A lion statue was present because it was believed the sun rose in the east in the jaws of a lion and set in its jaws in the west. Hathor, the goddess of love, stood near the statue of Horus, the falcon-headed all-seeing god of the sky, all requisite sentinels to ensure an appropriate royal realm in the afterlife.

When we completed this most memorable exhibit, the executive director of the film company approached me.

"We would like you to appear in this scene. The actors are very popular in Egypt," he said in impeccable English.

"What do I have to do?" I asked.

"Stand behind this glass case and look at the objects while the leading man and woman perform. Don't stare at them; pretend you are a tourist."

Viewing the pyramids in Egypt.

"That will be easy because we arrived here a few hours ago as tourists."

He led me to a spot behind the glass.

"Lights, camera, action!" another crew member announced.

The actors began to recite their lines in front of me, and I did exactly what I was told.

"You did very well. Would you be available tomorrow to be in another scene? We will pay you," the same gentleman asked.

"No. I have no work visa and it would be against the law to receive money in Egypt."

"Would you be interested in doing it for nothing? We could make it up to you via a gift of some sort?"

"No, thank you. That will not be possible," I declared reluctantly but resolutely.

This would be like another Mexican adventure and Mom and Dad would be furious if I deviated from our planned agenda. If Vicki weren't here I might be tempted. Mom and Dad would never find out. I'd love to explore new dimensions in this mysterious, seductive land.

Another similar and even more tempting opportunity presented itself on our extensive trip. After Egypt, we flew to Jerusalem. The highlight of our four-day visit was strolling along the Via Dolorosa, where Jesus purportedly walked to His crucifixion. Another incredible site was the historical Rose-City of Petra, a former Nabatean community with rock-cut architecture, below the Dead Sea in Jordan. Beirut, "the Paris of the Middle East," and Baalbek in Lebanon completed our Middle Eastern tour.

India was the next stop where we stayed in Delhi and Agra for a week. Our third destination was Benares (Varanasi), on the left bank of the river Ganges. Vicki and I arrived at a relatively small, lovely hotel in the city, in which a large portrait of First Lady Jacqueline Kennedy hung.

"I considered this to be the best hotel I have ever visited," she had written on the front of her likeness.

No doubt her accommodations were vastly superior to ours, which consisted of a stark, single room with double beds, a desk and small bathroom. Our windows had wide, thick wooden shutters. As we unpacked, a knock sounded on the wooden slat facing my bed.

Upon opening it, a turbaned man stood holding a wooden flute. He grinned at me. I would not have been startled if there were no undulating boa constrictor draped around his neck nor a wicker basket brimming with slithering cobras on the ground next to him.

"Would Memsaab like to see me charm a snake?"

Before I could refuse he began playing on the roughly-chiseled instrument. A reptile slowly emerged from the basket, its swaying body stiffened with its head erect, as though mesmerized by the lilting melody.

"Thank you, but not today," I said hastily, handing him a coin. I bolted the shutters, blotting out the piercing spears of sunlight.

I wonder if he charmed snakes for Jacqueline Kennedy?

"Let's go see the river Ganges," Vicki said. "I don't want to waste time in the room."

I agreed. As soon as we went out of the hotel we were approached by a pedi-cab driver.

"I take you around the city first and then to the Ganges. I am good guide. If you want, I show you things American tourists don't see."

"Okay; you're hired," I said, although I should have inquired more about the 'things' to which he alluded.

The open cab moved slowly, but deliberately, which afforded us an opportunity to absorb the surrounding sights and sounds. As in most urban areas of the subcontinent, the streets were teeming with people, cows, shops and stalls creating a panorama of resplendent color. A blend of aromatic spices such as capsicum, curry, cumin, and turmeric hung in the humid air. Our diminutive but robust peddler led us swiftly through winding thoroughfares, then settled on a less traversed road leading to the sacred river. Moving along, we noticed a girl about 10 years old lying on the ground. She struggled unsuccessfully to raise her head by bracing herself on her elbows. The emaciated creature appeared quasi moribund. A vendor had a cart of produce on the opposite side of the road.

"Stop!" I shouted to the driver. "Let me buy some bananas and give them to that starving child."

"No! No!" he called, turning his head to face me. He was adamant, accentuating his refusal by waving his arms in the blistering air.

I slumped back into the seat, haunted by the vision of a helpless human being abandoned on the side of the road with passers-by taking no notice.

This is a strange place—so full of life, color and suffering.

A few minutes later, our conductor signaled we were approaching the water. Vicki and I marveled at his stamina as he increased his rhythmic pedaling.

"I take you where you can get on a little boat. You see more of the river and what is happening on the banks that way. It is harder for me to move my cab through the crowds. When your river tour is over, I'll show you a place most tourists don't see."

We agreed with our driver's suggestion and boarded a wooden row boat. The craft glided as the rower moved slowly, wanting to reveal the flurry of activity on the *Ghats*. These consisted of wide stairs leading to the river and circular structures, on which pilgrims bathed, exercised, prayed or conducted religious rites. On the beach, we saw a shrouded corpse elevated on a wooden platform, set aflame, its ashes to be sprinkled over the surface of the Ganges.

Suddenly, without warning, a mummy-wrapped cadaver bobbed up from the water.

"Oh my gosh! A body is by the boat!" I exclaimed, horrified.

I tried valiantly to control my shock, but for our guide, this was just another familiar way of life along the sacred river.

The short tour ended, and our dependable cabby was waiting as planned.

"Come with me. I show you something."

He led Vicki and me among the throng of humanity to a place where people suddenly parted to allow us access. I was behind our guide when he stepped aside, opening a wedge for me. There, fingerless hands waved in my face, begging for money. Deformed faces, exposed bones, seeping sores and diseased limbs surrounded me in this locale of the lepers.

Engulfed by ghostly bodies and pleading eyes desperately seeking alms, I felt myself grow limp; I was losing consciousness. It was my 14-month younger sister who propped me up and hurried me away. Our escort seemed unmoved and never explained his motive for taking us to such a place.

Securely seated in the pedi-cab, we were once again on the road leading to our luxurious haven. I felt so unworthy of privilege amidst such human agony. But the day was not over; it was late afternoon and there was more to come.

On the side of the road, a rickety wagon was ready for the seemingly lifeless body of the child we saw that morning. The creature's emaciated frame was tossed unceremoniously into the rough wooden cart to be taken where? Did no one care?

The events of the day left us feeling somber. The concierge at the hotel saw our dour expressions as we entered the lobby.

"You should go to see a happy Indian movie tonight. There is one within walking distance. It is full of singing and dancing. It's called *Mere Mehboob* (My Lover). Harnam Singh Rawail is the director. It will cheer you."

We agreed to go. When we arrived at the ticket booth, the theater was almost sold out. The only two seats available side-by-side were in the balcony under large, rotating fans. The place buzzed with excitement. Soon the area darkened and there was immediate silence as the three and one-half-hour film commenced.

The concierge was right. The high-pitched singing and gyrating dances choreographed in a twirling sea of shimmering magenta, gold and malachite-colored costumes were the escape we needed. There were no sub-titles and the plot was not coherent, but we enjoyed the brilliant spectacle, a wonderful diversion from the reality of the day.

The next morning, we flew to Calcutta in east India and stayed in another Oberoi hotel. In our room, we could hear excited chatter coming from the attached suite. I stepped out into the hallway to see what was happening and got the most pleasant surprise. Cast members of *Mere Mehboob* were there. They were preparing for a significant reception from the look of their clothing and preparations. I walked past, trying to appear nonchalant as they were fussing with their makeup, elaborate outfits and jewelry.

I went to the lobby and asked the concierge if I could meet the hotel manager regarding our flight to Karachi the next morning. The agent led me to the appropriate office and opened the door. Two men were seated, and stood upon seeing me. The manager identified himself and introduced the other gentleman so quickly I did not hear his name clearly. The manager was accommodating and supplied the advice I sought.

"*Shukriyaa,*" (Thank You), I said, and turned to leave.

"Wait! Don't go," the other man interrupted. "Instead of flying to Karachi, would you be interested in joining the cast and me in Bombay? We will be filming there, and I think I may have a spot for you in my new movie."

Not again! Of course, I want to go. What woman wouldn't jump at the chance of being draped in a scarlet and gold sari and gorgeous jewels? They could teach me a dance routine and some expressions in Hindi. Yes! Yes! Take me to Bombay! But then I'd surely hear Mom and Dad's familiar reaction: "Only puttane (women of ill repute) are in the movies. It's no place for a daughter of ours."

Apparently, I have the look Mexicans, Egyptians and now, Indians, prefer. It's not the blonde, blue-eyed type for them. At Beaver, I did not stand out. But, be sensible, Gilda; you don't know this man. So, what? At the least it would make a great cocktail party conversation at home. I bet if I had a brother who wanted to be in a film in Bombay, Mom and Dad would be encouraging, but not with me. Based on my experience in Mexico, they would strongly disapprove of my getting involved once again in the indecent cinematic world. Resist this last temptation.

"No, Sir. Thank you for the kind proposal but I cannot accept."

"You will miss a wonderful opportunity, young lady," he replied.

"Probably so, but I cannot go with you. *Shukriyaa.*"

With that salutation, I stepped out of the room. Hearing the familiar click of the latch behind me, I realized I had closed the door on ever appearing in movies again.

If only I could try once more. Why am I given rare opportunities I cannot accept? Should I grab this one, come what may? Yet, if things do not go well, Mom and Dad would never forgive me for disrespecting their wishes.

The concierge approached and asked, "You were in there a long time. Did you have an opportunity to speak with Harnam Singh Rawail, the famous Indian film director? He is here with the cast of his latest hit, *Mere Mehboob.*"

"Yes, briefly," I said, ending the conversation hastily. When I returned to our room Vicki was waiting. She did not ask where I had been, and I did not bother to tell her. What could she say but, "Again?"

BURMA: A VALLEY OF TEARS

On our Pan Am flight to Burma, I was unable to resist telling my sister about meeting the famous Indian film producer. I mentioned to Vicki that I had received an offer from him to appear in a film he was making in Bombay. As anticipated, she was unaffected, knowing I would not accept.

But I am affected. Rejecting this opportunity symbolizes the end of any more movie prospects. I long to do it, if it were possible, or should I say, permissible? I can hear Mom and Dad yell at me.

"It's indecent. No young woman from a good family appears in the movies."

Vicki and I anticipated the next adventure because we would be guests of a dear family friend, Dr. Saw Nyun, a prominent neurosurgeon at Rangoon General Hospital. Being with friends and family made sharing visits on our world trip more rewarding. If it were not for him, we would never have included this Southeast Asian nation on our itinerary. Dr. Nyun was another colleague of our brother-in-law, J. B. They met when the former was among the first group of four medical doctors from Rangoon completing residency programs at the University of Pennsylvania. His was in neurosurgery.

Mom used to await eagerly for Dr. Nyun's visits to our house for dinner.

"Set the table, Gilly. The Burmese doctor is coming. He prefers vegetarian dishes, so I prepared eggplant *alla parmigiana*, lentils and fried zucchini flowers."

Mom was an excellent cook. She prepared dishes our neighbors did not eat like tripe, kidney stew, sautéed chicken hearts and brains. They were the ingredients she could afford during the Depression days. Although they did not sound appetizing to others, when she worked her magic, they could please the most sophisticated palate.

The doctor enjoyed our repasts. He was a dear, shy man in his late 30s. His five foot-six frame, copper complexion and deep brown, soulful eyes were attractive. His smile reflected gentleness and kindness. Yet, even during his happiest moments I always detected a hint of sadness in them.

Our family readily embraced Dr. Nyun and he soon became an adopted member of our clan, joining us on holidays and on a winter trip to Gloria and J.B.'s house in Florida. He and I shared a bond of appreciation. We were instantly attracted to one another, but always maintained a respectable distance. We were realists and aware of the vast distance between our two worlds. Although he seldom spoke with me directly, he frequently took my picture with his prized Leica camera.

The captain of our Pan Am plane announced we were nearing the Rangoon Airport.

"I'm looking forward to meeting Saw Nyun's wife, Barbara."

"Me too," Vicki concurred.

I'm glad he married and hope he is happy.

A gracious stewardess served us a hearty English breakfast of lamb chops and scrambled eggs. Vicki could not look at food, complaining she was feeling queasy.

"Eat my share, Gilda. Don't waste it."

Feeling guilty to squander such a valuable commodity as lamb chops, especially after our trip to Benares, I managed to scoff down a portion of her bountiful breakfast as well as my own.

Our aircraft landed, and we were led to Customs at the International Airport. We were totally unprepared for the harsh greeting we received.

"What is the purpose of your coming to Burma?" a male staff member snapped as he scoured the contents of our luggage.

"Tourism."

"Why are you two young women traveling alone? Where are you going? Where are you staying and with whom? Exactly how long do you plan to remain here?"

The man's questions seemed to be more a hostile interrogation than routine questioning.

He makes me feel like a spy suspect, seated on a wooden stool under a bright light while he screams in my face, locks me up and throws the key away.

"How much money are you carrying?"

I told him, but he was not satisfied.

"Give me your wallet!"

He pulled out all the bills and travelers' checks, which he counted and recorded carefully. Returning our passports, he pointed sternly toward the exit, where it was a relief to see Dr. Nyun waiting, wearing a western suit and customary wistful smile.

"Welcome to my homeland," he said, although he had been born in India. A driver took our bags and led us to a vehicle.

What a relief to be among a familiar, friendly face. That customs officer made me want to bolt from here.

In the auto, I wanted to absorb everything surrounding this truly foreign land. The first inescapable impression was the stifling heat and humidity. It was still monsoon season in October and inhaling was like breathing warm water. The greenery along the highway was lush and bountiful. Raised houses of bamboo with dirt floors and roofs of palm fronds dotted the road. In the distance, golden domes of pagodas softly jutted through gently rolling hills.

The serenity was suddenly broken when our car struck a hard object and went sailing a foot into the air, then crashed down with a thud.

What was that?

No explanation was given.

"Look out the rear window," Vicki whispered, looking ashen.

Turning slightly, I was rendered speechless on seeing the longest, thickest python imaginable slowly sliver across the road. Between this and the Customs agent, the introduction to Burma would be forever etched in my memory.

"Pythons grow big here," Dr. Nyun exclaimed, looking at our stricken faces with concern.

After one-half hour, we arrived at the doctor's home. It stood out from all others we had seen. It was a single, two-story mahogany structure.

"Welcome to my humble home."

This place is not humble. It is massive, dark brown and square. There is no outdoor molding, columns or other adornments. I wouldn't know how to describe the style—plain?

We entered a spacious parlor where Barbara was waiting to greet us. She was a lovely woman with dark brown hair and almond eyes. Her gentle smile complimented her mint green *longy* (Burmese sarong).

"We are honored you are our guests. My husband speaks of you often."

Barbara summoned a servant to take our luggage and show us to our rooms.

"You must be hungry after your flight. We prepared an English breakfast. Come downstairs after you have settled."

"How can we eat again so soon?" Vicki asked.

"We'll have to force ourselves."

"You do it for me. I can't. I don't feel well and bumping into that python made me feel worse. I can't look at food. You go alone."

A full breakfast was prepared in the sparsely-decorated dining room. The table and chairs were of unadorned mahogany. No paintings were on the walls. What stood out was the formal table setting with a glistening, hand-hammered English sterling silver coffee set over a stiffly starched, lace trimmed linen cloth.

"Where is your sister?

"She's a bit tired and prefers to rest."

"Yes, of course; I will leave you to enjoy your repast quietly," our hostess said in flawless English with a charming accent.

I admired the abundant spread of freshly-squeezed fruit juice, orange marmalade, toast, sunny-side fried eggs and thick, plump lamb chops.

How can I manage more food? Surely most Burmese don't eat like this. Ingest something or our hosts will be offended.

Barbara reappeared after 45 minutes.

"Allow me to accompany you to your room to ensure you have all you need."

I followed the gracious lady from the dining room past the kitchen where a contingent of Buddhist monks sat in silence, flanking a wall, clutching begging bowls. I could not avoid staring at those men with their shaved heads, saffron robes and stoical expressions. They were waiting for servants to give them rations for their daily meal consisting largely of rice and vegetables.

Dr. Nyun (rear), Vicki, me and Barbara (front, from left).

"The monks come here every morning. They eat only once a day," Barbara volunteered.

Upstairs, we entered the bedroom where Vicki was lying down on one of the twin beds. The room was comfortable, with a desk, two chairs and a dresser. The walls were bare. There were no frills or pretension of any kind. Suddenly, a strange sound was heard coming from the roof overhead, a combined moan and low, guttural growl.

"What is that?" Vicki asked, her face resuming that ashen look.

"Oh. It is only a creature that stays on our roof. We never disturb it because that would bring bad luck."

Barbara is educated, and her husband is a neurosurgeon. Yet she is super-stitious, and he must be also to ignore whatever it is up there. From its mournful sound, I don't mind not seeing what it looks like.

"Rest, now. Come to the parlor in three hours; we will meet for lunch."

Repose was necessary in the blistering heat as the house was not air conditioned. Once Barbara left us, the clouds opened and a brief, torrential downpour fell. When the rain ended, it seemed to get hotter and steamier. My hair became a tangle of unruly waves and looked frizzy in the intense humidity.

At 1 p.m., we went downstairs to the parlor. My heart jumped when I spied an 8 x 10-inch photo of myself in a sterling silver frame, placed on a console. Dr. Nyun had taken the picture when he was visiting with us at Gloria and J. B.'s home in Florida. In it, I was standing beside an orange tree, holding a blossom.

How touching to see this photograph far from home; I feel honored they have it displayed.

The sound of animated voices was heard and soon, Saw Nyun, Barbara and a bevy of family members came to greet us. Barbara's father took our hands ceremoniously. The gentleman was decidedly taller and more robust than most men we'd seen here. His bearing was regal, that of a man used to commanding others and being obeyed. We soon were told that in the not distant past, he had held power over the life and death of his subjects.

Settling into the comfortable surroundings, we began the pleasant task of getting acquainted. We learned Barbara was the eldest of twelve children, eight females and four males. A daughter and two sons were abroad, studying in England. Their eldest offspring was not present.

"Is your other son coming?" I asked.

My question was greeted with uncomfortable, surreptitious stares among those gathered. No one spoke until Saw Nyun's sister changed the subject.

"How were you treated at the airport?"

Vicki was trying valiantly to make a good impression, but she was still not feeling well so she signaled to me to do the talking. I tried to explain the scene at Customs as diplomatically as possible when the relative interrupted me.

"You need not be polite. It's too bad you will never know the Burma we knew. Our beautiful country is in the hands of communists since the Chinese military takeover in 1962. Everything has changed. We feel sorry for our young people."

The family was justified in lamenting. Barbara's father had been a *Soboa*, a prince in the former princedom of the Shan States. The Shan chiefs manifested the same habits of royalty as the Burmese kings. Now he was deposed.

"I was lucky," Dr. Nyun said with a smile. "I am a commoner and it would not have been possible for me to marry a woman of Barbara's high rank."

The pleasant encounter ended because Barbara's father was going to rest.

After lunch, Barbara accompanied us to our room.

"Would you like to see some of my wedding jewels?"

We nodded affirmatively as a servant was summoned bearing square, wooden cases. When Barbara opened the lids, the interiors shone like a treasure. Complete sets of rubies and sapphires were unveiled. A set consisted of a hair ornament for the fashionable bun Barbara wore. Necklaces, earrings, bangle and ankle bracelets and buttons for the national *Engi* (blouse) seemed to brighten the dim room. Vicki and I had never seen anything like those gems outside a museum.

At this moment, I would gladly trade a bauble for an air conditioner. The heat is oppressive.

"After dinner this evening, Saw Nyun will show you our wedding movie."

"We would love that."

Evening came. At dinner, we were served Chinese-style meatless dishes. The Shan State is on the Chinese border and the culinary influence of that large nation was strong.

"Do you like Chinese food?" another aunt asked.

"Very much," we responded in unison. Vicki was feeling better and she ate heartily.

As we were at table, I noticed the six and eight-carat diamond buttons the women wore on their *Engi*. Precious gems were plentiful, even commonplace among them. It was time to view the wedding film. Our breath was taken away from the first frame. In it, Dr. Nyun was wearing the traditional silk *Longi*. Barbara's gown was that of a true princess,

Dr. Saw Nyun and Barbara's wedding.

encrusted with diamonds, sapphires, rubies and sea pearls. A hairpiece of strands of cascading diamonds flowed from her bun. Pearl necklaces and jeweled bracelets, rings and anklets made her delicate, five-foot frame glow.

The most beautiful aspect of the movie was the sweetness and respect which exuded from the married couple. Barring the brusque Customs Officials, the Burmese people were the personification of grace.

The fairy tale film turned grim when family members pointed out wedding guests who were no longer in their privileged circle.

"He was executed. She was thrown in prison. No one has heard from her since."

"Be quiet. Your voice is too loud. Don't let a servant hear you," someone said.

I whispered in Dr. Nyun's ear. "The servants don't speak English, do they?"

"Only when they need or want to."

How awful! People are wary of their own household help.

The conversation continued identifying victims of the government's oppression. Vicki and I were stunned. Nothing had prepared us for current life in Burma. Dr. Nyun was cognizant of our reaction. To be up-beat, he said, "Tomorrow is Saturday. I do not work. We will go sightseeing."

The following morning the sun shone brightly. We rose to the sound of a maid knocking on our door.

"Madame. May I serve you morning tea?"

The delicate young woman poured the warm brew and exited, walking backwards, facing us.

During the five days we were in this exotic land, we observed the strong imprint derived from Indian, British, and Chinese cultures. We enjoyed especially the British morning tea.

Outside, Saw Nyun was waiting for us with a car and driver.

"Barbara will remain at home today to oversee the preparation of the regional dishes she wants you to sample tonight."

The hospitality of this family makes us feel like princesses. Traveling along the bucolic Burmese countryside, we were encapsulated in lush greenery. Germantown seemed like a remote place on another planet. This natural beauty makes me feel calm. Time does not seem relevant here. The Buddhist monks appear oblivious to it. On the surface, you would never imagine the tumult that exists.

"We've arrived at the Schwedagon Pagoda Chaukhtatgyi Buddha Temple."

Entering the exotic interior, before us was a 100-foot-tall, 195-foot-long reclining Buddha. Worshipers respectfully parted to give us uninterrupted access to the breathtaking figure. On the base of the foot the lives of the Buddha were imprinted.

"We believe in reincarnation. Life is a valley of tears. Each successive cycle brings us closer to Nirvana," my host said as he lit candles and bowed before the massive, reclining figure.

"Nirvana is Paradise," I affirmed, but Dr. Nyun corrected me respectfully.

"It is nothingness, the end of all suffering."

Is suffering why I detect sadness in his eyes and smile? How has he suffered? He is among the rarely privileged class. It is a question I shall not ask and one he will most likely not answer.

The doctor did reveal a snippet of his childhood days as a Buddhist Monk.

"We learned discipline, selflessness and meditation. We were taught not to desire material things."

He never mentioned his experience as a monk when he was in Philadelphia. I often wondered why he didn't want to remain in "The City of Brotherly Love." As a neurosurgeon, he could have earned a lot of money, certainly more than here, which he said was about 35 dollars a month. Hearing about his childhood training in the monastery offered me that insight.

In the temple, followers of the Buddha were reverent. They brought flowers and kneeled before the awe-inspiring figure. Their devotion greatly impressed me.

"It is time to return home. Barbara is expecting us."

When we arrived at the house, the familiar scent of Chinese culinary delights greeted us. Barbara had supervised the preparation of a wonderful meal consisting of assorted dumplings, spring rolls, roast duck and various rice dishes brimming with colorful vegetables.

Dr. Nyun pulled me aside after dinner.

"Tomorrow morning, I am scheduled to perform brain surgery. Gilda, would you like to come to observe?"

"Of course, if I would not be in the way. Vicki does not like to visit hospitals."

"You won't be in the way. Besides, no one will comment so long as you are with me."

The following day we left the house, passing the familiar row of silent, saffron-clothed monks clutching begging bowls. A soft mist hung over the pagoda-dotted hills. The serenity was soon broken when we approached the bustling capital.

We entered the three-story, Victorian-style red brick Rangoon General Hospital and followed a dim corridor to a brightly-lit operating room. An assistant brought me a pale green hospital gown and cloth cap for my unruly hair. I watched as Dr. Nyun scrubbed his hands in preparation of the procedure.

"Sit on the stool behind me. You'll have a clear view of everything."

Positioning myself on the stiff, wooden seat, I looked directly and uneasily at a shaved human head.

This is unlike any operating room I've been in at home. The sanitary conditions are lax.

My surgeon friend's hands moved with alacrity as he sliced through the opaque scalp, separating it into two neat folds. An assistant handed him clamps to keep the thick skin secure, exposing the bony sheath beneath. He put a chisel-like instrument into the doctor's right hand. I controlled a gasp as Dr. Nyun deftly cut out chunks of skull, tossing them, clanging, into a metal bowl by his side.

Don't be squeamish. Watch and learn. You are fortunate to be observing this.

A swath of ridged brain tissue faced me as the physician's skilled hands excised the invading tumor. Every motion was exact. None was extraneous.

He is such a mild man, but his operating style is powerful.

The assistant whisked the offending tumor away while Dr. Nyun reached into the bowl, replacing the missing bony material. The folds of scalp were sutured together, ending the hour-long operation.

"You were fantastic. I never saw anything like the way you work."

The doctor smiled humbly.

"This patient will not occupy a hospital bed because they are all full. He will be placed on a mat in the corridor. The hospital does not provide food. Relatives must come to care for the sick. It's not like your country."

"What about sepsis? Do many die from infection? What if there is no family to look after them?"

My questions went unanswered. He motioned for me to follow as we walked into another operating room with an experienced surgeon. His medical student had anaesthetized a 13-year-old girl with a severe cleft lip.

"So, you're from Philadelphia? Dr. Nyun told us you might be coming."

I felt a sense of revulsion as the surgeon cut into the child's deformed mouth. It was also disconcerting for me to watch without having to wear a hospital gown, cap, or even washing my hands.

"Yes, you do wonderful work here," I said, turning my head slightly to avoid observing the gushing of blood.

"We do the best we can with what we have. In Philadelphia, I was offered a faculty position where I could have done research and made a lot of money. Here we carry a heavy workload and earn about 35 dollars a month."

The doctor's face says it all. He regrets not having stayed in Philadelphia. Here he doesn't have the facilities and the resources to do his work more effectively.

"How do you live on 35 dollars per month?"

"We get by. I am one of very few U.S. surgically trained doctors, but this government doesn't care. I felt it was my duty to return to Burma and serve my people regardless of what was happening in my country."

My escort did not want the conversation to continue in a political vein.

"We have to leave now," he interrupted politely.

In the car, we returned through the same bucolic countryside.

"Your colleague seemed unhappy at having to come back to practice here. You are heroes to me. You are all highly skilled surgeons. You should be considered national treasures and granted special facilities and privileges for your valuable work."

"Not really. If we do or say something the government doesn't like, they would throw us in jail or have us killed."

"Killed? But you are the only neurosurgeon at this hospital, perhaps in the entire country. You are indispensable. U Thant's son died in your arms."

Burmese family, Vicki and me.

"No one is indispensable here. Another example is that we no longer own our home. Recently, officials came and said the house now belongs to the government."

His words shocked me. I thought of how we Americans take for granted our freedom of speech and our private property and demand that government meet our needs.

Now I know what is behind that look. Contemporary life in Burma is a valley of tears. Everyone lives with apprehension—fearful of being overheard or misinterpreted. They all seem wary of an unseen oppressor. Since our experience with the customs officer at the airport, I too feel vulnerable.

"Dr. Nyun, I admire you and your colleague I saw this morning. You could have chosen the path of a more secure and financially rewarding professional life, but you chose to serve your people. I repeat: you are heroes."

As expected, my host said nothing.

The following day I enquired about the patient, wondering how anyone could recover from such an intricate operation, lying on an un-sanitized mat in a hospital hall.

"He's doing very well, without any complications. By the way, be-cause you are leaving tomorrow, Barbara has arranged a full family din-ner this evening."

That afternoon, Barbara came to our room with a servant.

"We would like to give you these silk *engi* and *Longi* as a gift. Perhaps you would like to wear them this evening?"

"They are beautiful. Thank you so much."

The entire family congregated in the parlor, awaiting our arrival for the farewell dinner together. Admiring glances greeted us as we entered wearing the Burmese national dress. It felt like being with my Italian family in Mays Landing or Margherita di Savoia, where all the genera-tions were assembled. I loved interacting with everyone from the chil-dren to the grandparents.

Our final meal consisted of Burmese specialties, including: *Thali*, a rice soup, *chapatis* served with a variety of vegetables, fish with curry and grilled okra, tofu and assorted greens. The flavors were a blend of Indian and Chinese cuisines.

After our wonderful banquet, an aunt asked Vicki and me to fol-low her into a private room. She brought out a square, wooden box. Opening the lid, our eyes widened. There was another display of shim-mering gems.

"As a sign of our esteem, we would like to give you a parting gift. Unfortunately, we are not able to give you a valuable gemstone because the customs officers would seize it and we would suffer the consequenc-es. Instead, we have a pin for each of you that is inexpensive. The offi-cials will not take them from you."

"Vicki's was a silver flower with small sapphires and mine was a floral spray consisting of three stalks dotted with cabochon rubies. Their value in the United States would be approximately 300 dollars, but they symbolized friendship, which was beyond price.

We joined the others who awaited us. Once again, one son was missing.

"Our family gathered here and hopes you enjoyed your visit and that you will have a safe and wonderful continuation of your journey," the patriarch said.

"We are sorry we didn't get to meet your other son. Please extend our best regards to him," I said, attempting to be inclusive.

My statement caused a wave of unease among the group. Eyes rolled, and some members fidgeted in their seats. It was Saw Nyun's sister who took the initiative to speak out in an agitated voice.

"You will never meet him. We no longer welcome him as a member of this family. He disobeyed our wishes and married an unsuitable woman."

A silence ensued. I was curious to know more but did not want to be the one to ask, "Is she nice? Does she make him happy?"

Composing herself, she continued.

"He married a movie actress. She is very beautiful and famous, but such a woman in that indecent line of work is not fit to be among us. He is now disowned."

Murmurs of assent were heard among the group.

Oh, Lord. I had asked for a sign on the plane and this is it. The old time Italians have a lot in common with the Burmese. It's good I never mentioned my recent movie offers in Egypt and India. In fact, I'll be careful not to speak of them in future.

Dr. Nyun and his driver took us to the airport the next day. It was a sad farewell because I knew I would never return to his lovely land of pagodas and would never see him or anyone in his family again. But his parting statement uplifted my spirit to an unexpected height.

"Gilda, if Barbara and I ever have a daughter, we will name her Gilda." I was speechless. My eyes welled with tears of gratitude and pride. Saw Nyun stood, held my hand and smiled gently. His, and all the loving smiles I received in Burma would always remain so dear to me.

I will regret not knowing what kind of creature was on their roof.

CHAPTER NINE

EDUCATION: THE RIGHT CHOICE

TENDER

After our global adventure, Vicki and I arrived home in Germantown, each with five dollars in our pockets. What to do? It was now January 1964. Our trip around the world was to last one year, but after seven months our resources, both fiscal and physical, gave out. My sister and I needed money fast, but temporary help was not abundant in Philadelphia.

"I have an idea," Vicki said. "Let's go to Manhattan with our five dollars and get a day job as 'Kelly Girls.' We can earn 20 dollars each."

"What do 'Kelly Girls' do?"

"They type, silly."

"While we're there, we can invite Aunt Millie to dinner at Luigino's Pizzeria on 42nd Street," I suggested.

My mother's sister, Carmella, who everyone called "Millie," lived in Staten Island and always enjoyed a junket into the "Big City." Vicki also loved New York. When she left home at 19, she worked on 38th Street until our world excursion. I did not share her enthusiasm of going there for the day because I was already fatigued from constant country hopping, but I consented to join her. After all, 20 dollars was 20 dollars.

We rose early the next morning and boarded the train for the great metropolis. Mom was worried we would go hungry, so she gave us each 10 dollars for the fare and lunch. She always came through.

On arriving at Penn Station, Vicki proved herself adept at taking the correct bus to lead us to the 'Kelly Girls' office.

"Good morning, ladies. Are you seeking one-day employment or longer?" said the receptionist, matter-of-factly.

"One day, ma-am," we replied in unison.

"Proceed to a vacant typing station and take the 10-minute qualifying test."

"Vicki, I didn't know there was a test. My typing is not that good. I wasted my money coming here."

"Keep quiet and do your best," she snapped.

Vicki always liked clerical work. She had been a secretary in New York for a travel agency for three years before our trip. I, on the other hand, never memorized the keyboard and always looked at the keys, which slowed me down. The inevitable occurred. My sister was hired and I, rejected, deemed unfit to be a 'Kelly Girl.'

"Telephone Aunt Millie and tell her to meet us at 5 o'clock at the restaurant," Vicki called out. Walk around the city until then, Gilda. Try to stay warm. Too bad it's so cold out."

Oh, well, I guess there is nothing for me to do but walk the streets of New York with the few dollars I have left from the train fare.

I strolled for an hour, admiring the bronze statue of Atlas supporting the world on his shoulders: Radio City Music Hall was always inviting.

It would be nice if I could afford the show, hear the organ and admire the Rockettes, but I can't indulge. It's really cold.

I turned a corner where a long line trailed the RKO Building. Curious, I went to the end and asked a woman ahead of me what the queue was for.

"We're here to see Merv Griffin's Anagram Show on TV."

"Who's Merv Griffin?" I queried.

"You don't know the famous game-show host. Where have you been?"

I didn't explain I had circled the globe. She continued.

"This program is so popular you need a ticket to get in. You have to write in at least two months in advance, but it's worth it."

"Oh, I have no ticket."

"Too bad," she said.

At that moment, a young man in an RKO uniform came out, asking to see the required permit from those gathered. He came to me, and smiled.

"Ticket, please."

I seized the moment and poured out a passionate account of my rejection as a Kelly Girl and having to pound the frigid pavement.

"Come with me."

I followed as he led me from the back of the line into the building. He opened a door revealing a large area where familiar television personalities were assembled, chatting. Florence Henderson stood out, wearing a dark-brown mink coat as Don Knotts looked on.

"Come into the studio," said my guide. We entered a large, cool grey room with bleacher-style planks to sit on and a rectangular stage in front.

"Stay here and sit near the aisle. Don't move because this place will really fill up in no time."

He winked and left me alone in that still, solitary space. I was sorry to see him go, but the excitement thus far distracted me. He was right: within 10 minutes, the area was abuzz with the happy, cacophonous banter of excited people waiting to be entertained. A crowd "animator" came out, coaching us on how and when to applaud. He had us laughing and clapping in no time. Soon, bright lights filled the stage. A disembodied voice made an enthusiastic announcement.

"Ladies and Gentlemen, here's America's favorite TV game host, Merv Griffin!"

The 'animator' signaled for us to shout, whistle and put our hands together as loud as we could while the star took his seat in front of the audience. All this commotion piqued my curiosity as to what the show was about.

Four, pre-picked contestants were summoned to a microphone on stage. They each stood before a lectern with a bell-ringing device. An overhead screen projected an anagram. The one to unscramble the letters first would ring the bell and earn points. Of course, the participant with the most points at the end of the program would be the winner. At first, the words were not difficult to decipher. The challenge was to respond quickly. The answer time became shorter and shorter, building tension among the four and the audience. If the players were stumped,

Merv Griffin would ask a member of the audience to "take a crack at it."

That happened! None of the players could guess the next word, but I could. My arm waved wildly from my aisle seat. The animator chose me from among all others and motioned for me to stand.

"What's your name and where are you from?" Merv Griffin asked with his infectious smile.

"Gilda Battaglia and I'm from Philadelphia."

"All right, Gilda from Philadelphia, can you solve the puzzle?"

"The word is tender," I said demurely.

"Wouldn't you know a pretty young girl would know the word 'tender,' he said. "Congratulations! You have won 20 dollars. Come in front to pick up your check."

I couldn't believe it! I made 20 dollars without having to sit behind a typewriter all day looking down at the keys. When the show was over, the room cleared, and I strutted proudly toward 42nd Street and our favorite Neapolitan eatery. Luigino's was the most authentic pizzeria outside Naples, as far as I was concerned. There were long brick ovens staffed by good-looking, dark-haired Italian *pizzaioli who* delighted the patrons by twirling and tossing pliable discs of dough above their heads.

A waiter passed, balancing a bubbling pie headed for Vicki and Aunt Millie's table.

Good timing!

"What did you do alone all day in the cold?" Vicki asked.

I pulled out my check and waved it in the air.

"Where did you get that?"

"From Merv Griffin. I was on his TV program and I won because I unscrambled a word."

Aunt Millie and Vicki looked at me in disbelief. I swaggered up to them.

"If you doubt me, watch channel WFIL tonight and you'll see how I earned my slice of the pie today. This pizza is on me."

IS THIS A SCHOOL?

Following the Kelly Girl attempt, I needed to start making money and plan seriously for the next phase of my life. There were no full-time teaching positions open in mid-January 1964. I decided to be a substitute while looking for a steady job. Substitute teaching was a ready option.

My first temporary assignment was teaching Spanish at Cheltenham High School in the suburbs of Philadelphia. What a building! Carpeted corridors and oil paintings lined the walls for the enjoyment of students, faculty and the public. Several of the teenagers seemed a bit haughty, conveying the feeling the teachers were there to serve them. After class, they'd drive past in their long-finned Cadillacs without acknowledging us. They did not demonstrate the deference we held for our educators.

At 7:30 a.m., on a clear, blustery January day, Dad drove me down Broad Street from our house in Germantown. We were headed toward Thomas Alva Edison High School where I had accepted a one-day teaching position. A protective Italian father, Dad wanted to escort me to the building to check it out as neither of us had ever heard of the place.

My father stopped at the light on Susquehanna and Dolphin, a "colored section" of the city. My mind instantly recalled tutoring Betty there last year after teaching at Upper Moreland High School. I remembered another Spanish teacher at Upper Moreland, Larry Pinni, who would drive me after the school day to the corner of that neighborhood and drop me off on Broad Street.

"I'm not going any farther. Are you sure you want to go in there?"

"Yes," I replied, unfazed.

"Suit yourself," and Larry sped off. Dad would come two hours later to take me home. I recalled my shy, high school pupil, Betty White. She lived with her parents in a modest row house in the neighborhood. "Betty is failing Spanish," her mother informed me. "She is very timid and doesn't want to speak in class." "I understand. Let's see what we can do."

Betty was sweet, and so were her parents. In fact, hers was the only family of a child I tutored who ever offered me anything to eat or drink.

"Would you like a cup of tea?" her mother asked.

Being up since 6 a.m., a hot drink at 4:30 p.m. sounded wonderful.

When the steaming beverage arrived, it was accompanied by a sandwich.

"Do you like Graham crackers?" her mother queried.

"Yes, I do."

I seldom ate them, but I savored the crispy, crunchy, brown wafers at that home. After the light repast, I had a renewed burst of energy and was grateful to Betty's mother for providing it.

One rainy, wintry night, while Betty and I conjugated irregular verbs, her father put on his raincoat, and left the house quietly. He later returned, drenched, carrying a small package. I saw in my peripheral vision that Mrs. White was unpacking Graham crackers to place on my saucer.

"You should not have done that!" I exclaimed when she brought the traditional tea. "I would never want your husband to go out in the rain on a night like this to buy me anything."

"That's all right; we know you like them," said her thoughtful mother. Her father grinned with satisfaction.

What a loving, caring family. Betty is fortunate to have such parents. It's no wonder she is such a sweet young woman.

A month after my tutoring assignment, Mrs. White called to notify me Betty got a B plus in Spanish.

"We owe it all to you," she said, gratefully.

"I owe it to Betty's hard work and your Graham crackers," I said, jokingly. Of all the neighborhoods where I tutored, I experienced the most gracious hospitality in Susquehanna and Dolphin, a place in which Larry Pinni feared to tread.

The traffic light changed, jolting me back to finding the assigned school. But Dad was not paying attention.

"Dad, the light is green."

Approaching the city, I admired the familiar landmarks of City Hall and the Union League, both buildings in the Second Empire style, richly ornamented and graceful. The Union League did not accept Italians as members. I resented the discrimination.

Dad also had recollections at traffic lights and sometimes needed to be reminded to move on. We passed *"Father Divine's Hotel."*

"Father Divine was a patient of mine. Not many white doctors would accept colored patients, but I welcome everybody."

"That's nice, Dad."

How could a physician refuse to treat any person? Wouldn't that be against the Hippocratic Oath?

We continued until we arrived at our destination at Luzern, the Thomas Alva Edison High School. We were in an inner-city section I had never seen. Boarded, neglected houses and store front churches were abundant, but where was the school?

Dad parked in front of an austere building without any of the usual indicators of a place of learning. It reminded me of the plain fascist buildings we saw on our recent trip to Rome. In contrast to the artfully ornate City Hall and Union League, nothing was visually appealing here. There were no flags, signs or the usual adjacent playground.

"This is the address, but is this a school?" asked Dad. "We must be in the wrong place. Let's get out of here!"

"Wait! I'll go in and find out," I said, determinedly.

Opening the heavy front door, a short flight of stone stairs led up to glass doors. There was no sound. An American flag was at the top right of the steps. It was unlike any flag of this country I had ever seen. The red, white and blue stripes had become torn, frayed strips of faded orange, beige and purple.

Dad's right. This cannot be a school.

I turned to exit the shabby, unwelcoming place. A loud bell squealed, and waves of young men passed behind the glass doors.

Could it be? Maybe this is the location.

I poked my head outside the front door and signaled to Dad to leave.

"Dad, I'm staying. It's all right; this is the place."

"Are you sure?" he said in disbelief.

"Yes. Pick me up at 3:30."

My father left reluctantly to open his office and I proceeded to the Principal's Office. Like the entrance, the hallway was dark and uninviting, but the principal was pleasant and obviously glad to see me.

Viewing sardines drying in Nazaré, Portugal.

"We don't get many substitutes to come here," he said, smiling. "Welcome!"

I soon found out Thomas Alva Edison was a high school for males, many of whom were 21 years old, and some, married with children. Most educators shunned such institutions, but I was eager to begin. The principal introduced me to the vice principal who escorted me to an empty classroom.

"This is where you'll be today."

Going to a small corner closet, he pointed to a telephone on the wall.

"If you have a situation in which you need help, just call me and I'll rush over."

"That shouldn't be necessary," I said, naively.

The administrator then took a seat in the front row of the class and waited with me for the room to fill, and soon it did. Many of the "boys" were strapping men, sauntering in and instantly commenting on my anatomy. When they saw the disapproving stares from the VP, some took their seats. Others slammed their books on top of the desk and used them as a cushion for their heads to nap on. One wiry lad called out in the hall.

"Hey! Come see the *mamacita* teaching us today."

When I asked for their attention, several pupils ignored me and started to doze off. Slam dunking tightly-wrapped paper balls in the trash can was a favorite activity. A few paper airplanes sailed past my nose.

How am I going to get them to quiet down?

"They won't listen to you, teacher. They work nights and sleep in class all day," a young boy told me.

I took roll call in English. Most of the pupils had Spanish names and spoke the language but I was soon to find they were not literate in that idiom or in English. The text books were worn. The yellowish pages had been handled countless times over the years. Unlike Cheltenham High School, no posters or paintings decorated the drab, brown classroom, just an orange, rusty streak spread down a corner of the beige ceiling, caused by a neglected water leak.

My charges continued to be unruly, until the magic happened.

"Buenos Días. Me llamo Señorita Battaglia." (Good day. My name is Miss Battaglia).

This was a Spanish literature class, but the pupils were unaccustomed to hearing an Anglo teacher speak in their idiom. The room became suddenly quiet. The drowsy students in the back lifted their heads in curiosity.

"Our assignment is to read about the life of a fisher in a small village in Galicia, in northern Spain. How many of you know how to fish?"

They shouted their answers uncontrollably. I told them we had to abide by classroom etiquette, meaning raising their hands to be called on to answer. There was silence and hands politely waved in the air.

I can't believe this. They are listening and responding.

"I visited the small fishing village of Nazaré in Portugal, where, for 25 cents (US), you could buy a quarter-pound grilled sardine, accompanied by a fresh roll and a glass of wine. In Italy, I saw three generations of fishers along the Bay of Naples, repairing their nets against the angry Vesuvius looming in the background."

The boys' hands swayed feverishly in the air as they were eager to recount their experiences in volcanic Costa Rica, Guatemala or Peru. Seeing all was under control, the vice principal excused himself.

The room was electric with comments and ideas. Observing a class full of disinterested students come to life gave me a rush of adrenalin. My students had keen insight into the role of fishers and other tradesmen. They were "street smart" and, in many ways, possessed life skills far above those of their more affluent counterparts.

If only the innate abilities of these inner-city youths were unleashed! They are so intelligent.

When the final bell rang, I was tired, albeit exhilarated. The room emptied; the telephone rang.

"Are you all right?" asked the vice principal, in a concerned voice.

"Oh, yes," I replied, collecting my things.

He soon appeared and led me to the front of the building where Dad was dutifully waiting. "Thanks for coming. Like I said, it's hard to get a substitute teacher into this neighborhood." "I don't know why," I answered. "This is one of the best days I ever had subbing."

"Gilda," Dad said." I still can't believe this is a school."

"It is, Dad. Believe me; it is."

RETURN TO ROOSEVELT JUNIOR HIGH SCHOOL

Tomorrow you are to substitute at a beautiful building, Roosevelt Junior High School. Do you need directions?" my supervisor asked. "No. That won't be necessary because I attended that school for three years and am familiar with it."

It will be exciting to go back to Roosevelt Junior High School after 10 years.

As I contemplated the visit, vivid memories of my middle school days flashed through my mind.

Junior High made me feel grown up. Having different teachers for different classes was far more interesting than being in one classroom all day with the same teacher. What I loved most was visiting the school library. Reading the classics was the ultimate escape for me.

As a student, I had consumed avidly great works of literature there. Reading in that peaceful place transported me to wondrous worlds where people had daring adventures. It also provided a vehicle for expanding my vocabulary. Words were fun. I kept endless lists of the new ones found in the books and practiced my burgeoning lexical repertoire on my family and friends. Some of them were impressed while others were annoyed. It didn't matter. Nothing could hinder me.

"When you speak to me like that I feel flummoxed," I'd say, with an opinionated air.

"Stop using those big words. Talk normal," several friends and family members would scold.

Alexander Dumas' *Man in the Iron Mask, The Three Musketeers* and Victor Hugo's, *Les Miserables*, were replete with lengthy French phrases. How I longed to learn that language. I'd sit for hours trying to decipher its pronunciation and meaning.

Someday I'm going to learn French even if I'd have to teach myself. I want to know what these words mean and how they sound.

"Miss Battaglia, I'm pleased to see you finished the 1,400 pages of *Les Miserables* this week. Let's talk about it someday," the librarian exclaimed, admiringly.

We never had that conversation, but ten years later I returned to the building as a 23-year-old substitute teacher. Who could have imagined such a thing?

My heart beat fast when I set foot in the front door of my alma mater. The entrance looked familiar. The hallway seemed unchanged with its shiny brown linoleum flooring and cream-colored walls. I wondered if I would see any of my former teachers.

"Good morning, Miss Battaglia. Welcome back. I am your contact person here today."

How wonderful it was to hear the voice of my former American History instructor, Mr. Moss.

"Mr. Moss, you remember me! I am so happy to see you."

"You're so grown up. I am glad to see you too, especially since you decided to enter the teaching profession. Didn't you want to be a nurse?"

I explained briefly my change of career. He listened with interest. Mr. Moss had aged. His five-foot-three-inch frame seemed the same, but his dark brown hair and mustache were speckled with white. The most obvious change was in his facial expression. The sparkle in his eyes had dimmed, and he seemed distracted as though my presence made him reminisce about past times at the school.

"Your assignment today is library duty. Don't worry; the kids are quiet there. The last period of the day is American History. I would like you to come to my class."

"I can't wait to be an observer this time, Mr. Moss."

I went to the library where students were waiting. The majority were kids of color. Very few were white. They knew the routine of silence and they adhered to it. Being with them in the space I had enjoyed in my youth was a joyful experience. As the youngsters settled in to their reading, I was eager to seek out the treasures that captivated me in my youth. There it was, Victor Hugo's *Les Miserables*! I pulled the book from the shelf and opened the front cover. On the inside card was my name, Gilda Battaglia. I was dismayed to see that I had been the last student to take it out in 10 years.

Hadn't any pupil been introduced to those wonderful thoughts in a decade? They were missing the elegant words Dumas set down on those pages.

Lorna Doone was still there but the cover had faded. I recalled how it became my favorite novel when I was 14 years old. A young woman of noble birth, captured by brigands and ultimately rescued by a handsome, stalwart farmer, John Rudd, was the ultimate romantic fantasy. My youthful thoughts were often on romance, especially with good looking protectors. I read that book 16 times, mostly jumping to the parts that made me sigh when Lorna and John fell in love. I suddenly had a flash-back to when a classmate asked me a serious question.

"You read all those classics. What's your favorite book?" The answer was easy.

"*María Pearl.*"

"That's not a classic. We read that short story in class the other day."

"No, but it's the one that reminds me of my life."

I am María Pearl. I'm that girl who was hustled between two sets of grand-parents—one was highly organized, and they called her Pearl. The other, in contrast, kept a cluttered house without any order or routine and referred to their granddaughter as "Maria." To them her name meant a free spirit and a carefree life. The heroine kept both names and brought balance to her life. I too will select the best traits from both sides of my family and Italian culture and disregard the rest. Common sense is not only found in classical literature.

When the last period arrived, I went to Mr. Moss' classroom. Un-like the library, I was greeted with cacophonic babble. My tired mentor approached me, his shoulders bowed and his face reflecting resignation.

"How things have changed. Students aren't like they were when you were here."

Mr. Moss was a weary veteran educator. At one time, he had been very strict and highly respected in our American History class. Speaking aloud without permission was strictly forbidden. I looked forward to observing him once again after almost a decade.

No one noticed my presence through so much loud talking. Mr. Moss tried to calm everyone down to take roll call, but the noise did not diminish. In frustration, he resorted to doing the routine task silently. When finished, he tried to make an announcement, but the chatter con-tinued for 15 minutes.

"Boys and girls, please pay attention. Today's lesson is about our flag and the battle at Fort McHenry in Baltimore. In what state was that fort?"

No one answered because no one was listening. Students had bro-ken off into intimate discussion groups where a few arguments took place. He tried valiantly to draw their attention to the chalkboard where there were facts written about the battle at Fort McHenry, the War of 1812 and the meaning of the flag.

"Please, pay attention. As Americans, we all should know the American National Anthem, the *Star Spangled Banner.*"

"Oh, that. Taneesha can sing it real good," a student said.

Seeing a glimmer of interest in the group, Mr. Moss consented.

"All right. Taneesha, will you sing our national anthem for us. The young girl rose and went to the front of the class. She was poised. This time there was no clamor. Her classmates looked on attentively. Taneesha sang in a beautiful soprano voice. When she ended her rendition, the class cheered. The bell rang and the room cleared without a formal dismissal. Sadly, I realized that no teaching or learning had taken place in the American History class. Mr. Moss turned to me wearing a forlorn expression.

"Miss Battaglia, as you can see, I can't reach these kids. In the days when you were a student, I loved my job. I've been in teaching over 30 years and it's time for me to retire."

How sad for him and his pupils. He is giving up after long years of service and his charges aren't being educated. There must be a way for him to hold their interest before he stops teaching. All educators face some sort of challenge and need to find a strategy that works. I hope Mr. Moss does soon.

"Mr. Moss, in the library today I saw no one had taken *Les Miserables* out in 10 years. I bet your pupils would be interested in the life of Jean Valjean and the injustice and suffering he endured on the galleys. His experience could be related to slavery in this country and the American flag, a symbol of freedom. Do you think that might capture their interest in both European and American History?"

"I'm not sure, Miss Battaglia. Tomorrow I'll see what I can do."

Mr. Moss' dejected look brightened ever so slightly as he pondered the suggestion. I left his class feeling empathy for him but energized thinking of possibly effective strategies to teach those students.

It might work, and it might not. These students are bright. We've got to stimulate their minds, and, in return, they will stimulate ours.

THE DOOR

Substituting was hard work. I liked socializing to clear my mind. During another hiatus from Louie, a blind date was arranged for me with Dr. Ferdinand M. He was "Man of the Year" at the Philadelphia College of Osteopathic Medicine in the early 1960s. Ms. Constance Bennett, a well-intentioned nurse at the college, and our family friend, suggested I meet the young physician. She described him as affable, intellectual, talented and an all-around nice guy. Dr. M. was to come to my house, according to custom, to meet my parents and hear what time my father wanted me to return home.

I was often embarrassed by our house in Germantown. My father, who was often described as having "Hands of Gold" when it came to homeopathic manipulation and Chiropractic adjustment of the human body, was inept at hammering a nail, an incompetence he nurtured with a sense of pride.

"My hands were destined for other things," he'd often say. This resulted in cracked mirrors or loose doors being abandoned in that condition.

I was 24 years old. Tonight was my blind date: I wanted everything to be perfect. Considerable time was spent selecting the right dress, light and cool to combat the 90-degree heat. The outfit was not too revealing, a pastel pink linen, not garish. Makeup was applied in moderation. My nose should not shine and my upper lip could not be dotted with droplets of perspiration in the excessive humidity. There was no air-conditioning in our house and the downstairs window fan gave little relief. It seemed everything I applied was melting.

My lipstick was a soft shade and I dismissed mascara, which could surely run down my cheeks in the torrid summer air. Appropriate salutations ran through my head. I practiced aloud, the usual awkward dialog of blind dates.

All preparations complete, I ventured downstairs to await the big moment. To my surprise, I saw Jake, our neighbor, adjusting our large, green, wooden front door. No one locked their doors on McMahon Street. Our neighbors came and went on a continual basis, as did Vicki and I in their homes. Jake became more like a member of the family than a neighbor.

"What's the matter, Jakey?" I asked.

"I was coming in to look for your folks, but they're not home yet. This door is a little wobbly, so I set it back on its hinges. I'll come back later when they're in."

Jake departed, leaving me in silence, except for the sound of my rapidly beating heart.

Soon my makeup will melt, and this heat will wrinkle my well-ironed linen dress. I'll look a mess by the time the "Man of the Year" arrives.

Suddenly, I heard a car motor turn off outside. Peeking through the curtains, I eyed an athletically-built young man clamber up the front steps, eagerly approaching our porch. I neared the door, but stood a distance back, not wanting to appear too quick to respond to the sound of the metal knocker. Timing is everything.

The second round of knocking commenced when suddenly, the door crashed onto the living room floor revealing a stupefied young man.

Dr. M. stood speechless at the gaping arch, his eyes darting toward mine in disbelief.

Though mortified, I felt compelled to make light of the situation as though this was a frequent occurrence in the lives of the Battaglias. The door was not the only thing to become unhinged. Smiling nervously, I kneeled to lift the rigid, six-foot frame.

What to do? Where should we put all this bulk? How can I act as though this nightmare isn't happening? Why are my parents taking so long to come home?

The young physician came to the rescue by flexing his hypertrophied muscles.

"Where do you want me to put the door?"

"On the sofa."

I watched in amazement as he jockeyed the heavy wooden object onto the soft, middle cushions. The bottom half of the door spread out, covering most of the carpet.

"Like my father tells visitors, our door is always open," I chuckled nervously, in a vain attempt at levity.

"Yeah, I see what you mean," he said with a bewildered smile.

We sat, flanked on each side of the wooden behemoth in awkward silence. The idle chit chat I rehearsed fell by the wayside.

"So where would you like to go tonight?"

I always disliked that question, preferring that my date would take the initiative to plan ahead.

"We can't go anywhere now and leave the house with no front door," I retorted nervously.

Silence!

How I wish Mom and Dad would come home and rescue me from this humiliating dilemma. Dad doesn't mind if things need repair, but this is too much.

"Would you like a cool drink?"

"No. I'm fine," he answered politely.

Sure. Fine, sitting here acting like having a huge door between us is normal. It reminds me of the trundle bed the Amish use to divide the sexes. But this separation will be fleeting because Ferdinand will soon leave skid marks on the carpet in his haste to flee our "Dream Castle" house with a gaping hole at the entrance.

A car was heard parking on the street. The metallic clang of the doors opening and closing signaled Mom and Dad were finally home. When my parents appeared at the hollow entrance, they stopped in their tracks and gazed directly into the open living room. My father seemed surprisingly unaffected by this debacle. He graciously approached the new doctor, shook his hand and gestured for him to help put the door on its hinges.

Ferdinand readily lifted the heavy object and set it upright. Dad thanked him.

"What time would you like me to bring your daughter home, sir?"

He's not taking off. There are no skid marks. I was sure he'd be gone by now. Ms. Bennett was right; he's a fine young man. Dad appears unfazed by this first awful impression. No doubt, his having been born in a one room dwelling in Margherita di Savoia, did not prepare him to become a handy man.

Dr. M. bid goodnight to Mom and Dad. Extending his arm, he led me to his immaculate new Dodge.

Strange, but I kind of miss Louie now, although he would undoubtedly rant all night about the potential danger of having a heavy door fall in on someone, expanding on potentially broken bones. He'd then wax about neglecting essential repairs in my "Dream Castle" house and declare he would never let such a thing happen. Dr. M. was too polite to make any negative comments, although he must be thinking of a few.

"Have you decided where you would like to go tonight?"

"How about the Kon Tiki Restaurant in the Marriott on City Line Avenue?"

I suggested that place because the lighting is always subdued and soft music from tropical islands plays soothingly in the background, an anodyne to my jangled nerves.

"Good choice; I like that too."

En route I made small talk, trying valiantly to hide my embarrassment at the scene we left behind. The episode could have prompted a lively and fun conversation had I been in the mood, but not tonight.

Dr. M. pulled into the driveway of our destination and we entered the pleasant Polynesian environment. As anticipated, the music swayed, and fountains gurgled gently. A smiling waiter escorted us to a small table where an orange candle emitted a flickering golden flame.

Ferdinand looked directly at me for the first time. I felt uncomfortable because I was still a bit flustered.

"I've heard so much about you from Ms. Bennett."

"All good I hope."

"Yes. And now that we've finally met, I know she did not exaggerate."

What a nice guy! Ms. Bennett did not exaggerate about him either.

"So, you just finished your internship at the Philadelphia College of Osteopathic Medicine? Why did you select that school?"

"I applied and was 'wait-listed' at Hahnemann. PCOM accepted me right away, but in my first week there, I received a letter from Hahnemann saying they had a place for me. I turned it down because PCOM had treated me so well."

I'm impressed. He's got character and is loyal. Most people do not know what osteopathy is and he could have taken the easy way out. Few People know what Naturopathy is. Some consider it a cult. I often wish Dad had become a plumber or something easily recognizable. I don't like prejudice toward a profession.

We continued chatting when the waiter served us the signature fruity cocktails of the house with a slice of pineapple and a skewered maraschino cherry. A miniature paper parasol topped off the tall, frosted glass. I sipped slowly as my date initiated the conversation.

Ferdinand spoke freely about his family and life goals. His father was a pharmacist, his mother a homemaker and he had a brother. During the summer, he had been a lifeguard at the Jersey Shore for several years. He was powerfully built and of medium height. He had honest, dark eyes, well-coiffed dark hair and handsome, rugged features so why didn't I feel an attraction? Any girl would be proud to be with such a man. He was a great catch and I could find none better.

"I want you to know, I expect to have six children," he said, staring intently into my eyes.

"That's nice. A large family is lovely."

Oh gosh! What if I presented him with six girls? Would he demand I keep producing until there was a son? Dr. Gorelli's brother had 10 daughters until his wife 'got it right.' And what if I can't have children? Will he divorce me like the Shah of Iran did to Soraya or Napoleon to Josephine, not to mention Henry VIII? I won't ask because I don't want to know.

I miss Louie right now. Each time we have a spat I vow never to see him, but I always go back. This young man is exceptional and more my age. Why am I thinking of Louie tonight?

Dr. M. kept talking and I feigned attention as I sat, twirling the flimsy blue paper parasol dotted with yellow and white flowers between my thumb and index finger. The tiny object made me reflect on how fragile human relationships can be.

Later that night the door closed on my blind date with the "Man of the Year."

TV AND THE FINAL PROPOSAL

Substitute teaching was interesting, but I needed to find a full-time job. This time, I wanted employment closer to home. Now, in 1964, it was once again time to job search.

A certificate was required for a permanent teaching position in Pennsylvania. An applicant as a language teacher was required to undergo a competitive written and oral examination in the target language. Subsequent school placement would be contingent on the test results. The document would only be granted upon working full time for three years and one day. Both examinations were administered at the Philadelphia Board of Education on 21st Street and Parkway in Center City Philadelphia.

All prior preparations had been made and I went to the Board Office on a designated morning. I was directed to an area where a bevy of prospective educators had gathered. All appeared anxious about meeting the rigorous standards.

The first section of the examination was three hours in length, covering basic grammar, comprehension, useful phrases and a 350-word composition on the Spanish Renaissance, all to be written in that idiom. It was not difficult, thanks to my additional academic experience in Mexico. I wrote from nine to 12:30 and stopped because Mom and Vicki were waiting in the lobby for me to join them for lunch.

"How did it go, Gilly?" Mom asked.

"Not bad."

"I know you did great." Mom was always giving me more credit than I felt I deserved, but I loved her for it.

At lunch I was quiet, thinking about the oral section. When I returned for the afternoon speaking portion, a panel of five expert educators greeted me and subsequently drilled me for a half-hour in Spanish. My linguistic fluency impressed them and they, as did I, enjoyed our session. At the end of the formal Castilian conversation, a panelist addressed me in English.

"Have you ever appeared on television?"

"Yes. I did modeling and appeared on a morning variety show called

Solar de Vagabundos (Yard for the Homeless), in Mexico City where I sang and acted.

That one question opened a floodgate of conversation to which my interviewers paid keen attention and said that they would want to see proof of my experience the following morning.

I returned home after the interview and saw Louie's white Dodge parked in front of our house. Although I had intended not to date him for a while, seeing his automobile sent the familiar tingling sensations throughout my being. Vicki and I had met many fine young men during our global travels. Some were American tourists, graduate students and dashing locals. There were lovely dates where we were wined and dined in exotic settings— but no sparks were ignited as with Louie.

Louie was waiting for me in his car. Seeing me, he got out of his car and slowly approached. We stared at each other for an awkward moment, both of us attempting to conceal our pleasure on being with each other after seven months.

"You're back."

"Yes."

"You look the same."

"Did you expect me to change drastically?" I said, semi-sarcastically, still feeling miffed at his abrupt declaration at the Dunnes' home.

Louie followed me to my front door and then into the living room. Our attempt at conversation was interrupted by the sudden ringing of the telephone.

"Hello!"

"Is this Miss Battaglia?"

"Yes."

"I am calling from the Philadelphia Board of Education. The interview Committee wants to ask if you would be interested in teaching Spanish on television Station WHYY?"

"Yes. I would be very interested," I responded, trying to control my voice.

Teaching on television should be exciting. I enjoyed appearing on TV in Mexico. I'd love to do it.

"Bring any publicity you have from the media in Mexico and report to the Board of Education at 9 a.m. on Monday morning to discuss this matter further."

"I will be there. Thank you."

Regardless of what Mom and Dad say about not mentioning the movies, I'm going to take my entire portfolio there.

When I returned the receiver to its cradle, Louie looked at me quizzically. He appeared to have something on his mind he wanted to say, but I interrupted him.

"That call was from the Board of Education. They may want me to teach Spanish on television. Isn't that fantastic?"

Whatever Louie had intended to tell me was forgotten because he saw I was too excited to concentrate on any other topic.

"Let's go eat Chinese," he said, unemotionally.

Fumbling with the chopsticks at the South China Restaurant near Race Street, I told Louie I wanted to keep this possible, incredible opportunity a secret between us. I did not want to tell anyone until I knew the job was mine. Keeping secrets was a forte of his so I knew my confidence was safe. I could think of little else as I twirled the *lo mein.*

Monday morning came, and I was again in front of two of the individuals who were on the original panel. One was Dr. Eleanor Sandstrom, a stellar bilingual educator in the Philadelphia area and Director of Foreign Languages at the Philadelphia Board of Education. The other official was Dr. Robert Coates, an administrator.

"Let's see what you have in your portfolio."

I unzipped the case and showed them several magazines with my picture on the cover. I pulled out rapidly a stack of articles from Mexican newspapers.

"Take your time. We want to see everything you brought today."

As they examined each piece of publicity and read the Spanish text, their facial expression showed approval. I felt confident they were going to say the job was mine, but it proved not to be that easy.

"There are nearly 400 applicants for this position," Dr. Coates remarked. "It consists of two, 14-minute programs, geared to the junior high school level. The successful person will be the producer of each segment and responsible for all audiovisual materials and the delivery of instruction in participating middle schools. The candidate must also develop a curriculum based on the lesson of the day with weekly follow-up materials for use in middle schools in the Tri-State area, comprising, Delaware, Pennsylvania and regions of New Jersey. The programs must be of interest to the public and be intelligible and entertaining for middle school students and all age levels. Ongoing school visitations are required to ascertain how well the program content is utilized and enjoyed. Do you still want to apply?"

I really want to run but I know I would always regret not trying.

"Yes."

"Very good! We want you to prepare the first sample 14-minute lesson. Bring in all the props and visuals for the segment. Gear the material for grades 7, 8 and 9. Be prepared to perform your work before three of us next Monday morning at 9 a.m."

"I will be ready."

I thought one lesson would not be too difficult, but Dr. Coates raised his hand to indicate there would be more directives.

"In addition, you will have lesson five prepared and you will itemize the contents of lessons two, three and four."

This is far more complicated than I thought. I had experience teaching high school for one year. Junior High must be different. After all that work, I could be rejected. There are so many applicants who may have much more experience. But I must not allow myself to think negatively. I must be prepared and decide how and where to begin.

The remainder of the week I composed five, 14-minute lessons I hoped would be of interest to younger students. I practiced them in front of a mirror in my bedroom, pretending it was a camera lens. For props, I took all my souvenirs from our trip to Spain: the swirling, brilliantly embroidered *mantón* (shawl), assorted lace mantillas, fans, a bullfighter belt from a *traje de luces* (suit of lights), the cap of a matador and castanets I learned to play in Madrid. I cut long strips of yellow composition paper and printed the Spanish phrases to be taught. White would have produced a glare on camera. I had learned that tip in Mexico. The stack of strips was slipped under my bed lest Mom and Dad wonder what I was up to. The fact that they were seldom home made my covert actions go undetected.

The day of my first audition arrived. I was nervous, but determined to use my jitters to appear to be in complete control. My planned program centered on a map of Spain, which, when laid flat, resembled the skin of a bull. My interviewers seemed to approve of all I prepared. Two more trials ensued. At the end of the third, Dr. Coates told me something I did not want to hear.

"You have done very well. The committee eliminated all other applicants except you and another young lady, Miss Irma Schwarz. Come back next Monday and present lesson number five."

Oh, no! After being put through all this for a month, I may not get the job? I should start contacting local school districts, but I can't afford to spend the time. I must concentrate on this; it represents the opportunity of a lifetime for me. This job has it all, the perfect combination of television and academics. No more being portrayed as "sexy," which I never liked. Mom and Dad would surely approve of this position on TV. I want it for them as well as for myself!

The challenge was greater than I thought. Louie came to my house and watched me assemble more props and materials for the final interview.

"You're really intent on doing this, aren't you?"

"Of course! Wouldn't you be?"

His eyes met mine and once again, he looked as though he wanted to express something unrelated to TV, but he withheld it.

"I'll leave now because I see you are busy."

That's just like him. He leaves abruptly without wishing me luck when I really need it.

Monday morning arrived, and I presented myself at the Board of Education for the final ordeal. I was determined to try even harder and not be discouraged, but I knew this was the deciding round. Thoughts of Irma Schwartz kept plaguing me.

Does she have more experience than I? Does she specialize in the junior high level? Stop thinking! Compose yourself and look professional. That's all you can do now.

I gave my fullest at the final session. It felt like I was auditioning for a Broadway show. I did my utmost to look relaxed while suppressing the "butterflies" in my stomach. The 14 minutes passed, and my lesson ended exactly at the designated time.

"Thank you, Miss Battaglia."

A committee of three, Drs. Coates, Sandstrom and Miss Martha Gable, chairwoman of the Philadelphia Board of Education, conferred among themselves for the seemingly longest five minutes of my life.

"We like your technique, presence and clarity on speaking Spanish. We have only one question."

"Yes. What is it?"

I can't believe they want me to do even more.

"Would you be available to also teach Spanish on Channel 6, WFIL? The series is *University of the Air*. It is broadcast for one-half hour, once a week, from September to June, at prime time in the morning, from 8:30–9 a.m. You must capture the interest of viewers of all ages, from youngsters to seniors. You will be in competition with *The Today Show*. Dr. Sandstrom will help you develop the curriculum."

"Yes. I would like to do it."

I'll do whatever you want to get that position—sing, dance, you name it.

"Congratulations are therefore in order. You are now the producer and presenter of three weekly TV programs."

"You mean I've got the job?"

"That is why we are congratulating you," they said, smiling and shaking my hand.

I couldn't believe my ears and felt as though I were walking on air when I left the building.

I got the job! Thank heavens I went to Mexico and acquired all that publicity and media experience. It's good I went around the world and especially to Spain. It seems as though everything is falling into place.

On the way home, I rehearsed several scenarios to inform Mom and Dad. No longer would I have to keep the arduous process a secret. I decided, however, to postpone the announcement until after Labor Day, and break the news the night before my first appearance on *Hablando Español,* (Speaking Spanish), the name given to my junior high-level series.

Of course, Louie had to know, or I thought I would burst.

"So, you got the job? It's what you want." he said, with the usual lack of emotion.

His reaction is expected, and I detect he is more than a little impressed by the shine in his eyes. He won't dare say he thinks it is a great opportunity. I know he is glad and secretly admires me. He may brag to others, but not to me. So many Italian men I know don't like their women to get a "big head."

"Yes. It's exactly what I want for now."

I was ecstatic as well as more than a little scared. It was a relief to express my feelings to him. There was now much work to do. Lessons had to be written and props prepared.

Dr. Sandstrom proved to be wonderful to work with. She helped me create the curriculum for *The University of the Air* program I would present on WFIL. By the end of the summer, the program booklet was completed.

September arrived and the night before my first scheduled appearance, I couldn't wait to tell my parents. Keeping the secret was incredibly difficult. They thought I was going to be a substitute teacher until a full-time position could be found.

We were seated at the kitchen table when I told my parents I had an important announcement.

"Mom and Dad, I have a job."

"It's about time," Dad snapped, good-naturedly. "What and where is it?"

"You won't believe what I'm going to tell you."

"Oh, no! It better not be some acting or modeling thing," they said disapprovingly.

"You're going to be surprised and so happy when you hear."

"Well, out with it, for goodness sake!"

How liberating it was to pour out my story to them. The surprised delight on their faces increased my excitement.

"Your time in Mexico panned out after all," Dad said with satisfaction.

"I always told you it would, Angelo," Mom inserted. "Didn't I?" It was the first time I ever heard her make that statement and it made me chuckle inwardly.

"Teaching on television is decent and respectable. That's all we wanted for you, not modeling and movies," Mom added. "We wanted you to have a real profession."

I appreciated my parents' beliefs. In my heart, I knew they always had the best intentions. Louie was like-minded.

That night, I could barely sleep. The lines I memorized for my first program kept running through my mind. I must have rehearsed that 14-minute program 14 times in bed.

I entered the WHYY Television Station the next day at 9 a.m. It was on the same street where American Bandstand was broadcast, with the original host, Bob Horn, followed by a soon-to-be national M.C., Dick Clark. A large shopping bag bulged with my script and props. I was feeling excited.

"Miss Battaglia, welcome! Follow me to the director's studio," an employee guide said. "Your program begins at 1:30 p.m. This is your first time here, so we wanted you to come early and observe your colleagues who go on the air before you."

He led me into the control center, where I could observe the director, as well as the complicated equipment utilized for the broadcasts. I was fascinated to observe everything and anxious to see how my colleagues would perform.

The first program was junior high-level science in which an experienced female instructor taught photosynthesis. Her delivery was clear, concise and seemingly effortless. I enjoyed watching and for a brief while forgot my churning stomach.

Basic French was featured next. The instructor was a pleasant woman I was briefly introduced to that morning. She was also making her TV debut. Unlike the science teacher, she appeared nervous before going on camera. She bit her lower lip and wrung her hands repeatedly. I sensed her uneasiness as I watched from the darkened control area.

"Five, four, three, two, one!" a voice announced to the teacher who smiled forcedly into the lens of the camera.

The woman's distress grew so quickly she could not utter a word, not a *bonjour mes enfants* or anything. She peered into the black square with an expression of sheer panic.

"She's going to faint. Stop the camera! Span to the backup documentary at once!" commanded the director.

Two male employees rushed to rescue the unconscious teacher and offer her a sip of water.

The poor thing! How is she going to perform the series after this? I know how she feels. Whatever happens, I must not faint. If my knees turn to jelly, I'll prop myself onto something, smile and go on as though I know exactly what I am doing.

The agonizing morning ended. I was too nervous to eat lunch. I preferred to treat myself to something after the program. Finally, my time had come.

"You're next, Miss Battaglia. Get ready. Stand on the yellow-taped square on the floor and when you speak, maintain good eye contact and don't let your gaze wander," the director advised.

In my peripheral vision, I noticed the same two staff members who came to the aid of the French instructor were poised in the wings as I was to go on.

I did exactly as I was instructed. Looking into the camera's square opening I imagined I was peering directly into the eyes of a student, a well-behaved, bright and eager one. The trepidation subsided, and I began my dialogue with confidence.

Buenos días y bienvenidos al programa, Hablando Español. (Good day and welcome to the program, *Speaking Spanish.*)

As I went through my routine, I sensed I was doing well and enjoyed the experience. When the camera man signaled the time was ending, I knew the segment went without a hitch and that Mom, Dad and Grandpop would be watching with pride.

"*Muy bien,*" said the director, as he patted my shoulder. Members of the crew congratulated me, and I exited the studio on Market Street elated. I felt as though I were floating, my feet barely touching the asphalt.

On arriving home, the telephone was ringing before I could put my key in the door. The jangling continued until I answered.

"Hello," I said into the receiver after the ninth ring.

"I saw it," the masculine voice commented laconically.

"What did you think, Louie? How did I do?"

"I followed it. I understood everything."

"Then you're saying I did well?"

"It was good. You know it was."

He is proud. I can hear it in his voice, although he is trying not to show it. There must be a smile on his face too. I can tell; I know him so well.

The moment my predictable conversation with Louie ended, the phone rang again.

"Gilly. You were great! Your father and I are so proud."

"That's good to hear Mom, and thanks for sending me to Mexico."

"We were against your acting in a foreign country. You never know what could happen to a girl in a place like that, especially in the movies, but as a teacher on television you have a dignified profession."

"I understand, Mom. I'm glad you and Dad are happy with what I'm doing."

Inwardly I empathize with them, although I will always regret not having been able to pursue the opportunities I had south of the border a while longer. I know I will never find out if I have what it takes to be an actress, although teaching on television is a form of acting.

Two weeks passed, and my camera fright disappeared; in fact, I was relaxed when the red light appeared, signaling the program was on. Live television was a venue I thoroughly enjoyed. A language teacher had to be prepared and engaging to her invisible audience. I grew to love it.

Louie was still coming by. His routine coincided with his office hours. Every Wednesday and Sunday he would be at my house about 3 o'clock in the afternoon. We'd often go to the Pub Restaurant in Camden, the Latin Casino, or to Chinatown on Race Street in Philadelphia.

Teaching Spanish on television.

I was still pursued by other Italian American gentlemen who, in those days, were looking for a "good girl" to marry.

A fine candidate was a cousin through marriage. His name was Bill Ferrante, from Rhode Island. He had earned a Ph.D. in mathematics and had returned from a special academic assignment at the University of Baghdad, in Iraq. In September 1964, he resumed his teaching position at Lehigh University. He came to spend a weekend at our home. His manners were impeccable, and Dad admired him greatly. Mom was also impressed but remained a staunch Louie fan. I used to tease her saying she liked him more than I did.

On Sunday morning Bill and I walked to the local Catholic Church to attend Mass. I enjoyed his company and admired the fact that he was devoutly religious. Louie did not belong to a parish nor did my parents. I, however, used to attend Mass every morning at 5 a.m. when I was in Junior High School. A strong motivation was for me to pray to the Virgin Mary that Miss Mauger, the algebra teacher, would not call on me or humiliate me in class. She took delight in insulting her less capable pupils in front of everyone. Despite the fervency of my prayers, they were not always answered when Miss Mauger had me stand and be ridiculed for all to see.

After Mass, Bill and I walked home. As we turned the corner where my house was located, a white automobile was parked in front of our lawn.

Oh, no! It's Louie. No matter what I do, he somehow appears on the scene. Every Sunday he arrives in the late afternoon. Why is he here so early on this day? Stop fighting it, Gilda; he's your destiny. You got that message the first time you met him by the elevator at the Osteopathic Hospital on 48th and Spruce Street. He IS the man you are going to marry.

Louie stepped out of his car as we approached.

"Bill, this is Louie."

"Nice to meet you," Bill said, extending his hand. Louie performed that formality with predictable reservation.

Louie is so straight forward; he cannot conceal his feelings.

Bill followed Louie and me into the house. He immediately apologized to Mom and Dad saying he had to return to Lehigh University to prepare for classes the next day. Mom was disappointed because she had been cooking all morning in anticipation of enjoying our Sunday meal together.

"Bill, won't you at least stay and have lunch with us?" she pleaded.

"No. I must leave now, but thank you. I had a wonderful time being here." He glanced my way before leaving.

Bill departed quickly. Mom turned toward Louie.

"Won't you join us, or do you have other plans?"

"I want to take Gilda out to eat Chinese."

Mom learned not to try to coax Louie. When he made his mind up he was inflexible. He relished Chinese cuisine. It was the only food he would eat apart from Italian. His real reason that day was that he wanted to be alone with me.

At the South China Restaurant, I looked across the table at the handsome face ordering one serving from Column A and another one from Column B. His dark brown almond eyes and exquisite smile were particularly attractive, but I maintained a cool demeanor until Louie initiated the conversation.

"Who is Bill?"

"A cousin through marriage. He's my Aunt Annie's nephew from Rhode Island."

"He can't get serious with you if he's a relative."

"I told you, he's a cousin through marriage. Who says he's serious about me?"

"Are you interested in him?"

"I like him very much except he's so good at math I feel intimidated. If he finds out how ignorant I am in that subject I'd feel awful. He also knows exactly when to stand or kneel at Mass. He's perfect in everything. I don't live up to those standards."

"My parents and family are going to be with my sister Faye at Women's Medical College for Thanksgiving. Do you want to come to Trenton? I'll take you to eat at the Roman Hall?"

"Okay."

Louie often took me to that landmark for special occasion dinners. It seemed half the *Capital City* went there.

When Thanksgiving Day came, I spent the morning and early afternoon with my parents, then drove to Trenton about 4:30 p.m. The Roman Hall Restaurant on Butler Street was one block from Louie's house on Hamilton Avenue, so we walked to it. I excused myself and went to the ladies' room. While there, I saw a "well-intentioned" acquaintance who couldn't wait to tell me that when I was on my worldly venture, Louie had dated a local artist named Peggy. I feigned disinterest, but the resulting feeling of jealousy was disconcerting. What if he leaves me for her? How would I feel? After all these years, life would not be the same without him. This game must end, and winner takes all.

The dinner was traditional, but it took on a special quality because I was with my handsome doctor. After the meal, we returned to Louie's classic, cream-colored Georgian-style house with grey trim. The site used to be *Mrs. Young's Maternity Hospital.* It specialized in maternity cases; for that reason, there were many small, single rooms in the house, ideal for the expectant mothers. Now the building was empty. It felt strange not being among his parents and siblings who lived there. Another sister, a physician, married a doctor the previous year and lived elsewhere.

Louie and I sat in the parlor in dim light. He stared at me but didn't say a word. He took me in his arms and kissed me gently.

Why couldn't I feel this way with the young men who were much more attentive to me than he? I understand he will never cater to me like Jamie or Xavier and others. He would probably consider it a sign of weakness. I know he would always be faithful and devoted and actions mean more than words. Who knows? It's chemistry, I guess, and I won't fight it any longer.

Louie pulled away. Reaching in his pocket, he extracted a small, navy blue velvet jewel box.

"Here! You want to get married. Take it!" He extended the diminutive square object toward me.

No! This cannot be another abrupt proposal! I feel the same frustration as before welling up, but I don't want another protracted separation.

Curious to see the contents, I slowly lifted the lid where a glistening light emanated from a beautiful solitaire diamond ring. It was exactly what I wanted but never mentioned to him. I knew he had given a lot of thought in selecting it. This was his ultimate silent, romantic gesture.

I did not respond verbally to this final, non-proposal proposal. I slipped the ring on my finger and Louie flashed his signature dazzling smile.

THE JACKET

Louie and I were honeymooning near Bern, Switzerland, in July 1965, standing at the base of the towering peaks of the Jungfrau Mountain. As we gazed up at its spire-like snow-capped peak, I thought:

I am 27 years old. It took me nine years to arrive here. At our wedding, my cousin Cathy congratulated me saying, "You are lucky. He gave you his name."

Louie and I are wed.

I am fine with the one I was born with, but society thinks differently. Now I am a married woman and this towering landmark makes me feel like Sisyphus. How many times I'd made progress pushing the rock of my relationship with Louie upward, only to have it crash. I wonder how many young couples go to the altar after having experienced multiple ups and downs? Now it will be different! We are married, and everything will be smooth as the chalk-white crests of the Jungfrau.

A cable car would soon swoop down to take us to the summit, where I anticipated the awe-inspiring view of the three mountain peaks: the Jungfrau, Eiger and the Monch. My two prior visits convinced me of that. I remembered vividly the scenic splendor of azure lakes, rushing waterfalls and rolling crystal glaciers of the region.

"I'll go buy the tickets, Gilda. You wait here and hold my jacket; it's getting warm."

I took the linen garment that wrapped the man I loved. It retained his faint essence, the same scent that intoxicated me while we danced at our wedding to the sound of *More*. Clutching it, I closed my eyes and thought of our special day.

I was influenced to have our wedding reception at the Barclay Hotel in the City of Brotherly Love. I had planned the wedding in the spirit of the 1959 film, *The Young Philadelphians*, in which Paul Newman and his bride had their nuptials at that upscale landmark. Its Crystal Room provided the perfect setting.

In the movie, the bride and groom were to sail off on the *Mauritania* for their honeymoon. Instead, my groom and I chose to return on the "Maiden Voyage" of the luxury-liner, the *Raffaello*. We explored England, France, Italy and Switzerland for six wondrous weeks. What bliss!

Yes, Louie and I were lucky! Everything went as planned, from the beautiful religious ceremony at the Basilica of Saints Peter and Paul to the sparkling Crystal Room in the Barclay. I never wanted the typical Italian-style wedding in a hall with hot roast pork sandwiches and pitchers of beer on the tables and stacks of cookies dotted with colorful confetti and Jordan almonds. Our orchestra, with the sweet sound of violins, replaced the typical loud band at most receptions. One must admit, however, those raucous celebrations in the halls were great fun, but ours was elegant.

Louie's voice calling in the distance startled me from my daydream. I was back in Switzerland on a brilliant, July day.

"Gilda, I got the tickets." He smiled, waving them in the air as he strode near.

Still clinging to the jacket cradled in my arms, an overwhelming feeling of joy welled within me. This jacket belongs to him and now I belong to him as well, as we ascend this glistening mountain together!

CHAPTER TEN

UNSETTLED DOWN

CONSTRUCTION

My honeymoon with Louie ended and we returned to Trenton in mid July 1965. We were to stay at my in-laws' home until our apartment was ready in Morrisville, a small town directly south of Trenton, across the Delaware River in Pennsylvania.

Living for a few weeks with Louie's folks was a pleasant experience. I felt at ease with them and the Chambersburg section of Trenton, with its sizeable Italian American population. Louie and I would stroll the streets around the Immaculate Conception and Saint Joachim's Churches and shop at local Italian delis. We'd pass rows of pristine clapboard houses where women swept the square of pavement in front, while men tended the miniscule gardens in the back, bursting with tomato, pepper and *zucchine* plants. Bouquets of fresh parsley and basil scented the warm air. These were uprooted Italians who maintained prize fig trees and shared the bounty with family and neighbors.

"In the winter, you know who has a fig tree because it will be covered by a bucket or burlap and were bent over to protect it from the cold," Louie said.

The succulent aroma of bread baking at the *Colonial, Barbero* and *Italian Peoples* Bakeries saturated the streets. Landolfi's pastry shop showcased fresh cannoli, *sfogliatelle* and other tempting confections. We'd stop at the *Panorama Musicale* for an espresso or Italian lemon ice and chat with one of the owners, Signora Concetta. We would speak Italian; she, in her Sicilian dialect of days past and I, in my limited Florentine variety. We had no difficulty understanding each other and she always expressed herself wearing a benevolent smile.

I loved watching the old timers, who would gather outside her shop to indulge in the ancient hand game of *Morra*, where, like the Roman soldiers of old, two players would call a number and flash out their fingers for odds or evens. It was fascinating to observe their digits move with such speed. The language and customs of the Old World seemed to be fossilized there, from the arrival of the first Italian immigrants in the late 1800s. Contemporary Italy was becoming more modernized. To me, this ethnic Chambersburg area was charming and welcoming.

My sisters used to tease me: "What is it about Trenton you love so much? Philadelphia is certainly more cosmopolitan."

They were right, but the close-knit Italian community in Trenton felt homey to me.

I often joked with the locals.

"Trenton is like a community of incest. Almost everyone is related to someone. If you are not blood relatives, you know each other from public or Catholic school." They readily agreed. But that was not the case for me in sprawling Philadelphia. The Italians here were drawn together in the Burg and I was swept along.

During those summer evenings, Louie would drive me aimlessly through the streets of the Burg. It was a romantic experience for me and I believe it also was for him, although he never expressed it verbally.

And so, I soon realized I would have to abandon girlish romantic notions with Louie. He had married me and that stood as sufficient proof of his feelings. Verbalizing them was not necessary to him.

Uttering words of love would probably make him feel less manly. After all, he is the first-born son of five children, the primogenitor, and now the boss of his own family of one—me. That's how it is, and he will not change.

I appreciated the adage, "Actions speak louder than words," but I would have liked to hear my man say, just once, some of the lines actors recited to their lady loves in the movies.

I used to tease Louie, saying that I would write a book titled "Italian Lovers and Other Myths." As expected, he did not break a smile.

"It doesn't cost anything to say something romantic. After all, the best things in life are free." Again, silence.

THE TRENTONIAN

New Jersey APR 1 1966

Mrs. Gilda Rorro Cited Outstanding Young Woman

Mrs. Gilda Rorro, 295 Hamilton Ave., has been cited as an "Outstanding Young Woman of America." The wife of Dr. Louis M. Rorro, she is included in the annual biographical compilation of "Outstanding Young Women of America," a publication headed by Mrs. Lyndon B. Johnson and Mrs. Margaret Chase Smith.

The book honors women for their outstanding achievements and contributions to the community. Mrs. Rorro's selection, recommended by her alma mater Beaver College, was based on her professional service on educational television.

Mrs. Rorro appears on WFIL-TV's University of the Air series, "Say It in Spanish" and on WHYY-TV's "Hablando Español."

A graduate of Beaver College, the Philadelphia native studied and taught at the University of Mexico. While in that country she was in a number of documentary films and in three full-length motion pictures that were shown in Mexico.

Mrs. Rorro, a member of the National and International Associations of University Women, represented that group on a world tour, meeting heads of various countries and officials of the organization.

MRS. GILDA RORRO

Receiving a national award.

To me, Louie's reticence was a form of romance. He was methodical and determined to provide all the appropriate necessities in our state of matrimony. He obtained a lovely apartment at the Canal House in Morrisville, prior to our honeymoon. Upon its completion in the month of August, we occupied a first-floor unit located on the New Hope Canal.

At times, we'd shop in Philadelphia for household appliances and on several occasions, Louie bought me pieces of jewelry. One day, a multi-tiered pearl bracelet in a store window caught my attention. It had a removable diamond clasp that could be worn as a pin. I tried it on several times at Barsky's Jewelry Store on Delancy Street. It cost 450 dollars, a high price.

Two weeks later, my spouse spontaneously confessed, "I had thought of purchasing that bracelet and surprising you, but decided it was not practical. We could buy a vacuum cleaner and a lot of other items we need for that amount."

I agreed with him verbally, but in my heart, I would have cherished that bracelet more than any Hoover. I contented myself by his sheer thought of the purchase.

The days and months passed as we both adjusted to married life. Louie had an easier time than I because his family lived in the house where his medical practice was located. He interacted with his parents and siblings daily. My parents were always working in Philadelphia and my sisters lived at a distance in New York and Florida. I had not culti-vated lady friends in my new area and I was alone most of the day in our apartment across the river.

September arrived, and the second year of my Spanish television series began. I was initially informed that my program may only be aired one semester, but I kept receiving fan mail about "the sweet voiced Spanish teacher," and my series gained significant popularity. I was the only recipient from Beaver College for the prestigious national award, "Outstanding Young Woman of America."

This year, however, I felt differently from when I started. My prior-ities were changing.

I know I am lucky to have this job, but what I want now is to have a baby. I've longed for one since I was 25, when Cousin Cathy came from New York with her newborn daughter Jennifer, and asked me if I'd like to hold the baby. When I sat in a rocking chair in our house on McMahon Street with the infant in my arms, I looked at the sweet, tiny face: an overwhelming maternal desire to have my own surged through me. I wanted one so badly, but I knew I'd have to find a husband first. Now I am two years older and the time is right.

After 11 months of marriage, in May 1966, I suddenly began to feel sick. I was constantly nauseated and concerned something was seriously wrong.

"I'm going to have you tested," Louie said, not appearing alarmed in the slightest with my unpleasant condition.

Several days later, I was cooking in the kitchen of our apartment, when Louie entered.

"Here! Look at this," he said, passing a sheet of paper into my hand.

It was a medical report and I did not understand the terminology.

"What does it mean?" I asked.

"You're pregnant," he answered in a clinical tone. "Now I need to build a house before the baby arrives."

I was overjoyed with the news and proud that the baby's father would want to provide a fitting domicile for our little one. Surely the baby would not know if it were in a new house, a drawer or a shoe box, but Louie knew, and it was important to him.

I had to inform the good people at the Philadelphia Department of Education of my condition. Traveling to Philadelphia was difficult because my "morning sickness" lasted 24-hours a day. When they heard the news, they were congratulatory but displeased.

"You can't appear on television pregnant; it is indecent," I was told. "But, we have another great offer for you. We want you to produce a series for *University of the Air: English*. We will provide you with the scripts. All you need do is present them. We are now able to videotape the series. You can perform the lessons in the studio here in advance, before your pregnancy becomes obvious."

I declined, and stood before my small group of benefactors praying I would not have to throw up on the well-polished hardwood floor. They were insistent, but so was I. I couldn't fathom teaching before cameras feeling so awful.

We need a substitute for your Spanish program until you can return," they conceded.

"My sister can do it. She was also a Spanish major during her one-year at Beaver College."

Although Vicki had not finished her college education, they gave her the temporary job because she matriculated to the University of Pennsylvania. Mom and Dad were glad Vicki would have to leave New York City and move back home with them.

At last, I could concentrate on the building of our new home. Dr. Angelo Guglielmelli, my mother-in-law's brother, boasted a thriving medical practice in Chambersburg as well as a hefty, black, handlebar moustache. One of his patients, Joseph DeLotto, was a builder and had a double plot of land for sale in nearby Hamilton. Louie purchased the nearly one-acre property. He researched architectural journals and found the perfect house for us—a two-story, red brick dwelling with a sloping lot. It would be ideal for our residence, his office space and park-

Our first house.

ing lot. I was so excited about having the new home for our expanding family. I was content.

Louie hired a local builder, Christopher Walsh. Every day we would go and watch him and his crew construct our dream castle from its foundation, to framing and sheet rocking. It was thrilling to see every nail hammered and phone jack installed from June to February 1967. As finished rooms took shape, we would go to clean them to make everything ready before the baby arrived.

The house was completed on the 11th of February 1967, and we moved in eagerly. Initially, I thought I might miss our apartment on the canal, as I loved living near the water, but our new home offered a spaciousness that the apartment could not duplicate. The living room, dining room combination was 42 feet long. The kitchen appliances were a soft turquoise; it was a real dream come true.

11 days later, at 7 p.m., on 20 February, I started to feel sharp cramps. They grew progressively worse by the hour.

So, this is what's it's like? I never felt anything like these jabbing pains. I hope the ordeal ends quickly.

"You are in labor. Let's go to the hospital," Louie said with satisfaction.

He drove in the snow to the Osteopathic Hospital in Burlington, Pennsylvania, where the obstetrician had been his classmate. I was immediately examined and received unwelcomed news.

"You are not nearly ready to deliver. We're sending you home until the contractions are closer together."

They have no idea how painful the spasms are, or they would not send me home. This is really rough.

As we rode home, I winced with every sharp pain. The rest of the night was agonizing as I tried to record the contractions. Sleeping was not possible.

The next day brought more of the same unrelenting pain, but I had to bear it. The phone rang at 5 p.m. Louie answered.

"Dr. Folmer is on the phone. He wants to know if you can tutor his daughter, Marilyn, with her Spanish homework. He said it will only take a few minutes."

Oh, Lord! How can he ask such a thing now? I'm miserable.

"Sure, tell them to come over now," I said.

What else can I do? Dr. Folmer is one of Louie's best friends and our dentist. I must consent, even under these circumstances, because he is going to come anyway.

When the pair arrived, the dentist said, "Gilda, this is so nice of you. We hope it isn't too inconvenient with your labor and all."

"No, of course not. I'll do my best."

Marilyn was a freshman in high school and a lovely young lady, but I was understandably not happy to see her as the contractions were increasingly frequent and bordering on unbearable.

"Let's go into the kitchen, Marilyn; the light is brighter there."

"This is the chapter," she said, opening her text book. "The title is *El violín metido.*"

"The title means 'The Violin Placed.' The reference to the violin being put in its case," I said. "Please excuse me for a second."

I exited the kitchen and entered the adjacent living room doubling over. As soon as the pain subsided, I returned to the tutoring task. This scenario was repeated several times until I could stand it no longer.

"Excuse me, Marilyn but the lesson is over. I must go back to the hospital."

The duo left, and Louie and I rushed to our car and drove off. This time, the hospital staff put me on a bed in a private section of the maternity ward. It was 8 p.m. The raging pain persisted throughout the night. Moans from other women filled the air, but I was determined to bear my suffering in silence, biting my hand in order not to scream.

At 7:30 a.m., after 36 grueling hours, the doctor arrived and exclaimed I was ready for delivery. I was wheeled into a bright room where the father-to-be and several of his physician pals were preparing for the big moment. As the men chatted away, an unknown doctor sat next to me and took my hand.

"I feel for you in your pain," he said. "I'll make you comfortable."

That act of compassion meant so much. Mercifully, he was the anesthesiologist and administered an injection which brought welcome relief.

A hearty cry pierced the air.

"It's a boy! Congratulations, Lou; you did it!"

"He's beautiful! He looks just like me," the obstetrician joked.

Our son Michael was named after his paternal grandfather, according to Italian custom. My father-in-law had passed away when I was four months pregnant, therefore, the name acquired added significance for the family. The newborn was held up for me to see. He ceased crying and his eyes were wide as he scanned the panorama of his new environment.

"How do you feel now?" the doctor asked, grinning.

"Charlton Heston is starring in the movie, *The Agony and the Ecstasy*. I feel like the actor. The last 36 hours were agonizing, but now I am ecstatic."

"Congratulations again on having a boy. There are 18 baby girls in the nursery and he's the only male. The little ladies will be happy."

"As a patriot, I am proud he was born on 22 February, George Washington's birthday." After three days in the hospital, it was time to take

Baby Michael.

our son home. It continued to snow, but despite the chill, we stopped at Louie's mother's house where she and my sisters-in-law exited to greet the new family member. I felt proud.

What a relief! I did my duty. I produced a male child the first time. Now I can relax with the next one.

When we left them, we were excited to show the baby his beautiful home. As we entered the front door, I held Michael up to display his new surroundings.

"Look! This is where you live." Michael passed gas, followed by another biological contribution.

"That's not how you are supposed to respond," I gently scolded.

Back at our house we put the little bundle into a bassinette in our bedroom. I sat on the edge of the bed and peered at his perfect, beautiful body. Louie stood next to me.

"You can confess now. You always wanted a son, didn't you?"

"No. I told you it didn't matter."

"That's what you said, but you really didn't mean it. You wanted a boy. Admit it."

"How many times did I have to tell you it didn't matter to me?"

Louie was convincing, and I loved him for it. All my life I resented the gender preference among Italians and others for that matter. Louie's stock escalated a notch on making that declaration. My dream of having a family and living in a beautiful house had come true.

MY MARY

December is a special month for me, mostly because of what happened when I was 30 years old. On a frigid day on 11 December 1968, I made a large pot of *pasta vazul* (dialect for pasta e fagiole). Louie, my mother and sisters-in-law devoured it. My in-laws came to help me decorate the house for Christmas. Until that time, I always adorned the place myself, but that day was different, since I was nine months pregnant with Michael's sibling. My physician estimated the infant would arrive on New Year's Day and was hoping to be featured in the *Trenton Times* paper for delivering the first baby of the year.

While everyone was trimming the tree, I started to hang a garland of tinsel on the living room mirror. "Ooh, Ooh!" I exclaimed on experiencing a sharp, bearing pain.

I shouldn't have eaten all those beans.

I resumed decorating when another agonizing jolt struck. Again, I blamed the piercing jabs on the soup. A few minutes and another aching episode later, I wondered.

Could it be happening now? The child isn't due for at least two more weeks.

The idea of a New Year's delivery with the fuss and gifts was abandoned. I announced to all present, "It is time for me to go to the hospital!"

We rushed to *Saint Francis* Hospital in Trenton, where I was placed immediately on a gurney in the hallway. The pains were becoming increasingly strong. The obstetrician examined me and gave me an unwelcome prediction.

"This baby won't be born until 11 o'clock tonight."

Much to my dismay, it was only 3 p.m. How could I endure eight more hours of this arduous labor? I managed a feeble smile at the doctor, trying to be brave, summoning my high tolerance for pain.

Well, I'll just have to grin and bear it, but this is worse than the first time.

After a few minutes, however, I could no longer endure the excruciating pain.

"Louie, tell the physician I can't stand this," I moaned.

My husband knew I typically suffered in silence, so he rushed to locate Dr. Fiorello. To my relief, the two returned quickly.

"Take her to the delivery room at once, the doctor directed. She's giving birth right now."

They wheeled me in, where, upon a quick examination, the doctor blurted, "It's a frank breech; prepare the anesthesia!"

Oh, no, not a breech! I recently saw the movie "Hawaii," in which the husband was trying to deliver their baby. When he told his wife, "It's a breech," a gasp filled the theater. Be prepared: now you'll know what that gasp was all about.

An otherworldly pain consumed me as the baby arrived. There was no customary cry. I wanted desperately to hear a sound from the newborn, but instead, a mask for nitrous oxide gas was placed over my face. I struggled to have it removed so I could know what was happening, but I succumbed. When I awakened in my hospital room, I instinctively searched for my newborn, but there was no infant.

"You have a daughter," the doctor declared gravely. "She had a difficult birth because she entered the world as a *frank breech*, that is, bottom first, upside down. She was not breathing, so we are giving her oxygen and she is in an incubator. You are lucky she only weighs six pounds."

"When can I see her?" I murmured.

"Soon."

I was disappointed I was not conscious to hold her. Why "knock me out" right after she was born?

Baby Mary.

My in-laws entered the room and congratulated me on having a daughter.

"She'll be your right arm, Gilda."

I was happy to hear something positive after that ordeal, when a voice from behind interrupted our conversation.

"Would you like to see your child?"

I looked at the tiny, white bundle the nurse handed me. A crop of dark, thick, hair surrounded a diminutive face. No sooner did I look, the woman in her white uniform took her from me, insisting I had to rest. I did not contradict her. Later, I found out she and the doctor were displeased that I was the only mother in the maternity section who wanted to nurse. Both attempted to talk me out of it, but I persisted.

I fell asleep until 8 p.m. I called for the nurse, who told me in an irritated tone that I would have to wait because I was the only mother who wanted to breastfeed.

"We have to prepare all the other infants before we can bring in yours," she said curtly.

"All right, I'll wait," I answered with determination.

Wait I did. At 8:45 p.m. I still did not have my daughter. I got out of bed and peered into the long, silent corridor, but still no baby.

Is she all right? Could something have gone wrong?

I rang again for the nurse and was finally successful. With my infant in my arms, I gently lay the little one on the bed in front of me. This was a magical moment. She was encased in swaddling , which the Italians call "*la fascia.*" In fact, she looked like an ice-cream cone, wrapped from her feet to her vanilla face with strawberry cheeks, topped with a mound of dark chocolate hair.

"We're going to call you Mary, after my mother, your aunt and your cousin," I said.

To me, you'll be Mariuccia (Little Mary)."

My mother-in-law's name was Filomena. It has a mellifluous sound in Italian, but everyone in Trenton called her "Fanny," and although I too had an Aunt Fanny, Louie and I would not impose it on a child of our own. "Gilda" was uncommon enough. I wanted to call her Mary Faye, after both mothers, but Louie preferred Mary Celeste.

Little Mary stared at me with suspicious eyes.

"How will this person treat me?" she seemed to think, wearing a quizzical expression.

"I will be very kind and gentle," I said aloud and began unraveling the stiff white linen, revealing the correct number of delicate fingers and toes. Thoughts of my mother's best friend raced through my mind.

Did Rosemary in Mays Landing have a magical moment like this with her baby girl? Did she marvel at the diaphanous skin covering miniature digits? Did she coo at her precious infant before it was taken from her? Oh, horror! I must not think of that, now.

My baby's inquisitive gaze followed my every move as though she comprehended my role in her life. I cradled her in my arms.

Mary, it may still be a man's world, but I am going to give you every opportunity to realize your fullest potential.

The nurse appeared saying she must take the newborn to her bassinette, where the other neonates were already asleep. It seemed my initial memories of Mary were of separation: first, because she wasn't breathing, and then because of my choice in feeding her.

No matter, she will soon be mine full-time.

When I nursed her, she became instantly mine. It was a joy for me to know I could nourish my baby as nature intended.

The next morning, Louie came to take his expanding family home. Before we were to leave the hospital, a pediatrician wanted to examine our offspring. We watched as he tested her reflexes, the fragile arms and legs flailing at his touch.

"Her responses are excellent. There's no problem with the initial lack of oxygen," he said, smiling with confidence.

He chose the right profession because he seems genuinely happy to work with little ones.

On leaving the hospital, Louie carefully drove us home. When we walked up the front steps of our house, my parents opened the door, where our 22-month-old son Michael stood looking at us and the new addition with wide eyes.

Mary was placed in our bedroom in a frilly bassinette strewn with white ruffles. Little Michael kept peering into its contents with curiosity and wonder. But *Mariuccia* was fast asleep, oblivious to all the activity.

"Gilly, get some anisette," my Dad said.

He poured the Italian liquor into the delicate, crystal glasses. Holding his glass high, he exclaimed, "Let's make a toast to the most beautiful baby girl we've ever seen!"

Mary may not have been the first New Year's baby, but she was our family's most cherished Christmas gift.

THE END OF INNOCENCE

All was right with my world after marriage and I settled in a routine revolving exclusively around home and family. Both children were all we could ask for: beautiful, bright and benevolent little beings. That was how my life was and would undoubtedly continue.

Living in the suburbs, I had everything the media told women they needed and wanted; but something was lacking. I recalled the protagonist in Gustav Flaubert's novel, *Madame Bovary*, in which boredom set into Emma's life with her country doctor husband. Unlike Emma, I did not know why I felt unfulfilled and I tried valiantly to conceal those feelings from others.

My mother was very astute. She had the annoying knack of reading and verbalizing my thoughts and was seldom mistaken. "What's the matter with you, Gilly? You have everything a woman could wish for, a home, car and children, yet you don't seem completely happy."

"That's not true! I am happy. Why do you say such things?"

Mom was right. I felt guilty about my unsettled feelings, but I defiantly denied her insight. It was ironic she, of all people, considered the ideal life for me was to stay at home. She was seldom present when we were children.

When I was working full time as a television teacher, the travel from Trenton by train and the Elevated Line to the studio, and the fast-paced schedule were at times very tedious. I preferred to stay in Trenton and watch our home being erected. Now, as my daily routine consisted predominantly of self-renewing domesticity, I lacked the excitement and vibrancy my past employment and travel experiences afforded.

Personal interaction was another part of life I missed. While making the beds or sorting laundry, I would recall meeting Pennsylvania Governor William Scranton at the WFIL Studio on City Line Avenue. He observed my *University of the Air* program one morning before he was to be interviewed. I confided to him that I had dated his nephew, William Scranton, while he had been a student at Princeton University. We both laughed at that.

My companions now were two toddlers and two neighbors. The neighbors were lovely young women, hard-working, responsible and caring. We'd meet over our fences and discuss what detergent was most effective, or what we would prepare for frequent family visits or whose children were potty trained first. I won the prize in the toilet category because while my three-year-old Michael kept resisting being diaper free, Mary became impatient and abandoning her 'nappy' taught herself the process at only one and one-half years. That significant act made me the talk of the neighborhood, a distinction I held until the next childhood coming-of-age event.

Like Proust, many times a taste, texture, or an object would make me recall extraordinary moments in the past. Changing sheets, I would experience all sorts of flashbacks. Jamie's claim of never allowing me to hold a mop was constant. How often I dreamed of how my life would have been as a woman of privilege in Caracas.

One morning, while straightening out our red velvet bedspread, I recalled my world trip and first port of call. Dore Silverman, a journalist I befriended at the *Acapulco Film Festival,* had told me to contact him if I ever went to London. The day Vicki and I arrived in that giant metropolis, I called Dore. He had us to his home to dinner, and after dessert, handed me a wonderful gift.

"Here, I want you to have these two tickets."

"What are they for, Dore?"

"They will take you to the hottest spectacle in town. You'll be in for a big surprise with the seating."

The tickets read: *The Bolshoi Ballet Production of Romeo and Juliette.*

"People have been sleeping on the sidewalk for days with the hope of obtaining entrance. It's completely sold out," Dore informed.

"Aren't you going too?"

"No. I was given another assignment. I want you to enjoy it."

The next evening my sister and I were anxious to enter the theater. We could never have prepared for what we were about to experience.

"Tickets, please," said an usher.

I handed ours over. When he saw the location, we were told to wait a minute. A tuxedoed escort came to greet us and led us along a red carpet through a corridor of secluded, private boxes. He unlocked a door that opened into a posh area of gilded, red velvet chairs. We were the sole occupants. As we sat, it seemed all eyes looked upward, at us.

"Do you notice everybody's staring, Vicki?"

"Yeah, they must think we are young VIPs or something."

I examined the luxurious quarters from side to side and realized why we were being ogled. We occupied the Press Box situated next to that of Her Majesty the Queen of England. Although the Royal Box was vacant, it was exhilarating viewing it at such close range.

The burgundy velvet and gold-trimmed curtain of Covent Garden opened to the strains of Prokofiev's magnificent score. The flawless performance of the ballerina earned her 22 minutes of curtain calls from an adoring audience. Dore was right; we were astounded. It was magical.

My children's voices snapped me back to reality.

"Mommy, can Billy and David stay for lunch? Their mother wants to watch soap operas."

"Sure, they can."

Such a mundane occurrence would fling me back into my day-dreaming. One day, as I filled my family's water glasses, another London memory was triggered. That time was when Dore took Vicki and me to a cocktail reception at the German Embassy. We wore our basic black dresses and joined a group of young, handsome people.

A young staffer approached and introduced himself as Mr. Jung-fleish. He was quite charming and praised my ten-word vocabulary in German. As we spoke, I noticed an elderly gentleman standing alone near us, looking isolated and uncomfortable.

"Do you see that poor man all by himself? I feel sorry. Let's go over and cheer him up," I said.

"Poor man: You feel sorry, did you say?" Mr. Jungfleish laughed. "He is definitely not poor. That solitary figure is John Paul Getty."

At that moment, the German Ambassador strode up to the billion-aire, embraced him and whisked him away.

Those and other memories haunted me time and again. When I'd see Ernest Borgnine on TV, I would think of when I had met him and his wife, Kati Jurado, at the *Acapulco film Festival.* Louie had joined my mother in making any talk of my movie experience a taboo subject, but I still had my memories.

"Never mention you modeled or were in the movies in Mexico," my husband would insist. "You can talk about teaching on television because that was decent."

I realized those fleeting days of glamour and excitement had long ended. At my parents' urging, I burned those bridges. I had done everything I was told a good Italian woman should do. I resisted all temptation. I never succumbed to the vanities of the world. I married into a good family and settled down to reap my reward. But why couldn't I have done more? Why couldn't I have taught English on television while rearing my children? Why was it always all or nothing? And now, why was I not in a perpetual state of bliss? Surely it was shameful not to be. Mom's critical pronouncements attested to that.

I feel as though there was another me who lived a different life. Part of me mourns that woman. Here, I have no identity other than being the wife of a physician. Our Lady of Sorrows Parish sends contribution envelopes to Mrs. Louis M. Rorro. I don't even have a first name or middle initial any more. My status in the community is wholly dependent on that of my husband— for good or bad. Like Ralph Ellison's "The Invisible Man," I too feel invisible, without an identity of my own. Why educate a woman and deny her full self-expression?

I was grateful for my family, however, and took pride in caring for it as best I could.

We were fortunate in many ways. Louie's medical practice flourished. After we were married four years he had become physician to the Mercer County Community College and both Chris-Craft and Congoleum Industries. He worked a 12-hour day and continued to make nightly house calls.

A chronically ill patient always seemed to call at 3 a.m. I used to get out of bed on snowy, January mornings to clear our car of the white powder and ice.

"Why are you doing this?" I'd complain. "They are not even going to pay you. You're killing yourself."

"It's all right. Don't worry."

"Well, I care!" I retorted in a bad mood caused by sleep interruption and frustration. At the same time, I was proud my husband would do so much for a sick patient, even if he were not financially compensated.

At 6 a.m., in 1972, seven years after we were married, Louie woke me.

"Get me two aspirin and a glass of water."

What! Louie take aspirin? He has never had an aspirin in his life. Something must be wrong.

"What's the matter? Are you ill?"

"I have pain in my chest. I think it is indigestion."

"Then why not take Tums?"

"Just get the aspirin."

After I did as he instructed, we waited fifteen minutes for the pills to take effect.

"How are you?"

"No different."

"I'm going to call your brother John and sister Mary (the other doctors in the family)."

Louie told me not to, but I realized I must not listen to him. His devoted siblings came quickly, and my spouse was whisked to the hospital where he was diagnosed with a massive myocardial infarction.

"What is a myocardial infarction?" I asked the cardiologist. He explained the condition was a heart attack caused by plaque buildup in the arteries which impedes blood flow to the heart.

"This is very grave; prepare yourself," the doctor said, putting his arm on my shoulder. "You know what you must do."

"Yes. Take it one day at a time," I said, weakly.

"No! Take it one-half day at a time. He may live for three months. If he does survive that amount of time, it is possible he may live longer. We don't know."

This cannot be! It took so long for us to marry. We constructed a home and family and now it is all crumbling. Louie has so much to live for. It's not fair for him or for us. I refuse to let it happen. Oh God, please don't let it happen.

The news was like a lightning bolt. At that moment, I thought of the passage in 1 Corinthians 13:11: ". . . When I was a child . . . I thought as a child . . . but when I became a man, I put away childish things . . ."

My age of innocence had ended abruptly. I would have to assume most responsibilities to keep our family unit together. There would be no more frivolous romantic ideas or daydreaming. I had to put away all childish things.

The 23rd Psalm also ran through my head. "The Lord is my shepherd . . . He leads me beside the still waters . . . He comforts me."

How thankful I was to have had Bible readings each day in public elementary school and at Mrs. Mac Crea's. They took on new significance now and would help me overcome the genuine panic I felt. I thought of other women who had received devastating news and how they had become stronger and prevailed. I would do no less. God would guide my path.

Louie stayed in the hospital for a week. He would require a long convalescence. When he returned home, I was attentive to his every breath and movement, always on edge that something untoward might happen. One afternoon, I went to look in on him as he napped. Mary was there sleeping, her four-year-old body across the headboard where her Daddy lay, the two almost resembling a crucifix.

Dear God, please don't take this child's father away. Let her grow to know him.

"Don't tell anyone about my condition. I want it to be a secret," Louie insisted.

"Why? You haven't done anything wrong, but I'll do as you say."

As a doctor, he doesn't want to be perceived as physically vulnerable. I must respect his wishes.

My prayers were answered once my husband survived the three prescribed months. He survived beyond the initial expectations, but significant changes in our lives began to unfold.

"You cannot return to Saint Francis Hospital because your condition makes you a liability," an administrator informed. Louie was understandably upset by the news but accepted it. He also had to relinquish all his other positions.

COMING OF AGE

The time arrived for me to acquire new responsibilities. In addition to caring for a home and family, I assumed a full-time job as an *English as a Second Language* (ESL) teacher in the Hamilton Township Board of Education. To qualify for a possible salary increase, I attended graduate school at night at Trenton State College (now The College of New Jersey). After being home with my children and husband for 11 years, I was taking on all the responsibilities of a "liberated female." It was 1976, the *Women's Movement* was in full swing and, at 38, I would become someone who had it all. I was glad that I would no longer hear my ophthalmologist, Dr. Pica, ask me this frequent, irksome question.

"What are you doing these days?"

"I'm taking care of my family."

"Yes. I know that, but what else are you doing?"

While I did not like his questioning, I knew he had higher expectations for me. Being at home with its relentless chores, a husband and two children is a full-time job under the best of circumstances, if one tackles it conscientiously. People think if a woman is not formally employed, she's taking it easy. That is not true. I had adjusted to be a homemaker and felt a bit of trepidation at the prospect of embarking on a new, full-time job and graduate school.

At Trenton State College, I hope I can keep up with the young students. I haven't been in a classroom since 1962.

A sister-in-law gave me this directive. "Rorros only get A's."

I'll take that challenge toward my Master's Degree. Teaching ESL is another matter. There are virtually no materials developed for that subject. I'm going to have to start from scratch and develop my own. Traveling to seven schools daily will not be easy either! Oh well, as they say in Italian, Speriamo (Let's hope).

Regarding my first preoccupation, I found returning to college far easier than expected. I was mature: my experiences in the classroom, on TV and in the home, served me well. I grasped the subject matter in educational research, curriculum development and multicultural education easily.

Returning to teaching a controversial subject was a challenge, though. From the first day, in each school I entered, most male building principals greeted me with this scenario: "Come in! Sit down! I want you to know I don't believe in your program. My father (or grandfather) came from Sicily and couldn't speak a word of English. He went to work, reared a family and did just fine. Nobody helped him; he had to learn English and he did."

I never knew so many building principals had Sicilian relatives.

At this, I went into my spiel about how education in the past did not encourage youngsters to graduate from high school. One could enter the workforce and the middle class because non-skilled jobs abounded.

Of course, I am swaying no one. That makes me more determined to have the administration and faculty realize the importance of my program. It may take a while, but they'll understand the need for helping non-English-speaking youngsters from kindergarten to high school.

My pupils were a delight, yet many of their classroom teachers were frustrated at having to accept them.

"I am not a dumping ground for these kids," some would say. "It's hard enough teaching English speakers. What am I supposed to do?"

I assured the instructors that we would work together to meet the students' needs and that having children from other countries in their classroom would be an advantage for everyone. Some were not convinced, but in time, I was certain they would be.

The ESL project was like the *Tower of Babel*. Eighteen different language groups were represented. I had youngsters whose linguistic proficiency varied from knowing no English to ability in intermediate and advanced levels. They came from disparate countries such as Korea, Indonesia, China, Egypt, Germany, India, Pakistan, Poland, Russia, Greece, Italy, Mexico and Venezuela. Communicating with them reminded me of my trip around the world, and it was exhilarating. My world language skills improved as my pupils learned English and I found the experience mentally and emotionally stimulating.

I had developed a curriculum that was based extensively on what I utilized for teaching Spanish on television. I translated those materials into English, and they proved to be extremely useful. On TV, there was no personal feedback. Working with ESL students demonstrated how effective my television lessons were, and I felt gratified. Concomitantly, I learned much more about their cultures and each day was an enriching experience for everyone.

Soon I learned a holistic approach to language learning was more important than just English language acquisition. The psycho-social aspect of teaching students separated from their homeland was a critical component to consider. Many were taunted by their counterparts and some were painfully shy, all were homesick.

"I look at the moon every night and hope my friends in Seoul are watching it too. That way, I am not lonely," a Korean girl confided.

Three Indonesian teenage siblings were living alone in a small apartment.

"We do odd jobs after school to support ourselves. It's hard but we manage."

A Chinese family, named Tse, had arrived from Hong Kong. Four of the children were in my program. They were shy, avoided eye contact and seldom spoke in class. Their father had opened his own Cantonese style restaurant in Hamilton Township.

"Miss Rorro, do you like Chinese food?"

"I love it and so does my family. We often go to Chinatown in Philadelphia and New York."

"Then come to our restaurant and try my Dad's Cantonese cooking."

That night I mentioned it to Louie, who was eager to sample a new Asian establishment. I was happy he had adjusted well to my schedule and enjoyed hearing about my experiences each evening at dinner. He accepted our invitation to the new eatery.

"Did you like our food, Miss Rorro?" the owner asked, as steaming mounds of *lo mein* and sweet and sour chicken were brought to the table.

"It was some of the best we've ever eaten, and we've sampled a lot."

The gentleman confided he had worked 364 days a year in a restaurant in Hong Kong, a practice he carried on in his new establishment in New Jersey. On his one day off a year, at Christmas, the father delivered a whole Chinese roast turkey and dumplings to our home as a token of respect. His children became less shy and made significant progress in English. I admired how hard working and united the family was. All the siblings and even the mother worked together in the restaurant. Theirs was a recipe for success.

My students were a beautiful addition to the school district, and I was determined to showcase that fact as many negative attitudes toward "otherness" still lingered. I held parent-student evening meetings and recruited fathers, mothers and caregivers to help design display cases in each school building showing artifacts, fashion and cuisine of their countries.

I organized multicultural assembly programs to introduce native dress, folk dancing and music to the general school population. With mini grants from the New Jersey Department of Education (DOE), my pupils developed a bi-yearly, multicultural publication titled *Hamilton Mosaics.* That activity brought forth a flurry of artistic and linguistic creativity which won praise from New Jersey Governor Brendon Byrne and the Office of Bilingual Education at the New Jersey Department of Education.

"Miss Rorro, nobody used to like to have us in class, but now we are famous. Our teachers want us to be in a lot of programs and talk about our first country," a middle school girl from India said.

My formerly shy youngsters were blossoming and so was I. Our ESL Program attracted statewide attention and became a model for districts throughout New Jersey. After one year I was asked to serve on the DOE's Bilingual Advisory Committee.

After teaching two and one-half years, I was designated *the Hamilton Township Teacher of the Year.* Simultaneously, I became a finalist for *The State of New Jersey Teacher of the Year.* The district's publicity person had missed the application deadline for the state award and submitted my forms to the DOE 12 days late. The first-place winner had already been selected, but I was honored to be a finalist.

This recognition means a great deal to me because I respect educators and appreciate their hard work and dedication.

Another ESL teacher, Ronnie Sternberg, was hired to teach in the elementary grades. She was of considerable help to me. I continued to expand the program and after being in the district for three years, the board decided to provide me traditional classrooms in all my assigned buildings. My work load had been reduced from seven to six schools a day since the second year. Now I would travel to four. No longer did I have to instruct in a ticket booth, boiler room, supply closet or on a stage. Two fine teachers working toward their ESL certification were assigned to me for mentoring and instructing: Judy Kolpack and Carmine Nalbone. It was wonderful!

The largesse of the board of education was beyond my expectations and I was appreciative, except something disturbing was happening. Gone was the overwhelming challenge. The program was running smoothly, and I was experiencing a normal teaching routine that most educators would relish, but not I. I started to feel restless and needed new peaks to conquer. The prospect was unsettling. The answer was soon to come.

Cav. Gilda Battaglia Rorro Baldassari, Ed.D.

III

Middle Age and Beyond

CHAPTER ELEVEN

CIVIL RIGHTS: OFFICE OF EQUAL EDUCATIONAL OPPORTUNITY

THE APPLICATION

The time had come. I was mentally ready to leave the Hamilton School District.

It's 1978. I've worked for the Hamilton Township Board of Education for the past three years where I enjoyed overcoming all odds—especially hearing building principals insist their grandfathers came from Sicily and learned to speak English without help from anyone. Now they welcome the ESL Program. I've been awarded for my teaching. I'm popular here, but I'm getting antsy. I need to embark on something new, but what? Where?

The opportunity arrived while I was still a member of the New Jersey Bilingual Education Advisory Committee. At our monthly meeting in the DOE in December, an ESL supervisor from the Perth Amboy School district gave me intriguing news.

"Congratulations, Gilda, on being a finalist for the New Jersey Teacher of the Year. It seems like you just started in Hamilton Township. That is a huge professional leap for you."

"Thanks, Fred, but to tell the truth, I need to do something else now, but what and where?"

"Do you have a specific position you would like in education?"

"Yes. I would like to become the Director of Bilingual Education for the State of New Jersey."

"It's not possible now because there are no available positions in that office. However, there is a vacancy in the Office of Equal Educational Opportunity. You know, OEEO; they work in civil rights. They're advertising for a National Origin Coordinator."

"What's that?"

"It's a highly experienced educator who conducts professional development workshops on meeting the needs of multicultural/multilingual student populations. It's right up your alley. When today's meeting ends, go and get an application."

At the conclusion of the session, I rushed to the second-floor office of the OEEO to get the form. Once there, I heard a woman call my name.

"Gilda, what are you doing here?"

I turned toward the voice which emanated behind me. It was Pam Leggio, an affable young woman I had met at the Advisory Committee. She had always shown an interest in my work, especially my ESL student publication, *Hamilton Mosaics,* and had attended several programs I organized in Hamilton Township.

"Fred H. told me you have an opening for a National Origin Coordinator. I'd like to submit my resume, Pam."

"Sure. Let me get an application for you. You're in luck because the interviews start next week."

I left the building on West State Street with the document in hand, elated at the prospect of embarking on a new path, wherever it would lead.

On arriving home, I completed the form. It emphasized knowledge of languages by asking for fluency and working knowledge of multiple idioms. I held teaching certificates in French and Spanish and spoke Italian fairly well and added a working knowledge of Russian to the list.

I taught myself "tourist Russian" (useful words and phrases) in 1976, because Louie was planning to attend a medical tour to the Soviet Union. My psychiatrist brother-in-law, JB, Gloria, 18-year-old niece, Mary, and I were to accompany him.

I was determined to be able to express myself in Russian as we prepared for the trip. I had visited the Hamilton Township Public Library and took out a kit titled *Listen and Learn Russian.* It consisted of a phrase manual, corresponding LP's and practice work sheets. I devoured the contents and became proficient, on an elementary level, in reading, writing the Cyrillic alphabet and speaking."

"What are you doing?" Louie would ask as I conjugated verbs in the new script. "You can't learn that language. Don't waste your time. Cook lunch."

My spouse's doubting made me more determined than ever. Undaunted, I had continued to practice daily for ten weeks.

I'll never forget the moment we all arrived at the Moscow Airport. An agent announced in English that our tour group would be housed in two different hotels.

"Eez-vy ee-NyEE-tyeh (Excuse me). *Yah khah-Choo bweet s mah-Yah sy-est-RAH, pah-ZHAH-loo-stah!* (I'd like to be with my sister, please), I mentioned to the young, female agent.

"TAK (Okay). *Khuh-rah-SHAW* (Good)."

Upon hearing our brief, albeit significant conversation, Louie looked on, dumbfounded.

"What did you say to her? What did she answer?" he asked, with a look of utter stupefaction.

"I just told her I wanted to be with my sister and she said all right."

"And she understood you?"

"We'll all be in the same hotel, so relax. You'll see."

I chuckled to myself as I watched Louie run over to Gloria, JB and Mary. I smiled as I heard him blurt out what had transpired and that I managed to keep our little group together. Louie and the other passengers on the trip became dependent on my limited, basic knowledge of Russian.

"Gilda, ask where the bathroom is."

"Hey, Gilda, order some ice. The water here is warm."

"Gilda, tell the sales woman that this costs too much."

Most of all, a little of the language went a long way in opening doors to the Russian people. When we arrived at the hotel that evening, staff was lined up along the hall in attention as we searched for our rooms. They bore dour, suspicious expressions. I looked directly at each one and said, *"DAWB-rih y VYEH-chehr.* (Good Evening)."

On hearing a simple salutation in Russian, their body language was transformed. Gone were the stern looks. Each smiled back, amicably. I was profoundly grateful for the Hamilton Township Library's "Listen and Learn Russian" kit.

Going to the Soviet Union opened another window to the world for me. Now I want more. I have enjoyed working in Hamilton Township, but I would love the job at the Department of Education. I pray that I get it.

HIGHWAY TO A NEW OPPORTUNITY

I submitted the application to the New Jersey Department of Education (DOE) in 1980 for the position of National Origin Coordinator. Three days later, Pam called to notify me I would be interviewed the next day at 3:30 p.m. in the OEEO office. The news was exciting. I did not say a word to anyone about the possibility of my leaving the Hamilton Township School District, not even to Louie.

The following morning, as I was reviewing grammatical paradigms with my ESL students, my mind kept jumping to the interview.

What will they ask? How shall I respond?

When the bell rang signaling the end of the school day, I rushed to my car and sped off to West State Street. Tingling with excitement, I entered the OEEO office at the DOE. I was told to be seated and wait for my interviewer. *Who could it be?*

"Gilda, come in," said a familiar voice.

It was that of Diego Castellanos, the host of the TV program "Puerto Rican Panorama," broadcast on Sunday mornings on WHYY. I'd met Dr. Castellanos and often watched his show. I was glad he was conducting the session. When I entered the conference room, there was another gentleman in attendance.

"Gilda, this is Dr. Paul, a colleague in the DOE. You checked on your application that you speak French, Italian. and Spanish fluently and have a working knowledge of Russian. Dr. Paul will interview you in all four languages; he has a doctorate in linguistics."

Good! I can handle the first three, but my Russian is limited. I've just got to wing it.

Dr. Paul started in French with the usual salutation.

"Comment allez-vous aujourd'hui?" (How are you today?).

I responded politely to that and a few other francophone inquiries with no difficulty.

He then switched to Italian. *"Perchè vuole lavorare qui?"* (Why do you want to work here?).

I rattled several worthy reasons and was relieved to know I was more fluent in that language than he. Dr. Paul never questioned me in my strongest idiom, Spanish. Instead, he asked me how I learned some Russian. I told him about the kit from the library. He listened attentively and then questioned.

"Vih ee Maw-zheh-tyeh skah-Zahty mnyeh . . ." (Can you tell me...?)

I decided to impress him with several expressions I'd memorized directly from a page in the "Listen and Learn Russian" manual.

"Shtaw vih DYEH-lah-yeh-tyeh syeh-VAW-dnyah VYEH-cheh-rum?" (What are you doing tonight?)

"Vih mnyeh AW-cheny NRAH-vy ee-tyes." (I like you very much).

"Yah vahs lyoob-Lyoo." (I love you).

I was hoping he wouldn't process it all in sequence and it was obvious to me the befuddled expression on his face indicated that he had not.

"She knows more Russian than I do, Diego," Dr. Paul exclaimed. Diego was satisfied and nodded his head approvingly. I was greatly relieved that my strategy had worked.

The remainder of the interview went well, and I left the session feeling confident.

I really want this job.

The next afternoon, Pam called with wonderful news.

"Congratulations! Welcome to the OEEO! Be ready to start here next month on January third, 1980."

YEAH! I am so happy to tackle something new. Now I can tell Louie, my parents and everyone.

When I informed the Superintendent's Office at the Hamilton Township Board of Education that I intended to leave, the Chief School Officer convened a meeting. They did not want me to go and offered me an increase in salary of five-thousand dollars. It didn't sway me. The time had come, and I accepted the position as a National Origin Co-ordinator in the Office of Equal Educational Opportunity. Of course, I would miss my colleagues and especially the students whom I had grown to love. We had become a little family and it would be wrenching to say goodbye to them.

To prepare for my new responsibilities, Pam sent me literature on the OEEO. Its mission was "to ensure non-discrimination in all New Jersey K-12 schools based on race, gender or national origin."

This was indeed a new focus and I knew I would grow in under-standing of civil rights issues, which I always found intriguing and very emotionally charged.

In preparation for my first day on the job, Dr. Castellanos called me on the telephone.

"Gilda, you are to report to the library in the East Orange School District tomorrow morning at 8:30, where you will make a one-hour presentation on meeting the needs of LEP (Limited English Proficient) Russian students. The Jewish Family Services is sponsoring Jewish youngsters from the Soviet Union to relocate with their families in New Jersey. Several school districts have requested this assistance."

"Fine," I said, trying to hide my jubilation, and began to prepare the presentation. Then I thought of driving there.

Where exactly is East Orange? Do I take the Turnpike? Louie always drove us on that highway. Oh, well. I better learn fast.

I looked at the map and located it. I had to take both the New Jersey Turnpike and the Garden State Parkway. For the past three and one-half years I hadn't left my comfort zone of driving to Hamilton Township schools. This would be different, but after all, I wanted a challenge.

The night before my presentation, I rehearsed in bed all that I would say in the allotted hour. I had to make a good impression. But it was how to get there that dominated my thoughts. Finding the school after exiting the Garden State Parkway might be complicated to say the least, but I was determined to do it.

"I'll leave the house by 7, to arrive on time," I said to Louie.

"Go even earlier, in case you get lost," he replied.

"I won't get lost," I answered with confidence.

The next morning, I was so excited. I left our home at 6:45, and sped off to the Turnpike.

Traveling this early, there won't be much traffic.

Wrong! Soon I learned that I should have avoided the "Trucks Only" lanes, where convoys of the metal monsters covered any signage indicating where I was going. To my horror, I found myself sandwiched between two behemoth tractor trailers going at breakneck speed.

If the one in front suddenly slows down, the one in back will crumple me.

"Hey, lady," an irate driver shouted out from the open window of his cab, as he drove by. "Keep movin'; you're too damn slow."

I wanted to obey the 65-mile speed limit, so I kept a good distance from the trailer in front, but the huge white cab in the rear kept tailgating. My heart pounded wildly. The loud horn from his vehicle blared, compounding my distress. There was no recourse except to keep going, and going fast. I purposely avoided glancing at the speedometer. Finally, a sign was visible, indicating "The Amboys."

Oh my God! Where are the Amboys? I may wind up in New York! Hamilton Township was easy. It was close to home and there was no stress commuting to six schools a day. Right now, I miss it. Look what I've gotten myself into.

My heart continued to race at the thought of getting lost in a sea of mean motorists showing no mercy. I managed to keep the steering wheel steady even in my heightened state of anxiety. There was no choice.

I arrived at the East Orange High School Library in a blur, emotionally drained. It was exactly 8:28 a.m.

"Oh, there you are!" Diego smiled as I entered the room.

I thought you might get here a little sooner to set up. How was your drive?"

"Just fine," I said nonchalantly. "No problem at all."

So, I've started this job with a lie. How many more will I be telling?

I managed to unpack all my handout materials and props and begin the presentation in two minutes. Thankfully, all went well. My fit of nerves was controlled. The teachers were receptive, the administration happy and Diego was pleased. I felt a great sense of relief.

On the way home, I was more at ease taking the Garden State Parkway, although cars zoomed past, oblivious to the designated speed limit. I joined the pack and felt emboldened until I approached a toll booth.

Opening the car window, I dropped the dime for the 35-cent fare. It fell between the driver's seat and the door, so I got out of the car to look for it, claxons clanging loudly behind.

"Lady, come on. Get movin!" Moving was the rule on those roads. There was no tolerance for slowing down.

The pounding in my chest accelerated with every beep of their rude horns. My palm felt sweaty as I knelt to retrieve the small coin. The blaring noise from the increasingly long line in back caused me to drop the dime again, generating more rage from the rear.

Somehow, I paid the toll and found my way home, drained of all emotion and energy.

"How was your first day?" Louie asked when I entered the house at 5 p.m., anticipating some degree of difficulty I would surely have with the commute without him at the wheel. "Did you have any trouble getting there?"

"It was fine," I answered smugly, "and driving there was a breeze."

The less he knows about it the better.

ANOTHER MOUNTAIN

The OEEO was divided into three divisions: Affirmative Action, School Desegregation and National Origin. The three units provided professional development to all New Jersey school staff and the community to ensure compliance with equity requirements.

The three offices were in separate rooms. This resulted in limited interaction among employees during the workday. We mainly socialized at lunch to exchange information about what was occurring in our respective fields.

"Are you a feminist, Gilda?" a female member of the Affirmative Action team asked over our tuna wraps at a South Broad Street diner.

"No; if you mean, do I get on a soap box, burn my bra and bash white men? I'm married to one and have a son with him. Three of my cousins were killed in World War II defending this country."

"Then, what are your thoughts on women's rights?" she asked calmly, ignoring my previous comments.

"I have a daughter and when she was born, I said to myself that although this may be a man's world I would do everything I could to have her reach her fullest potential."

"Bingo! You are a feminist, but you don't know it. Feminism isn't about bra burning or resenting male privilege. It's about ensuring equal rights for women in every aspect of society."

Her words impressed me greatly. I had much to learn, hailing from an atypical Italian American family where my sisters and I were given extraordinary liberties like going to college and traveling around the world, yet having to adhere to rigid moral restrictions. I appreciated working in a forward-thinking, progressive office that shared my views and aspirations.

"What are you focusing on in the Affirmative Action division?" I asked.

"Title IX drives what we do. It provides much latitude for equality of the sexes. We work closely with each district's Affirmative Action Officer, our counterpart for non-discrimination in the workplace. This year we will concentrate on ensuring that girls be given the same access to all sports that are available to boys."

"If a girl wants to play football on the boys' team, she should be given the chance?"

"Yes. She should have the chance."

I was doubtful about that, but respected her opinion.

Another member of the Affirmative Action group commented.

"We focus on encouraging female students to take more math and science courses. Girls are often told they can't do as well as boys in those fields and have been taught learned helplessness over the ages. They can do just as well as males if given the opportunity."

I liked her thinking and recalled my first day at Beaver College when the President told us there was no math requirement because it was accepted by society that women were naturally less capable in math than their male counterparts.

The desegregation component posed a conundrum for me.

Today I learned from the desegregation staff that there are 611 school districts in New Jersey. Home rule is sacrosanct with no one willing to change the status quo by incorporating several small districts into one large, metropolitan area. This is an expensive system to maintain and results in a plethora of segregated school districts. It doesn't make sense. I should advise them to combine Trenton with Hamilton, Lawrenceville and Ewing, like my school district in Germantown. It would be cost effective having only one superintendent and staff, but who would listen? All I can say is America will not be truly great until it unleashes the talent that is in our inner cities. Desegregation could play a large role in making it happen.

One morning I passed that office and noticed maps strewn across the walls and mounted on easels. Poking my head in the door, I asked an African American colleague what was going on.

"Why all those thumb tacks on the maps?"

"They show where the concentration of pupils is in the different schools in the district. Our job is to make sure the youngsters are re-assigned to balance the buildings racially and ethnically."

"Oh," I said. "You are going to bus them all over the district?"

"No! It's not about busing."

"That's good," I answered, though I didn't understand how else it could be achieved.

His unit was concentrating fully on implementing a desegregation plan in the Hillside School District. The office was a buzz of activity. Articles about Hillside's desegregation mandate began appearing in newspapers statewide and were creating quite a stir.

This issue is controversial. I heard that many white and some black parents are already transferring their children to private schools before the desegregation plan is even initiated. There must be a better way of accomplishing what the law demands other than forced reassignment.

National Origin was not puzzling to me at all. My co-workers were like-minded, and they welcomed me to the unit. My responsibility was to "train" teachers on meeting the needs of their culturally diverse, LEP students. My background made me a very effective instructor. I now traveled four days a week to different counties in the state. I gave professional development workshops on how to understand and reduce prejudice toward the burgeoning multicultural student population.

I took my job seriously and wanted to excel. After my first year in the OEEO I enrolled in a doctoral program at Rutgers University in Urban Education and Bilingual/Bicultural Education. The program would address equity issues head on with a strong concentration on school desegregation in New Jersey and the nation.

In Philadelphia, I attended desegregated schools, yet society remained racist. To me, the most important aspect of being in class with students of color was that we could interact on a personal level. We shared a lot of our feelings and perceptions. We often argued and disagreed about our experiences of life in America, but we respected each other.

I never forgot how I felt seeing the squalid sharecropper shacks along Route 1 when Dad drove us to Florida twice a year. From the open windows and doors of the dwellings, one could see the walls lined with newspaper. And those disgusting, rusty, water fountains for "Colored Only," at the rest stops that were offering all the orange juice you could drink. Those grim facilities affected me. If I had been born colored, I would have had to use one of those facilities through no fault of my own. My classmates told me what it was like for them to do just that. I'm proud to work in the OEEO, although not everyone in the DOE recognizes the importance of our office.

"What you people do is nice, but not necessary," an assistant commissioner once said.

He'll come to realize one day that it's more than nice. In Germantown, some of the most gifted kids in my high school were colored. Bill Cosby, for example, was a half-year behind me. I didn't know who he was, but I remember walking past closed auditorium doors with another student while the audience within was howling.

"Who's causing all that laughter?" I asked.

"It's Bill Cosby; he's really funny."

MY HAITIAN PHASE

Every day at the OEEO brought new experiences working with diverse student and teaching populations. Two years had passed with the same hectic, albeit stimulating routine. I was soon to learn that things were going to change. In December 1982, Pam convened a meeting with my National Origin colleagues, two females and one male.

"We need to determine what ethnic group to focus on next year," she informed. "How about the Asians?" one of the women asked. "Fort Lee has a sizeable Japanese community." "A lot of Indians from the sub-continent are gravitating to New Jersey, especially in Edison," another volunteered.

"That's a good idea," our supervisor stated.

I interjected.

"These suggestions are valid and should be addressed, but I think we should concentrate on Haitian youngsters. Every night on TV, we see boat flows of Haitians in rickety vessels fleeing the island to reach these shores, and too many are unsuccessful. I read that a large number are incarcerated in Texas, Miami and other places for coming here illegally. Their children must be traumatized when they arrive. Last night I saw that Haitian students are entering schools in Newark, East Orange, Princeton, Camden and other places."

"Good thought, Gilda," Pam said. "Do you all agree?"

Everyone nodded in approval.

"Who would like to work with Gilda?" No hand was raised.

"Okay, Gilda. It looks like you are in charge of this project. Write a proposal indicating what you plan to do and how you will do it."

Watch what you wish for! Why did you have to open your mouth? Won't you ever learn? You don't know anything about Haiti except it shares part of the island with the Dominican Republic. Remember when we saw President Trujillo taking a stroll in the capital, Santo Domingo, while we were on a cruise in 1958? We were invited on his daughter's yacht, the Angelita. Visiting the Dominican Republic certainly doesn't qualify you for an undertaking like this. I would like to get to know the Haitian people and learn more about why they are fleeing a tropical island to come to gritty cities in New Jersey. It would be very rewarding if I could help the youngsters in some way, but how?

The following day, Pam entered my work space. "Gilda, did you know we have a Haitian expert at the DOE? I'd like you to meet her."

I did not know, but I am anxious to find out who she is.

THE HAITIAN PROJECT

"Fasten your seat belts as we prepare for our landing in Port-au Prince," the captain announced. As we approached the airport, I was excited. It was July 1983 and I had prepared for this moment for nearly a year. Planning began the day after Pam put me in charge of the project.

"Gilda, this is Ms. C. She works in another division here at the DOE and is a member of the *New Jersey/Haiti Partners of the Americas*. She claims it is the largest volunteer agency in the Western Hemisphere," Pam said.

I never knew Haiti was the partner country to the state of New Jersey. It will be good to have a resource person in the DOE who could be of assistance.

Ms. C. was a lovely, tall, middle-aged woman with a thick crop of salt and pepper hair. She extended her hand and welcomed me warmly.

"You will love Haiti. It's a beautiful island and the people are wonderful. If you join our Washington-based organization, we will see that you go there."

"It sounds exciting. I will join because it may help me develop this project," I exclaimed.

To prepare me for the assignment, Pam found information regarding a six-week Haitian Creole immersion program at Indiana University in Bloomington. It was sponsored by the world-renown linguist and Creole specialist, Dr. Albert Valdman of Yale University. I applied and was accepted immediately into the comprehensive course consisting of six full weeks of immersion instruction in Haitian Creole. Louie supported my going and was willing to watch our 16 and 17-year-old children in my absence. With his help, my Haitian adventure had begun.

I learned to speak Haitian Creole quickly. Knowing French was an advantage, although the grammatical structure was different. After six weeks, I was sufficiently fluent to embark on a trip to Haiti, where I was to establish a partnership between schools there and in New Jersey.

When the plane descended, it revealed a beautiful, mountainous panorama. Haiti aptly means "Mountainous Land." Unfortunately, much of the landscape has been deforested. The population uses trees for burning wood for heating, washing and cooking. A Haitian proverb came to mind: "*Dye mon, gen mon*" (Beyond the mountains, more mountains). The saying refers more to the challenges of life in Haiti than to its topography.

On landing at the Port-au-Prince Airport, I was greeted by Dr. B, the middle-aged president of the *New Jersey/Haiti Partners of the Americas*. Dr. B. had been assigned as my mentor throughout the two-week visit.

"*Bonjour (Good-day)*, Madame Rorro. *Bienvenue en Haiti*," (Welcome to Haiti), the doctor said in French.

"*Bon jou. Ki jan ou ye?*" (Hello. How are you?), I answered in Creole.

"*Ou pale kreyol!*" (You speak Creole.), he announced incredulously.

We drove away from the airport and turned onto a bustling street with shabbily-constructed stores and dwellings. An acrid odor of carbon filled the air. Barefooted women were hawking live chickens or carrying baskets full of mangoes on their heads. Several men were pushing carts overloaded with rubber automobile tires. Children were also at work, selling what they could. All appeared weary under the blazing, mid-day rays of the tropical sun.

I smiled when a "*Tap Tap*" appeared. I had seen pictures of the *camionette*, or jitney. It was as I expected, a vehicle brushed with a rainbow of vibrant, primary colors. Each "*Tap Tap*" bore a religious name or prophetic statement, such as, "Love Thy Neighbor." The one nearing us stated *Dieu est juste*, (God is Just). An imagined image of God was painted across the hood. People needed divine intervention as the small bus was bursting with humanity from the inside out. Bags and suitcases perched precariously on the hood, bouncing wildly each time a *Tap-Tap* hit a pothole.

Suddenly, I stopped smiling as my eyes fixated on a man who ran into the gutter, fell prostrate into the sludge and hastily lapped water trickling from a broken pipe.

That man was desperate for a drink. How unsanitary! Are there no public water fountains in this city?

Dr. B. noticed my facial shock in his peripheral vision and wanted to divert my attention.

"You speak Creole. You are not American. You are one of us."

I heard that phrase often when I was in Mexico. The intention was to be flattering.

"Do you want to see the real Haiti, or do you prefer I take you where all the tourists go?"

"Show me all you can. I want to know how people live here."

"First, I'll escort you to your hotel where you must rest from this heat. Tomorrow, at 8:30 a.m., we'll visit a maternity hospital."

I had wanted to go to a school, but as a medical doctor, my escort was more interested in health care. That was fine with me, and I looked forward to accompanying him wherever he led.

When we arrived at the hotel, I called Louie.

"So, you got there all right. How do you like it?"

"Nothing I read or heard could prepare me for this experience. I feel fortunate to be here; otherwise, I could not tackle this project."

My compact, hotel room had an unadorned bed and bureau. The space was made lively by brightly colored native artwork strung along the walls. Pictures of children riding mules and women selling fruits and vegetables brightened the space considerably.

The next morning, I awoke to glorious bird calls from beyond my window. Never had I heard such a profusion of sounds of nature. I lay in bed for several minutes, relishing their wild songs.

After a breakfast of robust Haitian coffee and toast, Dr. B. appeared on time.

"Bon jou," he said. *"Ou byn jodia?"* (Are you well today?) By addressing me in Creole, he erased the need for our previous formality.

"M la-a," (I'm fine) I answered, anxious to begin the new day.

"The hospital is close by," he continued in his vernacular.

We moved through a tangle of crowded streets, some paved and some not, the majority in serious need of repair. There were signs of warning in French: *Cette Route Tue e Blesse* (This Road Kills and Maims).

"The hospital is close by."

We moved through the streets in silence as I absorbed this new world. My physician driver noticed my every reaction.

"I need to go to the bank," Dr. B. mentioned as he pulled up to a local one and parked in front.

"And I need to cash some traveler's cheques," I said.

"Not now. I am in a hurry. Just wait for me in the car. I'll only be a minute. Keep your window closed."

Close the window? It must be 95 degrees on this July morning. He must be kidding.

As I manually cranked the window up, a brown, bony hand jutted through the narrow, upper open space. Startled, I gently continued to close the glass partition, so the hand would retreat. Suddenly, the auto was surrounded by women. Some cradled babies; all extended hands, begging for a coin.

"Madame! Madame!" they cried in mild supplication.

I had no cash or change other than traveler's cheques. Even if I had some money, it would never be sufficient to satisfy the growing throng. The car rocked from the intense movements of their pleading bodies. I noticed several of the women wore their dresses inside out. The original exterior had long since faded from the flimsy cloth.

"*Madame! Madame!*" they continued to chant in a cacophonous chorus, their voices rising in frustration and need.

What can I do? I have nothing to give them. It seems like Dr. B. has been in the bank for an eternity. I can't bear to look at these poor souls. I'll keep my eyes fixed on the floor. I'm too embarrassed to open the window to tell them I have no money. Besides, they may not believe me.

"*Madame! Madame!*" they shouted ever more loudly, in growing frustration, causing me to feel desperately uneasy. Dr. B. witnessed the ruckus as he exited the building. He yelled something at the women which made them disperse. I told him what had happened.

"Don't worry. I understand," he said, unfazed. Such women were a familiar sight to him. "Let's go now to the *Hôpital de la Maternité* (Maternity Hospital). It was a relief to head off.

When we arrived at the building, the physician pulled into a parking space in front of the hospital. We entered. He told me once again to wait for him as he went to look for a staff member.

I remained in the stark, grey atrium where a five-foot portrait of Michelle Duvalier, the beautiful young wife of President "Baby Doc" Duvalier, hung. She was an elegant mulatto, richly bedecked in a stunning Dior gown and jewels. As I gazed at the oversized, dazzling gems, sounds of women moaning penetrated the corridors. Dr. B. re-appeared, accompanied by a nurse.

"*Vini isit!*" (Come here), she beckoned.

Leading us down a hall with deliberate steps, she knew exactly where we were to go. The disquieting sound of moaning accompanied us through the dim corridor.

"So many women seem to be in pain," I exclaimed, as the nurse conducted us forward at a rapid pace.

"Yes. They are in labor or are post-operative."

Do you give them anything for the discomfort?"

"No. In Haiti, we believe in natural child birth."

What she means is that they do not administer anesthesia to these suffering mothers-to-be.

"What about the post-operative patients?"

She offered no answer. I decided not to inquire further as we entered the pediatric ward. An overpowering smell of urine assaulted our nostrils, causing my head to reel in the humid, sun-filled room lined with rows of tiny, rusty iron beds. The sight of the emaciated bodies lying on saturated, yellowed mattresses was appalling. Flies nested on the eyes and lips of the pathetic, skeletal beings, too weak to repel the pests. Several of the malnourished toddlers screeched with their extended abdomens protruding in sharp contrast to their gaunt frames.

"Why do these little ones have sparse, orange-colored hair?"

"That is a sign of Kwashiorkor Disease, resulting from malnutrition. It is commonly seen here."

Their piercing cries and the fetid odor were unbearable. Thankfully, there was a balcony. I stepped onto it, anxious for a breath of air. Dr. B. followed me in silence, his eyes continuing to observe my every reaction.

He brought me here purposely knowing I would be horrified. At home, we see starving infants in Africa on television and conduct huge fundraisers to save them. It is an outrage to witness the same human tragedy only 600 miles from Miami. But what does Dr. B. want from me, surely more than shock value? Why reveal so much suffering without a reason?

I re-entered the infirmary where the nurse was ministering to an infant. "Don't the children here get fed?"

"We do what we can; food is expensive."

What upsets me most is the portrait of the First Lady with her opulent jewels, amidst so much adversity. Surely, she witnessed the misery in these halls filled with her impoverished citizens?

"There is one more section of the hospital to see," said the nurse.

We entered an operating room in which a Belgian surgeon was performing a procedure. His nurse turned to me.

"Hello! I'm from Wisconsin. I hear you come from New Jersey," the nurse exclaimed.

"Yes. You work here?"

"I belong to a Presbyterian church and the congregation pays for my room and board, so I may serve God in Haiti, among the poor."

"You don't get a salary?"

"No. It is a blessing for me to work here."

It is difficult to believe this young woman would spend her youth in a place like this for no pay and be grateful for the chance. She inspires me with her faith and selflessness. It's reassuring to know there are still good people in the world.

Dr. B. turned to me. "When you return to New Jersey, tell people what you witnessed here."

"Rest assured I will."

"We will go to a church now."

Dr. B. drove to *Citté Soleil* for our next stop.

"Sun City" is an appropriate name for this place," I said.

"Wait for me in the car a few minutes. I'm going to look for the Mother Superior."

I dreaded waiting in the vehicle for Dr. B., based on my earlier experience, but there was no choice. He left, and I took in the surroundings. His car was parked in front of an area where plots of earth, approximately six feet by six feet, were cordoned with ropes. A middle-aged woman had been sleeping on the ground. She was wearing a straight, faded skirt which hung below her knees. It bore the faint outline of once vibrant-colored flowers. She awoke and sat up. Her torso was completely bare. She registered no embarrassment as she noticed my observing her. Several men were sleeping in other designated areas, also lying directly on the dirt.

And to think, my sisters and I had the audacity to complain to Dad about our living conditions on McMahon Street. I wanted a big and beautiful house to entertain my friends. Seeing this unfortunate woman with no shelter, no bed and scant clothing, fills me with tremendous guilt. Thus far, everything here makes me ashamed of ever having been critical about anything.

"Hello!" a friendly voice called, breaking my reverie. It was that of the Mother Superior, her white habit flowing as she approached with quick steps, accompanied by Dr. B.

"Welcome to 'Citté Soleil.' Come; I'll take you to the Mother House."

It was a relief to be in the company of such a cheerful person after all I had witnessed that morning. She led us into her office, a stark 12 x 12-foot room with six wooden chairs and a desk behind which a foot-long, hand-carved mahogany crucifix hung. A picture of His Holiness, Pope John Paul II, was on another wall. Everything was spotlessly clean, in sharp contrast to the areas outdoors. It was obvious the Mother Superior was proud of her surroundings. A small table held a coffee pot and white demitasse cups.

"Isn't Haitian coffee wonderful?" she exclaimed, as we enjoyed the black brew. "What do you think of my office?" she asked, with pride.

"It's lovely. You must have been happy moving in when you arrived in Haiti."

"No, no! It took several years before this became a reality. When we first arrived in *Citté Soleil*, my sisters and I had no shelter at all. We slept on our *nats* (banana straw mats), on the ground."

I am shocked. Outside the window, I see flies in dense whirls like a black tornado, swooping along stalks of freshly-cut sugar cane. I never saw such darting swarms before. The horse flies in Mays Landing were a nuisance. There was fly paper in the kitchen of my grandparents' bar and grill, but the insects here are a formidable army. What do they do to a person who sleeps here in the open?

"Let's go outside now. There are some visiting nuns from Canada I want you to meet." The dynamic religious hurried us out into the brilliant sunshine where five young novices were sitting.

"This is Sister Leslie."

"Enchantée." (Charmed).

"Enchantée," I answered. "Mother Superior just told us about the circumstances surrounding her arrival. I feel ashamed because I could never do what you do. In fact, I feel unworthy of being in your company."

"Never say that, please. You are here because God has a plan for you as he does for us. What you do is just as important in His eyes."

The voice of the young, delicately featured Sister Leslie was sincere, compassionate and encouraging. She gave me comfort. I felt more secure in what I could accomplish in this land of contrasts and contradictions. Just then, a man approached saying that the shipment of milk and rolls had arrived for the children.

"We must go into the school now and feed the youngsters their breakfast. They each get a glass of milk laced with brown sugar and a roll. For many, it will be their only meal today," the Mother Superior remarked.

A bell rang, and several students came out of the building next to the convent and ran toward the nun. They smiled happily in her nurturing company.

After the incredible experiences of the morning, Dr. B. drove me back to my hotel where I ate lunch and needed a siesta.

Yes, the poverty in Haiti is indescribable, yet there is much to appreciate here. While riding with Dr. B., I noticed young boys and girls caring for blind and handicapped elders. People carried themselves with grace and pride, no doubt for being descendants of the first successful revolt by enslaved people in the western hemisphere. Children fortunate to attend school walk together, wearing well starched and pressed uniforms. Everyone seems respectful; many are cheerful regardless of their circumstances. The young are often supervised by observant adult eyes, as I experienced in my youth.

The extreme suffering, countered by acts of goodness, affects me greatly. Visiting this country leaves an indelible impression. I must find a way to contribute here and to the Haitians in New Jersey.

Haiti touch kè m. (Haiti touches my heart).

STRICTLY OFF THE RECORD

Returning from Haiti, I continued working on meeting the needs of that student population. I convened a statewide committee to devel-

On my graduation day as an Education Doctor with my husband, Louie.

op "A Handbook for Teachers of Haitian Students in New Jersey." The document was lauded throughout the state as a valuable tool for understanding this unique population.

Three years after my last trip to Haiti, I was recommended by the DOE to become the President of the Washington, D.C.-based, *New Jersey/Haiti Partners of the Americas* volunteer organization. I held that position for seven years. Interacting with the membership assisted me during my doctoral studies. At Rutgers University, the title of my dissertation was: *Academic Achievement of Haitian Limited English-Speaking Students in New Jersey Public High Schools.*

We established a Haitian center in the OEEO, with educational materials teachers could borrow. No matter what contribution I made, it would never compare to the unstinting dedication of the Catholic nuns, Protestant missionaries and medical workers I had met in Haiti. They would always remain a source of extraordinary inspiration.

Receiving the Doctorate in Education in 1988 in "The Science of Language" served me well because two weeks after I graduated, Barbara B. was promoted to an Assistant Commissioner position. Several staff had applied for the vacant directorship in our office. Assistant Commissioner Dr. Walter M. told me he would like me to assume the role of Acting Director of the OEEO. The permanent position had been originally earmarked for an African American or Hispanic candidate. I understood because at the time, there were few positions occupied by members of those minority groups. Dr. M. made the announcement at a general staff meeting.

"Dr. Rorro will be the Acting Director of the Office of Equal Educational Opportunity, until we find someone to fill the permanent position. I am of the opinion the final position should be given preferably to an African American woman."

He had mentioned to me in advance his intention of saying that, but now it is official. I could have disagreed with the criterion, but I am aware of the current political climate. When I have additional experience, other jobs may open for me where race or gender will not be an issue.

When I became a Spanish teacher, I never dreamed I would someday be the leader for School Desegregation, Affirmative Action and National Origin compliance statewide. I always accept a challenge, but this is the biggest in my career thus far.

"Do you want to comment, Gilda?" Dr. M. asked, in front of my peers.

"Yes. Although I will be in the "Acting" status, I would like to involve the office in the development of guidelines for education that is multicultural."

"Good, you've got it," he said, and exited the room.

It was obvious several of the African American staff were disappointed with my temporary appointment. Four had applied for the post. I knew that the Civil Rights Office had been headed by two women of color: Nida Thomas and Dr. Barbara B. Two of my African American male colleagues who had also sought the job called me aside.

"Gilda, congratulations! You can do more to further our cause as a white woman than we may be able to do."

"Are you sure of that?"

"Yes, we are. Having you as an advocate may be an advantage in desegregating school districts."

They convinced me. I had learned much from them, but until then I was not deeply involved with the highly controversial issue of desegregating schools. I would have to assume a great responsibility as fast as possible.

During my tenure, I learned that the Hillside School district became de-facto re-segregated two years after it integrated its schools. This was due to the "white flight" (white parents sending their children to private schools).

While there are stellar examples of successfully desegregated school districts such as Montclair, the mention of student reassignment is always controversial. I must find an option to assist districts to find a solution in a meaningful, non-disruptive way. But how?

That year, 1988, I was invited to serve on the National Committee for School Desegregation, in Washington, DC. All members were grappling with the same dilemma regarding the Supreme Court's mandate for racial balance. We learned there was federal money available to qualifying districts that would write grants to implement "Magnet Schools."

"What is a Magnet School?" I asked, naively, my first day on the committee.

"It is assigning a theme to a school to voluntarily attract interested students," the Chair answered. "For example, a school could be designated a "Magnet" for advanced teaching of science and mathematics, or performing arts. Students are selected by lottery and the result is a racially and ethnically balanced environment."

That makes sense. I'm going to share this with my colleagues in New Jersey.

When I returned, I discussed the option with Dr. M. He advised I should concentrate on the multicultural education project because I was only the Acting Director. Any new initiative would be at the discretion of a permanent leader. Hearing this, I did as he suggested.

I convened a statewide committee for the latter consisting of educators, parents, students and community members and, after a year and

Appearing on television as Director of OEEO.

a-half, I authored "GEM" (Guidelines for Education that Is Multicultural). One would think such a document would be readily approved and implemented. That was not the case in 1990.

"Diversity and Multiculturalism are controversial," Commissioner of Education, Dr. John Ellis, declared to me on his last day as Commissioner in New Jersey. "But I will put my signature on GEM."

When he signed, I breathed a sigh of relief because it had taken five administrations before the GEM document was finally signed by a Commissioner of Education.

One afternoon in 1990, Dr. M. gave me a surprise phone call.

"Gilda, I want you to apply for the permanent position of Director of the OEEO."

"But you told me I couldn't."

"Now I'm telling you to."

"Are you sure?" I asked skeptically.

"Yes, apply."

I did and was interviewed within the week. The session went beautifully. It consisted of my recounting the gains the office had made in advancing equity and GEM. I also mentioned the advantages of the Magnet School concept.

Finally, I was the successful candidate and I could explore new options for school desegregation. I realized that a bigger platform would be more effective in disseminating information on desegregation. This resulted in multiple appearances on local and national television and in five articles in *The New York Times*.

This is a great opportunity. Desegregation is the most challenging unit for me. People have died for Civil Rights. I must prove to majority and minority populations that racial balance can be achieved without turmoil, but this will not be easy.

My Italian grandparents always advised me to go to church when faced with a dilemma.

"Pray to *Il Signore* (God) or *La Madonna* (Blessed Mother)," they'd insist.

I went willingly to Our Lady of Sorrows Church in my parish and prayed with eyes fixed on the cross for divine intervention.

Dear Lord, take my hand and guide me in this job. Please help me to be effective.

Little did I know how much I would be tested as Director. I found out on the first day after Barbara B. paid me a visit.

"Gilda, the Hamilton Township School District needs to develop and implement a new desegregation plan. Meet with the superintendent and staff ASAP."

Oh, no! I was a popular teacher when I left the Hamilton Township Board of Education. Now I will return wearing a different hat. Desegregating the school system will not be welcomed.

An appointment was made. All parties were cordial, albeit strained, as everyone was aware of the potential commotion this could stir throughout the community.

A day after the Hamilton meeting, a young reporter from the *Times of Trenton* newspaper called my office, requesting an interview regarding the desegregation mandate for Hamilton Township. A half-hour prior to her arrival, I received a phone call from a concerned parent who spoke at length of the hardship of having her child transferred to a school other than that in her neighborhood. I listened attentively and attempted to assuage her concerns when she finally made a revealing statement.

"The bottom line is: the races aren't meant to be together. It's unfortunate, but that's the way it is."

Just then, my secretary signaled that the reporter arrived. The journalist informed me she was new to the job and this was an important story. The interview focused on the law requiring desegregation and districts in the state that were implementing plans. She also asked why *white flight* often occurred and what parents in Hamilton Township had to say about the new directive.

I told her that shortly before she arrived I had a conversation with a student's mother.

"This is strictly off the record," I said, thinking that statement would be honored. "The mother confessed the real reason she did not want her daughter reassigned was because she did not want her to be seated next to a black child."

That weekend, my family had a lovely house guest from Margherita di Savoia, Anna Rita, the daughter of Cellina and Gennaro. On Sunday, we drove to Our Lady of Lourdes Cemetery to pay respect to deceased family members. Anna Rita sat in the front seat of the car where my son was driving. I was in the back as I read *The Times*. My heart sank.

"Department of Education Official claims Hamilton parent does not want her child to sit next to a black child," the text began.

"Oh, no! You may as well dig my grave here, because this article will kill me," I blurted.

I was extremely upset throughout the day and dreaded what I would have to face in the OEEO and the community. I could not sleep that night in anticipation of the negative reaction that statement was sure to arouse. My fears were justified because the telephone rang continuously the following morning with irate parents and community members.

The headline in the Tuesday edition of the *Times* read in bold letters, *Mayor Seeks Education Official's Resignation.*

Every news article printed regarding the desegregation plan ended with the same damaging sentence about sitting next to a black child. I ceased to defend that it was taken out of context. No one was listening.

The following Sunday, a full-page ad appeared in the same paper featuring a school bus and a caption stating not to 'bus' the children away from home. Several parents called me saying their youngsters were having nightmares about leaving their school and friends.

"My child feels sick now because of what you are doing," a mother exclaimed, angrily.

One evening, I arrived home in an exhausted state and asked Louie and the children to grant me some quiet time. I wanted to look at a mindless TV program and forget the trials of the day. When I turned the television on, it revealed a town meeting at Grice Middle School with the Hamilton Township Superintendent, Mr. Callahan.

"Where is Dr. Rorro?" an irate man called out from the crowd. Is she on vacation at a time like this? Make her come here. We want to talk to her."

I turned the set off, too emotionally drained to respond.

How quickly one can fall from favor. When I left Hamilton, I was a respected, popular teacher. Now I feel like public enemy number one. I can identify with how the superintendents in Selma and Boston felt when riots occurred because of desegregation.

Individuals began to stop me in the supermarket and on the street, all expressing concern about where their children would be attending school. The situation became so distressing I didn't want to leave the house when I returned from work.

I was certain I was going to be fired over the damaging article. I spoke with Dr. M. He was understanding and advised me to keep working with the district and "to hang in there." His reassuring words restored my confidence. I promised never to make the mistake of speaking "off the record" with a reporter again, as it almost made me go "off my rocker."

RED LIGHT

The Assistant Commissioner of Education informed me I had ac-
cumulated 42 vacation days, and that I needed to take some of the time
or I would lose it. I did not plan to use it, until my sister Vicki offered
me a tempting adventure in Taiwan. I had an opportunity to take my
two children to another interesting corner of the world. This time, we
would explore a part of Asia.

We were not prepared for what we were about to see in Taiwan.
Taipei seemed like a city on amphetamines. It was as dynamic on a Monday night as a Saturday in Times Square. Michael, Mary and I meandered among the hordes of people milling about this energetic, frenetic
scene. We were glad Vicki had invited us there in December 1988. I
remembered with gratitude her words of invitation from Taiwan.

"Gilda, come visit us in Taipei. It's really a fascinating city. My husband Seth is working for a Chinese architectural company designing
metro stations here. His firm gave us a spacious, four-bedroom furnished apartment and you are more than welcome."

Fortunately, I had been able take to take a vacation from the OEEO
during Christmas break. Michael, Mary and I had spent the last 20 days
in Taipei visiting museums, attending concerts and various social events
sponsored by an international women's group to which Vicki belonged.
We had seen the Chiang Kai-shek Memorial Hall, the National Palace
Museum, the landmark Dalongdong Baoan Temple, and the Shilin
Night Market, boasting 539 stalls. The latter featured a vast variety of
local and international products. We sampled exotic foods in its cafes
such as: sea slug soup, sautéed frogs and deep-fried crickets. We were
happy to hear that our "last supper" menu at home with Vicki and Seth
included a familiar favorite.

"Tonight, we will have dinner late because of Seth's schedule. I'm
making a roast leg of lamb," my sister said. "A British couple we know
volunteered to escort you to town while I cook. They will be fun-loving,
adventurous companions."

"I am glad not to be eating more "UFO's—Unidentifiable Floating
Objects" like sea slugs."

The outgoing man and his wife arrived at 6 p.m. They were in their mid-40s and wore broad smiles. Their British accents were charming.

I was looking forward to sharing several pleasant hours with our new tour guides.

"Since you leave for the States tomorrow, you probably already saw the usual tourist attractions. We've lived here for two years and decided to take you and your children to a place few Americans ever see. Are you up to an adventure?"

"Of course, where will we be going?"

"We're not telling. We want it to be a surprise."

I thought it best not to press the issue because they appeared excited at the prospect.

They whisked us off in their car and after a half-hour ride, we arrived at a remote market beyond the center of the city. When we exited the vehicle, they led us past stalls of produce where bins of sea cucumbers and assorted fruits and vegetables were displayed on beds of colorful tissue paper. Our hosts escorted us to the back of the stalls and opened a rickety wooden door.

"Sit at one of the tables and we'll have a drink together," the wife said.

While her husband went to the bar to get the three of us coca cola, I took in the surroundings. The unfurnished room was approximately 30 x 40 square feet. Unadorned wooden tables and chairs occupied three-quarters of the space while the other third was taken up by a bar on which glass cases were strewn across the top. In each container, distinct varieties of live snakes were held captive—weaving furiously among themselves in a vain attempt to escape their cramped quarters. There was a rack behind the bar on which several of the live reptiles dangled on hooks protruding below their heads, their entrails exposed. Michael and Mary looked at me—sharing my silent revulsion.

"What is this place?" I asked our hostess.

"It's known as Snake Alley Night Market."

Before she had a chance to elaborate, a group of six men, in their 30s and 40s entered and sat roughly at a table.

"Watch what happens here and your question will soon be answered," she exclaimed with an anticipatory grin.

One of the men went to the bar, pointing to a case of Chinese cobras. The barman opened it and skillfully twirled a snake around a stick. Grabbing its head, he impaled the wriggling reptile on one of the available hooks. He then picked up a knife and made a long, vertical gash through its cool skin. Quickly recovering its blood and bile into a four-ounce glass, he mixed the cocktail with rice wine and served it to his impatient customer. The young man eagerly consumed the mixture. Turning toward his table companions, he grinned broadly and flexed his biceps as his friends cheered.

"Now you know what this place is," our guide said.

"Is it believed that a snake's bile and blood have curative powers?" I responded, trying to mask my disgust.

"You are partially right," she laughed. Nodding affirmatively at her husband, she said, "We think you need to see more; follow us."

We stood quickly, grateful for an opportunity to leave the dreadful place. Our escorts did not exit the door in which we entered. Instead, they led us through the bar, into an outdoor locale, illuminated by a round, hazy red light. We were walking on uneven ground, so I kept my eyes down, careful not to trip and fall. Vicki's friends walked in front; Michael trailed behind them and Mary walked by my side.

On seeing the British couple and Michael, female voices called out loudly in Chinese from platforms on which women and girls stood, ranging in age from late teens to five-years-old. A stern-faced "madam" stood watch in the center of the group.

When they saw my alarmed facial expression, their cackling stopped. An eerie silence pervaded the dank alley where the youngest girls huddled together like frightened fawns in frilly, pink pinafores. They and I stared at one another for a few seconds. Not bearing to peer at their pathetic plight any longer, I kept my eyes downward and walked on slowly with a heavy heart.

What are those children thinking when they see my daughter, protected at my side? Are they wondering about their mothers giving them up to a place like this? Now I realize the drink spiced with cobra blood and bile was a purported aphrodisiac. After the snakes have been abused, feeling emboldened, those macho men will soon follow us, in turn abusing one or more of these forsaken young women and children.

Arriving at the exit I controlled my sense of anger and disgust. It was not the place or time to make a scene which could ultimately upset my sister. I could not imagine how this light-hearted British couple could take us to such a depraved site. Did they believe we would be amused by this type of adventure?

"Well, what do you think?" the husband asked.

"It was utterly appalling," I exclaimed. "I have never experienced such a sense of disgust and pity."

On hearing those words, our host appeared disappointed.

"How do those children end up here?" Mary queried, in a hollow voice.

"Their parents often trade females in exchange for gambling debts. On occasion, a girl may escape, but a parent or caregiver returns them to the brothel as quickly as possible in order not to suffer consequences."

As we approached the parked car, mature prostitutes were posing provocatively before male passers-by, in hope of luring customers. The women were beautiful and obviously proficient in plying their trade.

Mom always said we were unbelievably lucky to have been born in the United States of America. Although we are still striving for equality among the sexes, a female in our country has rights only dreamed of elsewhere. I'll return to the OEEO with renewed motivation for enforcing Title IX of the Civil Rights Act. It is a struggle we must never abandon.

We three did not utter a word to Vicki's friends on the return trip. My children seemed to be in shock by what they had witnessed. Michael was then in his junior year at Vassar; Mary was a freshman at Bryn Mawr. I was proud they were attending traditionally female institutions. The unfortunate members of the group we had just seen would be getting an education of a different kind.

When our British hosts bid us farewell, we entered my sister's apartment building. The rich aroma of roasted lamb permeated the hallway.

Vicki opened the door and greeted us warmly.

"Did you have a good time? Dinner's ready. Let's talk about what you saw after we eat."

Sitting at table and looking at the roast reminded me of those little lambs huddled in the dank, metal containers—their youth slaughtered irrevocably. I felt neither appetite nor wish to describe where we had been. One thing was certain: those frightened, fragile faces would accompany me throughout my lifetime.

THE PRICE OF POLITICS

Education is a curious hybrid of politics and pedagogy. Although I was relentlessly attacked by the press for one month, Dr. M. supported me. I had the Hamilton Township School District develop a desegregation plan for approval of the OEEO without moving youngsters from their neighborhood schools. It consisted of having students meet throughout the district on designated days, to work together on specific projects. It also required the integration of the GEM Guidelines. With that approved plan, the controversy over desegregation ceased.

From that day forward, each district's desegregation plan was to have a twofold component: implementation of Magnet Schools and the GEM Guidelines. The OEEO would thus ensure the inclusion of the voices and world views of all people, in every student's learning experience.

The controversy regarding desegregation plans in New Jersey ended. The DOE was pleased with our accomplishments and in 1993, the New Jersey Equity Hall of Fame designated me "Equity Leader of the Year."

Louie was proud that I was working in civil rights. When I was to speak in the community, he often accompanied me, especially when the events were distant and late at night.

I felt good about what was transpiring during the five and one-half years I was director of the OEEO, but after a much-needed vacation at my cousin's hotel in Margherita di Savoia, everything changed abruptly.

On my return from "The Old Country," Louie met me at the airport, looking agitated.

"You'll never guess what happened?" he said, nervously.

"Was there a reorganization of the office in my absence and I'm no longer the director?"

"How did you know?"

"Such things happen on a regular basis."

"They named an Hispanic woman as director and you are now the manager at the same salary."

I anticipated that move. It was inevitable. Looking back, I had dared to defy the system. I knew it would be impossible for me to prevail once Barbara B. had paid me a visit after hours. I remember vividly when she had shut my office door and asked me to sit at the round conference table with her.

"Gilda, as a white woman, you can no longer remain as the director of this office. The position must go to an African American or Hispanic woman. It doesn't matter how hard you've worked or what you've accomplished. It's politics."

She emphasized the last words by tapping her long, red fingernails on the surface of the table.

"Tomorrow morning you will find a letter of recommendation I've prepared for you to be transferred to the Division of Urban Education. Take it and contact that office. I'm sorry, but as I said, it's politics."

I was not surprised nor was I angry, although inwardly I disagreed.

To achieve equity, it is my opinion no position should be set aside for any racial, ethnic or national origin group. Apparently, the DOE and other organizations all over the country are not ready for that to be the norm. I am not going to contradict Barbara, but I am not going to comply with her order. I too have the right to make a statement.

The following day, I did not retrieve the letter of recommendation. I went to my office, business as usual.

It took those five months for them to find a way to replace me and they did it when I was out of the country. Poor Louie! He looks so upset. He knows how hard I've worked, but it doesn't matter. I will accept whatever I'm asked to do. His reaction is another matter.

Louie became more agitated as he uttered even more serious news.

"They've done away with the OEEO. Now it's the Office of Bilingual Education and Equity Issues."

That's a different story. I feel Equity should be the overarching rubric in the DOE and not be subsumed under Bilingual Education. Again, it's not my call; it's politics, but now is the time for me to quietly leave the DOE. But where will I go?

When I returned home, I called Barbara B. She was apologetic.

"Gilda, I had to appoint a minority to be the director. This time it was an Hispanic."

"Don't worry," I said. "I understand the situation and I want you to know I will do all I can to make the new director's transition as smooth as possible."

"Gilda, thank you so much. You are somethin' else, Lady. I really appreciate those words."

I don't have a problem with that, but Louie does. Blacks and Hispanics have struggled to gain these opportunities. What concerns me most is that, as a white woman, I don't want to be a member of the Civil Rights Office subsumed under Bilingual Education. What I also worry about is Louie's health. His heart is weakening. He gets short of breath easily. He never complains, yet I can see him suffering. I always warn him that if something ever happens to him, the world will go on in its imperfect way.

No. Louie did not need anxiety, but he could not deal with the situation calmly, even though I refused to speak on the topic to protect him.

"Gilda, your husband called me in the office yesterday to ask what was happening with the reorganization. In fact, he rings me up on a regular basis."

"Oh, I'm sorry, Marcellus. I refuse to talk about anything with him at home because he gets easily upset. I know how things are and I accept them, but he can't. I'll tell him not to contact you anymore."

I was going to a retreat with the Commissioner of Education in nearby Jamesburg on the topic of Multicultural Education. It was a Friday evening and our daughter Mary wanted to accompany me because the hotel had a swimming pool and family members could attend. Louie called to me as I was leaving.

"Be home tomorrow by 5:30. We have to be at my sister's house for a cookout. Don't be late."

"I'll be back on time."

The following morning, while in the meeting room, a hotel staff person entered.

"Is there a Gilda here?"

"Yes, I am she"

As I followed the cheerful young woman in the hallway, my mood was apprehensive.

Who would be calling me now? Something untoward must have happened.

"Gilda, come home!" Louie's sister Celeste's voice quivered on the line.

"Is it Louie?"

"Come home!"

Hurriedly, I rounded up Mary from the pool area and rushed her wet body beside me into the front seat of the car. I sped along the highway only to find an accident had halted traffic. Flashing lights and police cars lined the road. That did not slow me. I careened onto the shoulder and raced past the officers who, amazingly, did not attempt to stop me. It was as though they sensed my urgency.

When I arrived home, Michael was outside, teary eyed, conferring with our cousin, Joseph. "We've taken him to the funeral home, Gilda. You can visit his body later."

"Thank you, Joe."

I stood there frozen and silent, unable to react. For 23 and one-half years, I was on pins and needles every time Louie was short of breath or anxious. I always tried to protect him from another heart attack. Not this time. He died without saying goodbye.

CHAPTER TWELVE
SILENT GOODBYE

FINALE

I was led from the brilliant sunlight of the June afternoon into a darkened, frigid room in the Chambers Funeral Home in Trenton. Michael and Mary had cried with me all morning and they took much needed naps. I, however, wanted to visit with Louie alone, regardless of my exhaustion. Louie's cousin and mortician, Joseph D'Errico, shared my sadness as he escorted me into the quiet area where my husband's lifeless body lay.

The surreal setting reminded me of a Fellini film. In the middle of a stark grey room furnished by a single wing-back chair, a muted, supernatural light illuminated Louie's still face, accentuating its ghost-like pallor.

Speak to me. Don't just lie there. We didn't even have the chance to say goodbye. How can you leave me like this?

I sat, continuing to ponder the fragility of life in a silent, internal dialog.

How many women have peered at their husbands who died in combat or accidents? How many never saw the bodies at all? They didn't have the chance to say farewells either and I have joined their ranks. It's often said that before one dies, their entire life flashes before them. It's strange, but that is how I feel about Louie's and my life together. I remember the first time I saw him smile near the elevator in the Osteopathic Hospital and the night I introduced him to Chinese food. How he loved lo mein!

Yesterday he seemed fine when I left for the staff retreat. There was no clue he was so ill. I am not going to join a bereavement group. I know what I must do—get up, dust off my skirt and move forward. That's what he would have wanted.

With those thoughts bombarding my mind that awful day, I lingered, melancholic and motionless as the cadaver. I felt cold and drained. My children were left fatherless and Louie was cheated of all the happy moments their lives would bring. I didn't know how long I sat by my husband's side, but after an hour, Joe signaled gently that it was time for me to leave and return home.

Michael was waiting at the door when I arrived. He followed me into my bedroom. It was he who had found his father's body slumped on the bedroom floor. My son was visibly upset.

"Mom, I didn't know what to do when I saw him lying there," he said, apologetically.

"I just went around in circles for several minutes before calling Aunt Celeste."

He rubbed his forehead in disbelief.

"It must have been so hard for you." I put my arm on Michael's shoulder, trying my best to console and compliment him for doing what was needed under the circumstances.

"I will earn my second Master's Degree soon and that may be enough right now. I'm not going for the doctorate, yet," he said, staring at me with confused eyes.

"Well, I worry that if you stop you won't go back for the doctorate. Give it serious thought, please."

No sooner had Michael left my room, his sister entered.

"Mom, maybe I should wait a year to mourn Dad before starting my psychiatric residency at Harvard."

"Mary, what do you think your father would want you to do, cry a year or prepare for your goal in life? Think about it. Don't make any serious decisions just now."

My poor children! They are in their 20s and have lost their father. I was 44 when my father passed, and it was hard at that age. At least Louie saw Mary graduate from medical school. He was incredibly proud to give her a party in the Officers' Club at Fort Dix, an event which he had enjoyed last week with all his friends and family. A picture we saved of him smiling with her showed how happy and healthy he looked. How did this happen?

My children are disoriented right now. I've got to be strong to help them as well as myself. I've been concerned about my future, but theirs is even more important at this moment.

I took a week off from work at the new Office of Bilingual Education and Equity Issues to make the funeral arrangements. Simultaneously, I knew I had to make a life-altering change. I would need more income to maintain the house and pay for my children's graduate education expenses. Our life savings would easily be gone otherwise. Where could I go? Everyone said it was almost impossible to be hired after 50. I was exhausted and there was no one on whose shoulder I could lean. In a way, I was grateful I had to fend for myself throughout most of my childhood and young adult life. It made me more resilient and my strength was certainly being tested at this moment.

Louie once said he would want a small, quiet funeral, so I followed his wishes. It was held at the Church of Saint Joachim in the Chambersburg section of Trenton, on Butler Street. It was amidst a "little Italy" enclave where he had received his first sacraments. Built in 1903 by Italian immigrants, the lovely structure was a monument to their faith. I loved the interior with its hand-carved and hand-painted wooden statues of saints, the Blessed Mother and Jesus. I also admired a colorful, stained glass window dedicated to the "Apostolate of the Laity," featuring the steel mill of John A. Roebling, in Trenton.

A priest from the Philippines celebrated the funeral mass. Although he did not know Louie personally, his homily was very fitting as he mentioned my husband's dedication to family and community. He had been unaware of all the times Louie had gotten out of bed in the middle of the night to make house calls to patients who were unable to pay him. The priest allowed me to say a few words before the Mass to those who did not know how much my husband had given of himself as a friend and physician, even after suffering a severe heart attack at age 45. In honor of Louie, I felt the message should be delivered.

"My husband would get out of bed at 3 a.m. to make a house call on an indigent patient in inclement weather. Money was not the issue to him; the well-being of his patient was."

When I finished, the congregation appeared moved.

The day after the funeral service, I found a few minutes to reflect. Thankfully, Mary had decided to go directly to Boston and begin her psychiatric residency. Michael was off to NYU in New York, still unsure about the doctoral program. I then pondered where my future would lead. I was 57 years old. I could remain at the DOE, of course, but I considered the current reorganization untenable.

The answer to that question came suddenly, with one phone call.

A NEW CHALLENGE

The day after the funeral service I sat alone on the living room sofa, imagining Louie inserting his key in the door and entering with his radiant smile. My rational mind knew he never would, yet emotionally I was yearning that he could. It was so strange. The shrilling of the telephone woke me out of my reverie.

"Dr. Rorro, this is Dr. C. from the Elizabeth Board of Education. The district has created the position of Director of Multicultural Education, with you in mind. Because you are a statewide leader in that field, we want to know if you would be interested in applying? If you are interested, please come to the district tomorrow to discuss the details."

How wonderful! They created the perfect spot for me.

"Thank you. I will be there." When I hung up, my melancholic mood changed to one of anticipation.

Louie would have wanted this for me. How many times have friends told me no one wants to hire someone in their 50s? It'll be good to prove them wrong.

The following day I rode one-hour by train to Elizabeth and was interviewed.

"Are you interested in the post, Dr. Rorro?"

"Yes."

Within the week, I returned to Elizabeth to sign the contract. The directorship afforded me a substantial raise, enough to meet all my current expenses and those of Michael and Mary. I was to begin the following month.

When I told my colleague Marie about the new job, she was happy.

"This calls for a celebration. Be my guest at Joe's Old Time Tavern at Five Points, in Hamilton. I'll treat you to their prime rib special."

"Sounds great!"

At dinner, we drank wine and toasted to a brighter future. The next day, I was reading the newspaper and saw an ad that read, "Seeking an Assistant Superintendent for Human Resources in the Trenton Board of Education." It called for extensive experience in school desegregation and equity issues. There were many other requisites with which I was not as familiar, such as contract negotiations, but the notice was still intriguing.

Hmmm. I should apply. Someday I may want to be an assistant superintendent and the interview would give me an idea of what the position entails.

I submitted the application. It was June 17th, 1997, one-week after Louie's death. I returned to the DOE intending to announce my contract with Elizabeth, yet something made me hesitate. I decided to wait.

The following week, I received a phone call notifying me I was to report to the Trenton Board of Education for a preliminary interview at 4:30 p.m.

After a full day of work, I went to the district's Administration Building on South Clinton Avenue and met Bernadette, a young, dynamic assistant to the superintendent. She noticed I looked tired. My fatigue was becoming chronic after my companion's demise, as I never took time off after the funeral to mourn him.

"Take a seat at the table in the corner. Write a 350-word essay on why you think you are the perfect person for this job. Mention all your qualifications and experience. Are you hungry? Have a banana."

She pulled the fruit from a drawer in her desk and extended it to me. Her hospitality put me at ease and with the help of the nourishing fruit I composed the text, submitted it and politely left.

The following day, I received a second phone call at my desk saying

I was to return to the Trenton Administration Building for another step in the application process.

They must have liked my essay. I wonder what they'll want today?

"Dr. Rorro, please complete this questionnaire. When you finish, there is another composition for you to write," Bernadette said.

They certainly require a lot of information. I never expected to get this far.

A third phone call came the next day informing me I was to meet with the members of the Trenton School Board for their individual interviews in two days. It was then that I realized I was being considered for the position.

The superintendent, Dr. Bernice Venable, called me at home that evening. She congratulated me for having passed the first stages of the process. She was highly professional, enthusiastic and encouraging.

"Be available to come to the Administration Building the day after tomorrow. The meeting with members of the board is very important."

I had met Dr. Venable before. She and I had been panelists at a desegregation conference in northern New Jersey and I liked and admired the charismatic educator. We had both completed doctoral studies at Rutgers University and we spoke Spanish. What impressed me most was that she had attended the viewing of my husband to show respect.

On the appointed day, I was led into the first-floor Conference Room to meet members of the Board. Dr. Venable introduced me and I subsequently went around the room shaking each person's hand. I noticed the composition of the Board was diverse, with one Italian American male.

It was immediately evident that while I was attempting to make a good impression, not all assembled were going to share Dr. Venable's enthusiasm regarding my candidacy. They fired questions at me, which I answered competently, yet two showed outright displeasure at an administrator from the DOE assuming the position.

"Having statewide supervision of districts is not the same as direct experience in an inner-city school system," one male member blurted. "You live in an 'Ivory tower' in the DOE. You give directives to districts without realizing all we go through." The Italian American concurred with his African American counterpart.

"That certainly may be the perception, but we work in tandem with our school systems, especially those having desegregation plans. The advantage of being a DOE employee is the broad, statewide perspective we bring to the table."

My detractors seemed unimpressed with that or any of my remarks. My composure remained intact despite the verbal onslaught. I knew they were playing hardball and I had to defend myself as well as prove my ability. The OEEO had provided me a good training ground.

This is not the same environment as Elizabeth, where I'd be welcomed with open arms. A Board member may have another candidate in mind— perhaps even a friend. There are rumors about who they want in Trenton for the job. Those things happen and as always, one needs to be cognizant of the politics. It could also be that they mean exactly what they say about DOE experience versus district experience. Oh, well, I don't like to be easily defeated and I am resolved to see this interview process through to the end. Whatever they throw at me, I'll throw back—diplomatically, but swiftly.

I left the building feeling discouraged and wondering what to do. On the way home, I was passing the Trenton Central High School, built in 1932, when I felt an impulse to stop the car and walk into the building, and so I did. I received permission to enter the auditorium. The area was large, with white walls and 1500 brown, wooden folded seats. A very distinctive feature, hanging above, was several massive, shaded chandeliers with light bulb cups made of Lenox china. I sat, gazing at the beautiful fixtures.

Louie must have looked up and admired these when he attended school here. He saw the same stage and sat on these chairs, chatting with classmates. This is where I want to be. I feel close to him in Trenton. There is no history in Elizabeth, no matter how well I may be treated. I've made my decision and I will deal with the dissenters on the Board.

Once again, the superintendent called me at home the following evening and said mine was the only name she would submit for the Human Resources position, regardless of the opposition.

"Do you know what that means?" she asked.

"Yes, and I appreciate all you are trying to do on my behalf. But while I value your support, I would be willing to accept the directorship in Elizabeth to avoid your having a conflict with the Board."

"I endorse you and I am up for the battle," she said.

There was undoubtedly going to be a struggle. The night the tele-vised Board Meeting arrived, I was appointed Assistant Superintendent for Human Resources by a 5–4 vote. Although it was hardly a landslide, I was in.

That close a number is not a reason to celebrate, rather, it signals there will be a rough road ahead. I am inwardly jubilant that the position is mine. The salary is substantially more than that at the DOE. It puts my career on a higher level and who knows where it will lead?

After polite applause sounded in the room, Mr. M., a male Board member took the microphone and admonished me from the podium in a booming voice.

"Dr. Rorro, I want everyone in the room to know I oppose your candidacy. The Department of Education does not prepare someone sufficiently to work in an inner-city school district."

How humiliating! He blurted that on television where my in-laws and the entire community could see. Why is he so against me? Maybe he really means what he said, but perhaps not. I may never know. My stomach is churn-ing, but I cannot allow that to show. He is determined to make my experience here miserable.

When everyone poured out of the room and into the hallway of the Administration Building, a reporter from the *The Times* approached me for my comment.

"Congratulations on your appointment. But tell me, how do you react to Mr. M's opposition toward you?" "I respect Mr. M. I can only strive to prove him wrong. I always look forward to a challenge." Little did I realize how daunting that would be.

PINK SLIPS

"Congratulations again, Gilda! Let's go back to Bill's Old Time Tavern and I'll treat you to another prime rib dinner."

"Thanks, Marie. Celebrating there every time I get a new job is becoming a habit."

Marie and I felt giddy from wine and my tales of signing a contract with both the Elizabeth and Trenton Boards of Education within a two-week period.

"When you announced you were leaving the DOE, Barbara B. wanted to give you a big "going away" party. Why did you refuse?"

"I was not in the mood to party so soon after Louie's death. Besides, I oppose the merger of the Civil Rights Office under Bilingual Education. It would be hypocritical."

"I understand, but it would have been a sendoff to remember. So how did you get out of the contract with Elizabeth?"

"I simply told them about the unexpected offer in Trenton and they were impressed. It was not difficult at all. I was relieved because I did not want to cause the district any inconvenience after all they had done for me."

"You were lucky. Let's drink a toast to a great new future!"

Marie's good wishes were appreciated, but during the first week on the job I learned that working in Trenton was going to be the biggest challenge of my career. For example, the hours specified in the contract were 8:30 a.m. - 4:30 p.m., but I worked most nights until 10 or 11 p.m., as did the superintendent. Even then I could not complete all the assignments because of one crisis or another.

I took copious amounts of work home, even after a routine 14-hour day. In the morning, I would awaken with papers splayed over the bed and on the floor. I decided it was necessary to keep even longer hours, so I started on the job site at 7:30 a.m. Rarely did I stop for lunch. A few times I tried to eat a tuna salad that Angie from the school cafeteria provided. I ate it in my car in the administration parking lot to avoid phone calls or office walk-ins, but that strategy was ineffective and knocks on the automobile window interrupted me. I would wearily abandon the tuna salad and exit the vehicle to attend to the latest issue.

One night, I was going to leave the building at 8 p.m., having started again at 7:30 a.m.

"Dr. Rorro, where are you going at this early hour?"

I turned in the direction of the stern voice belonging to Mr. M.

"You are cheating the Trenton Board by leaving so soon. I am still here, working."

I did not argue. I was too tired. I just turned and went into my office until the customary 11 p.m. My only concern was that I could not take my little shih-tzu Tiki, out for his much-needed walk.

The staff was wonderful to work with, however, and I was blessed with an Assistant Secretary, Angie, who had been in the district since she was 19 years old. Angie was feisty and very intelligent. She knew more at 48 than I, or anyone, would ever learn about the Trenton school system. She was also cognizant of the extremely high attrition rate of assistant superintendents.

"Your predecessor lasted only two weeks," she said.

"Sorry, Angie, but I intend to stay much longer." We both chuckled.

I was determined to remain and prove Mr. M. wrong, so I worked ceaselessly toward that goal. My attempt was futile because toward the end of my first year, disaster struck. The district Business Director claimed there was a multi-million-dollar shortfall, necessitating all staff to be let go until the restoration of funds. The Board and community demanded Dr. Venable verify the Business Director's report.

At a subsequent Board meeting overflowing with irate union representatives, staff, parents, students and community members, the superintendent concurred there was a critical lack of funding exceeding 20 million dollars. It was incumbent upon my office to issue 3,300 pink slips, signed by me in one day. One day!

Whenever I passed Mr. M or a union rep in the hallway, they glowered at me.

Hey! I'm a nice person. Do you think I want to do this? This is the worst possible assignment. I came to Trenton eager to make a difference and unfortunately, this is it. Instead of helping, I am hurting good people. Once all the certified school librarians, nurses and the 18 bilingual teachers are fired, other districts will gobble them up and they'll never come back to Trenton. It will be a disaster of long-range proportions.

The pain in my hands from the extensive signing worsened, but I continued working at a feverish pace, albeit never hearing a word of encouragement. There was so much to be done in Human Resources when confronting a situation of that magnitude.

I asked staff to persevere with me on a Saturday in a volunteer capacity, to ensure all personnel files were current. They dutifully came to the office at 8:30 a.m. and toiled until well past midnight on Sunday, without complaint. My son Michael prepared and delivered lunch and dinner for them. I was proud to be with such dedicated personnel. By 1 a.m. I was getting groggy, but the staff toiled on.

"Come on, Dr. Rorro. Don't fall asleep. We'll keep you going," they laughed, bringing me a steaming cup of coffee.

"You have all done yeomen's jobs. It's unfortunate that neither you nor I will be congratulated for our efficiency."

"That's alright, Dr. Rorro; we know what we need to do."

I admired and loved them all. On Monday morning, I was summoned to Dr. Venable's office. Her secretary informed me the superintendent was in Texas at a conference. In her absence, I was required to sign her name and title on over 400 documents.

"Can't another administrator do it? My hand hurts from writing my name and title on all those pink slips," I complained.

"Here, rest it on this pad for support, but you must put her name, title and your initials on each of these papers," her secretary said matter-of-factly, while sliding a black rubber square under my right hand.

"We're sorry for you, Dr. Rorro. Things are really bad here right now."

I did as I was instructed, but the pad helped only a little. The pain became so severe I decided to seek medical help from a doctor who would see me that evening.

"You have Carpal Tunnel Syndrome," the physician said. "I recommend a procedure be done to correct it on both hands as soon as possible or you are going to lose the use of your hands."

"How long would that take?"

"About 45 minutes under local anesthesia."

"I don't have time to schedule it now."

"Then at least wear braces for support and I will prescribe some anti-inflammatory medication."

I don't have time to take care of myself. The Trenton Board is becoming "The Killing Fields." I didn't see the movie, but working here must have similarities. If Louie were alive life would be very different, but he isn't and I don't know what else to do. I've got to get through this tough time alone, hurting hands and all.

I did as the doctor said, but the anti-inflammatory medication he prescribed made me drowsy all day. I drank copious amounts of coffee to stay alert, but the caffeine was ineffective. This condition, coupled with chronic sleep deprivation, made my life extremely difficult. I was not managing my time wisely nor delegating efficiently. I continued to take on too much work. At this rate, something untoward was bound to happen.

ROMAN HALL

There was no time for an uninterrupted lunch in my office, but one day I felt I had to leave the building. The Roman Hall Restaurant in the Burg would be a welcome change of scene. When I arrived, a member of the wait staff led me to a table for one. "Good afternoon. My name is Victor and I am your server today," said the handsome young waiter in a starched, white shirt and black pressed pants. His dark hair was slicked back Valentino style. The black cummerbund around his trim waist gave him the air of a tango dancer.

"What would you like to order?"

"The lobster Francese sounds good."

"Great choice," he nodded and walked off.

The crusty Italian bread placed before me looked inviting. Lifting the butter knife, it fell onto the white, porcelain plate. Its loud, metallic rattling caused all eyes to focus on me.

Darn these hands! The cloth braces I wear for my carpal tunnel condition aren't helping a bit. Everything falls from my fingers. It's so embarrassing.

I sat alone in this Trenton landmark that was established in 1938 by the Roman Society for immigrants from the region of Lazio. Its motto was, "One for all and all for one." In those days, if you did not work, you were not paid. Widows had a particularly hard time and the Roman Society was there to assist.

Louie had taken me to eat at the Roman Hall on a regular basis before we were married. In the 1960s, for $1.35 patrons were served soup or salad, one-half a roast chicken or a stuffed breast of capon with baked potatoes, a side of pasta, coffee and rum cake. The eatery resembled a capacious brown barn to me then. Splashes of color were provided by red and white checkered table cloths and traditional Chianti bottles half-covered by cascading, multi-colored candle wax. The bountiful food compensated for the sparse decor.

As I sat at a table now, in 1995, I was astounded at the transformation of the "barn" to a "glitzarama," thanks to the manager, Giovanni (aka John) Baldassari.

I faced a Palladian window framed by beige antique satin draperies. The sky had turned an ominous black. Torrential shafts of water crashed onto Butler Street. The raging summer storm was in sharp contrast to the bright, uplifting interior where crystal chandeliers reflected pastel prisms onto mirrored walls.

One side of the dining area was glass, allowing a lovely view of the cream-colored patio beyond, flanked by ornate moldings. Encrusted niches held miniature busts of Roman emperors. A hand-painted mural of the iconic Roman fortress, "Castel Sant'Angelo," dominated the surface of one, while another featured bas-relief friezes of Roman Legions dressed in incongruous, varied-colored uniforms. A large, decorative Capodimonte lamp with pink cherubs and dangling crystal fringes on the shade completed the fanciful ambience.

This is the most ornate restaurant I have ever seen in this country. When I set foot in here I forget the outside world. The workmanship is impressive. I feel content in this place.

"Here is your lobster Francese and Mr. Baldassari sends you a glass of Chardonnay with his compliments."

"How lovely, Victor. Thank you and Mr. Baldassari."

The lobster entree looked appetizing and I eagerly raised my knife and fork to cut into it. Clang! Both utensils fell from my hands, simultaneously striking the sides of the dinner plate, sending a new wave of startled stares in my direction.

"Is something wrong?" A deep male voice asked in an Italian accent.

"No. I have trouble with my hands," I said, indicating the braces.

"Vittorio, come here!"

Victor reappeared, watching as Mr. Baldassari deftly sliced the crustacean into manageable morsels. "When this lady comes to the restaurant, make sure all her food is cut before you serve it." "Okay, Boss," Victor replied.

What a nice man! He's so accommodating. I'll be back.

Little did I know the influence Mr. Baldassari and the Roman Hall would have on me from that day forward.

DO ME THE HONOR

The atmosphere in the Trenton Board of Education became increasingly tense. Staff complained in whispers among themselves. Everyone was justifiably on edge because their contracts might not be renewed. Administrators were disgruntled, having to deal with the brutal business. Staff meetings became more frequent, consisting of heated debates regarding the financial shortfall. We slept less, ate poorly at irregular hours and tried to conceal our raw nerves. A phone call from Marie brought a welcome respite from the strained atmosphere.

"Gilda, I am hosting a birthday party for my sister at the Roman Hall. I'd like you to join us Friday night because we consider you part of our family."

"Marie, I would love to."

Friday came, and I met my friends in the patio area of the eatery at 7 o'clock. It was raining but the scene inside brightened my spirits. Marie motioned for me to sit next to her. Donna, our middle-aged server, whose alabaster face was topped by a crop of unruly blonde hair, made a pleasant announcement.

"Mr. Baldassari would like to treat everyone to a complementary glass of *Asti Spumante.*"

"Isn't that nice?" the guests said in unison.

Marie smiled with satisfaction as we lifted our glasses to toast her sister.

Dinner was served. My entree had been pre-cut before serving. When we finished our main course, Mr. Baldassari appeared with a second bottle of *Asti Spumante.*

"I want you to enjoy this as an after-dinner drink before I bring you my surprise," he said, in his Italian accent.

"What is the surprise, Marie?"

"I didn't order any," she said, with a combination of curiosity and excitement.

While Donna poured the Asti, other wait staff entered, carrying a large birthday cake decorated with multicolored citron and *"Buon Compleanno!'* (Happy Birthday!) written in green gel across the white frosting. They burst into song after Marie's sibling blew out the candles.

"I ordered this special cake from Rome. It arrived today from Italy," the manager said with pride.

"Marie, you really rate," all exclaimed.

Marie was ecstatic at the heightened attention. Victor, her favorite waiter, came to slice the confection, which revealed layers of chocolate cream and hazelnut filling. A hint of Kermes liquor infused each segment and the overall combination of flavors made our palates explode with pleasure. Mr. Baldassari leaned over and whispered in Marie's ear.

While I was concentrating on the delightful pastry, she turned to me with a question.

"Did you hear what he said?"

"No. What?"

She whispered, "Do you think I have a chance with your friend now?" We both laughed at that.

"And your family thinks he did all this just for you," I teased.

He is such a nice man. I haven't experienced this kind of pampering for so long. It brings back beautiful memories of my youth.

While I was thinking to myself, Mr. Baldassari approached and said he would like to see me in his office when I finished dinner. Marie overheard the conversation and looked at me, grinning.

"What should I do?"

"You heard the man; go meet him!" she answered, smiling broadly.

I stayed with the family until everyone departed, then made my way through the crystal chandelier-studded hallway to the manager's area. I knocked on his solid oak door. Mr. Baldassari opened it and motioned for me to be seated. He asked if I enjoyed the meal and made other small talk for a few minutes. When I stood to go, he came close to me and closed the door. I felt slightly uncomfortable, wondering what would happen next.

"Would you do me the honor of having dinner with me, sometime?"

I'm flattered but uneasy. It's strange. For over 30 years I have never been with a man other than Louie. I still feel married to him, but I like the way Mr. Baldassari asked, with "Old World" respect.

"My husband has only been gone for over a year and I haven't been out with anyone. I don't think I am ready just yet."

"I understand. Take all the time you need."

Gathering an umbrella, he escorted me to my car. My heart beat discernibly faster. I felt confused but content.

The next day the assistant superintendents were called to Dr. Venable's office with the business administrator at 11:30 a.m. That meant no lunch, just diet Pepsi and the district's signature peanut butter bars.

"The fiscal crisis has reached alarming proportions," Dr. Venable said. "As pink slips were distributed to all staff, you administrators may also want to explore the possibility of finding new positions."

Where could I go now? If I find a slot, how far from home would it be?

At 3:30 p.m., the contentious session ended. I was in a foul mood, hypoglycemic and frustrated at the looming, massive layoff. When I got to my desk, those negative feelings changed instantly. A colorful bouquet of two dozen thick, fat red roses in a crystal vase covered its entire surface. Tiger lilies in glorious bloom stood out proudly among the scarlet, quivering blossoms. A two-pound box of Perugina chocolates lay at the base of this grand floral display. The card inserted read, "Do me the honor."

For the first time that day, I smiled.

ITALIAN EASTER BASKET

Events at work took precedence over my social life. There was no time to think of dating with people's livelihoods at stake. The day before Holy Thursday in 1997, Dr. Venable called a meeting of her senior staff. As usual, the session started at 11:30 a.m., with no breaks or lunch hour. Amidst the standard Pepsi and peanut butter bars, we listened to the bleak accounts from the School Business Administrator regarding the mass layoff. The disheartening task put me in a foul mood, and I again returned to my office feeling agitated.

"Dr. Rorro, someone is here to make a delivery," a secretary exclaimed.

Not another problem! What other crisis could this day bring? It's probably a subpoena or worse.

"Is there a wagon or something to put this thing on?" a man called out from the front counter.

A nearby staff member jumped up and produced a cart from the supply closet. All eyes turned toward the men as they strained to hoist a heavy load onto it. Once it was secure, they wheeled the contents toward me.

All work stopped at that moment and mouths were agape as the enormous parcel was lifted onto a table in my office. We looked in wonder at a wicker basket the size of a washtub. Two, four-foot Easter eggs in shimmering silver and gold wrapping flanked each side of the container, which was filled with fresh, golden daffodils, cobalt dahlias, crimson tulips, cuddly pink bunnies, fluffy white lambs with bobbing heads, coconut eggs and assorted jelly beans. The twin towering eggs and candies were imported from Italy by Perugina.

"Dr. Rorro, who sent this?" The staff queried me in unison.

There was a note. I asked the congregation to please leave as I read it. Opening the envelope, the message, in neat script, but inaccurate grammar, read: "You make my heart dance. *Buona Pasqua* (Happy Easter)!" Giovanni.

Mr. Baldassari had told me before that when he sees me enter a room, "His heart, she dance." What a dear, whimsical way he expresses himself. It's funny, but I don't feel hypoglycemic anymore.

"Dr. Rorro, the staff on the second and third floors want to come to see your Easter basket. Is it all right?" Angie asked. "I'll see to it that they enter in shifts and form a straight line to avoid confusion. They won't believe their eyes!"

"Of course," I said, returning the note to its envelope and securing it in my handbag.

We all need some pleasant diversion around here.

A smile crossed my lips as I focused on this oversized colorful assortment. It was a reminder of the meaning of the season: peace, renewal and hope. The joyful Easter basket made my heart dance.

A DINNER TO REMEMBER

The day after the Easter basket was delivered, a bountiful bouquet of red roses arrived in my office. The blossoms exhaled a deliciously sweet scent into my work space, soothing my jangled nerves. Enclosed was the familiar message: "Do Me the Honor."

I called the Roman Hall and asked for the manager.

"Hello," he said, in his Italian accent.

"Mr. Baldassari, I'd like to thank you for the beautiful flowers."

"Did you read my note?"

"Yes, but please understand: this is all very new to me."

"I know. Take all the time you need but let's at least have dinner."

"We'll talk about it soon, I promise."

I spent most of the day on Sundays with Dr. Venable visiting African American churches in the Trenton area. I loved the fiery sermons and impassioned oratory of the ministers, like Rev. S. Howard Woodson, at Shiloh Baptist. I had the privilege of getting to know several ministers rather well and enjoyed their interpretation of the Gospel. I prayed in their churches for guidance and strength to confront the scheduled Board of Education meetings, which I knew would be painfully difficult.

The spiritual uplift I receive, first at Saint Joachim's Catholic Church, where I read in Italian, and then at the various black churches, brings me necessary tranquility.

One Monday morning, the atmosphere in the office was eerily quiet like the calm before a storm. Everyone seemed to move about without speaking or in hushed tones, in anticipation of the dreaded Board Meeting. In the evening my prayers would be tested. I saw from my window busloads of people pouring into the Administration Building for the public portion of the meeting. There were several adults bearing large placards. One made my blood run cold. It featured skull and crossbones. The caption read "Alive or Deddy." The last name of the Business Administrator was Deddy.

This is going to be brutal. The staff told me there is standing room only in the auditorium and people have filled the hallway and are pouring out into the parking lot where there are loudspeakers for the proceedings. What can I say tonight to assuage this level of anger? I am feeling anxious.

The dreaded meeting time arrived, and I assumed my place on the dais with the rest of the Board. I looked out onto a sea of hostile faces. We were in the line of fire, targets for the imminent attack.

"Dr. Rorro, how do you propose to bring back all the staff you sent pink slips to?" a furious voice shouted from the rear of the auditorium.

"We're hoping funding will be restored and we can remedy the situation," I said meekly, to the sound of universal boos and hisses. The furious onlookers pounded their fists and stomped their feet in protest. Union reps scowled at me from below the platform.

I feel faint. I am experiencing the fright and flight syndrome. All I want to do is run out the exit door and never come back, but it's impossible. I must sit here and take the heat.

It was the most grueling public portion of a Board meeting possible as the irate crowd vented its justifiable rage. The misery lasted into early morning. Dr. Venable called for a Cabinet meeting at 3 a.m. By then we were all quasi comatose. We knew the situation was desperate and the inevitable had to be addressed. She warned us of the mounting anger from the Board and the community and that our contracts might not be renewed. We all expected her words to materialize.

It was 5 a.m. when I finally arrived home. I barely had the strength to listen to my telephone messages, but the sound of the familiar Italian accent from the receiver uplifted my flagging spirit.

"Did you decide, yet?" was the message he left.

That man is insistent but charming. Right now, I can't think about anything. I need some sleep.

When I returned to the office at the rare time of 10:30 a.m., Angie greeted me.

"That was some Board meeting last night! It was one of the worst ever, Dr. Rorro."

"It surely was."

"Mr. Baldassari wants you to call him back today. I have the number."

"Please dial it for me and pass it through."

I lifted the receiver happily on hearing his warm, friendly voice.

"Mr. Baldassari, I accept your invitation to dinner on Monday, your day off."

"Benìssimo!"

"Va bene," (That's fine) I said.

During the week, I was too distracted to contemplate my first date in over 31 years. On Sunday evening, however, the realization hit me.

Oh gosh! Tomorrow I am going out with Mr. Baldassari and I am not sure if it is the right thing. I want to and, at the same time, I don't want to.

On Monday, my date called me at work.

"I will come to your house at 5:30 p.m. We are going to a specialty restaurant at Caesar's Resort in Atlantic City."

"Atlantic City! That's far. It's pouring rain and the wind is raging. Let's do this another time."

"Non piove in macchina, (It doesn't rain in the car)," he said, in such a determined way I knew that we would be on our way to A.C.

I left work early to arrive home by five and change clothes. The two-hour ride was punctuated by my driver's humor, telling me stories of his childhood in Italy. I liked hearing how he used to ride a donkey and go trout fishing in the mountains of Umbria in the summer. He transported me to a serene, saner place.

He's happy to be with me and I'm relaxed with him. It's a good feeling.

It seemed like no time had passed when the glitzy skyline of the ocean resort loomed, and we soon approached the white and gold exterior of the behemoth Caesar's Casino and Resort. The rain and wind had stopped, and I inhaled fresh, ocean air. The valet parking attendant knew Mr. Baldassari and readily took charge of his green Cadillac.

We entered the gigantic glass doors of the casino, where the metallic clang from slot machines assaulted our ears. My host apparently enjoyed the jangling, but I did not. No one in my family or Louie's was a gambler. The flashing lights and the sound of coins crashing were to lure people, but they repulsed me.

"Here! Put a quarter in the machine, Gilda. They say if you win the first time it brings good luck."

He placed the money in my hand, but I refused to accept it.

"I've never gambled, Mr. Baldassari. I rely on every penny I earn, and I never jeopardize losing it."

He registered slight disappointment, inserted the money himself, and lost.

I must seem like such a prude. Putting a coin in a slot would have made the man happy, even if I didn't win anything. What's wrong with me? I am too straight-laced.

"Are you hungry?" he asked.

"No, not very."

"So, do you mind if I stop to play a little blackjack first?"

"Of course not."

We entered the Baccarat section where bets began at 100 dollars. I sat beside him as he plunked down ten, one hundred dollar bills and ordered a round of drinks. The Pit Boss came and greeted my date. The Croupier also recognized him. They exchanged brief smiles but then focused on the serious business at hand.

There were three other players at the table. The dealer started a new sleeve of cards and no one spoke. I held my breath as I saw $100 chips disappear and reappear until Mr. Baldassari had won several high stacks of them.

"I'm cashing in, as I have a dinner reservation with this lovely lady."

He put several one-thousand-dollar chips in his pocket and led me up a winding, red-carpeted stairway to the mezzanine.

"First, let's enjoy Campari in the lounge overlooking the ocean before going to the Primavera Restaurant."

How does he know Campari is my favorite aperitivo?

The moon cast a soft glow onto the calm water below. We sat, sipping and smiling, comfortable in each other's company.

"Time for *cena* (dinner)," he said, taking my arm.

We strolled across the aisle to the Primavera, where the Maître d' was stationed.

"O, Giovanni, *come stai?*" (How are you?), he blurted, giving Mr. Baldassari a hearty, bear hug. "Where would you like to sit tonight?"

"Give us a private table in the back."

"*Va bene.* Come this way."

The ornate decor was replete with multi-colored Venetian chandeliers and brightly-painted murals of Italy's treasured sites. We were motioned to a small, secluded table by a scene of "La Serenìssima" (Venice), with its graceful gondolas.

Mr. Baldassari gave the Maître d' a generous tip, while a member of the wait staff quickly brought extensive menus.

"What will it be tonight, Mr. Baldassari?" the waiter asked.

Everyone knows him here.

"Take these menus away and tell the chef to come out."

"Very good, Mr. Baldassari."

In a flash, the head cook appeared, clad in his toque blanche and white apron. He was a tall, handsome Italian with dark, chiseled features and professional demeanor.

"What can I serve you, Signor Baldassari?" he said, in a lilting Italian accent.

"Say hello to Dr. Rorro, from Trenton. I want you to prepare your best meal for her."

"Of course! How do you do, Signora? Do you prefer meat, fish or vegetarian?"

"Seafood, please."

"*Benìssimo!* Your lovely guest and you will not be disappointed; I promise."

The sommelier approached and poured chilled Prosecco into our crystal flutes.

"For you and your guest, Mr. Baldassari, chilled just how you like it."

After we raised our glasses for a toast, a young female photographer approached.

"Would you wish to have your picture taken?" she queried, with a broad smile.

"No!" I retorted, instinctively.

I do not want my photo with a man other than my husband. I already feel uncomfortable as though many eyes are upon me for being seen in public without Louie.

"Yes," Mr. Baldassari interrupted, disregarding my objection. "We want to remember this special night."

The area was softly lit, and, for the first time, I looked directly into my escort's eyes. Until then, my gaze was always half diverted because of my uneasiness being alone with a man other than my spouse.

Mr. Baldassari was good looking. The slight wave in his full head of brown hair was attractive. His hazel, Saint Bernard eyes were large, and kind, and his nose was aquiline. He looked elegant in his blue, pin-striped suit and Gucci tie of the same deep color. He was older than I, perhaps eight or ten years? If he lost 50-pounds he would be strikingly handsome. But his weight did not matter to me; how he treated me did.

He peers into my eyes and makes me feel secure. He caters to my every whim and wants me to be happy. I have not had this sensation for years and thought I would never experience it again. It's beautiful and almost makes me forget what is happening in Trenton.

"For your appetizer, the chef prepared a seafood medley," our waiter said with justifiable pride.

The platter consisted of a bevy of bivalves and crustaceans, including grilled *langostinos, scungilli and* sea urchins piled high.

"This is more than a meal," I exclaimed.

"Enjoy! *Buon appetito!*" Mr. Baldassari said, with anticipation.

Steaming bowls of *linguine alla vongole* (linguine with white clam sauce) followed. It was an outstanding dish, made from the liquor of the fresh clams. We savored every strand.

The entrees, consisting of two, one-half-pound lobster tails on each plate, were then served.

"How can we devour all this?" I asked, incredulously.

"Have only what you want. Let me cut it for you because I remember you have difficulty with your hands."

This reminds me of my gourmet meal with Xavier at Le Pavillion in New York City. It is even better because everyone knows and apparently likes the man I am with.

"Do you enjoy being here?" he asked.

"It's lovely! You certainly are familiar with the place and the staff. You must come often."

"Yes. I feel at home here, but most of all I want you to be happy. I don't like to see you sad. I miss my wife. When I go home alone at night, I feel depressed, so I go to places like this to forget for a while. I understand how you are suffering too, so tonight let me help you think of good things."

We were finishing our dessert of *zabaglione* (egg custard) with mixed berries and glasses of chilled *limoncello* when the friendly photographer approached.

"Before your espresso, would you like to purchase any of these photos? You both look great. Select the one you want."

"No, thank you," I muttered, foolishly.

"How much for all of them?" my escort asked.

"129 dollars."

"Good. I'll take them all."

"But Mr. Baldassari," I started, until he interrupted me.

"I'll take one; the rest are for you."

We did not look at the pictures because our coffee arrived, accompanied by miniature Perugina chocolates filled with assorted Italian liquors. When the feast finally ended, we headed back to Hamilton. For the first time in a month, I had a wonderful surge of energy from having consumed such an incredible meal. It was 11 p.m. but I was surprisingly wide awake and happy as Mr. Baldassari serenaded me with *"Canzoni Romane"* (Roman songs) for most of the ride home. His voice was surprisingly good and made me forget the Trenton Board of Ed. Well, almost.

Arriving at my front door, my date kissed my hand and thanked me for a beautiful evening. We stood for an instant, looking into each other's eyes. He bid me good night.

As soon as I entered the house, I placed all the photographs, which were in cardboard folders, on a shelf in my bedroom closet without looking at them. I didn't want to see myself in the company of a man other than Louie. It did not seem right.

Tired, but happy, I went straight to bed. Thoughts of the memorable evening lulled me to sleep.

CHAPTER THIRTEEN
A NEW LIFE BEGINS

Tuesday morning Angie was waiting for me when I arrived in the office. "Okay," she said, her arms folded with determination across her chest. "Tell me all about it."

I closed the door and sat.

It was fun relating the events of the night before with John. It provided a temporary respite from all the unpleasant work we had to face daily.

"What do you think of him?"

"He's nice."

"Just nice? If you ever tire of him, send him my way."

"Angie, are you serious?"

"You bet I am!"

We both laughed. The moment of levity ended abruptly as I was told to attend a meeting in the evening with the Mayor of Trenton and selected officials from City Council. My day would be spent preparing for it and my stomach began churning in anticipation.

When the appointed time arrived, we senior staff entered the conference room in the Administration Building facing the stern-faced Mayor Douglas Palmer and his entourage. I had taught with the mayor's mother, Dorothy, in Hamilton Township. She was pleasant and often boasted that her son was friendly; but he was not jovial now. We sat, stone faced, while the city officials fired accusations and questions at us for an hour. They vented their outrage at the turmoil the lay-offs were already causing the school district and community. Then the bombshell came.

"Dr. Venable, an outside audit of the district Business Office will take place to determine the extent of the fiscal crisis. We will get to the bottom of the cause of the multi-million-dollar shortfall," the mayor informed.

I don't blame them. Who could?

When the agonizing session finally ended, Dr. Venable, who was always calm and collected, looked visibly flushed. I felt sorry for her. She was extremely hard working and cared about the district, but it didn't matter to our inquisitors. The monetary shortfall and its consequences had impacted all personnel. It would now include us administrators.

Several days later, the subsequent audit indicated there was no fiscal crisis! The Business Administrator confessed she had miscalculated, but it was too late. All pink slips had been sent and many staff including school nurses, librarians and certified bilingual teachers had found positions elsewhere within a three-week period. They were not coming back to the Trenton School District.

Now it was June, time for our contract renewals for 1997–1998.

I know I will be the first to be fired, well, maybe the second, after the Business Administrator. The saddest thing is I will not be able to prove Mr. M. wrong. He will gloat at my defeat.

During the past few years, I have had to confront several near disasters in my life; I will face this one as well. What other options are there?

Ironically, things did not all turn out as I had expected: Dr. Venable was permitted to retire with her pension; the Business Administrator was indeed fired; the Assistant Superintendent for Curriculum had accepted a position as principal of an elementary school. My assistant was fired and I was re-hired by another 5-4 vote. It was hard to believe I was the only cabinet administrator who survived the purge. I attributed it in large part to the black ministers, who were a major source of support for me. When I visited their churches, they knew how hard I worked and how distressed I was at the layoffs. I was very grateful to have them on my side, and most of all, because they dismissed Mr. M. from the Trenton School Board.

Oh, happy day! At last, life can attain some normalcy. I will now be able to accomplish things without his constant harassment.

An Interim Superintendent was brought in. He left the building at 5 p.m. every day and expected the administrators to do likewise. At first, I was disoriented, thinking it was far too early to leave the jobsite. Life was taking a positive turn, except for the increasing pain in my hands. The discomfort was becoming unmanageable. I returned to the doctor and he conducted sensitive nerve tests.

"As I told you, if you don't have this taken care of, you will lose the use of your hands. You've waited too long, and your condition is now chronic," he declared.

After a Board meeting, I told the new Acting Chief School Administrator about my need to have a carpal tunnel procedure done immediately.

"With your permission, I'll go to the hospital tomorrow for the operation and then work half-days the rest of the week until my left hand heals."

"Gilda. That will be fine."

The following morning, at 4 a.m., my in-laws drove me to the Hunter Hand Center in Philadelphia where Doctor Hunter himself operated on me for 4 and 1/2 hours under general anesthesia. I originally thought I required an in-office procedure, but it turned out to be more complicated.

When I awoke, my body felt strange. I couldn't return to the Trenton Board of Education because I had been stricken with sudden onset polyarthritis. Every joint in my body swelled and screamed in agony. I could hardly move. Walking was difficult due to the swelling in my feet. Getting dressed or lifting anything, even a bed sheet, was torture. I could not go out the front door of my house because I could not turn the key in the lock. Driving and cooking were impossible. I lost 23 pounds in one month and resigned on disability.

I never dreamed this could happen. I earned my doctorate at age 50 and now, eight years later, I am retiring. This was not part of the plan.

Mr. Baldassari had sent me a five-foot peace lily after the operation. He called me several times to go with him to the Roman Hall, but I told him it was not possible for me to leave the house. My rheumatologist gave me grim news.

"Your condition is chronic and progressive. I regret to inform you that you will only get worse."

Vicki called me from Seattle and suggested I take aquatic classes for arthritis. I signed up at the Hamilton YMCA, where my in-laws drove me at 8 a.m. and brought me back home at 9:15 a.m., three days a week. The classes were exhausting and sapped me of energy. When I arrived home, I went to bed and slept until 12 or 1 p.m. When I awoke, I was no longer drowsy, but I had no energy. In short, I was a worthless mess.

At 3 a.m. one Saturday morning I awoke suddenly with unbearable pain in my right arm.

Please God, either help me to get better or let me die because I can't continue to live like this.

I fell back to sleep and had the most comforting dream. I had entered a dimly-lit, stark room where three men were seated at a desk: one was facing me, one was at his left side and another was positioned at the right angle of the table. As I approached, I recognized the man in the front. It was Louie. His cousin, Francis Brenna, was at the right corner. The outline of the man next to Louie was blurry and remained indistinguishable.

Louie smiled broadly as I neared and gave me a clear, non-verbal message, as his lips did not move.

"Don't worry. I'll take care of everything for you from now on; right, Francis?" His cousin nodded vigorously in agreement. The other figure remained a blur. The men disappeared, and I drifted deeper into sleep. In the morning, I awoke to the telephone ringing.

"Hello!" said the deep voice with the Italian accent.

"Good morning, Mr. Baldassari."

"I haven't seen you in a long time and I want you to come to the Roman Hall today and buy me Sunday lunch."

He liked to kid about my buying him lunch. "I never let a woman pay for anything in my life," he later mentioned.

"I can't drive yet, Mr. Baldassari."

"I'll send a cab for you at noon."

Don't argue with him. The sun is shining, and it is a beautiful day, so go.

Getting dressed proved to be a problem because I wanted to wear pantyhose for the first time in a month. Tears streamed down my face as I made the attempt. The struggle was too much so I donned sandals instead. The day before my operation I had worn stiletto heels. I would never strut in those again.

The cab horn sounded. The driver locked my front door and I was off to the Roman Hall. I had not told my children, who were in graduate school out of state, about my health conditions and asked my in-laws not to tell them about the extent of my incapacitation. I didn't want to disrupt my children's studies, so I suffered in silence. Now it was comforting to know there was someone who seemed to care for my well-being.

"You look so skinny," Mr. Baldassari remarked as I entered the restaurant. "I must fatten you up. Eat! You'll get better."

We dined in the beautiful patio area his friend Joe Damiano constructed. The atmosphere was elegant and inviting as we enjoyed the bountiful luncheon, gazing into each other's eyes and giggling like teenagers.

"When I look at you, you squeeze-a-my heart," he said, with the innocence of a schoolboy.

How many men would express themselves freely that way? Who cares if his English is not perfect; his words squeeze my heart.

When I arrived home from our lovely repast, a beautiful bouquet of flowers was at my front door.

He's romancing me, and I will not be indifferent. I feel so much better and stronger now.

The following day was Monday. Mr. Baldassari did not call. My phone rang mid-day but it was a former colleague inquiring about my health. I told him I was being "plumped up" at the Roman Hall by the manager.

"That's nice, but you should know John Baldassari is spoken for by a woman who was a friend of his wife. He has known her for a long time." When the conversation ended, I felt confused and sad.

I thought he liked me? Today he must be in Atlantic City with her. I really shouldn't care, and I certainly won't lower myself to find out where he is or with whom. But I do mind, and this miserable feeling is jealousy.

The beautiful June day made my solitude intolerable. I couldn't resist. I dialed the phone number of Mr. Baldassari's son.

When the young man answered, I asked if his father were available.

"No. He is not in Trenton today."

"Did he go to Atlantic City?" I asked, hating myself for betraying my interest.

"Yes," he answered, not offering more information.

"Thanks; good bye."

I knew it! He is with that other woman. He will probably take her to the Baccarat table and then to the Primavera restaurant for dinner. Gilda, no matter what you say about just being friends, if you feel this vulnerable and miserable, you must be in love.

The door to my bedroom closet was open. I entered and removed from the shelf all the pictures that were taken on our dinner date in Atlantic City. For the first time, I carefully studied each and smiled as fond memories flooded back. I must have gazed at the images for over an hour before returning them to their perch. They filled me with a sweet sadness. That mood lingered until I went to bed.

On Tuesday morning, the phone rang.

"Hello! Do you want to buy me lunch today?"

"Yes, Mr. Baldassari, I do."

GRANITA WITH LOVE

Lunch at the Roman Hall was delightfully habit-forming. Mr. Baldassari called me to join him almost daily. Each subsequent repast made me feel stronger and more pain free, a more powerful medicine than medications.

In July, I received a delightful telephone call from Cellina from Trani. Since I first met her when she was eight years old and I, 13, I always enjoyed her company. In 1951, in Margherita di Savoia, we were hosted by her family, who lived together in a palazzo facing the Adriatic Sea. I loved being in their home. During that visit, after Vicki and I romped on the beach in front of their house, servants washed our feet before we went indoors.

"Boy, Vicki, isn't this a far cry from our traipsing through Grandpop's house with sandy toes in Mays Landing?"

"It sure is."

I liked the animated Cellina the moment I met her. Her cherubic face, framed with curly auburn hair, reminded me of a Botticelli angel we saw in a museum. She would come up to me speaking Italian. When I could not respond, she'd laugh and say, "*Non capisci,*" (You don't understand). She got that right. I felt frustrated at my lack of knowledge and was determined, after my papal promise, to learn the language and converse with her someday.

The opportunity arrived in 1959, when I was 21 years old. Mom and Dad returned to Margherita di Savoia with me. We stayed at the family's newly-renovated Grand Hotel Terme. My sister Gloria was then married, and Vicki was working in New York City, so I was the only daughter traveling with them.

Before the trip, I took a basic course in Italian at Beaver College, taught by the French Professor, Dr. Proux. She stressed the grammar/translation method more than conversation, so I was still very limited in my ability, but Cellina and I managed to communicate and we became inseparable. She was my *Cicerone* (Guide), taking me all over town, showing me off as her guest from across the sea from America.

At 19, Cellina married a distinguished man, Gennaro Lalli, who had studied diplomacy. They soon had two beautiful daughters and I spent many joyous summers as their guest in their "Grand Hotel Terme" in Margherita di Savoia, and in their lovely villa in nearby Trani.

When I called Cellina to tell her of my sudden onset arthritis attack, she invited me to her resort for thermal treatments.

"Gilda, come to the "Terme." The *Aqua Madre* (curative water) in Margherita di Savoia is very high in sodium, sulphur and bromine. When you bathe in it, it will relieve your inflammation."

The thought of indulging daily in a Jacuzzi with the *Acqua Madre*, followed by a full body massage and sun bathing on Cellina's private, pristine lido, appealed to me.

With "sunny Italy" on my mind, I met Mr. Baldassari for lunch in the bright patio area of Roman Hall. I told him of my plans to go to Puglia on August 3rd, 1997.

"What a coincidence! I will be in Rome at the same time. You must come to visit with my family first for a few days."

"Oh, no! That would not be possible. My relatives invited me to join them for two days in a hotel in Fiuggi, where they are on vacation. After that, we will go to Puglia."

"That's alright, but first, you'll be with me at my cousin's summer villa in Marina San Nicola, near Ladispoli."

"Ladispoli! Where is that?"

"It's north of Rome, on the Tiberian Sea. You'll love it."

"I can't be alone with you in someone's house. What would my children think?"

"You'll share a room with my niece. All the family stays there together. It will be very proper."

There he goes again. He's taking charge. He's already planned for me to go with him to Italy without knowing about Cellina's phone call today.

"I know an agent with the airline and you will have a first-class ticket for the price of coach. Do you accept the offer?"

"Yes."

How can I resist that price; besides, I like the idea. I know what it means when an Italian invites you to meet his family.

After our lovely luncheon, I called Cellina and told her I would be with friends before going to Fiuggi, so she needn't send Valerio, her driver, from Trani to meet me at the Rome airport. She sounded a bit suspicious, but as expected, she pleasantly acquiesced.

Mr. Baldassari made the first-class arrangements on Delta Airlines from JFK Airport. The plane landed at Fiumicino Airport. Although my flight accommodations were comfortable, I felt "stonata" (groggy), from trying to sleep in an upright position. That all changed the moment I exited the building, greeted by the gleaming Italian sunshine and a radiant Mr. Baldassari. He looked well rested. Being in Italy, albeit for a few days, had obviously done wonders for him. He introduced me to his relative.

"Gilda, this is my cousin Mauro," he said in Italian.

"*Molto piacere* (very pleased to meet you)," I responded.

Mauro reminded me of a Roman centurion. He was tall, muscular, lean, with thick brown hair and matching eyes. He had the air of a leader, a man always in charge. As the "Primogenito" (first born male) in the family, that was generally the case as they were nurtured by their mothers to be the latter's heir and caregiver in case the father died. Mauro, Louie and Mr. Baldassari were primogenitors, used to being shown deference.

Mauro lifted my heavy suitcase with ease and put it securely in the back of his Mercedes SUV. Mr. Baldassari helped me into the back seat and we were whisked off to Ladispoli.

Later I learned Ladispoli was the artichoke capital of the country. To Mr. Baldassari, it was the summer resort of his dear family. I could understand the provenance of his pride once we arrived at the iron gate of their villa. The portal opened to a beautiful property where the entire family, Mauro's mother, wife, four children, a fiancée and a dog had assembled to greet us. We kissed Italian style, on both cheeks, as though I were a returning relative. All in the family were glad I could converse in their language.

After I settled in my room, Mr. Baldassari was waiting for me in the downstairs parlor. I passed along stately palms and a wall covered by a flurry of magenta bougainvillea, before seeing him.

"Let's go out for a coffee. I'd like to be alone with you for a while," he said.

I happily entered another of Cousin Mauro's Mercedes and we sped off to a local café. It was the type of day that gave "sunny Italy" its moniker. The cloudless sapphire sky and brilliant sun made our surroundings shimmer.

We arrived at a small café in front of the Villa Nova, the secluded palace of Prince Odiscalchi. It had been converted to an exclusive hotel hidden by shrubbery.

"Let's go to the rear garden area," my escort said.

I followed him onto a paved, intimate courtyard where metal bistro tables were shaded by *Cinzano* umbrellas. He led me to a chair next to a graceful, three-tiered terra cotta fountain. The sound of the cool, warbling water was soothing.

"What would you like?" a waiter asked.

"*Due granite di caffè con panna* (Two iced coffees topped with whipped cream)," Mr. Baldassari ordered.

Soon, two tumblers of shaved, iced espresso arrived topped with a generous dollop of crème Chantilly. It was the best frozen espresso I ever tasted. As we enjoyed our treat, I asked Mr. Baldassari to tell me about his status with Gina, the woman he had been seeing.

"She is still a good friend, but I have decided I want only to spend my life with you. You are the 'vincitrice' (the winner)."

I like that word. I feel so happy.

As we were finishing our *granite*, I asked him to tell me how he was related to Mauro.

"I was born in 1927, in Trenton, New Jersey. It's funny because I am the only one among my two brothers and two sisters who speaks English with an accent. Life in Trenton was hard during the Depression. When I was three years old, my father, who was born in Rome, took the family back to Italy to live near his brother. My mother had a baby each year although the financial situation in Italy worsened. My father's brother was a successful businessman and offered to take me to live with him and his family in the city. Having one less mouth to feed would lessen the financial burden on my parents. I lived with my uncle until I was 18 years old, working as a butcher in one of the family's many stores. We were accustomed to prosperity although most of Italy was suffering terribly during World War II.

My father died when I turned 18 and my mother was pregnant with her sixth child. My older sister had died in Italy of kidney trouble. My mother wanted to return to Trenton, her birthplace, where several members of her family still lived. I cried because I had a girlfriend and I loved my life in Rome, but one day my uncle pulled me aside and put his arm around my shoulder."

"You are now the head of the family and have to be a man. Take the family back to America and do your duty."

"You were 18, knew no English, and had to support your mother, four siblings and yourself?"

"Yes. I worked double shifts at the Trenton Doll Factory and for Roebling's Steel."

"Weren't you exhausted?"

"No, I was strong. In one month, I bought a house for us on College Avenue in the Burg."

"How noble you were."

"No. I just did my duty. Everyone worked, even my younger brother, Eddie."

"How many 18-year-olds today could, or would support five other people?"

Mr. Baldassari shrugged at my question and continued talking about his cousin.

"Mauro was my uncle's son. We were always close," he said.

"I can see how well you get along. There is much love in your family."

This man is so kind and in many ways extraordinary. He dotes on me. I never thought that would happen again.

I know that some people back home criticize me for dating someone with a limited education and no profession, but I don't care. What matters most at this point in life is how he treats me. Making my own decisions is one of the perks of being an independent senior.

We finished the *granita*.

"Would you like another?" Mr. Baldassari asked.

"Thank you, but I couldn't."

I looked at him, studying his face in the sunlight. Emerald cypress trees in the background highlighted his masculine features. His eyes were hopeful, and my heart responded. A euphoric sensation welled within me.

Cav. Gilda Battaglia Rorro Baldassari, Ed.D.

Vacationing at Hotel Hermitage in Monte Carlo.

I haven't felt like this in decades. I think I'm falling in love with this man over a granita di caffe.'

GIOVÀ: THE DREAM MAKER

Mauro invited us that evening to a lovely restaurant in the hills outside of Ladispoli, called *La Mimosa*, named after a fragrant tree growing there. His mother Marcella, raven-haired wife Loredana, four grown children and their fiancées and friends attended, 16 in all. I loved being with the different generations. It reminded me of the Chinese restaurants on a Sunday afternoon in Philadelphia, where entire families, from great-grandparents to infants, gathered to enjoy a meal. Most Italians also prefer being with friends and family to dining alone. For them, togetherness is a joy in life.

At dinner, Mauro informed Mr. Baldassari and me that we would accompany him and Loredana to an enchanting place.

"Tomorrow morning, we will go to Monte Carlo, where we will spend two nights. I will then drive us directly to Fiuggi, where Gilda can meet Cellina and her husband Gennaro."

The entire Baldassari family enjoyed gambling and Mauro often frequented the Casino in that famous playground. I had traveled to Monte Carlo four times in the past and the thought of returning was enticing. My first visit was in 1951, during our family's three-month European tour. The American dollar was very strong then, enabling my parents to provide extraordinary experiences that would be financially prohibitive today, such as eating every day in the finest Parisian restaurants and occupying posh suites in well-known hotels.

Mom, Dad, and Gloria took Vicki and me to the Casino one night. Vicki and I were not permitted in the gambling hall where women seemed to float by dressed in elegant gowns and diamond tiaras, accompanied by gentlemen in formal black tuxedoes. We were made to sit in a gilded salon until our family would join us.

"You kids can't imagine what it was like in there," Dad said when he exited the gaming room. "King Farouk of Egypt was betting with 1,000-dollar chips. Everyone was quiet as he plunked down a small fortune. You could hear a pin drop."

I always remembered Dad's comment and I had wished to see the forbidden chamber for myself. On subsequent trips, I was of age to go inside but the patrons no longer donned such fine attire. They dressed in "smart business" style. The gowns, tiaras and tuxedoes were relegated to a bygone age that I will always remember.

The following morning, we packed overnight bags and headed along the majestic mountains of Liguria en route to France. We spoke only Italian because Mauro and Loredana knew little English.

"How do you like your trip so far?" Mauro inquired in his idiom.

"It's been very enjoyable. Your family is wonderful," I exclaimed. Mr. Baldassari smiled approvingly at my comment since I knew he wanted me to feel at home with his relatives.

We arrived at our destination in mid-afternoon. Mauro drove his Mercedes to the front of the legendary "Hermitage." I had never stayed at that Five Star hotel in the heart of Monte Carlo on the Place du Casino, but I always admired its elegant *Belle Epoque* façade and lobby on previous visits. When Mauro and Mr. Baldassari went to the registration desk, I joined them.

"I wish to have my own room and I am paying for it," I said.

"But you are our guest," Mauro protested.

My insistence won the day and I signed for a place of my own. We were led to our quarters located on the same floor. My room was decorated in pale mauve and silver. White orchids bloomed in a pewter vase next to an inviting pink settee. A grey mural of bucolic trees and sloping hills adorned the wall behind the bed's headboard. An inviting private balcony overlooked the courtyard where graceful palms swayed in the Mediterranean breeze.

The telephone rang, and the familiar voice informed me that the four of us would be going to the Monte Carlo Sportsmen's Club at 7 p.m.

"Is the dress casual?" I asked, contemplating an informal environment.

"Nothing is casual here," Mr. Baldassari said, amusingly.

At 7, we gathered under the hotel's floral stained-glass skylight and then departed for a night on the town. When Mauro arrived at the club, the valet parking attendant recognized him.

He must be a regular here like Mr. Baldassari is in Atlantic City. I'm really impressed.

We entered the building, which opened onto a series of ante rooms strewn with intricate Persian carpets in swirling patterns. Hosts in tuxedoes directed us toward a set of large doors. As we approached, the portals opened, revealing an enormous dining hall with a stage on which musicians sat cross-legged, playing seductive rhythms on Middle-Eastern instruments. In the background, whole lambs rotated over wood fires. Women wore Dior gowns and fine jewels. Most men were also formally dressed. I felt a bit self-conscious in a basic black, modest cocktail dress amid the splendor, but I still reveled in the beauty of it all. Mauro looked quietly elegant in a dark suit. Loredana did as well in a turquoise, tight-fitting silk ensemble complemented by a sinuous, spiral diamond bracelet that coiled from her wrist to mid arm. Mr. Baldassari, in a black silk suit, appeared perfectly comfortable, concentrating more on the lamb than the ambiance.

We were seated at a long, rectangular table occupied by several guests who spoke Arabic. Mauro and Mr. Baldassari took charge of ordering to surprise Loredana and me. We knew that whatever would appear on our plates was bound to be superb. Suddenly a francophone voice on a loudspeaker told everyone to gaze at the top of the room.

"Keep your eyes fixed upward," it exclaimed.

We did so and to our amazement, amid the strains of lilting music, the ceiling slowly folded outward revealing a star studded open sky. Everyone applauded the special effect which left us gazing at the moon while being caressed by the cool, night air and dazzling stellar display.

Platters brimming with generous portions of succulent, roasted lamb accompanied by hummus, pita and *tabbouleh*, were passed along to eager diners. Before dessert, another announcement was made.

"Ladies and gentlemen, the long-awaited Monte Carlo Fashion Show will now begin.

How strange to have a fashion show in a setting like this.

"You are going to like what they model," Mr. Baldassari said.

"Why do you say that? Are they going to highlight fashions from the Middle-East?"

Mauro, Loredana and Mr. Baldassari just looked at me and smiled.

Attractive, bone-thin young women arrived at the tables, their bodies completely covered in black leotards from neck to toe.

Where are the clothes? Don't embarrass myself by asking another silly question.

Handsome men in tuxedoes went up to the young women, handing them each a thin, black box. As the contents were revealed, gasps were heard throughout the room. A profusion of dazzling necklaces, bracelets, earrings and rings were lifted from the black velvet linings and placed on the models. Additional containers were opened and circulated among the guests.

"This is a fashion show of exclusive Cartier jewels," Mauro exclaimed.

Masterpieces in diamonds, rubies, emeralds and sapphires were given to me to touch and to try on. I decided not to because the temptation of being offered an item might be too much to resist, and resist, I knew I must.

"Is there something you would like?" Mr. Baldassari asked.

"Everything is stunning, but I seldom wear jewelry," I said, nonchalantly.

This is a scene from the Arabian Nights. Almost everyone speaks Arabic as well as French. I've never seen more beautiful jewels. Where would anyone wear such finery in Trenton?

I wonder why they call this a "Sportsmen's Club?" What do they hunt here?

The overwhelming display ended and so did dinner with baklava, assorted figs and dates. We returned to our palatial hotel. It was 11 p.m. and the men wanted to go to the famous Casino adjacent to the hotel to play baccarat. I excused myself because it was my usual bedtime and the events of the day made me fatigued. The trio left, and I returned to my cozy cocoon, where the delicious sights, sounds, smells, and tastes of the evening lingered in my mind.

I awoke at 8:30 to the welcome aroma of rich coffee and fresh-ly-baked French pastry. Wait staff were preparing the *petit dejeuner* buffet *al fresco*.

Mr. Baldassari will still be sleeping, no doubt, so I'll have breakfast alone and then I'll try out the pool.

Demitasse on the veranda was delightful and so was sampling the rich assortment of French cheeses. I savored each bite of the Camembert de Normandie, the Gruyere and Roquefort. Being in that enchanting setting was utterly delicious.

It was 10:30 when I went into the bathing area. It was a capacious open space where chartreuse water reflected on white tiles and chaises, creating soft warmth. The main wall, framed in the shape of a sea shell, was completely open, affording an uninterrupted view of the splendid Palace of Monaco and Monte Carlo Marina.

An instructor was conducting an aquatic exercise class in a far cor-ner of the pool, so I joined the group in the water. The movements were extremely gentle, not like the vigorous water aerobics sessions I was used to at the Hamilton YMCA.

Everything here is geared to pampering hotel guests.

The water was pristine; lacking was the smell of harsh chemicals and chlorine. I was gliding in a side stroke in a state of poetic dreaming. The air held a faint sweetness from the exhalations of a profusion of flowers in bloom on the outdoor, spacious veranda.

This is the life! After my experiences with the Trenton Board of Education, I feel as though I am on another planet.

"Hello," I heard from behind. I turned to face my traveling compan-ion, who stood by the pool.

"Mr. Baldassari! I thought you would still be sleeping."

"It's 11:30. I am always at work before then even if I haven't slept all night. Let's have an early lunch here on the veranda overlooking the Grimaldi Palace and then we will go sightseeing. You must take a siesta today because I have a surprise this evening."

"With you, there is a surprise *de jour.*"

Sitting under a parasol in the glimmering outdoor sun was delightful. Mr. Baldassari ordered champagne and Dover Sole for lunch. Mauro and Loredana joined our lovely repast. We chatted about future travels together.

"My brother, Francesco, has a yacht. He likes to go fishing in Sardinia. Let's plan to join him on your next visit," Mauro said.

The trio looked at me for confirmation. I smiled at them without saying a word.

It's too soon for me to make that kind of commitment, although it sounds grand.

That evening, I met Mr. Baldassari in the lobby. Once again, he wore the black silk suit. I had on my favorite, form-fitting black dress with a V-neck, long sleeves, quarter-length skirt and a smart, satin sash which accentuated my waist. It was from an upscale boutique in Lawrenceville and I always received compliments on it.

"Tonight, we are going to be alone," he said.

"Where are we going?"

"To a special place."

He is always in charge and knows exactly what he wants. I admire a strong man like that. At home, I am the one who organizes all my family's affairs. This experience is easy to get used to, but where is he taking me?

That evening, my escort took my arm and we exited the Hotel Hermitage and walked a short distance to the Hotel de Paris, also at the Place du Casino. On previous trips, I had visited the lobby of the majestic landmark, but not beyond. I recognized areas of its luxurious interior in Alfred Hitchcock's movie, "To Catch a Thief," with Grace Kelly. Now I was in that setting, being led to its famous "Louis XIV" restaurant. I had once read this was arguably the finest restaurant in the western world. Escoffier, the renowned chef, sat from a vantage point, observing every dining table from which he orchestrated impeccable service for each guest.

The restaurant's glass door with gilded lettering opened, leading us to a visual feast. An intricate tapestry served as a backdrop on one wall.

A lovely, svelte blonde singer in a sleek black satin gown was performing on a stage, accompanied by a piano and violins. Floral centerpieces
and crystal candelabra adorned each table. The guests wore *haute couture*
and most women were bedecked in singular sparkling heirloom gem-
stones. As we passed the diners, they exuded elegance. My favorite black
dress did not stand out in that crowd. In fact, we seemed invisible to
them, but that did not deter my enjoyment as I admired the wait staff in
their white morning suits and gloves. While I was impressed, Mr. Baldassari appeared nonchalant. He was ready to be seated and experience
the famed service and cuisine.

"This is indeed a memorable surprise," I said.

"You deserve this and much more," he answered.

I was entertained watching the sommelier pour wine and the waiters lift silver domes covering our entrees with a flourish of their gloved
hands. I savored each bite, but not Mr. Baldassari. In fact, he complained
his *tournedos du boeuf* was too gamey; this brought the *Maître d'* to us,
apologetic and eager to compensate with another choice of entrée. Mr.
Baldassari dismissed the suggestion settling for dessert and coffee.

*I would never have the nerve to complain in a place like this, yet, I admire
his Chutzpah. He is not intimidated by the sophisticates of the world.*

When we exited the restaurant, Mr. Baldassari took me to the
famed gaming salon where my parents had observed the Egyptian King
Farouk. I wanted to absorb each detail of the stately, formal setting but
surprisingly, my date was not in the mood to gamble. He then led me
through another area of the Casino where slot machines for the hoi-pol-
loi were installed.

*This is certainly a change from the exclusive, posh place we saw in 1951.
That era is gone forever.*

We strolled back to the Hermitage and ascended on the elevator to
our floor. When the door opened, we walked through the hallway. I
headed toward my room when Mr. Baldassari took my arm and steered
me gently in another direction.

"Where are we going?"

He remained silent. We stopped in front of the door to his room.

"Will you spend the night with me?"

"I can't. All my things are in my place," I answered, hedging, vacillating between nervousness and curiosity.

"I've taken care of everything. Your bag is here, and you are my guest for last night and tonight."

Oh, my God! What would Louie and my family say? Gilda, face it; you knew this was bound to happen sooner or later. You've never slept with a man other than Louie. Times have changed. Look at it this way: You were taught always to be pleasing to your husband; determine if this man is pleasing to you. Of course, you're nervous but control it. After all, this is the 21st century. You're an adult in Monte Carlo. You have to play to win.

I remained silent, yielding to his request. Mr. Baldassari opened the door and motioned for me to enter. His room was considerably larger than mine. My eyes darted from one angle to the next, taking in a wall covered with bright blue blossoms on a white background. The inviting color scheme was carried from the bedspread to the carpet and provincial chairs. A graceful antique satin azure drapery framed the long, glass patio doors, which opened onto a spacious veranda with robust balustrades. My overnight bag had been deposited unobtrusively near white closet doors.

Mr. Baldassari's eyes rested on me in a penetrating gaze. He came closer. His arms were incredibly strong.

"What is your name?" Correcting myself, I said, "I know people call you John. Is that your birth name?" "It's Giovanni. Call me John, Giovanni or whatever you like." "Giovà. I'll call you Giovà," and smiling seductively, I turned out the light.

DISAPPROVAL AND DECISION

After spending a delicious night with Mr. Baldassari, the following morning Mauro knocked on the door. "Get ready. We're leaving for Fiuggi soon," he said, then walked away discreetly.

The ride from Monte Carlo to the south of Rome took most of the day. Mauro drove on the *autostrada*, where we passed scenic hill towns perched along the Apennines. Frequent stops at charming cafés and a leisurely lunch of pasta with the famous pesto of Liguria, extended the travel time. We were living *La Dolce Vita*. Gennaro and Cellina were expecting us at *La Fontana Hotel*, where I would be their guest for the continuation of my trip. They invited John and his cousins to dinner there that evening.

It was nearly 8 p.m. when we arrived at the gracious landmark. Our hosts had invited the parish priest from Margherita di Savoia, Msgr. Emanuele Barra, to join them during their weekend stay. We gathered at the hotel bar, where Gennaro ordered Campari.

An open-air dinner was served by the pool. Everyone seemed relaxed and friendly and I was very content to be in the presence of those I loved. After the meal, Mauro, Loredana, and John left for their summer villa in Ladispoli. I felt happy that our mutual time together had gone well only to be surprised at what came next.

"Gilda, that man and you come from worlds apart," Cellina said.

"What do you mean? We are just friends," I said, defensively.

"No! Friends don't look at you that way. You two are so different."

My heart sank, as I felt they were chastising me. I didn't want to listen to their reasoning, so I said nothing more. I did not mention him to my hosts again. Instead, I concentrated on being an ideal travel companion. As a result, two lovely nights were spent at the hotel in Fiuggi. There was dancing in the evening with a live combo for the guests.

One night, Monsignor Barra invited me to be his partner in an elegant waltz, and later, to the rhythms of a Latin Samba. As we sauntered to our seats, I overheard several dowager onlookers whisper their disapproval of a dancing priest.

"It's scandalous!" one protested. "A dancing priest is not accepted behavior in my church in Brindisi." The others nodded in agreement.

Social strata and taboos still thrive in southern Italy. A major drawback of all this 'togetherness' is that everyone knows each other's business and renders an opinion. Gennaro and Cellina didn't accept Mr. Baldassari. I wonder how many promising relationships have been destroyed because of the "caring" of concerned family and friends. Yet, they may be right; he and I come from diametrically opposite backgrounds. All I know is that, during my excruciating bout of arthritis, Giovà picked me up like a bird with broken wings and for the first time in two years, I feel rejuvenated. But their disapproval has confused me. I must think this through carefully, but not now. Tomorrow is another day.

We left Fiuggi and traveled to one of my favorite places on earth, Margherita di Savoia. Gennaro's driver, Valerio, took us along the familiar *autostrada*, partially built by Gennaro's construction company. As our chauffeur sped along the highway, I felt as though I was returning to my second home. The brilliant burst of color from the oleander blooming along the highway signaled we were approaching the vast, open landscape of Puglia. We had left the congestion of major cities such as Naples, and sped along rolling hills where shafts of golden wheat undulated in the warm, limpid air. How I loved this agricultural region studded with orchards of olive and almond trees. I admired the Masserie (Italian farmhouses), with white stucco walls and terra cotta tiled roofs dotting the countryside. My heart quickened as we approached Margherita di Savoia, that small town by the sea.

The one-room house where my father was born still stands. Roaming the narrow streets, I imagined Dad in front of his boyhood home. Tourists enjoyed the summer in this popular resort because of its expansive view of the Adriatic flanked by the mountains of the Gargano range. Lounging under a huge, white beach umbrella on the lido of Cellina's hotel, I always marveled at how the violet sky meets the transparent, chartreuse sea, the two seeming to blend into a single, shimmering element. The sand sparkles like a carpet of miniature diamonds. In the warm evenings, outdoor discos blare international rhythms while entire families stroll, arm-in-arm, along the mosaic promenade *lungomare* (seafront).

The Grand Hotel Terme is a handsome, centrally located oasis. Each accommodation is furnished in cheerful, soothing pastels. The spacious bathrooms are lined with white tiles and complementary mint-green

Cellina visiting with me in New York.

accents. All quarters face the resplendent sea and the private lido where guests spend restful days on padded chaises under broad parasols.

The regional cuisine features simple, fresh ingredients prepared exquisitely. *Frutti di mare* (assorted seafood) are caught daily and cooked to tender perfection. Carrots, potatoes and zucchine have an uncommonly rich flavor because of the high concentration of sodium and other minerals in the soil.

One of my favorite delicacies is a peasant dish of *cozze, patate e riso* (mussels, potatoes and rice), covered with a mixture of bread crumbs, parmesan cheese, a hint of garlic and finely chopped parsley. The subtle, sweet liquor from the bi-valves infuses the roasted potatoes and rice, while the parmesan cheese forms a delectable, golden crust.

Being in my father's town always filled me with joy. This time, however, because of Cellina's previous declarations about John, there was a pall over my stay, until the second night, when the phone rang in my room.

"Hello," the familiar voice said.

My beating heart signaled that the chemistry between us was strong. For the first time, I wanted to leave Italy and return home, but I remained for the planned 10-day visit where John called me daily. The night before I was to return to Trenton, he told me that when my plane landed, he wanted me to go directly to the Roman Hall from the airport.

"I am not sure I can do that. My children are home from graduate school for only two more days. They must go back on Monday and I want to spend time with them."

"I have been sick, and I want you to come. Please bring your children with you."

"I am sorry to hear you have been ill. I will call you when the plane arrives," I replied.

Cellina and Gennaro were quintessential hosts. I was always sad to depart from them, but this time, the thought of seeing Giovà filled me with anticipation.

Michael and Mary met me at the Alitalia terminal in New York.

"We prepared a good dinner," my son said.

"That's nice of you but Mr. Baldassari called and wants us to eat with him tonight at the Roman Hall."

"But we spent so much time cooking," they protested.

"I'm sure you did, and I appreciate it, but Mr. Baldassari said he has been sick and he wants to be with us. Let's go there to say hello for a few minutes."

Michael and Mary were fond of John and they were genuinely concerned about his health.

We arrived in Trenton's familiar landmark two hours later. When Michael opened the front door of the restaurant, Giovà was waiting for us.

"Welcome home," he exclaimed, warmly, giving everyone a kiss on both cheeks.

"You seem healthy. You don't look sick at all," I said.

"Oh, I had a little cold, but I am all right now. Come to the patio; food is already on the table."

He said he was ill and that had me worried. What a pleasant ploy to get me here!

Bountiful antipasti awaited us. I noticed that although the restaurant was full, no one else was dining in the popular patio area. I excused myself to use the ladies' room and when I returned, I was in shock by a comment from John.

"I feel better now because your children gave me their permission."

"Permission for what?" I asked, my eyes scanning Michael and Mary for a clue.

"They gave me permission to marry you. They have no father now, so I asked them for your hand and they said yes."

Both children, who were in their mid-20s, exchanged perplexed glances with me. This was as unexpected for them as it was for me, but they liked him, and they appeared excited at the prospect of having a new father figure in their lives. I wanted to ask them exactly what John had said, but John gave me no opportunity to do so.

"After dinner, before you leave, please come to my office alone."

Another surprise? I wondered.

While Michael and Mary were waiting for their dessert, I went to the familiar command center, where John sat in a capacious 'captain's chair.'

"Please sit down," he said, graciously.

He opened a large, red ledger book, scanned it, and pointed his finger at a spot.

"That is it!"

"It is what?"

"July 12th. That will be our wedding day."

"Our wedding day? "John," I blurted. "I can't marry you. I don't really know you that well."

"This is October 23rd, 1997; by July 12th, you will know me."

"This wedding is going to take place whether I say yes or no, isn't it?"

"Yes, it is," he retorted, with confidence.

"What about the weather? July can be hot and humid."

"Don't worry. It's going to be a beautiful day."

Believe him. Everything will be just as he says. It always is.

Of course, I could have refused John if I wanted, as doubts persisted. This feeling was reinforced when, soon after I announced the possibility of marrying him, in lieu of congratulations, I received warnings from many well-meaning friends. The first was from Hank, a highly-published Professor of English at the College of New Jersey.

"Gilda, have you any idea what you are getting into? Do you know what it means that he is an Italian, owning and managing restaurants in Trenton?"

"It means he is a man who works long hours in that business."

"Oh, stop being coy. Of course, you know. You can't get mixed up in that element. It's dangerous. Don't do it!"

There was no convincing the upstanding WASP educator that John was simply a hard-working guy.

Two neighbors approached me on different occasions.

"You can't marry John Baldassari. You two are too different. It would never work."

I know they are genuinely interested in my welfare, but their comments are troubling.

The next day, I talked to John about my concerns, starting with the reference to his working in the restaurant business.

"People think because I'm Italian, I'm connected with organized crime? If I were, would I need to work so hard and wouldn't I have more money?"

He gazed at me with those pleading, Saint Bernard eyes. I hoped I hadn't offended him. He gave no further details and I did not question him. I wanted so much to trust that sincere man who was completely detached from my "white doily" world. Louie was from my world; but with John, it was different. He called me his *reginella* (little queen). In my weakened physical condition, his attention to my every need had comforted me and made me feel secure.

John's self-confidence was energizing. Returning home, I decided to embark on a new phase of my life. For starters, I needed to make repairs and upgrades to my house. Louie's protracted illness had precluded him from doing so and I never pressed the issue. Now I was ready and eager to make necessary changes.

The wall-to-wall deep green wool carpet in my living/dining room area was the first thing that had to go. My little *shih tzu*, Tiki, had been left alone 14 to 18 hours a day when I worked in Trenton and the rug was subsequently stained with unsightly yellow blotches. I thought of replacing it with ceramic tile but when that proved considerably expensive, I decided to look for linoleum which had a similar appearance.

"What did you do this morning?" John inquired, over lunch in Roman Hall's bright patio area.

I recounted how my canine companion ruined my carpeting.

"I went looking for ceramic tile, but I think I'll settle for linoleum instead."

"How much material do you need?"

"Enough to cover a 42 x 12-foot space."

"What if I could arrange for you to have marble installed for the same price as linoleum?"

"I wouldn't believe it, except that the statement is coming from you."

"Well, you can. My friend Leo Pignat is a master of marble installation. He owned the Pignat and Visintin Marble Company on Liberty Street. His company's workers laid all the marble at the National Shrine of Our Lady of Czestochowa in Doylestown. Can I send him to your house tomorrow?"

"Of course," I said, skeptically. "I've been to the Shrine and it is beautiful."

"If you marry me, I will convert your entire house into an Italian villa."

Ha, sure he will.

The following morning, Leo Pignat appeared at my front door. He was a tall, distinguished man in his 60s, with a cosmopolitan air, hailing from the Friuli/Veneto region. His accent was charming and his manners impeccable. John was right. This skilled craftsman was willing to transform my floor, parts of the kitchen and bathrooms, for an incredibly reasonable price.

John and I are engaged.

John's good friend proved to be a consummate professional and the beautification project was happily underway. While I was overjoyed with the change taking place in my home, I was still plagued by doubt about marrying John. After two weeks, I felt more comfortable with Leo and mustered the courage to ask him a personal question that was vital to me.

"Leo, you are one of John's best friends and aware he wants to marry me. Would you be willing to tell me something about his character since you've known him for over 20 years?"

"Of course," he said good-naturedly, smiling as he answered.

"First, you will never be hungry. Second, your life will always be exciting."

"Without a doubt, but how did he treat his wife?"

At that question, Leo's demeanor and voice took on a serious tone. He emphasized his words by patting his hand over his heart.

"Johnny was very loyal to her. She was sick most of the time they were married, but he was always faithful and never once complained about the situation."

That last statement mattered to me. I wanted a husband like Louie who I could rely on unconditionally. Louie had never looked at another woman once we were wed. In fact, he always said that if I predeceased him he would never remarry. Was I being disloyal to Louie's memory to contemplate marrying again? I had never pledged not to do so, and I was 57 when he passed away.

That evening, I had dinner with Marie. I recounted how the comments of others contrasted with the encouraging words of Leo.

"Gilda, listen to your heart. Remember that dream you told me you had a while ago in which there were three men in a room: one was Louie, one was his cousin and one was a blurry figure in the middle? Remember when Louie said not to worry, that he would take care of everything from then on? Well, I think that fuzzy figure in the center was John."

Marie's words startled me. Could that be? Could my dream have been a cosmic message from Louie? It didn't matter if it were fact or fantasy; I yearned to believe her interpretation: it made me feel at peace about my relationship with Giovà and I felt Louie's acceptance.

Despite the negative comments, these last few months have been the happiest I've known in a long time. If I heed the advice of "well-wishers," I will be isolated once again, concentrating only on my aching joints.

With Giovà there will be romance and much more.

"Marie, you have great insight and have truly helped me. Would you like to be a bridesmaid?"

CHAPTER FOURTEEN

DIPLOMACY AT LAST

DIPLOMACY AT LAST?

My life changed dramatically once I retired. While I was contemplating re-marrying, another significant transition occurred.

From the moment when the Consul of Uruguay introduced me to the world of diplomacy in 1962, I secretly yearned to be part of it. The diplomatic life was immersed in exciting high level social and cultural events. The foreign representatives in Philadelphia were politically connected men so I thought it impossible for a middle-class Italian American female to aspire to that exclusive domain. However, the desire lingered in my subconscious mind.

Surprisingly, the opportunity presented itself when I was 56-years-old, in 1994, working in the OEEO. The Cultural *Attaché* for the Office of the Italian Consulate General in Philadelphia met me at an educational reception in the *City of Brotherly Love*. We chatted, and I confided my fantasy of working in diplomatic circles. We stayed in contact socially and one day he called me with exciting news.

"There is an opening for the post of Honorary Vice Consul for Italy in Trenton, Gilda, and I want you to apply. You would be perfect. Do I have permission to nominate you?"

"Yes, of course, but what does the post entail?"

"All sorts of things: passport renewals, pension matters, preparing power of attorney documents, elopements in Italy and other duties."

That doesn't seem as glamorous as I always imagined, but what is? Contrary to public perception, life for young women in the movies was not all glamour either. This will be a challenge because the responsibilities are new, and I still need intellectual growth.

"Do you think I have a chance? Doesn't one have to be well-to-do and have certain political affiliations?"

"You need to be financially independent because there is just a small stipend. Of course, it helps to know people, and after all, you know me," he chuckled. "An honorary situation is not the same as being a career diplomat, but it does command respect as a representative of the government of Italy. Go for it. You will never know unless you try."

Apply I did, and within a few days I was summoned to the Italian Consulate General in Philadelphia. Consul General Valentino conducted the interview in Italian.

"Tell me about your interest in assuming this position and what you would do to promote Italian culture if selected," he asked.

"The thought of entering the diplomatic field has been a dream of mine since I was in my twenties. I have accrued additional life experience through advanced study, developing multicultural guidelines at the DOE and frequent visits to Italy. I will contribute significantly to the position."

I showed him several documents and the three handbooks I had written, which were published at the DOE. He was sufficiently impressed to tell me then and there that I was his choice from among the other candidates. There was a drawback. There were no health benefits and the office stipend might be 10,000 dollars a year. That did not quell my enthusiasm. The monetary issue seemed insignificant at that time. All I could think of was that it was finally possible for me to fulfill a long-awaited dream.

"Thank you. You will be pleased you made this decision," I exclaimed on preparing to leave the consul's office.

"One last thing, write me a letter of your intention to accept the position. There is a caveat. Do not tell anyone about this for at least six months. It will take that long for your paperwork to be processed by the Italian authorities. Things don't function as rapidly in Italy as they do in the United States."

I left his office excited at the prospect of embarking on a potentially new full-time career and leaving behind the stressful working conditions at the DOE. I couldn't wait to tell Louie about the interview, which I had kept a secret in case I was not accepted. When I arrived home, my husband wondered why I was smiling.

"Guess what? I am going to be the next Honorary Vice Consul for Italy, in Trenton; isn't that wonderful?" In lieu of congratulations, he immediately put a damper on my excitement.

"You can't do it. How can you give up a good salary and benefits to do that kind of work? It's out of the question now."

Louie was right, as usual. He was the practical one. I had only wanted to spread my wings doing something I would love, but family responsibilities precluded that. I worried that if I did not accept the position then, it would not be available in the future. Regardless, I sent the letter of intent to Consul General Valentino, not knowing what might transpire in six months.

Time passed, and Louie died in 1995. I had been working as Assistant Superintendent in Trenton for almost two years without any word from Consul General Valentino. Out of curiosity, I contacted him, inquiring about the opening.

"I was told you had accepted an important position in education in Trenton, therefore I assumed you were no longer interested in the honorary vice consulship. Someone else in Trenton has been selected. I hope my decision has not caused you any inconvenience."

I wonder who told him about my leaving the DOE? It was in the newspaper, so he may have seen it there. The consul is a sensible man like Louie. I am the dreamer, and some dreams are not meant to be.

In January 1998, I had retired from the Trenton Board of Education because of my debilitating polyarthritis. I busied myself with making wedding plans to marry John Baldassari when Carl Carabelli, a local leader in the Italian American community, told me that a mutual friend, Josie Giaquinto, was selected to be the next Honorary Vice Consul of Italy. She was born in Sicily and was well-qualified. I stated to Carl that Josie was a fine choice, but I could not resist relating my story to him.

"Gilda, I had no idea you were ever interviewed," he said, genuinely surprised. "Send me a copy of your intention letter; I'm interested in reading it."

Of course, nothing will change because of the letter. I just want Carl to know I was previously interviewed and selected. When the Pope asked me to promise I would learn Italian and never forget my heritage, I felt becoming the Honorary Vice Consul for Italy would have fulfilled that pledge. Oh, well.

At lunch in the Roman Hall the following afternoon, I told Giovà what had transpired. I referred to my betrothed as Giovà, when I addressed him with affection; otherwise, he was John.

"Don't feel bad. If you were the vice consul you would not have as much time to spend with me, so I'm glad," he said, in a comforting voice. John was positive and always strived to make me feel better.

He's in the right business. He is perfect in the role of making people happy, be it with food or advice.

A few days later Carl invited me to a reception to welcome Consul General Valentino's successor, the Hon. Anna Brigante Colonna at the Trenton Club on West State Street. I accepted and on entering the building, Josie was waiting for me at the top of the staircase.

"Gilda, I need to talk to you. Let's go to a private place where no one will hear us," she said quickly. We found a deserted corner behind the kitchen.

"I don't want to be the Honorary Vice Consul now. It's a great honor, but the stipend is small and there are no benefits. We have two young sons to educate; besides, I heard about your interview and we think you are the right person."

Josie's remarks were totally unexpected. I thanked her but said she should think about it a little longer.

"No, Gilda, I talked it over with my husband already and we agree to support your nomination."

Josie rushed off, leaving me to ponder what had just happened, but there was no time to reflect because Carl was escorting the new Consul General toward me. I soon learned she was the widow of an Italian ambassador, hailing from a centuries-old noble Roman family, the Colonnas. Carl and several other prominent individuals had already told her of my prior application for the honorary position. She took my hand and smiled.

"I am conducting interviews next week at the consulate. There are 14 candidates. You must reapply."

As she departed, I felt surprised that my interest in the job had not waned after all that had transpired. Apart from planning to marry, I still craved challenges and mental stimulation. I was concerned, however, that I could be setting myself up for another disappointment.

Remember what the Cultural Attaché, Prof. Luigi Scotto said, "You'll never know unless you try."

The next week I went to the consulate for the interview. It was inspiring to see a woman in the role of Consul General. She proved to be a highly professional and gracious interviewer.

"All the applicants are fluent in Italian. In addition to regular duties, Italian consulate representatives are now expected to conduct activities to promote Italian culture as well. Why should I choose you from among the others?"

"I am in an advantageous position in that I belong to many Italian American organizations, which encourages me to promote the cultural patrimony of Italy."

I expounded on my connection to the New Jersey Department of Education, being the Chair of the Cultural Theater of the Mercer County Italian American Festival and Chair for Programming for the Italian American National Hall of Fame, as well as membership in several other similar groups. At the end of the session she said that my consular jurisdiction would include southern and central New Jersey and that I would be hearing soon from her assistant regarding my status.

When I left her office, and walked down the hall toward the elevator, I felt assured all had gone well. There was no mention of a six-month wait period or letter of intent. This time the space had to be filled quickly.

Three days later, the assistant to the Consul General called me.

"*Congratulazioni, Vice Console Onorario d'Italia!*" the cheerful voice of the assistant to the Consul General announced. She told me to report to their office for my official swearing-in ceremony the following week.

Finalmente! This was meant to be. The Pope would be pleased; my parents would be thrilled and even Louie would be happy for me now. Somehow, I would like to think they know.

I called John as soon as I returned home.

"Brava!" He shouted. "After you are sworn in, we will host a big reception for the community to inaugurate the new consular office in your home."

"Oh, John, something that size will be difficult for me to manage with my arthritis. Are you sure it is necessary?"

"Of course, it is. Don't worry. I am going to take care of everything for you from now on."

Strange, they were the exact words Louie uttered to me in my dream.

"When we marry, you will never have to cook or clean again," John said, convincingly. "All I want is to see you happy and to get well."

Dear Lord, I hope this man is for real. If he's not, he sure has me fooled.

John accompanied me the following week to the Italian Consulate where my lovely, official ceremony was attended by all staff in a stately oak-paneled reception room overlooking Independence Hall. Prosecco flowed, and I was congratulated by each staff person, making me feel instantly a part of their diplomatic family.

On the way home, in the car, we were planning the open-house reception. My fiancé proved true to his word. For the first time in over 30 years, I did not have to prepare all the hors-d'oeuvres, clean or decorate the house. Instead, I watched in wonder as he sent a crew of workers to my home sporting long, crisp white aprons. They whisked past me, moving furniture, setting tables, arranging flowers and balancing large trays of beautifully presented food. It was like a theatrical production providing me a glimpse of how Giovà was transforming my dwelling and my life. I couldn't wait to see what was coming next.

WEDDING OF THE CENTURY

"Now, ladies and gentlemen," the MC announced, "you will hear from our guest speaker of the evening, Dr. Gilda Rorro Baldassari."

I began walking toward the microphone when a loud voice called.

"Stop! I have something to say first. Gilda; sit down."

The voice belonged to Monsignor Joseph Ferrante. Everyone attending the Roman Society dinner was stunned at the priest's abrupt announcement.

"After concelebrating the beautiful mass for John and Gilda last year at Saint Joachim's Church, there were 475 people having an unforgettable time here at the Roman Hall. From the 18-piece band, the surf and turf dinner to Dom Perignon Champaign, I've heard some comment that it was the wedding of the year, but I say it was the wedding of the century. Those of you who were fortunate to have been there know what I mean."

His unexpected remarks were greeted with a burst of applause, evoking a flash of happy memories, which took me back to planning the big event.

My first recollection took place in Giovà's office, with him asking me where I wanted to be married.

"In Saint Joachim's Church, where Louie received all his sacraments."

"I will do anything you say—priest, justice of the peace, whatever you want. What kind of reception would you like?"

"Giovà, you are 70 and I am 60 years old. Something intimate with just our immediate family and a few friends would be nice. A candlelight supper in the Black Swan Restaurant at the Scanticon, in Princeton, would be lovely."

"Whatever you want, sweetheart," he answered.

Of course, my first lesson of life with John was that his idea of small or intimate was big, if not grandiose, so the Roman Hall banquet room became the place of choice. I didn't mind. I was amused by my betrothed's childlike enthusiasm for making our bonding a community affair. His happiness was infectious, and I had never seen anything like its ripple effect on others. People in the Burg who had treated me with polite indifference in the past sought me out with displays of effusive affection, lavishing me with hugs and kisses.

It was also curious how attitudes toward my marrying John Baldassari had suddenly changed. No more did I hear that we were not well suited. On the contrary, the whole of Chambersburg was congratulating us and talking about our nuptials. The most important topic of conversation focused on who would receive an invitation. The capacity at the Roman Hall Banquet Room could not exceed 475 people. If it could have accommodated 1,000, there would have been no problem finding those who wanted to come. To me, the most meaningful change of opinion happened that March with an unexpected visit from Cellina and Gennaro.

"Gilda, we are coming to spend the night with you in Trenton next Friday, and on Saturday, we would like you to be our guest at the Saint Regis Hotel in New York City," Cellina informed me in Italian from her home in Rome.

When I mentioned this to John, he immediately said, "Have a wonderful time, but I don't want you on a train carrying suitcases. You will go in my car and I will send my staff person, Cesare, to drive you round trip."

According to plan, my wonderful guests arrived from Italy and the following day Cesare arrived at my door and drove Cellina, Gennaro, and me to the 'Big Apple.' I felt uneasy being in John's car because, when in Italy, Cellina and Gennaro had been so skeptical about my continuing a relationship with him. Their attitude was the only impediment to my feeling completely happy about my forthcoming marriage.

My discomfort was heightened when Cellina, being uncommonly astute, asked slowly and deliberately, "Gilda, who is the owner of this automobile? It's not yours. Does it belong to the man we met in Fiuggi?"

I had turned 60 years old that month and felt like an embarrassed schoolgirl being forced to confess my trespass to an authority figure.

"Yes, it does, Cellina, and we are going to be married in July."

I tried to control my voice and not respond meekly, bracing myself for her inevitable verbal rebuke. But Cellina's reaction startled me.

"Gilda, why didn't you tell me this sooner?" she asked, with disappointment.

"Because you and Gennaro were against my seeing him. I wanted you to know, but it was too awkward for me."

"No, Gilda. If that is what you want, we are happy for you. When is the wedding going to take place and where are you going on your honeymoon?"

"We'll be married in Trenton on July 12th and then travel to Rome to visit John's family. We will then go to Venice for a cruise to the Greek Islands."

"Doesn't that ship stop in Bari?"

"Yes. Bari is on the itinerary."

"Then our family and your friends in Margherita di Savoia will come to the ship to greet you there."

Oh, glory! Even Cellina and Gennaro are happy for me now. They have removed the last vestige of lingering doubt I may have had about marrying John. From now on, I am going to focus on our wedding and becoming a bride at 60. Giovà and I will show everyone how senior love can bloom in the Burg.

Monsignor Ferrante ended his discourse and with it, my reverie. When I returned home and readied for bed, Monsignor's comment about our wedding of the century continued to spark memories. Several persisted after I turned out the light.

Before dozing off, one scene stood out vividly in my obscure surroundings. I recalled that our 79-year-old friend Lola Rossi and I had been in my kitchen reviewing the final seating arrangements for the wedding reception. Red-headed, feisty Lola was the designated person in the parish for organizing such plans. She knew everyone and where and with whom each should be placed at every occasion. The jangle of the telephone interrupted us. Monsignor Thomas Gervasio was on the line.

"Gilda, I'll meet the wedding party this evening at 4:30 at Saint Joachim's Church for the rehearsal, after which I'll join you for dinner at 6 p.m. in the Roman Hall. Don't forget to bring the marriage license with you."

"License? What license?" I asked, incredulously. "Didn't we arrange everything with you at the rectory two months ago?"

"No. We discussed the church ceremony, but not the license. Don't you remember needing one when you were first married?"

"That was over 30 years ago, and I did not remember."

"I'm sorry, but if you don't have a license, I can't marry you."

"Oh, my God! It's 2:50 p.m. on Friday and the wedding is this Sunday. What am I to do, Monsignor?"

"Go to the Township Building right away and take a witness with you."

I slammed the receiver on its cradle. Feeling frantic, I turned to my bewildered companion.

"Lola, drop what you are doing and come with me."

Before Lola could speak, I had her by the wrist, leading her out the door to my car. In the vehicle, we headed on Greenwood Avenue toward the Hamilton Township Municipal Building in rush-hour traffic.

"Where are you taking me? What's happened?"

"It's what didn't happen that's important."

I explained the situation hurriedly to my flustered friend as we rapidly climbed the side stairs of the Township Building.

"I need a marriage license ASAP," I exclaimed to a clerk, panting for air.

"Wait here while I get someone to help you," he said, realizing my urgency.

A large wall clock indicated it was 3:15 p.m. I began to relax. *At least I got here before four*, I thought, feeling assured there was ample time to secure the precious document so I sat and made small talk with Lola.

Ten minutes later, an agent entered the room, speaking as he approached us.

"Sorry to keep you waiting. We can't issue you a marriage license. You must go to the Justice Department downtown. There isn't much time because they close at 4 p.m., and you have to see a judge."

"May I use your phone?" I asked, feeling weak in the knees. He led me into an office where I placed a call to John.

"Giovà, you won't believe what I am about to say. We may not get married Sunday."

I explained the situation and told him I was going to Trenton with Lola and I would call him from there.

"Okay, sweetheart, but relax. Everything will be all right."

Relax. How can I relax? How can John sound so calm in this situation?

"Come, Lola, you're going for another ride. There's so little time; I'll explain what's happening later."

My companion was not used to that much rushing, but she tried valiantly to control herself and not flinch as I swept through several yellow lights until we reached the destination. Luckily there was a parking spot on the street in front of the Justice Department, as workers were already exiting the building for the weekend.

"Hurry, Lola," I said, tugging on her arm as though it were a water pump as we ascended a new set of stairs.

We entered the empty lobby, when a voice behind us broke the silence.

"What are you looking for ladies?"

It was a guard. When he heard my prattle about the license, he cut me short.

"It's too late now. You can go up to the second floor and look for a judge if you insist, but I doubt you will find one available at 3:50 p.m. on a Friday."

Undaunted, I once again pulled Lola by the arm up a long flight of stairs to the next floor, not wanting to waste precious minutes waiting for an elevator. She asked no questions; she saw it was useless to slow me down and somehow kept the hectic pace.

At the top of the stairs, two guards were speaking with two other staff workers. When they saw us rushing toward them, they stopped their conversation.

"Please. I need a marriage license immediately."

"What? You can't be serious. It's five minutes to four."

"But I'm supposed to be married on Sunday and without that piece of paper it's impossible."

Our wedding day: July 12, 1998.

"Sorry, but there's nothing we can do."

I was so frustrated. I turned to Lola who took my hand in a gesture of consolation.

That's it. I give up. Nothing can be done now. What will we tell everyone at the church?

Suddenly, the group's attention shifted from Lola and me to someone behind us.

"Hey Johnny! How you doin' man? What's up?" the four shouted in unison, their dour expressions transforming into radiant, toothy smiles. John stepped forward where he received hearty *abrazos* and back slapping from the friendly foursome.

"So, you forgot to get a license, Johnny?" they laughed in unison.

"Come with me," one guard said, leading us down the hall to a room where court was in session. "Wait here a minute; I'll see what I can do." He was true to his word because he returned quickly.

"Go in. The judge is almost finished with a case. As soon as she's done, she'll come to address your issue."

The clock on the wall ticked to 3:59 p.m. John took my hand in his and squeezed it reassuringly.

I don't need to worry about anything. Giovà is taking care of everything like he always does.

I was too drained to linger on the unfairness of my being denied assistance while John was granted this big favor. My tension dissipated as Lola looked at us, smiling, albeit befuddled. When the prior legal business concluded, the judge addressed us with stern eyes.

"Well, well, what do we have here? You are expecting to be married this Sunday. You've made all the arrangements and you've invited 475 guests, but you forgot to get a license." Her demeanor morphed from serious to amused as she uttered the last phrase chuckling.

"Correction, your Honor," I blurted. We're expecting 476, because you're invited too."

At my impromptu declaration, all assembled began to laugh, then applaud. The license appeared; we signed. The judge kissed us and off we went to Saint Joachim's to meet Monsignor Gervasio. On the way, I quizzed John.

"Giovà, what would you have done Sunday if we didn't get the license?"

"It's simple. I'd be at the church steps and tell everyone to go to Roman Hall for the party because we were going to get married in Italy instead. You see sweetheart, you don't need to worry anymore. I'll always take care of everything."

Somehow, I believed him, and fell asleep and dreamed about my wedding.

What a glorious morning! Our wedding day was perfect, just as John predicted: 82 degrees with low humidity, under a cloudless, cobalt blue sky. The dazzling morning put everyone in a joyful mood to celebrate the nuptials of two seniors.

Saint Joachim's Church was overflowing with well-wishers. Some lined the sidewalk outside to greet us. The familiar strains from Lohen-

Consul General of Italy, Hon. Anna
Brigante Colonna, attends our wedding

John and I with John's good friend,
Leo Pignat

grin signaled the procession was to begin. The ushers looked dashing in their tuxedoes and the bridesmaids were elegant in navy-blue chiffon gowns. I wore a sleeveless, cream-colored straight silk gown with orange blossoms in my hair. My son was to "give me away."

He dutifully escorted me next to John, who appeared so pale I thought he would faint. I smiled more broadly and took on an air of confidence to bolster him. At the altar, Monsignor Gervasio, with three priest concelebrants, began the ceremony by making a statement. "How I would love to see such a crowd at every mass on Sunday."

Consul General Brigante Colonna attended with the Consular Accountant. Pope John Paul II sent a Papal Blessing on ornately painted parchment paper and had his Secretary of State forward a telegram saying all present were to receive a special blessing from the Holy Father. My daughter Mary played the *Ave Maria* on the viola and my talented friend from the DOE, Assistant Commissioner Jay Doolan, sang beautifully in Italian and English.

The reception that followed in the Roman Hall was overflowing with floral arrangements, gold candelabras, and gleaming crystal. Giovà and I sat at a "sweetheart table" in the center of the ballroom as the metal clangs of a spoon on a glass signaled we were to kiss. Between smooching, people came up to us with envelopes. Giuseppe (Joe) Damiano had constructed a 4 x 4 foot wooden Italianate mailbox with white columns at the corners, not the usual satin purse brides carried to facilitate the depositing of monetary gifts. It was full by the end of the evening.

Guests came to our table sharing pertinent anecdotes.

"Hey Johnny, it's 1998, remember how weddings were here a long time ago? Remember the pitchers of beer and wine on the tables and trays piled high with Italian sandwiches wrapped in wax paper? Remember how, if we wanted salami and it wasn't on our tray, we'd shout to a friend across the room. If they had it, they'd throw it to us and we'd toss our provolone back at them? They were fun days. But when you took this place over, you changed everything: no more sandwiches. You started buffets and sit-down dinners. Now look at all this class."

The conversation conjures up visions of torpedo-like missiles flying across the room at break neck speed. I wonder if the hurlers ever hit anyone accidentally, or intentionally? That would have caused quite a stir. It reminds me of similar receptions in local halls in Philadelphia, where roast pork and beef sandwiches were served. No throwing was possible with those piping hot rolls brimming with soft, juicy meat. How I admired then the huge trays of Italian cookies dotted with Jordan almonds and colorful confetti. I vowed, however, to have a sophisticated wedding when I first married, and I did, but people had a great time at those other affairs and they are having a wonderful time now.

Our reception dinner at the Roman Hall was an *abbondanza* extravaganza consisting of assorted antipasti, vodka rigatoni, lobster tails and filet mignon. Dom Perignon was poured for the *brindisi* (toast).

Several of my 90-year-old cousins from the Bronx, in New York, including my Uncle Ralph, from Mays Landing, came and their presence was a high point for me. My 92-year-old Cousin Helen went on the stage, took the microphone and sang in a booming voice, "I Ain't Got Nobody," to hearty applause.

Our wedding party in Kuser Park.

Giovà was in his glory; he relished the glitz, the laughter and the congratulatory back-slapping. He was king of this world and he wanted all assembled to welcome his "Queen."

I would have preferred the subdued, candle-light supper at the Scanticon, but I knew Giovà wanted me to have the biggest and best affair ever seen in Chambersburg, and he certainly succeeded. I love him for the enormous amount of preparation he has devoted to our union and I want to make him happy. Seeing all these smiling faces warms my heart.

When the five-hour celebration ended, a limousine whisked us to Atlantic City where Giovà had arranged for us to return to the place where we had our first date at Caesar's.

I'm exhausted. It would have been so nice to go home and rest before leaving for Rome tomorrow, but John wants every detail of our day to be special. He's so romantic; I could never disappoint him. I'm learning what Leo meant when he said, "If you marry John your life will always be exciting."

After a two-hour ride to AC, we entered our capacious suite in Caesar's. The room had bowls of fruit, cheese and cracker trays, bountiful floral bouquets and another bottle of chilled Dom Perignon. Giovà smiled at me, satisfied that all the nuptial arrangements he had made with assiduous care had been met.

Taking me in his arms, he said, "You are my *reginella*, (little queen). Pack your wedding gown because your new family is giving us another wedding reception in Rome."

"Another?"

Leo's words keep ringing in my ears.

The next day at noon, we returned to Trenton to attend to last minute details and farewells to family and friends before going to the Newark Airport. John booked a three and one-half-week honeymoon. All was going according to his plan. Our flight on Alitalia was on time. The captain sat and chatted with us a little before takeoff and the ride was wonderfully smooth.

Giovà fell asleep on the plane while my thoughts soared about how my life had changed dramatically in less than a year. I went from being isolated at home, barely able to walk and wracked with pain from rheumatoid arthritis to the belle of the ball. It was as though I landed on another planet and it was mostly because of the man snoring softly beside me.

Looking back, I remember Monsignor Ferrante's reference to "the wedding of the century," surely the largest and grandest ever staged in Roman Hall.

When we arrived at Fiumicino Airport, Mauro drove us to Marina San Nicola.

The sun was dazzling in sunny Italy. It was wonderful being in love and acting like teenagers. Perhaps Giovà and I were even happier than adolescents because we had been through so much in life and appreciated the rare gift we found in each other. As joyful as I was at that moment, I could never have imagined what more was yet to unfold.

SAVED BY TRENTON

Marriage to John Baldassari was delightfully life altering. My introduction was from the first day of our honeymoon in Italy and cruise to the Greek islands. It began with a meeting with the American Ambassador, Hon. Thomas M. Foglietta, at the Embassy of the United States of America in the sumptuous Roman Palazzo Margherita, converted into diplomatic offices. The second day, Helen Boehm, CEO of Boehm Porcelain Studios in Trenton, arranged for us to enjoy a private, guided tour of the Sistine Chapel as well as her two permanent exhibits in the Vatican Museum: Etruscan Art and Miniature Mosaics.

A second formal wedding reception had been planned by Mauro and Loredana at the *Ristorante La Monachina,* on the outskirts of Rome, where 70 family members and friends assembled. The festivities began with an outdoor cocktail under a violet Italian sky, followed by a joyful six-hour banquet and dancing.

On the cruise, when our ship on the Costa Line docked in Bari, Giovà had arranged a private luncheon aboard for Cellina, her family and four select friends. We had the entire 600-seat dining room to ourselves where the Maître d', a sommelier and abundant wait staff catered to our every whim.

John certainly knows how to impress family and he makes me feel like "Queen for a Day."

Those festivities were special, but to me, the most meaningful moments were having time to sit quietly and converse with my husband. I realized that I married the man without really knowing him and he truly didn't know me either. We had been caught in a whirlwind of lunches, dinners, banquets and parties at the Roman Hall where he was constantly interrupted by clients, vendors and phone calls.

John had asked me to marry him to fill a void after his wife died. He often told me, "When I go home to an empty house, I feel depressed." I don't think he cares about who I am as much as having a woman's presence in his home, and somehow I don't mind. He married me with a trusting innocence that I find endearing. I won't disappoint him.

One beautiful morning, the two of us enjoyed a relaxed moment alone by a Venetian canal at an outdoor café. While we sipped espresso, Giovà told me a shocking story which revealed a significant side of his character.

"Trenton saved my life."

"Trenton, what do you mean?"

"I was 18 years old in Rome during the war. Partisans had killed a German soldier. It was the custom for the Nazis to round up and execute 10 Italian men for every German shot. I was pulled off the street and taken prisoner. They threw me in a cell in the army barracks with nine other frightened men aged 16–70. After several hours, the door of the crowded, stifling room opened, and an S.S. officer entered, accompanied by two soldiers. The officer addressed us in a loud, harsh voice.

Domani, alles kaput (Tomorrow, you all will die), slashing the air with his right hand across his throat. I don't know what possessed me, but I went up to him, enclosed his hand in mine and shook it vigorously. The gesture startled him, and he slowly released his fingers, staring at me intently."

"Where are you from?"

"Trenton. He thought I said "Trento," the region in northern Italy controlled by the Nazis. He turned to his two men."

"This man is free to go."

"Guards escorted me from the cell behind the officer. I rushed out of the building and began running home as fast as I could, not daring to look back for fear someone would realize I was from Trenton, New Jersey, and not from Trentino-Alto Adige. As I dashed on, skirting past annoyed pedestrians, I felt guilty and cowardly on having left the nine other men to their grim fate. What did they think of me? Did I deserve to be spared? What I knew was that I would remember their frightened faces the rest of my life."

TRANSFORMATION

John was true to his word about transforming my rectangular ranch style house on a double sloping lot into an Italianate villa. He attacked the project with ebullient energy. It started with the 8 x 10 foot crumbling concrete patio.

"This space needs to be repaired."

"I know John, but I haven't had time to think about it, with my arthritis and the wedding preparations. I've concentrated on remodeling the inside before we married. The outside didn't seem as important."

"But it is. Relax. I'll take care of it, sweetheart."

These words are music to my ears. All my life I have had to care for myself and others. This is the first time someone says he will take care of things for me.

A few days later, on a busy Saturday morning, at 9 a.m., there were 24 people assembled in my consular office waiting room at home. When I escorted one Italian co-national to the door, I saw three men walking hurriedly into the yard area.

"Are you looking for the consulate?"

"No. Johnny sent us to see the patio," one exclaimed as he moved on.

"Oh, okay; it's back there."

The heavy consular workload distracted me temporarily. When the last person exited, at 3:30 p.m., I went to see what was happening outside. There, surrounding the patio, was a string measuring 26 x 26 feet.

"Why is this area cordoned off?" I inquired from the workman who seemed to be the leader.

"Johnny says he wants to enlarge the patio."

"But this much?"

"That's what Johnny told me, Ma'am. You gotta talk to him."

I called John immediately at the restaurant.

"John, the workers must have made a mistake. You'd better come home before they do anything else."

Surprisingly, my husband returned quickly, eager to see what was happening. He took two lawn chairs and said, "Sit down, sweetheart. I want to share my idea with you."

I dutifully took my place beside him.

"I've been thinking. You have a lot of room out here. Let's make a large, screened patio where we can sit and entertain. You'll love it, I know."

As usual, it was hard to resist those "Saint Bernard" eyes and his voice, pleading to please.

"That does sound nice, Giovà. You'll be in charge?"

"I'll do everything."

The following week, after concrete was poured on the expansive new area, John had me sit at the site once again.

"I've been thinking, sweetheart. Instead of screening the patio, we should enclose it and make it into a big sun room where we can sit and entertain all year long. How does that sound?"

"It sounds fine, Giovà."

John was not one to waste time. Soon the frame for the walls went up. For a third time, John led me to the familiar chairs outside for a consultation.

"Sweetheart, I've got another idea, but I will do it only if you approve. If you say no, it's no."

"What is it this time?

"Let's build a new bedroom over the sun room with a bathroom for you and me."

"Why do you want to make so many changes? Don't you think it's fine the way it is now?

"Yes, I like it but I don't feel as though I deserve to live here without contributing to the house."

That's a noble gesture.

"I also feel Louie is staring down at us in the bedroom. Let's build a room of our own."

That's the real reason.

Before long the framing was complete with insulation, plumbing, electric and sheetrock. The house was now undergoing a major change.

"We're traveling to Easton today."

"What for?"

"You'll see. Leo and Joe Damiano are coming too."

I enjoyed being in the company of John's best friends, who some people in the Burg labeled "The Dream Team" because of their extraordinary craftsmanship.

The three men and I climbed into the Roman Hall van with an image of "Miss Piggy" covering one side, and took off for Easton. The September day was bright, and our spirits mounted. On the Pennsylvania Turnpike, John led us into singing Neapolitan favorites until we reached our destination, which was a landscape supply company with a vast array of outdoor fountains, columns, statues and ornaments in marble, terra cotta, concrete, porcelain and other materials.

"It's good to see you, John. What brings you here today?" the proprietor asked.

"I need five, eight-foot concrete columns, a large fountain, four reclining lions and some balustrades."

"Is that all?" the owner laughed. What will you do with the columns?"

"I want to build a temple to the woman I love."

And so, my life continued amid the creative chaos.

WHAT GOES AROUND, COMES AROUND

After our honeymoon, our lives and responsibilities resumed. John worked long hours daily and I was occupied with Italian citizens coming to my consular office in the house. Although I tried to maintain a tight schedule by appointment only, people called me on the phone at all hours of the day and night. Often, we would be awakened at 3 a.m. while apologetic voices from Italy said they were not aware of the time difference. John never complained. He was proud of the work I was doing, as I was of his managing arguably Trenton's most popular Italian restaurant and banquet hall.

It was only at breakfast we had an opportunity to talk to each other, enjoying an espresso and holding hands. Those precious moments were the most meaningful to me. I often joked with my husband that he could have saved himself a bundle during our courtship. I told him I fell in love over the *granita di caffè* we shared in the courtyard of the cozy café outside of Ladispoli.

I listened attentively as John told me many stories about how he entered the restaurant business.

"I worked as a dishwasher in an Italian restaurant on Warren Street in Trenton. One Sunday evening, the chef quit. The manager needed a cook. I told him I had culinary experience."

"You can cook?" the owner asked. "Why didn't you ever tell me?"

"You never asked."

"All right. Start on Tuesday. Let's see how you do."

"Thanks boss. You won't be disappointed."

"I had never prepared two eggs in my life, but I didn't want to be a dishwasher any longer. I bought a cookbook and studied it all day Sunday and practiced making omelets and tomato sauce on Monday. When Tuesday arrived, I was ready."

"John, the first thing you have to do is to buy a new strainer for pasta. Ours is dented."

"Okay, boss."

I went to a local supply store.

"How can I help you?"

"I couldn't remember the word for strainer, so I tried to explain what it was.

"I want a water go, macaroni stop."

The salesman looked at me for a moment without saying a word. He disappeared and soon returned with the device. I knew I was on my way to a new career."

John's stories always fascinated me, and I found his way of speaking, endearing. One day he took me to the Roma Bank in Chambersburg. Everyone in the building knew and liked my spouse.

"Mr. Baldassari, what can I do for you today?"

"I want to put some money in *shcarol* (dialect pronunciation of escarole)."

Fortunately, the young male agent was of Italian background and understood instantly that John wanted to put money in escrow, not to buy the vegetable, and he and I could not suppress a laugh.

My life continued with a house under constant construction. I loved accompanying Joe, Leo, and John to Millhurst Mills in Freehold to buy building materials. One of my favorite pastimes there was to talk with Timothy Crawford, the young manager. His mother was a reading teacher and instilled a love of literature in her son. It was amusing for me to sit and discuss "The Scarlet Pimpernel" with Timmy while robust contractors would interrupt us.

"Hey Tim, give me two loads of WonderBoard."

The transaction finished, we resumed our discussion. Our conversations in that location were anachronistic, symbolic of my life with John, where I was living in a world out of sync to the life I always led. I felt each day was a new adventure into unexplored territory.

One morning in August, my phone jangled loudly.

"Gilda. It's Barbara. Are you sitting down? I have an offer you can't refuse."

It was Dr. Barbara B, now an Assistant Commissioner in the DOE.

"What a pleasant surprise. What can I do for you, Barbara?"

"Make sure you are sitting first. We want you to return to the DOE as the Director of the Office of Bilingual Education and Equity Issues. Isn't that great! What do you say, lady?"

"You know my original ambition was to head the Bilingual Education Office, but I've got arthritis now. I can't put in a full day without having to rest from time to time."

"Don't worry. We will accommodate your schedule the best we can; we will be flexible."

"Barbara, you don't know how much this means to me. If you had asked several months ago, I would have considered it, but my life is taking another direction now and I cannot accept the offer. I'm married, and I am the Honorary Vice Consul for Italy in Trenton. One thing I assure you is that while I am in this position, I will continue to be an advocate of civil rights for all people, not just Italians."

"I have no doubt, but think about it, Gilda. Don't make a hasty decision. This is a great opportunity."

"My decision is not hasty; it's definite, Barbara."

Wow! I can't believe it. She just offered me the job at the DOE I always wanted. It's good to know the organization is moving beyond designating some positions according to race and ethnicity. They also recognize all the work I did and would continue to do, but I would never accept a post where 'Equity' was subsumed under Bilingual Education. That is the reason I left in the first place. I can't go back, but it sure feels good to be asked. There is validity to the saying I often hear in the Burg: "What goes around, comes around."

From now on, I'll concentrate on being the Honorary Vice Consul for Italy and the contented wife of Giovà, who my friends aptly call "The Dream Maker."

The rest of the day I strutted throughout the house, glowing with satisfaction.

CHAPTER FIFTEEN

FADED DREAMS

Three and a-half years with John passed blissfully. We never argued. Our home, albeit under constant construction, was filled with family, friends and good times. John had added 2,500 square feet to the building which had become my 'Dream Castle.' I lived in a world of sheetrock, molding and cinder blocks. Regardless of the domestic disarray, Mauro and his family came to visit and we, in turn, went to stay with them in Italy each year.

Our social life was full, and we organized a variety of activities for the community, such as piano recitals at the Roman Hall. We were a popular couple. John was honored by the *Società Romana* for his contributions to the Roman Hall. I was recognized for my consular work in 2000, as the recipient of the *Citizen of the Year Award* by the Kent Athletic Association in Trenton. In 2002, I was inducted into the Italian American National Hall of Fame.

I had nominated Larry Paragano, CEO of Paragano Enterprises, to be an inductee. While we were on the dais at the Tropicana Resort for the ceremony in Atlantic City, Larry made an offer I readily accepted.

"Gilda, we recently signed legislation establishing the New Jersey Italian and Italian American Heritage Commission. I think you'd make a great commissioner. Will you accept?"

"Yes, I'd be honored to serve on the Commission."

"Good. I'll submit your name to the Governor's Office."

A few weeks later, I received notice from Governor Corzine that he had appointed me a commissioner. I was excited at the prospect of serving the Italian community in new ways. At that time, John made a surprising statement.

"Sweetheart, I am going to retire in January 2003. Mauro is giving us one of his new condominiums in Rome and we will alternate three months in Italy and three months in New Jersey. We will travel all over Europe. First, we'll go to Austria, then we'll sail with Mauro's brother, Francesco, on his yacht to Sardinia and from there, anywhere you want. We'll explore all of Europe and enjoy life."

I can't believe how fortunate I am to have found romance in my 6os. I never believed John would retire but he seems to have thought about it very carefully. We are blessed as we plan an idyllic future together.

On our trip to Italy that year, my 94-year-old uncle/godfather, Ralph Sorrentino, Jr., accompanied us. My mother's five-foot baby brother, who she affectionately called, *Falluch,* is a crackerjack, possessing an astute mind, agile body and keen sense of humor. If there were one word to describe Uncle Ralph, "quicksilver" comes to mind. Since my childhood, he has always been in perpetual motion, reminding me of a Keystone Cop in jerky, hurried movements.

We three were having a wonderful visit in Sicily, though often John complained of indigestion. I gave him TUMS, but they were not alleviating his discomfort. Uncle Ralph and I became increasingly concerned about his health.

When we arrived back home in Hamilton, the pain persisted, and my daughter Mary told me to take John to the Emergency Room at Saint Francis Hospital. There, X-Rays revealed advanced lymphoma. We went for a second opinion at Fox Chase Medical Center where an aggressive chemotherapy treatment was recommended.

"We prescribe two days of continuous chemotherapy to block the progression of the lymphoma," the doctor said. "Your husband will be admitted to Saint Francis Hospital today."

No. this can't be happening. John complained of indigestion, as Louie had done before his massive myocardial infarction. Louie lived over 23 years with a severely damaged heart. Hopefully John will live many more years. I am going to be optimistic.

I wanted to stay in the room with John for the duration of the first treatment. A young man with an opaque pallor, suffering from leukemia, occupied the other bed. He never uttered a sound. I spoke softly not to disturb him. A cot was placed in the room for me to spend the night. John, always wanting me to be happy, was in high spirits.

"The treatment will make me better, sweetheart; I know it."

Dear Lord, let it be so.

The next morning, I awoke to John's singing, "*Come sei bella di prima mattina, come il culo della padella.* (How beautiful you are in the early morning, like the bottom of a frying pan).*"

We laughed, but I put my finger to my lips, motioning to John not to disturb his neighbor. When I glanced at the other patient, a smile was visible on his wan, alabaster face. It was a comfort to know that John's song made him happy too.

John did what the doctors told him. He stopped smoking and lost weight but six weeks after the first diagnosis, a new form of cancer was found in his lungs. He was getting weaker every day. The robust, powerful man I married with the abundance of dark brown hair, like Samson, had lost both his mane and strength. It was a sad sight to witness such a rapid decline.

John kept his word and submitted his resignation to the *Società Romana* at the Roman Hall in November 2002. The Executive Board thought it fitting to give their loyal manager a rousing retirement dinner. Once the announcement was circulated, the banquet hall sold out in a week, with a waiting list to boot.

The event on 25 November was a grand affair. The hall glittered with its crystal chandeliers, gilded candelabras and the pomp of vivid floral bouquets. People from all walks of life came to pay homage to a man who had touched their lives. His relatives from Italy, *Zia* (Aunt) Marcella and relatives Maurizia and Francesco, traveled from Rome to attend his "big night." Trenton Mayor, Douglas Palmer, took the mike and said, "John's my man, my buddy." Senator Shirley Turner referred to him as "an icon" of the community. The festivities continued until after midnight leaving John, albeit exhausted, deeply moved and exhilarated by all the tributes and loving comments.

The chemotherapy continued, and blood transfusions were added to help alleviate my husband's chronic weakness. Although John was optimistic with each infusion, I became increasingly skeptical about his recovery. After the treatment sessions, he would say, "Let's go have a great lunch, sweetheart. We'll go to Rats at the Grounds for Sculpture. I know you like that place."

Poor John. He probably wants only to go home and rest. If I tell him it would be better to go to bed for a while, he'll pretend he is the one who wants to eat out.

His weakened condition worsened over the next month. The semester of nursing training I had in Philadelphia served me well. I could provide bed baths and change sheets without my husband having to leave the comfort of his bed. He was grateful for the attention and even in illness, managed to convey an element of romance. When I fluffed his pillows, and helped him sit up, our eyes mingled. His loving look enveloped me, and we'd embrace, more deeply in love than at any other time.

He became increasingly dependent on me and did not want any more nurses or assistants to attend him.

"I'm embarrassed with those other people here. I just want you to take care of me."

"Of course, Giovà."

John's doctor was always encouraging, offering him hope of a recovery. When she discovered the cancer had not invaded his bones, I had a celebration party for his friends and family at his brother Italo's (Eddy's) banquet hall, The Baldassari Regency. Any good news was an opportunity to celebrate and it lifted John's spirits, although I felt the time for cheering would be short lived.

During a subsequent treatment, I asked John's oncologist an important question.

"Doctor, please be candid with me. Is my husband going to survive this ordeal?"

"No," she answered gravely, but forthrightly. "We were hoping the aggressive chemotherapy would destroy the cancer, but it has metastasized."

The word, 'No,' vanquished all aspirations. How will John react to this revelation?

"Perhaps, doctor, it is best not to tell him yet. He is so hopeful of improving."

"All right. We'll wait a while longer."

The year was ebbing away, sadly. Early in the morning of January 1st, I peered out our bedroom window. There was not a glint of sun. The landscape was swaddled in a gray pall. Narrow bands of vapor rose from the frozen earth, causing me to feel melancholic. John was scheduled for another treatment, but the effort of taking him outdoors seemed futile.

"Giovà, the weather is terrible today. It's so cold and dreary. Let's reschedule your appointment."

"No, sweetheart. I must have a transfusion. I'll do anything to be able to live with you a little longer."

Your words pierce my heart, Giovà. If you only knew the truth.

"All right. I'll get your coat."

THE CAR

New Year's Eve had passed uneventfully, unlike times past at the Roman Hall. There were no silly, glitzy hats, noisemakers, feasting and dancing 'til dawn with entertainers like 'Johnny Pompadour,' until a continental breakfast indicated it would soon be closing time. To usher in 2003, I cooked and blended John's food so he could sit up in bed to be spoon fed.

"I'm going to survive this, sweetheart and this year we are going to Rome."

"Yes Giovà."

New Year's Day was bleak and blustery with what weather forecasters call a "wintry mix." At breakfast, John seemed impatient. "Sweetheart, let's go for a ride." "A ride in this weather?"

"Yes. I want to go; but you drive, please."

I did not insist. John seemed intent on getting dressed and going out, despite my protestations. Once in the car, I turned to the fragile man beside me.

"Where do you want to go?"

"Drive down Route 1."

"Route 1? Why?" I uttered incredulously.

"I feel like going there."

I had learned long before not to question or resist what John wanted. From Quakerbridge Road, we traveled on the familiar highway until he told me to take the jug handle and turn on the other side of the road.

"Where in the world do you want to go now?"

"Oh, stop the car here at the Mercedes Benz dealer. I have a question about brakes."

The weather was so nasty. I welcomed being indoors wherever it was. I hoped there would be a machine with hot chocolate inside. We entered through the large, glass showroom entrance.

"Go look at some of the cars. I will sit here until a representative comes."

I meandered, observing some of the handsome vehicles. A white one caught my eye. It was an S class 430, a designation which meant little to me. I admired the bright look of the auto and its cream-colored interior with mahogany trim. John was talking to an agent when a salesman approached me.

"Are you interested in any of these models, madam?"

"No. I'm just looking."

"We have other, less expensive samples in the back. Would you like to see them?"

"Yes. That would be fine."

I guess I am here to kill some time, so why not. While John talks about brakes, maybe this man will offer me a hot chocolate.

"Follow me."

As we were about to exit the area, John's voice interrupted us.

"Where are you going?"

"We're going to look at other, more reasonably priced cars, John."

On hearing that remark, my husband turned to the man with whom he had been talking.

"My sweetheart looked at that white car for a long time. I know she likes it. Don't show her anything else. If you want to make a deal now, let's talk business."

"But John," I protested.

"Leave this to me, Gilda."

Louie would review consumer magazines and conduct other research for weeks before purchasing an automobile. He was a pragmatic, sensible man who would never buy anything spontaneously. John is obviously not discussing brakes.

Twenty minutes later, we were driving home in the new Mercedes Benz.

"Giovà, why did you want this car so badly?"

"I watched you admire it and I want you to have the safest car possible when I am gone."

THE END OF A DREAM

The following week, on a blustery, grey January morning, harsh winds bent trees bare of foliage. John was scheduled for another transfusion. I feared the freezing temperatures would compromise his weakened immune system, but once again he was insistent.

"Getting blood today will make me stronger. My New Year's resolution is to take you to Italy. Remember how you loved Maurizia's wedding in the Castle at *Bracciano*?"

Yes. I was impressed to be able to touch medieval tapestries and coats of armor. I remember how we danced in the torch lit courtyard and watched fireworks from the garden terrace overlooking the lake. The colorful display looked like a cascade of stars glittering on the black water below.

"Remember the night after the wedding? Mauro invited the 'gang' and us to the *Cavaliere Hilton* for a dinner *al fresco*. The stiff, white tablecloth was strewn with plump burgundy cherries for us to nibble on before placing our orders. As soon as I am stronger, we're going back," he promised.

"It would be wonderful, Giovà."

Ever hopeful, he came with me to the hospital. While he was undergoing the procedure at Saint Francis, I decided to speak with the oncologist.

"Doctor, do you think it is time to tell my husband the facts about his condition?"

"Yes, it would be appropriate now."

When John's session ended, the physician and I approached him slowly, each dreading his inevitable reaction. Seeing us, John smiled.

"How am I doing, Doc?"

"Mr. Baldassari, I regret to tell you that the treatments are no longer effective."

"What do you mean?"

"I mean that the cancer has spread, and we can no longer help you."

"But you said you thought I could be cured."

"At the time, it was agreed that aggressive chemotherapy might destroy the cancer, but that has not happened."

"You mean I am going to die?"

"I'm afraid so; I'm very sorry."

John sat motionless for a moment, visibly stunned at the shocking pronouncement. Composing himself, he faced his physician.

"You did all you could, doctor, and I am grateful. How much time do I have left? Can I take my wife to Rome?"

"It won't be long. We do not advise you to leave the country now."

"Oh, I see," he said.

John did not flinch. He merely shrugged his shoulders and said, "If that's it; that's it."

A wheelchair was provided as my husband could no longer walk without assistance. We exited the building and entered our car. I was silent, too choked with emotion to utter a sound when John, peering upward, declared in a loud, pleading voice.

"I've worked since I was eight years old. These are the happiest days of my life. I want to live! I want to live!"

Restraining myself was very difficult. Being the caregiver of my parents, I was aware of the inexorability of life, but seeing John in this state, relatively soon after we had found each other, filled me with despair. Giovà and I shared a passion for the life we enjoyed together.

Before we married, doctors said we were healthy. How did this terrible thing happen to my companion? It's not fair!

John, sensing my sadness, stroked my hand.

"It is what it is, sweetheart; I will face it like a man. Call my family and have them come to the house tonight at 8 o'clock. There is something I must do."

Without questioning, I did as he ordered. John spent the afternoon resting, preparing for the later gathering. Promptly at 8, a steady stream of family members appeared, several of whom I had never met. The group of about 30 seemed to intuit the purpose of their visit. When all assembled in our new, spacious kitchen, John made several announcements: "Thank you for coming. I wanted you all here to say goodbye. Today the doctor told me I won't live much longer."

"No, Johnny! You'll lick this and see 100 years," several protested.

"*Magari* (maybe), but it won't happen. Some of us have had our little misunderstandings at times, but you know I always loved you, right?"

A resounding "Sure, Johnny, don't mention it," was heard in the room.

"I want you to know that I'll miss you. Also, I want you to know what my wishes are before the end. Gilda has space for her family in Saint Mary's Mausoleum and I want to be there with her. My son is resting beside his mother in another building and I don't want to disturb them. Mass will be at Saint Joachim's Church with Father Jeffrey Lee. Lastly, know that Gilda has taken very good care of me, and we have been truly happy. Without her, I would have died a long time ago."

Dear Giovà, he brought these people here as much for my well-being as his.

Since we were married in Saint Joachim's Church and Father Lee is now the Pastor, it is fitting his mass be there. He never discussed where he wanted to be interred and I'm very touched it will be with me. He is ensuring there will be no possible family conflict over these matters once he is gone.

Silence reigned in the room as the assemblage processed what they had heard. John poured wine for everyone. Smiling, he said, "I propose a *brindisi*: To life and family!"

The onlookers raised their glasses of Chianti, replying in unison, "Here's to you, Johnny."

My husband got up from the wheelchair, and shunning assistance, walked shakily to the door and stood erect, the quintessential *pater familias*. He kissed and embraced each person as they filed out into the chill night air.

"Thank you, Giovà," I said, after the last guest exited. "This is such a difficult time for you, and yet, you're looking out for me."

"You are all I think about, sweetheart."

To offset the gloom of winter, my husband wanted the house to be full of light and laughter. When news spread throughout Trenton regarding his condition, friends and relatives came every day, almost all day, from 8:30 a.m. to 11:30 p.m. Each afternoon at least 12-14 family members arrived for lunch where the table groaned under the weight of *abbondanza*. Some told jokes; others led us into song and John, at the head of the table, was in his glory. He never complained about his condition; his only thought was of making people happy; after all, he was a "dream maker" to the end.

I'm exhausted. After lunch, he tells me he is tired and must lie down. Next, he asks me to entertain the house full of people. No matter what, I must because it takes his mind off the inevitable and makes him smile. That is worth gold.

January 27th was one of the bleakest days of the cruel season. When I poked my head out the front door onto the frosty silence, frozen droplets stung my cheeks. A torpid mist hung like a shroud. John was scheduled for another hospital visit, but I intended to call and postpone it for the following morning.

"No, sweetheart, I must go."

"John, it is slippery and dangerous outside."

"I want to go," he insisted, but when he tried to get out of bed, he fell. Despite his rapid weight loss, I could not help him move so I called 911 and the paramedics came promptly.

"Hi, Johnny. Take it easy man; we're here to help you."

"John, you did our wedding reception at the Roman Hall. People are still talking about it," said one young, robust attendant.

How comforting it is that John has touched so many people's lives.

They lifted him onto a gurney and took him very carefully down the slick front steps into the ambulance. We rode holding hands, realizing the severity of what was happening.

When we arrived in the emergency room, John unexpectedly grabbed my wrist and exclaimed in a desperate voice, "Call the doctor. I need morphine right away. I cannot stand the pain."

My spouse had never complained of any discomfort until now. I ran to the desk, where I asked that someone notify a physician immediately. I then rushed back to John.

"I have to die now, Gilda. You know I love you, don't you?"

"Yes, John. Here comes the doctor."

Morphine was administered, and John was taken to the sixth floor Hospice Center. He never uttered another word.

I remained with my husband throughout the day until the next evening in the Hospice Section of the hospital. While swabbing his mouth, his breathing stopped. My happy, albeit short dream ended but made me believe in the invincible power of love.

Louie and Giovà will be with me throughout my life. I will never marry again. I cannot suffer this torment of loss for a third time. I will never allow myself to get so emotionally involved as to remarry. From now on, I will concentrate on my Consular and Commission work and strive always to bring honor to the Rorro and Baldassari names.

More than 2,000 people attended John's viewing in Saint Joachim's Church.

"After 2,000 signatures, we ran out of registry books, Gilda" Joe D'Errico said.

"That's all right, Joe. There is still a long line of people from the parking lot waiting to come in."

The viewing lasted almost six hours. My children and their spouses, my Uncle Ralph and my son-in-law's mother, Jeannette, were by my side throughout. Mourners represented all walks of life from dignitaries such as the Consul General of Italy from Philadelphia, senators, mayors to dishwashers in local restaurants. Men and women sobbed on my shoulder about the loss of their dear friend who touched their lives in so many ways. A young couple told me John gave their daughter a baptism party at no cost when they came to Trenton from Costa Rica, as they had no money. Similar stories were repeated by many others.

Music was provided continuously throughout the viewing with musicians taking turns at the organ and other instruments as a tribute to him. Although the pews of the church were packed, a respectful silence pervaded the atmosphere.

John left an extraordinary legacy in Trenton and beyond. He was a man who at 18 years old, returned to the capital city to support his mother and four siblings and gave selflessly to them and the community. He dedicated his life to making people happy and was my own true "Dream Maker."

CHAPTER SIXTEEN

NEW TRAVAILS

THE YEAR AFTER

After John's death, my days were spent performing consular duties. As a member of the New Jersey Italian and Italian American Heritage Commission, I became the Chair in developing a statewide curriculum project to infuse Italian cultural heritage into all schools, all subjects and grade levels K-16, which included the undergraduate level of college. While at the DOE, I worked with Dr. Robert Freda and his Office for Social Justice. We gave many statewide presentations on the topic of prejudice reduction. Dr. Freda was also on the Italian Commission and he had nominated me to become the Chair of the Curriculum Development Committee.

Producing *The Universality of Italian Heritage* curriculum was a daunting task but I took it on with gusto. Most of my professional career was spent advocating for the rights of minorities, women and the underprivileged. Focusing now on the Italian and Italian American experience would be the capstone.

It was possible to undertake these projects because I had renewed energy. During the past 14 months, I thought my poor sleeping patterns were due to advancing age. The constant worries regarding John's health and the frequent nocturnal interruptions to give him water and tend to his other needs were in fact the culprit. In time, the steady stream of daily visitors disappeared, providing time to concentrate on my professional interests.

Another outcome was that Leo Pignat and Giuseppe Damiano did not abandon me. When John passed, I thought they would be gone from my life, but they remained, helping me with the house. Leo had retired from his very successful marble installation business. He planned to spend his remaining years alternating between Italy and New Jersey, but he was willing to apply Dry-Vit (stucco) to outdoor areas of my home and assist with other smaller jobs for which Giuseppe needed help. The latter, on the other hand, dutifully came to my door every morning at 8:30 and worked until 6 p.m., seven days a week. He was determined the transformation project on my domicile would not be interrupted.

Giuseppe's gentle, efficient presence had a calming effect on me, despite the loud whirling of his red compressor, the staccato ping of his hammer and the shrill whining of the table saw. Those were sounds of life and progress and they became my steady companions. Giuseppe never spoke when he worked. I prepared his three daily meals and several coffee breaks in between with his favorite, a triple espresso. In warmer weather, we'd sit in the garden and enjoy surveying the surrounding masonry wall he chiseled by hand while he recounted endless stories of his adventures with John. As he spoke, I would examine his fine features, abundant silver hair and blue eyes.

He told me that he worked for William Levitt, the CEO of Levittown, for 23 years. From 7 a.m. to 12 p.m. each day, he and his three brothers would trim four houses for the sum of 35 dollars a house. Mr. Levitt gave them a turkey every Thanksgiving.

One February morning, while serving the customary espresso, Giuseppe made a startling statement.

"I have feelings for you. We are not from the same world. Nothing can come from it. Never will I bring it up again and I will never be out of line. I just want you to know. You should feel honored."

"Of course, I am honored. Your words will always be very precious to me. Let's always remain devoted friends. True friendship will endure and that is all I can ever offer you."

His revelation is completely unexpected. This could have been an awkward, even painful moment, but it ended as it should. Giuseppe and I will be like Dante and Beatrice, sharing an idealized love and a spiritual bond for the rest of our lives. Most people will not believe it, but we will know.

Giuseppe sipped his strong brew in agreement and no more was said.

That May, Cellina extended her annual invitation for me to spend a few weeks at the Terme.

"Gilda, come to Margherita di Savoia. You will relax, take our thermal treatments, eat our wonderful Pugliese seafood and vegetable specialties and feel good with friends."

Cellina is wonderful. She has always cared for me.

I readily accepted. Being recently widowed, I packed a predominately black wardrobe, which I believed was common practice for widows in Italy.

When I arrived at Cellina's *Gran Albergo Terme*, I wore a charcoal-colored dress and stockings. An outspoken friend of hers made a diplomatic suggestion.

"Your clothing is so obscure. Perhaps you'd feel more comfortable in something *più allegro* (more cheerful)."

"Don't widows wear dark colors for three years or more in Italy?"

"In the past. Now, not so much."

At dinner, I wore a blue silk flowered ensemble to my admiring hosts. Soon, however, I found that other restrictive Italian traditions persisted. The revelation came via three single women Cellina invited to the Terme. One was Valeria, the chic Roman proprietor of a fashionable jewelry store on the famous *Via Condotti*, near the Spanish Steps. She was accompanied by her 40-year-old staff person, Anna, who never wed. The third person was an elegant woman dressed in Italian haute couture, a chain-smoking recent widow, Gabriella, from Brindisi.

We ladies enjoyed dining together, lounging on the hotel's pristine lido and engaging in "girl talk," comparing our lives as single women.

I remember Gabriella from my first visit to the Terme with Louie. She was married to a dashing attorney. They appeared to be a perfect couple. Now she seems so nervous, lighting one cigarette after another.

"Life must be very hard for you as a widow, Gilda. Being alone can be a curse for a woman, but there is nothing you can do about it," Gabriella said.

"I do not consider it a curse. It is sad. My husbands will always be missed but I lead a very full life. In fact, it is so packed with interesting activities my children always tell me to slow down."

"What are you doing?"

I waxed on about my consular and commission duties as well as participating in various cultural and charitable organizations.

"That's incredible!" Gabriella exclaimed. "When my husband died two years ago, my grown children took me aside and gave me an order."

"Mamma, from now on, your life will revolve around *casa e chiesa* (house and church). I live in a baronial mansion, but it gets oppressive being alone in those huge rooms. A new boutique opened in town and I wanted to work there, not for the money, but to socialize..."

Gabriella's facial muscles tensed. Her hands twitched nervously as she fumbled to ignite a cigarette. After a long inhalation, her eyes narrowed to dark, thin slits.

"My mother-in-law ordered me to her home."

"If you want to work in that shop, you will never be able to set foot in my house again," she demanded.

"After your husband died she still tried to have authority over you? Couldn't you decide to stand up to her and live your own life?" I asked.

"She continues to control me. She is the grandmother of my children and they are on her side. In my community, women do not go out of the house unaccompanied. A decent woman should always be with a relative or another female companion."

Valeria jumped into the conversation.

"I am divorced. I have male friends and I go out alone. It is different in the big cities. In Rome, women are more emancipated."

I was relieved to hear that, when Anna broke into the conversation.

"I never married. I go to work by myself in Rome, but I don't go out much alone. It is always more comfortable for me to have another woman with me when I leave the house socially."

I'll make no judgments, but I value the freedom life offers to men and women in the United States. When I was in my early teens I used to tell Mom that I wished I had been born in Margherita di Savoia to be surrounded by so many loving people.

"Are you crazy, Gilly? A baby girl in her crib has more rights and freedom in America than almost anywhere else. There's no place like this country. You're too young to appreciate the advantages you have here."

Her words came back to me at that moment.

As much as I enjoyed my annual visit, I was not sad to return to Trenton. New ideas had sprung into my head concerning the curriculum project and I was also curious to see what Giuseppe had done to the house in my two-week absence.

On arriving home from Newark Airport, Giuseppe's green Ford pickup truck stood in the parking lot, a sign that he was on task. When I walked in the door, I heard a pounding sound emanating from the lap pool area. I followed it and there was the senior tradesman, putting the finishing touches to a splendid mural of the ruins of the Temples of Castor and Pollux in the Roman Forum. The remarkable hand-designed intarsia, consisting of inlaid marble, granite and travertine, was installed on the wall overlooking the pool. Never could I have imagined such a work of art on what used to be a faded yellow, cinderblock storage area.

Giuseppe looked at me without uttering a word. He knew instinctively if I liked what I saw. Gazing at his mastery of detail, I was speechless.

"You're pleased?"

"It's incredible, Giuseppe. There are no words. Nothing anyone could say would have prepared me for this. Your talent is extraordinary. Would you like an espresso?"

"It wouldn't hurt," he replied.

In June, I had attended a reception for the Boheme Opera Company of New Jersey. A young, attractive blonde woman and I were chatting while waiting in the buffet line. She had known my husband John and expressed her condolences. The following morning, I received a phone call from her husband.

"Dr. Rorro, allow me to introduce myself. You met my wife last night. I am Anthony D's son. You may know my father."

"I'm not sure. Does he need consular services?"

"Oh, no, it's nothing like that. You see, my mother died last year, and Dad has been alone. I know this may be awkward for you. It is for me but let me tell you something about him. He is a great cook. He likes to enjoy life and spends the winter months in his house in Florida. He's a retired engineer and, in short, he's a great guy. My wife thinks you would be a perfect friend for him. Could I give him your phone number?"

Mom always said one should mourn a spouse for at least one year. But I am touched by this young man's offer.

"Your father is very fortunate to have a son and daughter-in-law as caring as you. I'm flattered and proud you would consider my meeting your Dad, but my husband died only two months ago, and I am not ready to embark on another relationship so soon. I'm sorry."

"But if you contact him he may be willing to wait longer."

"Thank you, but I can't. If your father is so sad, perhaps it would be better for him to look elsewhere."

"Okay. But if you change your mind, write my number down."

"I will, and thank you again for calling me. As I said, your father is an exceptional man to have reared a caring son like you. Goodbye."

I can't believe you uttered those words without hesitating. You may have passed up an exceptional opportunity. The reality is you don't want to get serious with another man so soon. Since you were married at 27, you became a willing and happy caretaker for parents, husbands and children. Now you are free from those responsibilities. Don't listen to what you were constantly told from your youth. "A woman can't live alone. She must have a man to protect her."

Protect her from what? No one is attacking me. This is my chance to prove the "old timers" wrong. Yes, it's a little scary, but for now, spread your wings and fly solo.

ANNI HORRIBILI (HORRIBLE YEARS)

In February 2004, my daughter-in-law's mother, Betsy, and step-father, David, invited me to accompany them on a cruise to the Caribbean.

I had spent 13 months in mourning and decided to go. It was time to get back to enjoying life, and that we did. Ours was a delightful vacation visiting ruins in Tulum on the Riviera Maya, and those in Guatemala. Lounging on deck chairs under cloudless, azure skies was delicious. The change of pace and beautiful scenery made me feel rejuvenated, until our last excursion in Key West.

At the end of an eight-hour visit to that tropical hotspot, passengers lined up to board a tender that would take them to the ship anchored nearby in deeper water. The Caribbean was choppy. Large swells forced the crew to have passengers file aboard one-by-one on a narrow gangway.

My turn came. I stepped on the wooden platform which swayed above the turbulent water, clutching firmly my handbag and passport. A crew member extended his hand as the plank began to swerve. I reached to grasp it, when a startling thing happened. The gangway broke loose, hurling me outward, into the water.

Oh, my God, I'm going down deep fast. All I see are warm, murky green bubbles. I've got to swim to the surface as quickly as possible. What's that dark cloud overhead? It's the gangway. If that huge object struck my head, I would be dead. Steer away from it and whatever you do, don't panic or let go of your passport.

Swimming upwards, I was worried I wouldn't be able to hold my breath much longer, but I succeeded. Surfacing, I quickly took inventory of my surroundings. A sea of startled eyes stared down at me from the tender. To my dismay, a member of the crew wearing combat boots stood poised to come to my rescue.

Oh, no. He's going to jump in and land on top of me.

As I feared, his bulky frame struck squarely on my shoulders as his heavy footwear struck my hips, submerging me forcibly once again.

I struggled to get to the surface, and when I succeeded, my "rescuer" suffered a panic attack and began to babble: "Oh, my. What to do? What to do?"

"Sir, please, stay calm."

"Yes. Yes. Stay calm; Stay calm," he repeated several times, his eyes darting and lips trembling.

It's good I use the pool at home almost daily. This man is afraid in the water.

"I see a little metal ladder attached to the pier," I said. "Let's swim there. Here. Take my handbag and passport while I try to get out of the water." "Okay." Relieving me of the items, he swam off in another direction.

I turned toward the rusty, yellow steps when a far more frightening situation occurred. The swells grew more powerful, moving the tender rapidly in my direction. The vessel struck my side, forcing me violently onto a barnacle-covered water-column. The sound of passengers shouting and screaming pierced the evening air: "Move the boat; you'll crush her. Move the goddamn boat!"

Somehow the tender backed off, freeing me to swim as fast as I could to the only life salvation device at my disposal—the rickety, rusty ladder. But when I arrived to where it hung, the turbulent water kept me from reaching the bottom rung. Struggling and feeling sore and fatigued, I heard a familiar voice.

"I'm back," said my rescuer. "I'll stiffen my legs. Climb on them and try to reach the ladder."

The expanding water made it difficult; my energy was waning. A group of anxious onlookers had gathered around the dock. After three aborted attempts to reach the corroded rung, a swell propelled me upwards. Bracing my knees on my aquatic companion, I finally managed to reach the corroded rung and cling to it. My lack of strength and arthritis made it impossible for me to climb. Observing my dilemma, a burly young man prostrated himself on the pier, extending his arm to help me. I grasped his hand and he pulled me out of the water by my right arm. Cheers and applause greeted me. I felt both relief and embarrassment in my wet, clinging, yellow sundress. I was more concerned for the skirt traveling up to my waist than for my aching arm. My mother always said to wear clean underwear and her words rang in my ears as I tugged the wet cloth downwards. My embarrassment dissipated when a kind woman approached, carrying a blanket.

"I am a nurse. You are in shock. Let me wrap you in this."

I was very grateful for her attention as she helped me board the tender to the sound of more applause. I smiled at everyone as I was grateful to be alive. My rescuer returned my dripping handbag and passport, and once again our cruise resumed. When we boarded the ship, I was told to stand in line in my saturated garment and pass through the metal detector. I was too tired to protest and did as requested. My travel companions escorted me directly to the office of the ship's doctor where a middle-aged man swiveled in his chair.

"Everyone on board heard what happened to you. That must have been some experience. Are you all right?"

"Please, don't ask her; examine her yourself, doctor," David demanded.

"I'm sorry, but I am the physician for the crew. The doctor for the passengers is having lunch and will be back in an hour and a-half. Come back then."

"No!" David's voice rose in protest. "First you will give her a tetanus shot. See all the cuts on her arm and side from the barnacles? Next, you will send a wheelchair to her cabin when our doctor arrives."

The vaccine was administered. Betsy turned to me and said that everyone laughed when I kept telling my "life saver" not to panic.

"All I can say, Betsy, is that it is good I use my lap pool often and am not afraid of the water. There are a lot of elderly people aboard with portable oxygen. If it had been a child, someone who can't swim or an incapacitated person, a death would have occurred. Nothing was thrown into the water to help me, only the man who jumped in and landed right on top of me. What an experience!"

"And to think, you were the calm one while he and everybody watching was panic stricken."

We laughed at that. A little humor is always welcome, but little did I realize that the day's events were only a preview of the startling episodes to come.

A SHOCK

On arriving home, I threw myself full force into resuming consular duties and working on the Italian Heritage Curriculum project. Dr. Robert Freda and I went to lunch at a restaurant next to the DOE, where we had been planning a teacher writing workshop to develop the curriculum document. After placing our orders, Bob began the conversation with some disturbing news.

"Gilda, my wife Lilly has breast cancer. Tomorrow, she will be operated on at Sloan Kettering Hospital in New York. Say a prayer for her."

How horrible! Lilly is such a vivacious person. She must be suffering terribly right now.

"Bob, I'm so sorry to hear that. Of course; I will pray for Lilly. Give her my wishes for a speedy recovery."

THE BATTLE BEGINS

When we returned to the commission office in the DOE, I felt persistent pain in my right shoulder. That evening, when Mary made her customary visit home, she noticed something was wrong. "You don't look good, Mom. What's the matter?" When I told her, she gave me an order. "Mom, you must get an MRI right away for the shoulder as well as a mammogram. It's been almost two years since your last breast exam." "Oh, Mary, you worry too much. My mammograms have always been negative. I can wait a little longer."

"No. You can't wait. Make an appointment as soon as possible."

When my daughter hears about a complaint, she is insistent in her follow-up. Appointments were subsequently made for both tests the following week. The MRI of the shoulder was first.

"Dr. Rorro. You have a torn tendon in your right arm which will not heal on its own. I recommend you have rotator cuff surgery," a young orthopedist exclaimed.

I agreed to undergo the repair. Two days later, I went for the mammogram. In the past, I would be informed of the results the same day, but this time they said they would notify me later, at home. The following morning, an assistant to the radiologist called.

"The doctor would like you to come back for another mammogram. The images on this one are not clear. It happens sometimes."

I did as I was instructed, but became anxious when I received another phone call from the same assistant.

"The doctor wants you to come to his office tomorrow to discuss the results of the second test. Don't worry."

If the outcome were normal they would simply say so. Something is not right.

Giuseppe came the next morning before my appointment to work on his hand-carved bookshelves in the library. He had spent several months fashioning a replica of the room I had admired in the Columbus Citizens' Foundation in New York City, formerly the Austrian Embassy. Giuseppe's finishing touches to an inlaid wooden floor, cherry wood fireplace, crown moldings and now, two large bookcases, would complete the beautiful surroundings.

When I mentioned where and why I was going out, he said, "There is nothing wrong. You'll be fine."

"I sure hope so, Giuseppe."

It was March 15, 2004, my birthday. The weather was balmy, the sky brilliant and I felt in excellent health. While driving to my appointment, I forgot my apprehension and began singing a chorus of "You are my sunshine." At the doctor's office, however, that carefree mood changed drastically.

I was escorted into a darkened room, where a concerned looking physician sat. A series of five previous mammograms lined the wall. Seeing me, he rose and pointed to the grayish images.

"Good morning, Dr. Rorro. I wanted you here to see these results. Look at the past films and compare them to your most recent ones. You will see clearly what has changed. There is a mass in your right breast that didn't exist two years ago. I believe it is malignant and that you will need a mastectomy. I am sorry."

His diagnosis stunned me. I asked no questions and only muttered, "Thank you."

I left the office in a daze, my legs wobbling. I grasped a handrail at the exit in order not to fall down the three short steps of the building. I walked to the car like a robot. Once in, I sat motionless for several minutes, unable to think or react. When I gained sufficient composure to drive, disjointed thoughts darted through my head.

All you could say was "Thank You?" What an awful way to spend your birthday. Life is going to change drastically now. You may even die, though you feel good. First John and now you? You're going to have chemotherapy, get sick and lose your hair. But you're not ready to go yet. Do whatever is necessary to live. No doubt consular and commission work will be abandoned. Rotator cuff surgery will be on hold. There is no one to lean on now—no Louie or John. Michael is away at school and Mary works full time. You're on your own. Be strong.

This beautiful, sunny weather is disturbing now. Such news should be uttered on a grim, rainy day, not one filled with such bright light.

There was no singing in the car. There would be no birthday celebration tonight with friends.

Giuseppe was working dutifully when I arrived home. He saw me enter and stopped, his face bearing a quizzical expression.

"Well, how did you make out? You're okay, right?"

My forlorn expression said it all. Walking up to him, I began to sob uncontrollably. He and I had never had any physical contact, but at that moment, he held out his arms to comfort me. I was so grateful to be embraced by an empathic human being who disregarded the wet, salty stains saturating his shirt. My crying stopped. Giuseppe said nothing; his blue eyes expressed sincere sympathy.

Compose yourself. No more tears. Now I need to find an oncologist and take care of business.

"Would you like an espresso, Giuseppe?"

"It wouldn't hurt," he responded, not knowing what else to say.

As we sat, sipping the dark, rich brew, I remembered Bob Freda mentioning Sloan Kettering Hospital. I called Lilly and told her my plight.

"You too, Gilda? Perhaps God has given me this condition so that I could help you and others. Sloan Kettering is my hospital of choice. I'll give you the names of several surgeons there. The head of the department is Dr. Patrick Borgen. You won't be able to get him because he is booked for years, but here are some other physicians."

I thanked her profusely and called the hospital. When a staff person answered, I made a request.

"I would like Dr. Patrick Borgen to be my physician and perform the surgery."

Why did you blurt his name? Lilly stressed he was unavailable.

"The doctor's surgical schedule is full this year, but we will get back to you." The following day, the phone rang with unexpected news.

"You are fortunate. There is a cancellation next Tuesday. An appointment is scheduled for you with Dr. Borgen."

It was Wednesday. The next five days would be spent getting medical opinions locally. The radiologist in Hamilton already said he thought I needed a mastectomy. What was there to lose in seeking other diagnoses?

Mary was glad I could meet Dr. Borgen. She also advised me to get other opinions to compare to his. Two appointments were made. One oncologist confirmed a mastectomy was necessary. The other advised me to have more drastic surgery.

"It is my opinion you should have both breasts and your ovaries removed. That way you will not have to fear the cancer returning or spreading to those areas."

The disparate options were confusing and disheartening. I could only hope Dr. Borgen would have a different assessment of my case. I decided to follow whatever treatment Dr. Borgen suggested.

The following Monday evening, my son Michael came in from Manhattan, where he was soon to earn a second Masters' Degree. When I told him the situation, he said little.

"I'll drive you to New York. You shouldn't be alone now."

Michael was solicitous, offering me a cup of tea. I could see he was worried. He had found his father's lifeless body and was probably wondering if it was time to lose his mother. He drove me to New York during the Tuesday morning rush hour. A man of few words, we drove without mentioning my condition. He kept asking me if I was comfortable or if I would like to stop on the way for a cup of coffee. He was upset, but tried not to show it. I was not nervous, but thankful to be in competent hands.

In the hospital's oncology waiting area, an array of articles on breast cancer was splayed on several tables. I read a few texts, all stating that the quality of breast cancer care varies throughout regions of the country, the most progressive being in coastal areas.

Women in their teens to advanced age filled the room. There were those who wore head scarves to conceal the effects of chemotherapy, while others opted to expose their bare pates. Several were in wheelchairs, severely pale, weakened by the advancement of the disease.

This place is depressing. The worst sight for me is the young mothers cradling babies in their arms or wheeling toddlers in their strollers. They are battling to live to care for the new life they brought into the world. What anguish they must feel. At least I've had 64 years. Few people speak here, but the tension is palpable.

My name was called, and Michael and I met the personable, middle-aged, highly professional, Dr. Patrick Borgen.

"I've studied your records, and need to perform a biopsy to verify the diagnosis of breast cancer."

He performed the procedure that day. The following morning, he called me at home.

"The tissue sample is malignant. Please return to my office tomorrow and we will discuss your operation."

The news was anticipated. Strangely, I was not filled with dread; I had remained calm since my one crying spell.

"The cancer is less than one centimeter. It had been contained in the duct, but now has invaded the general area. It does not require a mastectomy or chemotherapy, so a lumpectomy will be sufficient."

"And what is a lumpectomy?"

"Only the mass is removed. The procedure was developed by a doctor in Italy. It is less drastic than a mastectomy and equally efficient. Although you will not need chemotherapy, extensive radiation treatment is recommended."

"How much is extensive?"

"Forty-nine doses."

"That seems like a lot. Is it one size fits all?"

"Yes. Currently, that number is considered the most effective for destroying malignant cells."

I am relieved I don't need a mastectomy, the removal of my ovaries or chemo. Radiation may be better, but Madame Curie died from radiation. Stop thinking negatively; you decided that whatever Dr. Borgen says, you will do.

When Vicki heard of my surgery she flew in from Seattle to be with me. It was good to have her by my side. We left for New York City the day before the operation, which was scheduled for 8:30 a.m., on March 30th.

On arriving at our hotel in Manhattan, a man from the hospital called, informing me in a curt manner that my operation was postponed until 2:30 p.m. the next day.

"They will perform a lymph node dissection. Don't have anything to eat and don't take any aspirin."

Up to that point, I had been composed. But the lymph node revelation sounded ominous. I didn't recall Dr. Borgen mentioning it. The news caused me so much anxiety I developed a raging migraine. Vicki looked on in dismay because of the aspirin prohibition. Her presence was comforting even if there was nothing she could do to lessen the severe pain. My head was pounding throughout the night and into the early afternoon of the scheduled procedure.

We were led into a waiting room where other patients sat until their names were called. A middle-aged woman, noticing my distress, smiled and spoke to me gently.

"We are fortunate to be here today. I've had a double mastectomy. A few years ago, I developed a brain tumor. Now I'll be treated for ovarian cancer, and I am going to be all right. You will be too."

I tried to smile back, but the pain in my head made responding difficult. "My sister has a migraine," Vicki explained, apologetically.

This kind woman is trying to reassure me, but her story is upsetting me more. She has been through far more than I, yet she is hopeful. Her positive attitude makes me feel ashamed. People go through tremendous challenges in their battle against cancer. Now is my turn. Just think, if I were in a country like Haiti, with no money, I would probably be left to die slowly and agonizingly on a mat on the ground. She is right; we are very lucky to be in this hospital.

"Gilda Rorro," a voice called. "What is your date of birth?"

The young female attendant led me to a gurney where I was wheeled into the operating room. Dr. Borgen welcomed me.

"Doctor, at this moment, you are the most important man in my life. I'm sure your wife would understand."

"Yes, she would," he said, smiling.

"Are you ready for some fun today?" the anesthesiologist joked.

"Indeed. Let the games begin."

When I was aroused after the operation, Dr. Borgen assured me all had gone extremely well. "Your scar will be barely visible. You are to rest and do very little exertion for at least two weeks."

"Thank you so much, doctor. I'll follow your orders. "

My migraine was gone. There was no adverse reaction to the anesthesia. After an hour, I went to get dressed to leave the hospital and noticed in a mirror that my cheeks were rosy.

I look and feel good again. It's as though I have been reborn. Radiation is the next hurdle, but that too will go well. There may be no need for drastic life changes after all. I'm going to live. I'm going to live!

FIRE

The day after my lumpectomy I rested at home, experiencing fatigue and sharp pains in the operated breast. Vicki and Giuseppe were attentive, but the telephone rang incessantly with Italians needing consular services. I explained I was recovering from an operation and most were very understanding. A few, however, spurred on by their anxious, elderly mothers, urged me to be of assistance.

Per favore, dottoressa, aiuti mia Mamma. (Please, help my Mamma.)

Their pleas were difficult to resist, so after two days Vicki left and I returned to work on a limited basis. Serving the people, I was still aware of shooting pains, but interacting with the public was a distraction that made the discomfort seem less severe. After the third day, I decided to resume my normal, daily routine and concentrate on others. It helped.

After 10 months, on 26 December 2004, Giuseppe completed the library. The result was outstanding. To celebrate, I opened a bottle of prosecco. The room exuded warmth replete with hand-carved cherubs flanking two bookcases, an inlaid wooden floor with star-shaped medallions, crown moldings and a granite-trimmed fireplace. We were in high spirits, oblivious to the five-degree temperature outside.

Deviating from his normal routine of working from 8:30 a.m. to 6 p.m., Giuseppe excused himself at 4 p.m. to go to Home Depot to look for additional materials. I decided to sit on my burgundy-tufted leather sofa and watch TV in the stately new surroundings. The view on the screen instantly changed my mood from pleasure to dismay. A massive earthquake in the Indian Ocean had caused a massive tsunami in Sumatra, Indonesia. Panicked people were fleeing in terror as everything in the wake of the rushing water was washing away.

Oh, how dreadful! So many people are homeless.

As soon as that thought flashed through my mind, there was a loud, roaring sound behind me. Standing up, I gasped in horror as a wave of flames darted rapidly from one corner of the ceiling to the other, leaving a trail of billowing smoke where my parents' portraits hung side-by-side.

Oh, my God! I must do something. What can I save?

For a second, I was mesmerized in disbelief and terror. Frantically, I grabbed a fire extinguisher nearby, but my arthritic hands could not activate the nozzle. I tried pressing it down with my foot to no avail. Knowing that time was vital, I grabbed my cell phone with trembling

My library with portraits.

hands and called 911. The operator connected me to someone in the Nottingham Volunteer Fire Department, which was down the street from my home.

"I'll dispatch my men as soon as possible."

"Hurry, there are flames everywhere," I shouted back.

"Lady, what are you doing in the house? Get out of there right this minute."

Yes, but first, I must save something. I must save the portraits of Mom and Dad!

My mother's painting was in front of me, the flames splitting into scarlet tongues lapping at its ornate, gilded frame. I loosened it from the wall, but a ribbon of fire nearly brushed my cheek, causing me to pivot and drop it upside down onto the floor. An ominous cloud of black smoke covered my father's likeness hanging on the other side of the blazing wall. I contemplated holding my breath and rushing to free it but realized the danger was too great.

In a few seconds, fire was enveloping the room, searing the edges of my portrait, a high school graduation present from Mom and Dad. This frame was lighter, making it easier to dislodge and carry onto the freezing patio. I wore a light sweater when a police officer had arrived to escort me to the back seat of his car, parked on the street where we could watch the glowing spectacle.

I couldn't save the portraits. What will my sisters say? Of all things, that is what I will always regret most. It's as though Mom and Dad died again tonight.

It was about 20 minutes before the firefighters arrived, but seemed like an eternity. They worked in rapid, coordinated movements. I watched an eerie crimson glow ominously in the windows of my home.

It's been said that when one is dying, their entire life flashes by. Vivid memories of the 38 years I've lived in this house are racing through my mind right now: watching the building being constructed, decorating it, bringing the babies home from the hospital, Thanksgiving dinners and John's converting it to an Italian villa. All the memories, so much effort, laughter and sadness; everything is gone. How could this happen?

I should be crying or even screaming, but all I can do is sit in this cold, cramped vehicle and watch the destruction. My body has undergone so many shocks recently it won't react now. This must be how some of the tsunami victims feel because I, too, am homeless.

The fire fighters smashed windows, climbed on the roof and tore through portions with hatchets to dispel the conflagration into the black night. The crashing sounds stabbed at my heart.

They're breaking Giuseppe's stained glass—so much beauty gone in a flash. How often you used to tell him that if something happened to the house you would be devastated. Well, it's happened and you're still here. You survived cancer; you'll get through this.

"Too bad. You had a nice house," the officer commented.

"Yes. So much love and labor went into it and now it's gone."

"Be happy you got out without a scratch. I was at a fire last week where a woman was trapped inside. She's in Saint Francis Hospital now, suffering from severe burns all over her body."

Mom's portrait.   *Dad's portrait.*

"If I had been in my indoor pool or some other place in the building I would have been burned too. I am grateful to be in the back seat of your car."

Edinburg Road was blocked off from my residence to Five Points, a half-mile away. When the valiant work of the volunteer firefighters ended, a new police vehicle was stationed on my property for the night. Mary and Joe took me to their townhouse in Princeton. Joe was a very thoughtful son-in-law. Sitting on the sofa, he presented me an offer with a sincere, concerned look.

"Mom, you can't go back to that big house now. Live here. We have all this room."

How kind of him, but I intend to live independently, as long as possible.

I called Vicki in Seattle.

"The worst thing, Vicki, is that I couldn't save the portraits."

"You are not hurt, Gilda, so nothing is more important."

Her words were considerate, but nothing could make me get over the guilt of my helplessness. When I finally fell asleep, I was plagued by

Fireplace, after the fire.

nightmares of paintings melting in swirls of raging flames and billowing, ebony smoke.

The following morning, Mary drove me to my property where a police officer assisted us into the darkened building. We donned hard hats, surgical masks and carried flashlights. We sloshed on the water-soaked floor of the downstairs kitchen. In contrast to the sunny day, the inside seemed like a carbonized cave where recessed light fixtures and sparkling crystal chandeliers had morphed into drooping charcoal stalactites. The air was fetid and produced a metallic taste.

This is heart wrenching. I'm glad Louie and John can't see everything scorched. One thing is certain; I have a humongous job on my hands and I don't know where to begin. This is harrowing.

We moved slowly and quietly until my right foot hit something solid on the saturated floor. The officer assisted me in carrying it outside. In the bright sunlight, we saw the back of a large picture frame. The policeman turned it around.

"It's my mother's portrait and it's perfect and beautiful!" I gasped.

Seeing Mom's benign smile, pristine and unscathed, I burst into tears, tears of ineffable joy.

Somehow, she's still with me. I can do anything now.

The police officer left as Giuseppe arrived in his green, Ford pickup. The stunned look on his face was pitiful. He stood for several minutes, staring in silent disbelief, his eyes vapid.

Giuseppe is in shock. His six years of incredible labor have been reduced to this smoldering, black mass. My heart aches for him. He doesn't express himself in words, only in his work. Now it's all gone. When Windsor Castle burned in 1992, Queen Elizabeth II said it was an Annus Horribilis (Horrible Year). John's demise, combatting breast cancer and now this dreadful fire, the term, "Anni Horribili ("Horrible Years") applies to Giuseppe and me.

My friend shuffled to the driver's seat of his truck without a greeting. I knew it was best to leave him alone at that moment. My children, in-laws, niece Lisa, and friend Leo came to my aid, boxing the few salvageable items remaining. Everyone offered advice, clothing and hospitality. I decided to stay at the Rorro's home on Hamilton Avenue because it was just 15 minutes away by car; being with them in familiar surroundings, somehow made me feel Louie's protective presence.

On awakening the next day in their large, Georgian-style house in Trenton, I felt happy, grateful once again to be alive and well, and began singing. I heard my brother-in-law John make remarks about my mood to his two sisters while they prepared breakfast in the adjacent kitchen.

"Listen to her. She's singing at a time like this. Can you believe it?"

Yes. I was content for my life and for having a caring family. But I knew lightheartedness would not solve the dark reality of dealing with a severely damaged property. Only four months had passed since my final dose of radiation. Whatever my state of health, I was confronted with making a life-altering decision, so I set out to assess the damage once again.

The insurance company informed me that my husband John had the property underinsured. I was always concerned about that and had contacted the company on five occasions to question the rate. Each time they told me it was enough. Now I find it is far too low.

What a disaster! Now I feel my only option is to demolish the house, sell the lot and move into a senior community. Life in my "Dream Castle" is over.

CHAPTER SEVENTEEN

FROM DARKNESS TO LIGHT

GRAN CANARIA

The State Farm insurance agent provided his assessment of the fire damage at the end of his inspection.

"It seems the fire was caused by a loose wire in the wall of the library. There was another fire about to happen in your bedroom where an additional wire was not capped. Who was the electrician?"

"The last I heard, he was imprisoned for embezzlement," I was embarrassed to admit.

How could I forget the day the electrician told me luckily, he completed the job in time because he was going to jail? Where did John find such a person?

"What do you plan to do now?" he queried.

"Demolish the house, sell the lot and move on."

"It would be a shame to tear down the structure," he proffered. "The framing is in excellent condition of fire-proofed Douglas fir. You don't find houses made with that quality wood today. If the blaze raged another 10 to 15 minutes, it may have been too late, but it was stopped just in time. Don't destroy it."

"Thank you for the advice. I need to do some serious thinking."

Soon after the insurance agent left, I was visited by people claiming to be sent by the insurance company to help me. The first to pull onto the property was a grey van on which *DRY CLEANING SERVICE* stood out in bold, white letters. A man in his early 40s exited with a male assistant.

"You've had a big fire, too bad."

"Yes. Why are you here?"

"We represent the insurance company, and will take your smoke-damaged garments and restore them."

This must be routine procedure. I'll let them see the clothes, as some may be salvageable.

Hearing about the loose wires was upsetting, and the enormity of the problem was sinking in. The two men followed, surveying the interior with considerable interest.

"Here is my closet. Can these clothes really be cleaned?"

The leader examined the soot-saturated camisoles, suits, jackets, skirts and dresses and gave me an extraordinary estimate.

"I can dry clean all of them and make them look like new. For you, there is a special price: 14,000 dollars."

"That is indeed a special price."

Stunned, I politely asked the men to leave. After their van pulled away, I called State Farm.

"Two men came saying they represent your company to provide dry cleaning services. They want a lot of money."

"We have no such representatives. It was good you told them to leave."

No sooner did I return the phone to its cradle than another van approached. This time the man said his agency was there to do internal cleaning. In my state of naiveté and shock, I allowed him to enter and explore the charred interior.

"We'll clean the ceramic tile, marble and other stonework upstairs and down. For you, the special price is 75,000 dollars."

I was feeling weak in the knees. All I wanted to do was lay my head on a pillow and drift off into oblivion. I told him he would hear soon regarding my decision.

The letter carrier's van was next to arrive.

"Wow! How did this happen? Where should I leave the mail?"

"Give it to me for now, please. I'll arrange for a new mailbox at another time."

There was a postcard from my German friends who had a time-share in the Canary Islands. On it, a scene of blooming bougainvillea and palms looked idyllic in contrast to this frigid, late December afternoon. The message was warm and inviting.

"Come to *Gran Canaria*. David and Betsy are arriving next week, and they would like you to join us for ten days. We will have a great time together. The weather is wonderful, and the sun will shine for you every day."

I wish I could go, but it is impossible. How could I leave all this mess?

I stood in the parking lot for several minutes, my eyes fixated on the colorful card, when my friend, Dr. Frank Campo, a local pathologist, pulled into my driveway.

"I was passing by and see you have trouble. Are you all right?"

"How kind of you. I'm as good as can be expected. Actually, I am joyful because my mother's portrait was spared."

"That must be very comforting, but my concern is that this dilemma might be overwhelming, so soon after your radiation treatments."

"It won't be easy, but others have gone through worse. I'll manage somehow. Look! This postcard just came. I've been invited to the Canary Islands; can you imagine? It would be nice, but obviously, I can't leave."

"Gilda, as your friend and as a physician, I advise you to go and get away. Clear your mind and when you return you'll be in better condition to tackle this enormous problem."

"Do you really think so?"

"I know so. Go! It's a doctor's order."

My children and in-laws concurred it would be good for me to have a respite. They and friends volunteered to watch the house in my absence. David and Betsy were happy I would be traveling with them as were my German friends who lived in Frankfurt.

David and Betsy arranged to leave in only seven days. There was much to do with travel preparations and addressing the pressing issues with the house. I did not want to leave without an idea of what had to be done with the property. The first thing I learned about was the role of an adjuster. I interviewed several that week, some of whom charged a rate of 15 percent. It was my daughter Mary who negotiated with the insurance company.

"Mom. You don't need an adjuster. Your policy was under-insured, and the company is paying you the full amount."

That is good news and certainly one less thing to worry about.

What disturbed me most was Giuseppe's mental and physical condition. He came to the site daily, but unshaven and silent. He refused to eat or engage in conversation and seemed shell-shocked. I knew it would take a good deal of thought to find a solution to his problem.

In the meantime, I was told a contractor would be necessary to oversee the reconstruction of the house. Several contacted me, requesting 75,000-100,000 dollars for their services. The estimates for interior cleaning, and a contractor, would exhaust the 200,000 dollars I would hopefully receive from the insurance company. These amounts caused me more concern and my head was in a whirl.

How I wish Louie were alive. He'd know exactly what to do. I cannot afford to make any mistakes, but how can I avoid them? Dr. Campo is right. The change of scene may do me a world of good right now, but sooner or later, I must face this challenge.

A week later, with the house securely boarded against intruders, I was on a flight to Madrid with David and Betsy. I drifted off to sleep 20,000 feet in the skies. My worries seemed to melt away as I dreamt of pink blossoms and turquoise waters of the Canary Islands. I was feeling a little unsure about leaving, but also relieved to escape the copious tasks that lay ahead.

From Madrid, we took another plane to *Gran Canaria*, off north-western Africa, where my friend Peter was waiting at the airport. He drove us to *Villa Florida*, a German-managed vacation compound consisting of small, charming, two-floor apartments. All accommodations seemed similar, with a compact living room, an eat-in kitchen and two bedrooms and a bath upstairs. A large communal swimming pool was outdoors. A restaurant included a full buffet breakfast daily and offered lunch and dinner menus for those who preferred not to cook.

Life on *Gran Canaria* was continental. Like the postcard, broad, pristine avenues were dotted with riotously-colored bougainvillea and elegant, majestic palms. Peter escorted us on our first walk to the beach.

He led me by the hand across shimmering sand dunes emblazoned with a sulphur-yellow light. Peter never prepared me for the sight that lay on them.

The sun was blazing, and so were nude bodies dotting the path. As we plowed along, several gay and lesbian couples popped out from behind sparse bushes, enjoying the glory of nature's pleasure to the fullest.

"Oh, my God!" I exclaimed, uncontrollably.

The scene became so frequent and my reaction so predictable that my friends referred to me laughingly as "Gilda, oh my God."

The more liberal attitude of the German and other tourists on *Gran Canaria* contrasted with the town of *Teror*, outside of the city. There, a beautiful Basilica was dedicated to the *Virgen del Pino*, Patron of the Diocese of the Canary Islands. We were told to purchase the famous biscuits of the cloistered nuns at the Cistercian Monastery nearby. It was a novel experience to order and pay for the sweets via a revolving "lazy Susan" device spun by an unseen, mute sister.

Visiting the Christopher Columbus Museum downtown was a special treat. It had a replica of the Admiral's sparse quarters aboard the *Santa María* and the limited navigational equipment used to embark on the "Dark Sea," as the Atlantic was called. The uncertainty he faced going forth made me identify in some way with the admiral.

I feel like a daughter of Columbus. I am embarking on a journey with an unknown outcome. He possessed courage and I must conjure it as well.

Basking in the sun, dining in fine restaurants, strolling with our German companions and their friends, most of whom spoke no English, proved to be a delightful diversion. At night, however, my sleep was interrupted by recurrent visions of black smoke enveloping my parents' portraits.

I knew it would take time to recover from that traumatic experience. I also knew I needed to return home.

We were alarmed about what appeared on television the day before our departure. New York City was struck by a blizzard. Transportation was extremely hazardous and long flight delays were to be expected at JFK.

This looks awful. Our flight may be turbulent and getting home from "the Big Apple" will surely be arduous.

I decided to make the best of the situation. We bid farewell to the lovely island where Columbus had set sail on his last westward voyage in 1502 to "The New World."

Returning to New York, our flights had been uneventful. On the contrary, it was uncommonly tranquil and efficient at JFK. The planes arrived on time and there was no chaos at the airport. A driver was waiting for me and escorted me to the car on the snow-banked street. I enjoyed a pleasant ride back to my in-law's home in Trenton. It was such a relief to enter the house where Louie had once lived, and I felt his fortifying and consoling presence.

The following day, I couldn't wait to return to my house to see what transpired in my absence. Happily, everything was as I left it, except Giuseppe was different. His pickup truck pulled into the parking lot only three minutes after I arrived. A gaunter figure exited. His beard was longer and bushier, his clothes, rumpled. He did not speak, so I initiated a conversation.

"How are you?"

He shrugged his shoulders in indifference and walked to the back of the property. I followed him.

"Giuseppe, I am going to get an estimate from one more contractor today. An appointment was made before I left. He'll arrive at 3 this afternoon."

He did not respond, but remained within earshot when the man arrived. We spoke outdoors, in a voice sufficiently loud for Giuseppe to grasp the conversation. The man's estimate was consistent with the fees of the other contractors.

Regardless of what the insurance agent said about not leveling the frame, I will not be able to afford to rebuild the house.

No sooner had the thought crossed my mind than Frank Gargione paid a visit. A retired rocket scientist, born in Italy and trained at Drexel and the University of Pennsylvania, he was a member of the New Jersey Italian Heritage Commission. Frank and his wife Lucille were fellow parishioners at Our Lady of the Angels Parish in Trenton, and we were friends.

"Gilda, I see you returned from the Canary Islands. I hope you had a good rest because, from the look of things, you're going to need to be in top shape to deal with all this. Have you decided what you are going to do now?"

I reported the prohibitive cost of tradesmen from adjusters to cleaners, to contractors.

"It's too bad, Frank, but there is no alternative. The insurance money will not cover the cost of rebuilding. There is no alternative but to tear down the frame, sell the lot and move. It breaks my heart; so many memories are here. My first husband bought the land and had the house built as soon as he heard we were expecting our first child. John added to it and Giuseppe worked here for six years before the fire. This place is my foundation, while so many other aspects of my life have been crumbling."

"Gilda, you may be able to stay here. Ask Giuseppe to do the work. What do you need a contractor for? He knows all the trades. No one is better. Ask him."

"Joe Damiano? No, Frank. He is in a depressive state right now. The poor man put his heart and soul in this place. He is more heartbroken than I and won't even speak."

"You have your hands full. If there is anything we can do, please let me know. But before you decide, ask Giuseppe."

"Thank you, Frank."

When his car pulled away, I went to the back of the house to see my friend, whose dour expression had not changed. I felt frustrated and decided to cease trying to coddle him out of pity, and use another tactic.

"Giuseppe. Enough is enough. I know how horrible you feel seeing your beautiful inlaid marble and woodwork go up in smoke, but if you want to come back here I insist that you go home now, shave, change your clothes and expect to talk to me. Otherwise, do not come back."

The pained look on his face made me regret my words, but I did not flinch in front of him. Giuseppe obediently walked to his truck and drove away.

Throughout the night I reproached myself for my sharp tone.

It was so unlike me to speak that way. My words upset him. He might never return.

I was too embarrassed to tell my in-laws what I had done. My remorse grew deeper the following day when I drove back to the site. I stood outside my car and stared at the side of the house where dark soot ran in rivulets down the cream-colored stucco. A door slammed behind me. Giuseppe arrived clean-shaven and wearing crisp clothes. My first impulse was to apologize for my harsh declarations the previous night, but he didn't give me a chance to utter a word.

"I'm going to rebuild your house. John was my best friend. I owe it to him and you to do it."

"Giuseppe, you're 72-years-old. You can't tackle a job of this magnitude."

"Read my lips. I'm going to build you a church."

"A church, what do you mean?"

"That's an expression in the Burg. A church is usually the most beautiful building in town. When you construct something special, we call it a church. We have a lot of work to do. Here, I bought you a hard hat. Let's go to Millhurst Mills to look at construction material."

Protesting seemed futile and I was relieved by Giuseppe's confident metamorphosis. Smiling, I donned the yellow hard hat, stepped into the driver's seat of my Chevy Tahoe and we sped off.

NO! NOT AGAIN?

Giuseppe proved true to his word. He tackled the job of reconstruction with enthusiasm, working 10-hours per day, 7 days a week. What-

Giuseppe begins rebuilding.

ever I suggested, he would readily and eagerly do. "Giuseppe, could you tear down the walls in the upstairs kitchen and make an open space?"

"I'll do it."

"Giuseppe, there is a four-foot crawl space in the roof. Instead of maintaining the standard eight-feet, could you elevate the living room ceiling?"

"If you like, I'll raise the ceilings in all the rooms upstairs."

It was exciting to watch his slender frame in a creative mood. He moved purposely, concentrating on every detail, not wanting to indulge in small talk while he was absorbed in his work. He never drew a blue print nor discussed a possible design. His modus operandi was to start a project and the inspiration would come. He did not know in advance what he would do, and I always loved the outcome.

One day, a friend from Princeton paid me a surprise visit. She observed Giuseppe and asked him to show her one of his designs on paper.

"There is none. I never draw anything in advance."

"If you worked for me, you would have to produce a blueprint."

"Lady, I would never work for you."

He uttered those words in a genteel way that was not insulting. He

421

Restoration results - front; back of the house; the garden.

merely wanted to convey the fact that his inspiration was spontaneous, not pre-planned.

After staying one-month at my in-law's home, the insurance company provided a new fully-furnished townhouse for me to occupy for eight months. I moved into Avalon Way on Quakerbridge Road, only a ten-minute drive from my house.

"You may love it there, Gilda, and never want to leave. Living will be a lot easier; you'll see," my sister-in-law said.

Being in the townhouse was convenient because there was no outside maintenance. The interior furnishings were functional Americana. A beige sofa and matching armchair occupied the living room, facing a gas fireplace. The dining room table was a light-brown oak with matching straight chairs. Small pictures of flowers adorned the walls. White tiles, tub and sink were standard in the bathrooms. When I entertained family and friends, they commented on the pleasant surroundings.

Yes. It is nice, but it is not home to me. Ferlinghetti understood this when he used the word "deracinated," or uprooted, to describe his feelings on being a transplanted Italian. I too feel disoriented. I can't wait to return to the firm foundation of my house.

Every day I went to Edinburg Road after my consular duties at my new office in Saint Joachim's church. I'd watch Giuseppe and tend to a plethora of chores. Observing the daily progress did me a world of good. I was happy and so was he. Springtime was glorious, and our spirits were high. We enjoyed ten-minute coffee breaks sipping espresso on the patio and watching the squirrels scamper in the trees. The simple things of life rendered a heightened sense of pleasure.

Vicki called me in in April 2005, informing me that Wagner's Ring Cycle was going to be performed in the Seattle Opera House that month. One of my dreams was to see the complete four masterful works of *Der Ring des Nibelungen* in that renowned facility. Following an impulse, I purchased tickets for her and me. Vicki's birthday was in May and that would make a great gift. Subsequently, I purchased an airline ticket to Seattle.

I would never do this if married. Being single allows me the freedom to be impetuous. When I told Vicki about her present, she was delighted.

The next day, the sun was gleaming as I planted geraniums, wearing a light green, strapless dress. Suddenly, I felt a stabbing pain in the right breast.

The doctors told me to keep out of the sun when I was undergoing radiation, but that was last August. I'd better avoid those rays and stay in the shade.

The following day, a Wednesday, I noticed a pink rash and slight swelling had formed in that area. In the afternoon, I went to the Princeton Medical Center for an appointment to be examined by both my radiologist and oncologist.

"Let's keep an eye on it," the radiologist said. "Come back in three months. If there is any change, call me."

My daughter arrived from work to meet me for the oncologist's appointment. Mary told the oncologist she was concerned the rash was indurated, or stiffened. He agreed and sent me to have an emergency MRI.

I began to feel alarmed at the concerned looks of Mary and the physician and dutifully went to submit to the test. Having an MRI was very unpleasant because of my arthritic condition. Reclining motionless, with limbs extended on a narrow cot, encapsulated for 45 minutes in a confined space, an inch from my nose with clanging noises, was an extremely uncomfortable experience.

On arriving at the medical facility, a female technician informed me she was new on the job and that I was one of her first patients for the test. She was pleasant and explained that if I should become uncomfortable, I should call out to her. After less than 15 minutes in that stiff position, my knee joints felt as though they were being stabbed by sharp blades.

"Please. Stop for a minute," I called out.

The technician obliged and within one minute, the test resumed. After what seemed like a half-hour, the pain in my limbs became unbearable and I stiffened my muscles to alleviate it.

"Don't move!" she shouted.

I endured. The session ended, and I felt exhausted. When I arrived back at the townhouse I went promptly to bed, too tired to talk.

The next day, the Korean oncologist, called me. The manner in which he said my name, haltingly, in a low voice, alerted me that he was the bearer of disconcerting news.

"Dr. Rorro, I regret to inform you that, the MRI results reveal the cancer has returned and metastasized. It spread throughout the breast area. You have lesions deep in the chest cavity. I recommend immediate aggressive chemotherapy and radiation to shrink the tumor, followed by a radical mastectomy. Please return to Sloan Kettering Hospital in New York for the treatment. I am sorry."

He hung up without giving me an opportunity to ask questions.

What! How could he tell me this devastating diagnosis over the telephone, and then hang up abruptly? When I taught ESL, I learned most Asians avoid giving bad news. This is a classic example. I think he has just given me a death sentence. I'm going to call my sister-in-law Mary. As a doctor, she will know.

I contacted her immediately and recounted the doctor's findings.

"It's very serious, isn't it, Mary?"

"Oh, my goodness! Go back to Sloan Kettering and do what they say."

From the sound of her voice, I knew she concurred with the gravity of my condition. I had to wait until Monday morning for an appointment. From Thursday evening to Monday, waves of uncontrollable terror surged from my abdomen to my throat. At rare moments when I was temporarily distracted, the thought of the cancer jolted me back to the frightening reality. I was acutely aware of every twinge of feeling in my body, thinking it was caused by the spreading tentacles of disease.

My daughter accompanied me to New York on Monday, where Dr. Borgen examined me, frowning.

"I have arranged for you to go downstairs for a biopsy."

Mary and I entered a cold room where a female physician sat, accompanied by a Filipino nurse. Their warm smiles offset the chill in the surroundings.

"Your records indicate the cancer has returned. We are going to verify it by a biopsy of the breast tissue," the doctor said.

Her empathic nurse held my hand as the physician's blade pierced my skin.

"If the cancer has returned, before starting any treatment, will I be able to go to the opera in Seattle? I want to hear Brunhilde sing before I die. I bought expensive, non-refundable tickets for my sister and me."

"No. That would be impossible," she said in a slow, deliberate voice. "If this is what we think it is, you have inflammatory breast cancer, which may be fatal within three days. You must cancel your trip."

Her words struck me like a lightning bolt.

What is inflammatory breast cancer? It must be deadly for those pronouncements. I may have three days to live? Could there be even less time? After 49 radiation treatments, the cancer has returned? I've got lesions deep in my chest and may need a radical mastectomy? Gilda; prepare yourself; this time it's over. There is no more room for levity about Brunhilde. I've got so much to do—funeral arrangements, gifts and goodbyes

THE RITE OF THE SICK

My disjointed mental ramblings ceased when I noticed Mary's diminutive frame beginning to quiver. Her eyes welled with tears as she tried valiantly to control them. Her reaction brought a flashback etched in my memory of my mother's imminent demise.

I've got to be careful how I react to this situation. Like my mother, I am teaching my daughter a life lesson. Although she's a psychiatrist, she's my little girl who may be about to lose her surviving parent. Remember Mom? How extraordinary she was when the doctor at Jefferson told her she had terminal colon cancer and could expect to live only a few months. Remember how she answered when the surgeon recommended chemotherapy, radiation, and an operation to prolong her life for perhaps a year?

"No, doctor! I do not wish to be baked, stewed or steamed. At the end, I want a morphine drip, that's all." I was devastated as she said that. When we went out of the doctor's office and into the hall, she startled me even more. "Mom, come to Trenton and live with me now. Leave your apartment in The Philadelphian and let me take care of you."

"No, Gilly. I always wanted to learn to speak French and Spanish. I'm going to enroll in courses at Temple University next week. There isn't much time to waste. Now let's go to the *Mezzaluna Restaurant* and have a wonderful lunch."

No word of complaint or self-pity ever exited my mother's lips. Her attitude was always positive and celebratory.

"Gilly, I've had a great life. Your father took me from the village of Mays Landing, had me go to Beaver College and travel the world. Never in my wildest dreams did I aspire to such things growing up in that small town. Going to college changed my life. My siblings respected me, but at the same time, I became somewhat alienated from my family. They treated me differently after I earned my degree, loving me, but always keeping me at a little distance. I understood and loved them the same. A woman had to pay a price in those days, whether she remained ignorant or educated. I wanted things to be better for you and your sisters, and they are. Your schooling has already rendered you rewards. As a mother, can you appreciate how great life has been to me? If you want to be of assistance, help me with my homework on the weekends. I intend to be a star student.

"The Bible promises us three score and ten. I'm 84-years-old and have enjoyed 14 extra years. When I go, it will be with a heart full of joy. I'm grateful for you, Gilly, because we always loved each other."

Mom's courageous confrontation to the inevitable taught me more than any lecture or sermon.

The night before she died, after attending Temple University for four months, I sat with her alone in the hospital room, where she told me her mother was with her.

"Where is Grandmom?"

"She's right by the door, smiling at us. She's come to take me with her soon."

"Tell her I said hello."

"She knows you are here, and she is happy."

The next day, Mary, Vicki and I were summoned to the hospital where the male physician was examining Mom.

"Dr. Battaglia," roll over onto your left side. Good. Now, roll onto your right side."

"Doctor," Mom retorted, "You had me roll over so many times I feel like a certificate of deposit."

We all laughed at those, her last words. Mom gave Vicki, Mary and me her final great lesson—never lose your sense of humor. Now the torch is passed to me. What lesson will I leave my children? Can I find humor in this?

Mary's shaking body interrupted my reverie. I held her in my arms before the examining room door opened and an energetic young woman oncologist, Dr. Debra Mangino, entered with quick strides. Her confident, staccato voice filled the room.

"I looked at your records from Princeton. We can treat you, but first I want you to have another MRI here tomorrow morning at 8 a.m."

"Why another? Do you think the first one is inaccurate?"

"I want you to return to this hospital for the test tomorrow. We'll then discuss the results."

She exited the area quickly, as did Mary and I.

On the street, Mary hailed a cab. I slumped into the back seat. The worrisome, weary weekend compounded by the dreadful possible prognosis, had taken a toll. I felt exhausted and closed my eyes. Per my daughter's instructions, the cab stopped.

"Mom, get out. There is something I have to do here."

"What! Where are we?"

"Get out, Mom. You'll see."

We were not at Penn Station, where I longed to board the train to Hamilton and rest. Obeying Mary, I exited onto Lexington Avenue, in front of the Church of Saint Vincent Ferrer, the majestic structure where Mary and her husband Joseph had been married.

"Why are we here, Mary? What is it you have to do? I want to go home."

Mary went to a side building and rang a bell. The door opened, and my daughter motioned for me to approach. I felt too tired to resist and joined her inside. A young priest was there to meet us.

"Good afternoon! I am Father Peter. Your daughter informed me you received distressing news a short while ago. She would like me to perform the *Right of the Sick* for you, if you consent."

Poor Mary. She is suffering more than I. She knows the church has always been an integral part of my life. She is so thoughtful.

"Father, I will be most appreciative to receive the rite."

Lifting a small vial, the priest said, "I brought this holy water from the River Jordan where I traveled recently."

"Yes. I also have been there. How wonderful!"

Being in the rectory with the calming presence of Father Peter and my loving daughter filled me with a sense of peace. I was ready to confront whatever challenge was set before me and, like Mom, I would try to do it with grace and class.

On the train to Hamilton there was no sleeping. Mary was too distraught. She wanted to console me, but the reverse happened. Cradling her delicate frame in my arms, I had to assure her I had no fear of dying. We discussed funeral arrangements, followed by maternal musings about how much she and Michael had always meant to me.

My greatest concern is for my daughter. Michael is much more independent; Mary will be greatly affected because she has always been very attached. When people say, life is difficult, it's times of sickness and death that make it so. Losing money, position, or even a house can be hard but ultimately overcome. Death is final.

The strangest thing is that I have no discomfort—no pain. Will the disease strike me in a day or two? No one explained inflammatory breast cancer to me. I asked no questions, so the doctors must have assumed I know how devastating it is.

At 5 a.m. the following day, I rose and prepared to be at Sloan Kettering Hospital by 7:30 a.m. for the MRI. My-son-in-law accompanied me. He was very attentive throughout the trip and during the protracted wait at Sloan Kettering. His efficient presence was reassuring. When the test was to begin, a technician gave me good news.

"The time for the MRI has been reduced from 45 minutes to a half-hour."

Having 15 fewer minutes to experience joint pain was a blessing. I lay motionless during the procedure, bearing up under the loud, crackling sounds in the metal tube and the stabbing sensation in my elbows and knees. When the test ended, Joseph took me for a cappuccino at a nearby Starbucks, after which he put me on New Jersey Transit, headed for Hamilton.

That evening, my phone rang. The voice was that of the young doctor who had told me to get a second MRI.

"Hi, Dr. Rorro. This is Dr. Mangino. Your MRI results came back, and they are negative."

"Negative? Is that good or bad?" *Negative* did not sound reassuring.

"It means you do not have cancer in your right breast. However, we detect a spot on your lungs and you will need a CAT scan."

I don't have cancer? After the fearful prognosis, it is hard for me to accept it had been an error or could I be cured by the Holy Water from the River Jordan?

"The original MRI was faulty. You are all right, but you should come back for the CAT scan."

"I will do so Doctor Mangino, but not now. I am going to Seattle to hear Brunhilde sing, spot or no spot. I'm alive, and for me, it's Miller time."

The physician chuckled, and I went to look for my airline ticket, happy I did not cancel the flight. I was also thankful I had not shared the cancer story with anyone but my children and in-laws. With a happy heart, I picked up the receiver and made calls to them.

Two weeks later, not only had I heard Brunhilde's robust voice, but Seigfreid's tenor and the entire glorious cast of characters of *Des Ring* cycle. Vicki and I were in a celebratory mood during my visit to Seattle. Every moment of life seemed precious. I was alive, pain free and able to savor Wagner's soaring score. A loving family surrounded me. Receiving an extension of life was remarkable.

On returning to New Jersey, however, I found I was not "out of the woods" yet. The rash on my right breast remained, requiring another biopsy, MRI's at three-month intervals, pelvic sonograms and additional CAT and Pet Scans. The latter, in which I had to consume a half-gallon of radioactive liquid, was needed to rule out possible cancerous "spots" found on my liver. In short, for the subsequent two and a-half-years, I was subjected to a continuous battery of tests, including a Colonoscopy and Brain Scan. All the spots proved to be benign and I was truly grateful.

Boarding the train to New York was always fun—anticipating new adventures in the world's most dynamic city. Now I dislike the ride which surely culminates in more anxiety and discomfort. Of course, I am also grateful to be the recipient of state-of-the-art treatment and technology, but all this testing is wearing on my nervous system. I long for this ordeal to end.

And end it did. In 2007, I was told one mammogram a year would be sufficient. All other testing would cease. The rash disappeared, its genesis unknown. I was ecstatic. An amusing episode awaited me.

FIVE CAMELS IN CASABLANCA

To celebrate my good news, my daughter and son-in-law invited me to join them on a Mediterranean cruise aboard the exclusive Oceania Line. I accepted their offer with joy and we departed in September that year.

"Today we dock in Casablanca," announced a voice on the ship's loudspeaker.

The Casablanca depicted in Rick's Bar in the 1940s is quite a different place in 2007. My sister Vicki and I traveled to this western Moroccan city in 1963. I was 25 and she was 24 at that time, filled with an insatiable desire for adventure. Casablanca seemed much smaller in 1963, without so many high rises and condominiums. But the minarets and muezzin calling the faithful to prayer remained familiar.

Vicki and her husband, Seth made plans to sail with Mary and Joe about three months ago. I told the latter to keep my booking a secret.

At 69, I still enjoyed an element of surprise. On entering the ship for our cruise, I instructed Mary and Joe to go to the dining room ahead of me and sit where my sister would have her back to the entrance of the Grand Dining Room. I would arrive five minutes later.

"Is there room for one more at this table?" I asked slowly.

Vicki spun around and when she saw it was I, she gasped and cried out "Gilda!" It was such fun deluding her those weeks before the trip. She never suspected I'd be on board for a family reunion.

Today we find ourselves once more in this city of contrasts. There are now over 3 million inhabitants compared to the approximately one million in 1963. Arabic, French, English, Italian and a variety of other tongues are widely spoken in this bustling metropolis. White, square, stark dwellings in the old Medina Quarter stand out anachronistically aside ultra-modern apartment complexes and mosques, where slender columns support strong, ornately decorated arches. Seth, the architect, admires the Hispano-Mauresque and art deco styles of buildings here.

The decorative motifs on facades, where delicate Islamic calligraphic forms are woven into lacelike patterns, are truly mesmerizing.

There is so much to see in Casablanca that we decided to hire a driver. We walked to a local taxi stand where a good-looking young man approached, promising us an extensive tour to points of interest such as King Mohammed VI's residence; the majestic Hassan II Mosque boasting the world's tallest minaret extending 210 meters in the air with space in its courtyard for 80,000 of faithful; the sprawling beach; the Jockey Club; the Ben M'siq Market, with its stalls of exotic fish, herbs and spices, and lastly, Rick's Bar of the movie "Casablanca" fame. We piled into the chauffeur's Mercedes, eager to see it all.

"I take you for four hours all over the city," boasted Abdel, our driver, deftly maneuvering chaotic streets under a blazing sun.

Traffic there made driving in New York City seem tame. We passed pedestrians wearing the gamut of fashion: Women donned the traditional, loose-fitting, ankle-length, hooded djellaba, to super short, abbreviated modern dresses; men sported black, western suits, casual wear, or full-length kaftans and skull caps. Flamboyantly clad water vendors with broad-brimmed hats and outfits splashed with bright magentas, greens, blues and gold, remained unaltered since 1963.

Of course, I've changed these past 50 years, but my age is not stopping our conductor, Abdel, from touching my hand from time to time as we speak French.

Perhaps it is a cultural thing French brings out in people. I prefer not to make mention of it to him, although he converses in good English to those in the back-seat sans physical contact.

"I am a Berber."

"Oh. Do you ride a horse?" I asked, recalling in 1963 a team of Berber equestrians galloping into the sunset beside the sea, their head scarves undulating in the warm North African breeze.

"Yes." He eagerly took his i-Phone and proudly displayed a photo of himself astride an Arabian steed.

"You are such a nice lady. Do not leave Casablanca. Remain here with me."

I asked suspiciously, "Tell me, Abdel, are you married; do you have children?" After a poignant pause, he reluctantly confessed.

"I am married and have one child. But I am Muslim, and you can be my second wife."

I did not respond.

"If you marry me I will give you five camels," he added enthusiastically.

We said nothing for several minutes until we passed our last stop, Rick's Bar. It looked exactly like the establishment in the famous movie, with two palm trees flanking an ornate wooden door at the entrance. Although the filming was done in Hollywood, it seemed Humphrey Bogart would exit any minute to extinguish a cigarette.

We arrived at the pier where the Oceania *Riviera* awaited, a symbol of our life in the West. Abdel helped me exit the auto. He appeared sad our tour was over and that I was soon to board the ship. Joe overheard and understood the marriage proposal.

He whispered in my ear, "Tell him to make it six camels and it's a deal!"

I wonder if I am only worth five camels in Casablanca? Or, is that a hefty sum for a cab driver here? Whatever the answer, Abdel has given my ego a boost. It is so good to be alive.

Abdel shook my hand, saying, "Goodbye, Gilda." "Goodbye, Abdel. Here's looking at you, kid."

CHAPTER EIGHTEEN

CONSUL TO CAVALIERE

Returning home from Casablanca, the best news of all awaited me. *Finalmente!* The New Jersey Italian Heritage Commission held its 2007 Annual Congress at the Rutgers University Student Center. The theme was the launching of *The Universality of Italian Heritage* curriculum. It took me five years of diligent effort to develop the document with Dr. Kevin Brady, former president of the American Institute for History Education. I felt proud. The Congress officially showcased its integration throughout schools statewide and beyond.

We were honored to have the Consul General of Italy in Philadelphia, Hon. Stefano Mistretta, attend. He extolled the project publicly. When the program ended, he called me aside.

I think he wants to tell me I did a good job.

I was not prepared for what he had to say.

"*Dottoressa Rorro*, on March 15th, you will have a birthday and be *una donna di una certa età* (a woman of a certain age). He pronounced those words with the typical Italian gesture of swirling his right hand into the air.

"Italian law does not allow anyone to hold the position of Honorary Vice Consul for Italy after they are 70 years old."

"Not even if the individual is capable of carrying out the duties?"

"It does not matter. But tell me, why are you smiling?"

"I am smiling because I worked for 15 and a-half years at the Civil Rights Office of the New Jersey Department of Education, where we confronted age discrimination."

"That may be so, but it is the law in Italy."

"Fine. I've held the position for 10 years. Someone else can do it now."

"I'm leaving soon for a new post in Alexandria, Egypt. Come to the consulate next week so we can discuss this issue."

His words reverberated in my head.

All things come to an end, I suppose.

The following week, I presented myself at the Consul General's office. He asked me to be seated and immediately lit a cigarette. He appeared agitated.

"You cannot continue as Honorary Vice Consul, but I can offer you a new title of Consular Correspondent. Unfortunately, there is no stipend, but there are also fewer responsibilities."

"Thank you, but I am not interested. It seems like a lesser position, and perhaps it is time to give someone else the opportunity."

"It is not downgrading; it is simply different. You would still be a representative of the Government of Italy."

"You are very kind, but I've served for 10 years and that is sufficient."

Consul Mistretta then lit his second cigarette. He stood, walked around the room and resumed his seat near mine.

"I received notice from the Italian Embassy in Washington, D.C., that they would like you to accept the title of Consular Correspondent."

It was apparent he was determined to follow his orders even if it took all afternoon. He was so intent on having me agree that I felt empathy toward him.

"You're going to keep me here all day until I say yes, aren't you?"

"*Sì, Dottoressa,*" he said, with a nervous chuckle.

"If it means that much, I will agree to become a Consular Correspondent, but let them know in Washington that I think the law is discriminatory."

"*Benìssimo*" (Very Good), he said, slowly exhaling a cloud of smoke.

The Consul General grasped my hand in his and the meeting ended. During the ride back to Trenton, I thought about what had transpired.

One must respect the law in Italy. In fact, isn't there a similar one in the United States stipulating judges must retire at age 70? What matters most is that I am valued by the Italian officials. Somebody must like the job I'm doing and it's flattering to be asked.

My consular activities always brought new surprises. One of them focused on Rose Alito, the mother of Associate Justice of the Supreme Court of the United States, Samuel A. Alito, Jr. Rose was a Teacher Supervisor when I worked in the Hamilton Township Board of Education. She and I became friends there. After I retired, our friendship resumed when the Acting Italian Consul in Newark asked me to identify the town in Italy where Justice Alito's father had been born. I contacted Rose, then in her 90s, by telephone and she was her gracious self.

"Come on over, Gilda. I will be happy to see you."

When I went to her house, which is near mine in Hamilton Township, a strapping Secret Service man greeted me outside. Justice Alito was undergoing the confirmation process at that time, and the home of his mother was being protected.

The agent was cordial and allowed me to enter. Rose met me with her warm smile and keen intelligence. She provided the name of the town in Calabria and I subsequently relayed it to the Acting Italian Consul in Newark, Hon. Paolo Toschi.

"*Grazie. Questa informazione è preziosa.* (Thank you. This information is precious)," the youthful diplomat related.

Rose asked me to call on her again. I did, and my visits became frequent, usually two to three times a week, conversing about education and a variety of other topics related to her life in Trenton. The hurdles she overcame as an Italian American woman entering the teaching field always inspired me. Rose was a true feminist trailblazer and I valued our friendship.

Like his mother, Associate Justice Samuel A. Alito, Jr. was committed to his Italian heritage. He generously agreed to participate in several Commission events. He was the Keynote Speaker in 2011 at the 8th annual Congress of the NJIHC, "Achievements of Italian Americans." He also was inducted into The Italian American National Hall of Fame, an organization Chaired by Cav. Carl Carabelli.

Rose Alito and I at Columbus Day Parade in Hamilton.

My life continued to concentrate on consular and commission work. I was content, feeling fulfilled with the intellectual stimulation of problem solving and speaking Italian. Socially, I was pleased to have an entourage of male friends who escorted me to various functions in New Jersey, Philadelphia and New York. My house was becoming truly beautiful with Giuseppe's expert touch and I had received a Certificate of Occupancy from the township. Life was good.

That year, I received a surprising phone call from the office of the Consul General in Philadelphia.

"*Dottoressa Rorro*, Consul General Mistretta wishes to nominate you to receive the *Cavalierato* (Knighthood) from the President of Italy who heads the *Ordine al Merito della Repubblica Italiana* (Order of Merit of the Republic of Italy). He is impressed by your service to the Consulate and your effort to preserve and promote Italian cultural heritage through your curriculum project with the New Jersey Department of Education. Do you accept?"

For a moment, I was dumbstruck. As Honorary Vice Consul for Italy, I had nominated individuals for the honor and a few had received it, often only one person per year, statewide. I recovered and responded calmly.

"Please inform Consul General Mistretta that I am deeply honored and grateful for his nomination."

When I hung up, I was overjoyed.

Wow! I will be like Julie Andrews, Elizabeth Taylor and Judi Dench, when, in 2000, Queen Elizabeth officially honored them as "Dames."

When they were knighted, it made national headlines. Their honor was on nightly TV stations and made headlines in the New York Times. I don't expect any of that, but being knighted by the President of Italy Giorgio Napolitano, and confirmed by Prime Minister Silvio Berlusconi, is arguably the biggest moment of my life.

What impressed me most was the wording of the letter sent in my behalf from the Consul General to the Italian Ambassador in Washington.

"She performs her many duties with honor and grace and her style can only be described as refined and elegant. She is a walking, talking, living example of good relations between Italy and the United States."

Tears welled in my eyes.

I never thought Consul General Mistretta appreciated me to that extent.

Bureaucracy moves more slowly in Italy than in the United States. In December 2008, I was notified all documents had been signed for me to receive the honorific title of *Cavaliere* (Cavalier). A new young Consul had been appointed in Newark, the Hon. Andrea Barbaria. He was affable, competent and unpretentious. He called me on the phone one day.

"Hello, Gilda. This is Andrea."

I like his informality, calling me by my first name as well as using his own. I will be working with him since they now changed my consular jurisdiction from Philadelphia to Newark.

"Gilda, let me be the first to congratulate you. Everything is finalized

*Joining the family of Associate Justice of the US Supreme Court, Samuel A. Alito, Jr.
in Princeton, at the Governor's Mansion, Drumthwacket.
From left to right: Martha Ann Alito, Justice Alito, Rose Alito, and me.*

to bestow upon you the title of *Cavaliere*. We are holding the formal Inauguration Ceremony for the Italian Consulate here at 1 Gateway Plaza in the ground floor Gallery. Your event will follow upstairs in the Consular Reception Room. Do you like the idea?"

"Oh yes. That would be perfect."

When our conversation ended, my heart raced.

Oh, my! I always enjoyed attending the knighting ceremony of people I had nominated. Now it is my turn. There are preparations to make: what outfit to wear; acceptance remarks and determining who will accompany me. Mary will come but Michael is in California. There are no immediate family members who could make the trip. Maybe I will ask my neighbor, Ann Pantaleoni, to be with me. She is a fellow lector for the Italian masses at Saint Joachim's Church and loves all aspects of Italian heritage. That's it. I'll just ask Ann.

As anticipated, Ann was thrilled at the prospect of going. She mentioned her invitation to someone at the parish, Our Lady of the Angels. Before long, I was to go to Newark with an entourage of well-wishers.

Two days before the big event, Consul Barbaria called me.

"Hello, Gilda. Everything is ready for your award ceremony. How many people will be coming with you?"

"Forty-two."

"Forty-two!" he exclaimed, as if in shock.

"Yes. Is that a problem?"

"I expected perhaps four, not 42." After a brief pause, he said, "Bring them."

I never thought of a limit nor did I anticipate so many friends would want to ride the train to Newark to celebrate with me. Consul Barbaria seems concerned with the large number. Please stop worrying and enjoy the moment.

The "Times of Trenton" sent a reporter to my home for an interview the day before I was going to Newark. The feature article appeared in color on my big day with the title, "It's Her Night of Shining Honor."

This is one of the most exciting experiences of my life, but being the center of attention makes me feel nervous. People often laugh in disbelief when I say I am shy, but I am. I force myself to overcome it through public speaking. I only wish Mom and Dad could see me; they would be beaming. With all the joy, there is also an element of sadness. I will not have those who would care the most by my side.

At the Hamilton Train Station, my spirits were uplifted by the smiling faces of my companions who almost filled an entire car on New Jersey Transit. They prattled in anticipation of what they were about to experience, and the time passed quickly.

"Gilda, when did the knighthood tradition begin?"

"From what I've read, there was a knightly class in Ancient Rome. The first European knights were during the reign of Charlemagne in the 8th century. In the 12th century, knighthood was given as a special prestige to a mounted warrior. *Cheval* means horse in French."

"Gilda. Will you have to kneel? Will the consul tap you on the shoulder with a sword?"

Senator Lautenberg congratulates me.

"Not from what I've seen. He makes a few remarks about the person, presents a formal parchment signed by the President and Prime Minister of Italy, confers the title and then gives the recipient a medal."

"That's it?" some said, appearing disappointed.

"That's it," I confirmed.

When "The Gang" arrived at 1 Gateway Plaza, a large crowd had already gathered in the first-floor Gallery section for the formal, televised ceremony of the opening of the Italian Consulate. Lovely paintings adorned the gallery walls while refreshments were being set up for a post-ceremony reception.

Soon, the spacious atrium filled with chatter in anticipation of the landmark event. A temporary dais had been erected from which politicians, including Mayors Cory Booker and Frank Lautenberg, made official remarks to the standing room onlookers.

Elda and Elisa Coccia, of the Coccia Institute at Montclair University, accompanied by Dr. Mary Ann Puccio, teacher of Italian at Rutgers University, came up to me.

"Congratulations, Gilda. We are so proud of you and brought a gift."

"How thoughtful! Would you like to attend my knighting ceremony after the Installation of the Consulate?"

"We'd love to."

Angelo Bianchi, the former prosecutor in Essex County, also approached me. I invited him to join my group as well.

I'm sure, after his initial surprise, Consul Barbaria will not mind hosting another four people. With Italians, there is always room for a few more.

The Installation Ceremony was a superb affair. Everyone was in high spirits, grateful to have the much-needed office in our state. After greeting and networking with statewide politicians and business people, my group was told to take the elevator one flight up to the new Office of the Italian Consulate.

On arriving, we were instructed to wait outside in the public area for Consul Barbaria. After approximately 20 minutes, the diplomat appeared and motioned for us to enter his reception area.

"Gilda, my staff has arranged a special reception with prosecco and hors-d'oeuvres. A reporter and crew from New Jersey TV are also here for this important occasion."

How thoughtful. I am fortunate to work with such a considerate consul.

His colleagues had set a splendid table with assorted Italian delicacies. Apart from my guests, there were other people in the room including consular staff, Senator Lautenberg and Antonino Ciappina, a reporter and editor of the widely-read Italian newspaper, *America Oggi,* (America Today).

I feel my knees will start knocking like they did on the stage at the San Diego Fort at the Acapulco Film Festival. Control yourself. Look cool and dignified.

Andrea Barbaria rose to address the attendees. He made many kind comments about my work and read aloud the beautiful message from Consul General Mistretta's letter to the Ambassador in Washington,

Consul Barbaria presents the award and pins the gold Cavalier medal on me.

DC. He mentioned the Cavalier designation dates from medieval times when a man, riding a horse, went about doing good deeds for the community (Most women did not gallop off alone in those days.). He finished by stating that the *Cavalierato* was the highest honor bestowed on an individual by the Italian Government.

Mom and Dad would be ecstatic on hearing those words. Dad would have gone around this room boasting that his daughter was now a "Dame" because he took us to Italy in 1951.

Mom would burst with pride. She would have notified everyone she knew, and maybe even strangers.

Consul Barbaria said, "Gilda, now please say a few words to our guests."

By then I was composed and began my address in Italian, followed by English. The words flowed, inspired by a sense of humility and fulfillment. I spoke about how learning Italian opened a door to the world, which enabled me to do the following: bonding with relatives in Italy; becoming the Honorary Vice Consul for Italy in Trenton; being appointed by the governor to the New Jersey Italian American Commission; becoming Chair of five Italian American organizations to promote Italian language and culture and Chair of the Commission's Curriculum Project, "The Universality of Italian Heritage." At the end, everyone stood and applauded. It was glorious.

This is the capstone of my career. I believe God has led me to this point in my life.

Consul Barbaria took the gold medal of the "Order of Merit of the Republic of Italy," and pinned it on my pewter-colored suit jacket Giovà bought for me in Rome. He then made a *Brindisi* (toast) with prosecco. Senator Lautenberg made laudatory remarks and an Italian poet followed with a recitation in his Florentine dialect.

The Consul led me to a table on which a square cake sat with the emblem of the Italian Republic emblazoned across the top. He held my right hand as we cut into the beautiful confection amidst the flashing lights of cameras. Once aside, a reporter from NJTV interviewed me, asking how I felt.

"Completely overwhelmed."

"I can imagine. I would be too," the interviewer exclaimed. "Consul Barbaria said the Cavalierato is the highest honor bestowed by the country of Italy. You must feel incredible."

"You cannot imagine how I feel."

Many attendees came up and congratulated me.

Everyone was in high spirits during the ride home. The train car was filled with their cacophonic chatter about all that had transpired. What a day!

Marie said, "Gilda, let's invite Diane Kubinski and Ann Panteleoni to your house to watch the program."

That evening, the four of us were glued to the TV screen when the announcer appeared on "NJ Today."

"This afternoon, a knighting ceremony took place after the installation of the Italian Consulate in Newark. Dama Gilda received the honorific title of Cavalier."

Mine was the feature story of the evening. Ann, Diane, and Marie cheered. I watched the TV screen, stunned. They were talking about me, yet I somehow felt disembodied. Could this really have happened to me?

I feel truly blessed. Learning Italian opened a beautiful window to the world. My work is meaningful, and I hope to continue promoting Italian language and heritage for years to come. I am grateful to have loyal friends who shared in this memorable event.

If only my parents were here, they would be proud that, after our audience at Castel Gandolfo 56 years ago, I am knighted by the president of Italy and have kept my promise to the Pope.

Epilogue

Just two words: "Promise me" uttered to me by Pope Pius XII in 1951, at his summer residence at Castel Gandolfo, changed the course of my life.

This extensive memoir is my roller-coaster venture to foreign places, dramatic heights and challenging paths undreamed of and censured for most women of my generation. But in the end, I kept my promise to the Pope.

Index

CPSIA information can be obtained
at www.ICGtesting.com
Printed in the USA
BVHW07s0957240618
519874BV00001B/18/P